THE PERFECT 10

THE PERFECT 10

10 LEADERSHIP PRINCIPLES
to Achieve True Independence, Extreme Wealth, and Huge Success

DAVE LINIGER
WITH LAURA MORTON

Forefront
BOOKS

The Perfect 10: 10 Leadership Principles to Achieve True Independence, Extreme Wealth, and Huge Success

Published by Forefront Books, Nashville, Tennessee.
Distributed by Simon & Schuster.

Library of Congress Control Number: 2024900380

Print ISBN: 978-1-63763-183-6
Proprietary ISBN: 978-1-63763-322-9
E-book ISBN: 978-1-63763-184-3

Cover Design by G Sharp Design
Interior Design by PerfecType, Nashville, TN

Printed in the United States of America

DEDICATION

To my wife Gail. You have been an awesome partner for more than fifty years in business, and the most wonderful, loving wife for forty years and counting. There is simply no way I would have become the success or man I am today without you standing by my side.

CONTENTS

INTRODUCTION

> ***If I have seen further, it is because I have stood on the shoulders of giants.***
>
> **—Isaac Newton**

THE STORYTELLER

A large oil painting entitled *The Storyteller* hangs on a wall in our home. It depicts an older Native American chief sharing his wisdom with the young men of his tribe. If you look closely at each adolescent's face, the boys appear captivated by the knowledge and insight coming from the elder wise man, as if they're hanging on his every word. After all, he has seen, heard, and done more in his lifetime than they have collectively.

As I've gotten older, I've grown to understand this painting more with every passing day. In many ways, I see myself as that elder statesman. I've lived a full and prosperous life—and I don't just mean financially. I've been enriched by experiences that I value far more than monetary wealth. The path to success hasn't always been easy, but that's what has made it so damned interesting. So, as I look back on the road that led me here, I feel that it's my calling—my responsibility—to share what I've learned throughout my lifetime. If

I've become an expert at anything, it's living. And, yes, I've become an expert at business too.

In the nearly two hundred thousand or so years human beings have existed in our modern form, it's only in the past few hundred years that we've begun to turn to people other than our local elders for advice and solutions to life's problems. Anthropologists believe that the accumulated wisdom of older people was an essential part of human survival. The elders taught the next generation how to farm, handle challenges, and care for their children. They were also sources of experience in times of crisis.

It's a good idea to consult older people, especially those who've lived through situations we haven't. They've dealt with financial stress, failure, harassment, war, illness, aging, and loss. It's these sorts of unthinkable, complex, and challenging experiences that lead to profound insight and great knowledge, and those who've lived longer and been through tough times possess a unique perspective that's incredibly valuable to younger people. It can help shape their view of their own lives and opportunities.

Why wouldn't we seek the advice of someone who's lived through much more than ourselves? When you think about it, it's an easy question to answer. There is *no* logical reason to pass up such an opportunity. I've always enjoyed the company of wiser, more experienced people than myself, whether as business mentors or military commanders. If you listen closely, they reveal so much. And the more experienced they are, the more they want to share. Henry Wadsworth Longfellow said, "A single conversation across the table with a wise man is better than ten years' mere study of books." The value of these relationships cannot be overstated.

The harder question is, Why won't some pay attention, listen, and act upon such advice when they do talk with someone who's more seasoned? Over the years, I've spent numerous hours mentoring people in their careers. I've heard their dilemmas, complaints, worries, and ideas too many times to count. I'm very deliberate when it comes time to share my thoughts, solutions, and suggestions. And I'm very attuned: I can always tell when the person I'm sitting with will just nod their head in agreement, get up, leave, and never use the experiences and advice I've offered. It happens more often than you might think. And yet there are many people, some of whom I'll talk about in these pages, who not only heard my words but also heeded my recommendations. What's the difference between these two types of people?

Action.

The responsive ones know that if you want a different result, you must change how you do things. If you keep making the same mistakes, you'll get the same results. It's that simple. But more on this later.

As a young boy, I loved reading Louis L'Amour novels. If you aren't familiar with L'Amour's work, he was a great author who wrote dozens of books portraying the lives of American frontiersmen and women so vividly that you could imagine yourself living on the range during that time. Many of his novels became motion pictures, drawing us even further into the power of his wonderful storytelling.

Most of L'Amour's Westerns start with some kind of tragedy. It might be the orphaning of a young child, the robbing of innocent people by bandits, or a mass killing. The main character is always a misfit too; he's usually an uneducated kid who doesn't fit in and has to work his way through life. L'Amour's writing typically features a good guy who changes as he ages, and by the time you get to the end of the book, the loner has become a successful hero. He might be a prosperous rancher or a respected sheriff. Everything he learns comes to him through life experiences. He doesn't go to college or have any formal education. I like to think of these characters as having graduated from the College of Hard Knocks, which is a hell of an education. Unfortunately, most people can't afford the tuition. I contend that the best education comes through the pain of failing, making mistakes, enduring losses, and so on. Someone or something must knock you on your ass once or twice before you can understand the value in each of those experiences.

The College of Hard Knocks will teach you that persistence is incredibly important in any endeavor.

As you read this book and move forward in your career, I hope the importance of this message will stick with you. There's no doubt that I've seen my share of challenges throughout the years, and like Louis L'Amour's protagonists, I've survived them all. If I can do that, you most certainly can too.

CHOICES

Two other authors whose work affected me, in part because they also recognized the value in life experiences and learning from those who've gone before us, were Dale Carnegie and Napoleon Hill. Carnegie's *How to Make Friends and Influence People* and Hill's *Think and Grow Rich* are must-reads for anyone contemplating becoming an entrepreneur. Both books are so inspirational that I believe they should be required reading in every high school across America. Hill once interviewed Carnegie for a magazine article he was writing, and during their three-day discussion, Carnegie challenged Hill to write a book about the philosophy of success. He suggested Hill meet and interview hundreds of Carnegie's high-achieving friends and colleagues, including people such as Henry Ford, Thomas Edison, Alexander Graham Bell, and John D. Rockefeller. He wanted Hill to pick their brains and learn the secrets of their prosperity in business and in life. The result was *Think and Grow Rich.*

In 1956, nearly twenty years after Hill's book was published, a man named Earl Nightingale released a spoken-word recording called *The Strangest Secret*, which sold more than one million copies and launched the fields of business motivation and audio publishing. He eventually released a forty-four-page book by the same title. Nightingale was motivated to produce *The Strangest Secret* by the words "We become what we think," which he read in Hill's *Think and Grow Rich.* At the time, Nightingale owned an insurance company where he often gave weekly motivational speeches to his staff. One week he recorded his speech so it could be played in his absence while he was on vacation. That particular speech focused on nonconformity and the power of self-education, presenting the notion that you are now, and you will become, what you think about. Moved by the message of the speech, Nightingale's employees spread the word, and demand for the recording grew so large that he and his friend Lloyd Conant formed the Nightingale-Conant Corporation to manage the record's sales. Nightingale went on to become quite well-known for helping people become more successful and for defining success as "the progressive realization of a worthy goal or idea." In 1956, this was a groundbreaking interpretation.

Over the years, however, the clearest definition of success I've ever heard was from Darren Hardy. Hardy is a serial entrepreneur, the former publisher of *Success* magazine, and a *New York Times* bestselling author who wrote *The Entrepreneur Roller Coaster*, *Living Your Best Year Ever*, and *The Compound Effect*. He said, "success is doing what you want to do, when you want to do it, where you want to do it, with whom you want to do it, and how you want to do it." The first time I heard him say this, I remember thinking, *He's correct.* That's the type of freedom every entrepreneur strives for. But it doesn't come easy or fast. Success is a collection of building blocks, cemented together one at a time.

At my age, with fifty-plus years of experience as an entrepreneur and all that I've accomplished in life, I now live by this definition of success. In fact, I've made it my mantra. I have wealth, money, and prestige. I have friends, businesses, and hobbies. You could say my life is satisfying and full. When I'm considering whether to give up an hour of my time for someone, the choice comes down to those factors. Am I willing to give up sixty minutes of my life for whatever their cause might be? Often these meetings are essentially requests for money—either loans, investments, or donations—so I know walking in that it could cost me both time and money. When you achieve a certain level of success, you face an overwhelming demand for both, especially from people you don't necessarily know, let alone care about. But sometimes those meetings can result in a paycheck. So when I heard Darren describe success that way, it hit home. I had an epiphany of sorts. I suddenly had permission to do what I wanted, when I wanted, where I wanted, and with people I wanted to be involved with. If something doesn't check *all* those boxes, I'm out. Everyone should live their lives this way, yet most people won't get to a place where they believe they can.

Today, I'm selective. I say yes to only a few requests because I can't say yes to fifty, one hundred, or more. There's great power in saying no. It preserves your value and resources. But there's actually another reason I'm particular about what I get involved with: You can spend all your time chasing what I call the monkey—that next bright, shiny thing—or you can be hyper-focused on the one or two things that are important to you and your business. It's easy to run after the next shiny thing, but in the process, most people end up destroying their companies. Steve Jobs once said something I'll never forget: "We're famous for what we did, which was executed brilliantly on very few products. What we're not famous for is how often we turn down a good idea, say no, so we can concentrate on the two or three things we do great." What you focus on is where you're going to get the best results. If you're constantly jumping from one shiny thing to another, focusing on the flavor of the day, you will inevitably lose. Why? That shiny thing is nothing more than a distraction. Of course, *everyone* is prone to distraction now and then.

Think about how often you check your messages or social media platforms in a day. But that's just a diversion from what you ought to be focused on.

If you've never been successful as an entrepreneur, you may argue with my opinion. You may try to persuade me (or others) that this gizmo or that boondoggle will save your company or propel you to great success. But it doesn't work that way. This book will demonstrate what I believe are the tried-and-true methods that will help you flourish in business and achieve the type of success you desire, and allow you to create an exceptional life.

THE PERFECT 10

When we chose the title for this book, we knew there were multiple associations with the phrase *The Perfect 10*. To me, a perfect ten is executing something flawlessly and in a way that cannot be imitated. Everyone wants a perfect ten in one way or another. We're all looking at our lives and trying to figure out, "How can I make more money? How can I make my business work? How can I make my marriage work when I've got all these demands at the office? How can I keep my kids from hating me because I work eighteen hours a day?" In some manner, we're all asking ourselves, *What is perfection?*

Of course, a very attractive woman (or man) immediately comes to mind. Or maybe you're aiming for a perfect-ten day, a perfect-ten event, or a perfect-ten life. A perfect ten, by the way, doesn't mean attaining balance, because there is no perfect balance. But it does ask whether we're happy with all parts of our life. And if we aren't, why not? A perfect ten can apply to performance as well—think of achieving a perfect score in sports. When I was in high school, I was a ten-meter platform diver. I remember popping up from under the water countless times after my dives with great anticipation of seeing all 10s on the scorecards. It never happened to me, although I broke my shoulder trying more than once. Receiving a perfect 10 in diving (or any other sport) is rare, but it does happen, and when it does, it's a beautiful experience. Over the years I've realized that the same is true in business—a perfect ten is someone who excels in multiple disciplines such as leadership, management, and marketing, as well as in key areas of personal growth and adaptability. Those, of course, are your A players, and the people I look for whenever I'm hiring or partnering with someone. I want the whole package.

My aim with this book is to help you become a perfect ten. To that end, I've divided the book into ten chapters, each addressing a different discipline or area of self-development that helped me achieve success. In each chapter I've identified the most significant lessons I've learned throughout my career to help you excel in that pursuit. You'll find that every chapter is chock-full of information, and all of them contain at least one list of ten takeaways that I consider to be the ultimate secrets to success in that discipline. That's at least one hundred useful tips for becoming a perfect ten in business, particularly as an entrepreneur, franchisor, or franchisee.

Part of my motivation for doing this dates back to 1976 when I read *Why S.O.B.'s Succeed and Nice Guys Fail in a Small Business.* It wasn't a big bestseller, but it was a truly amazing book. In fact, there was one paragraph that changed my life. It was so impactful that I had a plaque made with that paragraph inscribed on it. It has been hanging on the wall in my office for fifty years. It reads, "When you have made it up the mountain, reached the pinnacle, you can then do what the rest of those successful entrepreneurs have done before you. You can write a code of ethics, make speeches about morality to business and civic groups, and look down with a cold smile on all the scrambling, scratching little bastards below trying to find their path to the top. You can even do what some of the rest of them have done. Roll rocks down on them just for the hell of it and make the road a little tougher."

Now, *that's* a great quote.

For some time, I was one of those little scrambling bastards trying to make it to the top. To me, the bad guys were all the wealthy and powerful people in real estate who had hundreds of offices and were hell-bent on destroying any newcomers trying to climb the mountain. And then I made it. But here's why that quote mattered to me so much back then: From the first time I read it, I decided that I would *never* be a man who rained rocks down on others. Aside from my time in the military when I was given direct orders by my superior officer to act otherwise, I did my best to always help those around me thrive. You see, everyone you meet on your journey will impact you in one way or another. Some will empower you, while others will try to hold you back and get in your way. But I'm certain of one thing: You won't become successful without navigating the terrain at both the top *and* the bottom of the mountain, and you'll never do it alone.

Sometime in the early 1970s, when I was starting RE/MAX, I found another quote that profoundly impacted me. It's an old Irish blessing that reads, "May the road rise up to meet you. May the wind be always at your back. May the sun shine warm upon your face, the rains fall soft upon your fields, and, until we meet again, may God hold you in the palm of His hand." In Irish culture, the *seanchaí* were the traditional keepers of stories. They would travel from one village to another, reciting ancient lore and tales of wisdom. They often spoke of kings and heroes. This blessing was originally an Irish prayer, first written in Gaeilge, the language of Ireland. Like many traditional stories, it lost some of its authenticity when certain words were mistranslated into English.

Although there are many theories about who originally wrote the blessing, most attribute it to either St. Patrick or an unknown author. But whoever it was, most people agree that the prayer's message is not to worry. It assures us that God has our back and will provide us with a steady path through life with as few challenges as possible. It emphasizes that God is there to give us unwavering support regardless of the difficulties we may face, so we shouldn't spend a moment stressing about anything. Instead, we should live in peace, knowing that we're always safe in His hands. This blessing is often given at weddings or before one is about to embark on a journey.

Because I've never been a particularly religious man, when I read this blessing for the first time many years ago, I had a slightly different take on it. For me, it was a reminder that if you blaze a trail, you should remember to reach down and give the person behind you a hand up, making their journey somewhat smoother. If you do this, that person might be inspired to do the same for the person behind him. That's what I've always tried to do, and I want you to know that practice has never failed me.

Now, I want to be completely up front with you. I can't take credit for most of the ideas in this book. These pages are a compilation of what I've learned over fifty years of attending thousands of seminars, reading countless books, and listening to speakers and friends whenever they took the time to share their wisdom. I have an insatiable appetite for learning and reading. I still read at least five or six books a week, half for enjoyment and half for business. I always buy hardcover business books because I like to underline meaningful material and take notes. You learn better when you put pen to paper.

In addition to my own hands-on experience, the content comes largely from studying business in many forms and interacting with numerous top business leaders and managers across different markets. People like Darren Hardy, Jack Canfield, Jim Rohn, Zig Ziglar, Napoleon Hill, and many more have influenced how I think, act, and operate in business and in life. If I'm being completely honest, I wouldn't be where I am today without those influences. I'm a compulsive learner, and in the process, I've also been a teacher. So, you might say that there isn't an original thought in this book, because most of what I've learned over the years comes from someone else's experiences, which they've graciously shared along the way.

Another important point I want to make clear is that I, as an individual, did not make RE/MAX or any of the other businesses I've been involved with the incredible successes they became. There was always a *team* behind those accomplishments. We all learned together. Our success derived from the collective efforts of those I worked with and of countless others who influenced us. It truly has been the product of so many people's input, whether we worked side by side or not.

Several years ago, Phil Harkins and Keith Hollihan came to me wanting to write the story behind RE/MAX. They took five years to research and write their book. They honored me with a business-leadership award for excellence, which was really nice. At the time, I wasn't ready to tell the full RE/MAX story, but we agreed to cooperate with them, providing access to our archives and granting them interviews with key executives in the company. That book does a wonderful job of telling everything we did right over the years. In reality, of course, there was a lot we did wrong too. We made many mistakes. And so, as much of our story as that book tells, it isn't the whole story. When I set out to write *The Perfect 10*, I knew I had to address how to become the entrepreneur you dream of becoming, how to scale a business, how to deal with the inevitable challenges, and how to achieve ultimate success in your career and your life. The RE/MAX story is only as complete as the knowledge I pass along to you from my journey. I've done my best to note the original sources of those lessons, and wherever I haven't, please know that the omission was not intentional. I ask that if you find such an omission, please contact me through my website, daveliniger.com, with the appropriate source so I can give credit where it's due.

With so much collective wisdom included in this book, I hope that you'll return to it often, as I did with the many books that inspired me, and that you'll find something of value in it each time. As you and your business grow, I also hope the trail rises up to meet you—and when you achieve success, you remember to pay it forward.

1

Goal Setting and Planning

I grew up on a farm in Marion, Indiana, where hard work was as natural to me as breathing. My parents had a small business in town, so they leased their land for others to work, keeping ten acres for themselves. It was my responsibility to maintain those ten acres using a gas-powered push mower, which took hours. But I never complained. It was my job, and I took it on like I would everything in life—with fierce determination to do my best.

As a kid, I was a scrappy fighter. I had a chip on my shoulder and wanted to prove that I could kick anyone's ass. I suppose you could call it small-man syndrome; no matter the name, though, it contributed to my being a bit of a jerk. I used to throw erasers at my teacher and write bad words on the chalkboard. It wasn't anything so wrong that I deserved a beating, but I got one every time. This was back when teachers could paddle your rear end if you misbehaved. I'd be so bruised I could barely walk. When my parents asked what happened, I would tell them, but they didn't seem to care much about it. They probably thought I deserved it. And maybe they were right.

For reasons I was unsure of then, some of the bigger kids at school liked to bully the smaller ones. They would come after me all the time. I knew that the only way I could beat them was to focus all my energy on training harder. My goal was to get so strong that one day I would be able to take down the six-foot bullies who made my life a living hell. Eventually the harassment stopped, but those were tough years to get through. As a result, I developed a penchant for protecting the little guy, fighting for what I believed was just and right. And most of all, I learned never to give up.

There's always a solution waiting to solve any problem.

Fast-forward to adulthood. There's no doubt that when I went to Vietnam, I walked into the country naïve and stupid, but walked out a different man. When I got home from my tour, I was damn glad to be an American. I was proud to have served my country and appreciated how the military helped me mature. I was also ready to chase the American dream.

I did what most guys did when they returned: I went to work, started a business on the side, got married, had children, eventually divorced, fought through financial difficulties, and, despite it all, went on with my life. I learned early on that you could choose to wallow in self-pity or look inward to examine your flaws. You could point the finger of blame at yourself or point it at others. You could also choose to do destructive things with your life. But guess what? Those things wouldn't change the world. There were, however, ways you could impact the world for the better, and that's precisely what I set out to do. No matter what life threw at me, I knew that the only way to win was to put on my big-boy pants and go out and play the game as if my life depended on it. And it did.

As I grew older, I found myself looking back at how foolish and uneducated I had been, especially when I first started in business. No matter how hard I tried to take the straight path to success, the universe always had a different plan. It led me down a road full of twists and turns I didn't expect and sometimes wasn't ready to handle. But I learned—often the hard way. There were times when I succeeded, and even more occasions when I failed. And believe me, failure has been my greatest teacher.

LESSONS OF A STREET FIGHTER

Even if you're someone who grew up as a scrappy fighter like me, there comes a point when you realize that punching people isn't a great idea, and it's really not a smart strategy for growing a business. Once I finally matured, I no longer got into physical brawls. Instead, I learned to avoid fighting at all costs.

I began to study Tae Kwan Do, a martial art that involves discipline and conditioning. But because it also involves a lot of kicking, it's ideal for someone with longer legs. Since I'm a short-legged fellow, I eventually moved on to Kenpō, a Japanese martial art. From there, my study evolved to include Shotokan, a form of karate that proved ideal for my body type.

Of course, most people who take karate strive to become a black belt for the mystique and prestige. The reality is, becoming a black belt won't really help you in a street fight. You might be able to take an amateur fighter to task, but if you're up against someone who's a true street fighter, you'll be in the fight of your life. When I began studying and practicing martial arts, I was just hoping that if I were ever jumped in an alley or late at night, I'd have learned enough to be able to fight to the bitter end, because the only rule in street fighting is: *Do not lose.* It's win or die. Nothing else counts. The military taught me that too. Marital arts classes allowed me to hone my skills in the event such a dreaded death match ever occurred.

As brutal as that sounds, this mentality prepared me for the rough-and-tumble world of business.

A street fighter in business is someone who finds a way to make a profit no matter what the problems are. They don't always play by the rules. A lot of them are ruthless, though not all of them are. It was Ray Kroc who once said, "If my competitor were drowning, I'd stick a hose in his mouth and turn on the water." It's a harsh statement, yet an honest one. As for me? Well, I like to win. In fact, one of my favorite sayings is "Second place is the first loser." But I like it even more when *everybody* wins.

4 Lessons Street Fighting Taught Me

1. There are no rules.
2. The only acceptable outcome is to win.
3. If you ever go to a knife fight, make sure you bring a gun.
4. David can slay Goliath.

ARE YOU PREPARED TO BE RELENTLESS?

Type in relentless.com on your computer or smartphone and see where it takes you. Go ahead. I'll wait.

Did you get rerouted to the Amazon website?

Interesting, isn't it?

Jeff Bezos had the idea to name his online bookstore Relentless, so in 1994 he registered that domain, even though the original name of his company was Cadabra—as in *abracadabra*. His attorney dissuaded him from using Cadabra because he felt it was too obscure a reference for most people to get. It also sounded a lot like *cadaver* when people said it aloud. Of course, that business ultimately became the retail giant Amazon.com. Amazon, as you know, is also the name of the world's largest river by volume. And not only is it the largest river in the world but it's also many times larger than the next-biggest river. The metaphor cannot be overlooked.

There's no doubt that Bezos has always had drive, purpose, and passion. They're what helped him stay the course and build one of the most successful businesses in the world. Perhaps you have drive, purpose, and passion too. If you had the chance to pitch me on investing in your business, I'd expect you to walk me through your pitch deck and share all the reasons why you think I should give you startup capital. I might even expect you to have a strong name already picked out, and a logo to match.

But as we neared the end of our time together, I would also expect you to answer the one question that matters above all else: *Why are you starting this business?*

I would warn you to be very careful about how you respond, because there's only one answer I'm looking for, and it ought to be the same reason you give.

Before going any further, write your answer here.

The reason I'm starting my business is to ______________________

____

____

____

____

____

____

____

____

____

____

____

____

____

The answer I'm looking for is simple:

To change the world.

If that wasn't your answer, you may need some time to reassess where you are.

YOUR ENTREPRENEURIAL CALLING

Find something you love to do so much, you can't wait for the sun to rise to do it all over again.
—Chris Gardner

Chris Gardner, as some of you may remember, is the homeless-man-turned-successful-stockbroker featured in the film *The Pursuit of Happyness*. He believes that the most inspiring leaders don't just work—they follow a calling. If you're trying to figure out your entrepreneurial calling, there are several factors to consider. First, *what is most important to you?* Try to look beyond your current priorities, because those are bound to evolve over time. Ask big questions and then really sit with your answers. *What change are you trying to make in the world? How can you do that?* Talk with lots of different people, especially those who know you well. These are the folks who will be honest with you about your ideas and goals. Speak with people you trust and admire, and ask their opinions too. Seek out successful people who are willing to talk with you about their business journey. How did they get to where they are today? What advice would they offer you? And what would they change about their own trajectories if they could? I always encourage having these conversations with older people—those of us who have been there, done that. Hell, the sole purpose of writing this book is to share fifty-plus years of wisdom with you to give you a jump start and help you potentially avoid the pitfalls I did not. One question I strongly encourage you to ask is, "What do you look back on in your life, personally and professionally, and regret?"

Listen to what they have to say. Think about how it relates to you and your business quest. How do their answers make you feel? The closer you get to understanding what sets your heart aflutter, the closer you'll get to discovering your purpose. Not your next job.

Not your next business. In the grand scheme of things, both of those are easy to figure out. What I'm talking about is looking deeply into your soul and asking a lot of questions, examining your assumptions, calling your bluffs, and reflecting on what you find until you narrow it all down to the clearest answer about who you are, what you believe in, and what you want to create. The late Zig Ziglar, the renowned motivational speaker and author, put it this way: "What you get by achieving your goals is not as important as what you become by achieving your goals." I love that quote.

Know this: *You can have anything, but you can't have everything.* So be selective, be realistic, and honor your priorities. Consider the various roles you play—spouse, parent, friend, sibling, boss, employee, volunteer, and so on. All of these roles will divide your time, which means you'll have to become adept at saying no a lot. The best leaders in business understand the power of no. You can't do everything and expect to do it well, so prioritize these areas of your life and consider the choices you'll have to make to fulfill your goals and live your calling.

WHAT'S YOUR WHY?

The question "What's your why?" was popularized by Simon Sinek in his book *Start with Why.* The book was written after Sinek gave a TED Talk that went viral. In his talk he explained that as humans we are compelled to do things for our own reasons. Understanding those reasons—our *why*—leads to greater motivation and a sense of purpose. Essentially, the why we discover during self-reflection equates with our sense of personal fulfillment, clarity, and life meaning. Our why isn't about *why now* so much as *why for the long term*.

Sinek's book focuses on creating an organization that puts its values at the center of its business. The idea is straightforward:

"Great businesses know why they're doing what they're doing, and they use that mission as their guiding principle."

The book breaks the concept down into three parts:

1. Defining your why.
2. Understanding how your why affects your company on all levels.
3. Making sure you stay focused on your why in the long term.

Your why is all about what motivates you to get up and go to work every day. Your company's why is the reason you're in business. Think of it as your mission statement—the vision and motivation behind your company's existence. This why leads to your *how*—the various steps you'll need to take to achieve your why and the goals you must meet along the way. Finally, your *what* is the product or service that you're providing. It's the most tangible part of your business.

For example, if we look at RE/MAX, it can be explained like this:

Our *why* is to disrupt the real estate industry, putting our agents first.

Our *how* involves creating a 100 percent commission structure for our agents.

Our *what* is the real estate we sell.

I've spent my entire career chasing my dreams. Whether it was building a real estate company that would rock the industry, constructing a private golf course to be used to raise money for charity, or breeding the world's most sought-after Arabian horses, I had my *why* in mind. From day one, we were never in it for the money. Don't get me wrong—financial freedom was always a goal, but it was never our *purpose*. And I genuinely love what I do. I get excited by the work. Whenever I found myself bored or uninterested in a business, I knew it was time to sell.

All great entrepreneurs will tell you that if your sole motivation is money or fame, you likely won't achieve either. First, the odds that you'll achieve financial success are pretty low. Statistically, the average business owner earns 35 percent less over their first ten years than they would have earned if they had been gainfully employed by someone else. Starting a business is hard. It will challenge you in ways you can't imagine. These constant curveballs frustrate and discourage most people, preventing them from getting to where they want to go. Many entrepreneurs become so disappointed that they give up. If a paycheck is what you're after, you're far better off being on someone else's payroll. It's much more of a sure thing.

There's no shame in wanting to achieve monetary success and notoriety. A hell of a lot of fun comes with that. Just be honest about it, and then ask yourself if that's truly what you want out of life, or if there could be something more. For myself and many of the great entrepreneurs who've inspired me over the years, the allure of building something meaningful has far outweighed the financial rewards that come with success.

Some people seek fame, wanting to become the next Elon Musk or Mark Zuckerberg, without having the necessary ingenuity or drive. Nancy Gross, the operating manager of the MBA program at Stanford Graduate School of Business, has commented that in her previous role at the school's Center for Entrepreneurial Studies, it wasn't uncommon for aspiring entrepreneurs to come into the program aiming to become famous and enjoy all the perks of success without a clue as to what they were signing up for. They would often show up without a pen or a piece of paper, wanting to be fed the answers without doing any work. According to Gross, these budding entrepreneurs would never make it.

There have been many times when I've witnessed business owners who were solely driven by money make decisions that were bad for their businesses. These were decisions that fed their ego and/or the bottom line. In theory, such decisions feel right in the moment, but they usually end up costing a lot over time. This type of arrogant decision-making can easily drive away partners and employees who would much prefer to thrive in a "we" environment than to serve a boss in a situation with no upside.

> ***The best reason to start an organization is to make meaning—to create a product or service that makes the world a better place.***
> **—Guy Kawasaki, *The Art of the Start***

As the above quote indicates, most seasoned entrepreneurs and investors are in it to change the world in one way or another. This is the exact motive I look for in the entrepreneurs whose businesses I choose to invest in. I know individuals like this will persevere through the tough times every new company faces. These are the people who are willing to sacrifice whatever they must to make it. They're the smart risk takers who dare to push limits and challenge norms, and they believe in what they're doing so much that failure isn't an option.

Look—turning your ideas into dreams is hard work. RE/MAX was an idea that had been taking shape for years. It was a series of connected observations and discoveries made over time. A well-thought-out dream becomes possible only after the idea has been fully developed.

John Coleman, author of the *HBR Guide to Crafting Your Purpose*, contends that few of us have thoughtfully considered what success really is before pursuing it. Many people choose a career or a job based on what they're good at, what they studied in school, or even what someone they admire did before them—following in a family member's footsteps, for instance. For most people, this tends to overtake the more meaningful aspects of life. Some experts call this a work-life imbalance. Coleman suggests that it's important to consider how we can pursue success while maintaining joy and purpose too.

Psychologist Martin Seligman believes that when thinking about success, we ought to include positive emotions, engagement, and relationships on the list of the many accomplishments we hope to achieve. Doing this allows us to flourish, have more profound experiences, and live a life rooted in meaning.

In the Disney movie *Soul*, the main character discovers that life is not only about finding one's purpose but also about understanding the *why* within the day-to-day moments we experience. Knowing this early in your career will give you a head start in your pursuit of success. It will enable you to enjoy a life that includes meaningful love, positive relationships, a great career, and service to others. Don't wait until later in life or when you're at the top of your game to discover your purpose. Start today. Doing this will guarantee a more meaningful and fulfilling journey.

For me, the ultimate *why* in business is knowing that I'm doing something that serves others. As a species, we're hardwired to be of service. Knowing we have something of value to give can connect us in ways no other why does. It provides a sense of belonging, and it feels much better and more fulfilling than just being in something for personal gain. Plus, it connects us more deeply to whatever we're doing and selling, increasing our resolve to stick it out when times are tough.

Keep in mind that your why—your purpose—may change over time as your business grows and the needs of the market you're serving change. Staying in touch with your evolving why can help you successfully navigate those changes.

WHAT IS YOUR PASSION?

Okay, so let's say we're still in our interview, and I'm considering whether to make an investment in your business. I'm going to ask you another important question: *What is your definition of success?*

Before going any further, write your answer here.

My definition of success is ______________________________

____

____

____

____

____

____

____

Because we've already touched on the dangers of chasing money and fame, and why purpose and making a difference matter, I hope your answer doesn't suggest that you define success as a measurement of wealth, notoriety, and the accumulation of things such as homes, cars, watches, and so on. In fact, I hope your answer has something to do with following your *passion*, because those who factor passion into the equation are more likely to have a positive outlook and an easier time overcoming obstacles and challenges as they arise. Those who are passionate about their work also take great pride in themselves and work harder, and thereby increase their odds of success.

Follow your happiness.
—Mark Zuckerberg

Mark Zuckerberg has literally changed the world with his company Meta, formerly known as Facebook. Zuckerberg followed his passion—not money—when launching his unique vision. His philosophy was simple: Even if you don't end up making a fortune, at least you'll be doing something you love.

Know what success really means.
—Warren Buffet

If you have any doubt that success equates more with having a passion than having material possessions, consider this: Warren Buffet is one of the greatest investors of all time, but even with all his monetary success, he still lives humbly in Omaha, Nebraska. According to him, it's critically important to pursue what brings meaning to each day.

INTENSITY OF DESIRE

Howard Schultz, the founder of Starbucks, has often said, "Work should be personal for all of us. Not just for artists and entrepreneurs. Work should have meaning for an accountant, construction worker, technologist, manager, and clerk." I completely agree. No matter what career path you choose, whether you're an entrepreneur or an employee, you must find purpose and meaning to be fulfilled.

There's an old saying that goes, "Choose a job you love, and you will never have to work a day in your life." I don't think that's exactly true. If you find a job you're passionate about, it will motivate you to work harder, and when you do, you won't mind, because you'll be doing things you never thought possible. But if starting a business is something you're considering, remember that it's about so much more than that. It's a mission driven by a vision that is worthy of your time, energy, and intellect.

The term *intensity of desire* refers to the strength, passion, and fervor with which someone wants or pursues something. It reflects the level of motivation, determination, and dedication that an individual has toward achieving a particular goal or fulfilling a specific desire. When someone has a high intensity of desire, they're deeply committed to attaining their objective. This intensity can manifest in various ways, including a willingness to persevere through challenges and a drive to go above and beyond to make their dream a reality. A note of caution: It can also manifest as being restless. Patience is indeed a virtue when it comes to achieving goals.

At best, though, the intensity of desire is the fuel that motivates us. It's the driving force behind our actions and decision-making. Your intensity of desire in business can vary over time and be influenced by factors such as personal goals, values, aspirations, and the perceived importance or significance of the goal. It can be a powerful force that propels you toward success and achievement in pursuing your career ambitions, personal relationships, or personal growth. The Chinese believe that guanxi, or personal connections, are at the center of business. To truly succeed, you have to build a network of trusted and respected people you can reach out to whenever you need them. Guanxi is important and takes time to develop. It's also a reciprocal proposition. If you ask a favor of someone, be prepared to give one in return as well. Remember, what goes around, comes around.

OPENING NIGHT ELECTRICITY

For me, passion in business is a lot like romance and the thrill of the chase. You may be in a happy marriage or a career you love, but it's never the same as when you first started dating or working in that job.

You never get over the thrill of the pursuit.

I still go to events for RE/MAX that I find fun, and certainly they're essential to connect with our teams. But after so many years, the romance—the excitement—has faded.

On the opening night of a Broadway show, there's such intensity in the air. The anticipation is palpable, especially for the actors and dancers who were chosen for their roles and who've spent months practicing for this night. Everyone wants tickets to opening night, and the show is the talk of the town.

As an audience member, you have your ticket in hand, you see celebrities walking the red carpet, and you're dazzled by the bright lights of the paparazzi and the marquee overhead. Backstage, the performers are excited and ready to go. There's so much anticipation for the show that you can feel it throughout the building. That's what I call "opening night electricity." It's a true phenomenon. There's no replacing that feeling, that "Holy cow, this is so cool" excitement. When the curtain comes down, there's a standing ovation, multiple curtain calls, and everyone is ecstatic.

Three years later, though, the cast has changed several times, the show has been running for a thousand-plus days, and the thrill is gone. It's a gift when the curtains go up night after night and the cast can still feel some of the magic they did on opening night. Eventually, though, there isn't any more opening night electricity. And worse, no one expects it, so it eventually goes away. And when it does, it impacts every aspect of the show. That's when it's time for a change.

Every time you make a presentation, it can feel like opening night electricity. It's your chance to shine. Creating opening night electricity is the aim of most businesses. They have to figure out how to re-create the happy, warm embrace of the first time whenever someone walks through their door. The customer expects that opening night sensation. They anticipate adventure, experience, and the debut of something new that's as good as (if not better than) your last product, service, or offering. If you fail them—if you can't generate that level of enthusiasm—you're not pleasing your customer. That type of passion comes from within. It's really from your heart.

Think about a restaurant where people take pictures of their food and post them on social media for others to see. That too is opening night electricity. What they're really saying is, "Holy moly. Look at what I'm eating tonight!"

For an entrepreneur, there's also an opening night electricity. It's not so much that feeling of walking through the door as it is,

"What's next? What's my upcoming acquisition going to be? What new business idea will I launch?" For someone like me, it's a constant chase, and it will be until the day I die. This is my game, my purpose. If you're not in the game, you're a bystander. You're just sitting on the sidelines and watching. You've got to be in the game.

I'm a guy who enjoys going to Las Vegas. When I walk into a casino, everyone knows I'm there. I'm what they refer to as a whale—a big-stakes gambler. They comp my stay in a suite that runs $20,000 or $30,000 a night, serve me all the wine I can drink, and dish out all the food I can eat. They close off a private table where I can sit all night. I mostly play blackjack, and when I do, I bet six figures a hand—sometimes playing four or five hands at a time. I could lose, or I might win. It doesn't really matter. I'm a player who knows the odds favor the house. But you've got to play to win, right? I am one of those rare gamblers who has won more than I've lost. I claim my winnings with the IRS. And for those few days, I'm the king of that casino. It feels good. My ego is bolstered, and win or lose, I have a hell of a lot of fun. I've had big nights and bad nights. I don't dwell on losses any more than I do windfalls. It's just the game. It isn't the way I make my living. Walking into a casino, sitting down, and playing at the five-dollar tables just wouldn't ring my bell. It would only frustrate me. Why would I do that? It's all about the excitement—those opening night jitters—and the feeling of knocking one right out of the park.

My point is, we all crave that opening night electricity in our lives and careers. The mega wattage supercharges us for quite a while. Sometimes it wanes. Sometimes it returns, through luck and effort. But if it dies out, it's definitely time for a reset. A new goal. A new passion.

A goal properly set is halfway reached.

—Zig Ziglar

SETTING YOUR GOALS

James Clear's *Atomic Habits* is a book I very much enjoyed reading. It talks about goal setting like this: Athletes who train for the Olympics have the same objective, which is to win gold. Obviously, not everyone will take home the top medal. Some won't have the skill set; others won't have trained hard enough; and still others might falter, fall, get hurt, cramp, or just quit. Winning gold requires countless hours of practice and repetition that most people can't handle. These elite athletes train morning, noon, and night, seven days a week. Why? To meet their goal.

The same is true in business. Goal setting is fundamental to one's success, and it's a common theme throughout this book. Starting or running a business requires deliberate planning, and that requires goal setting. Your choice of goals will determine your direction and the steps necessary to get there. I always advise entrepreneurs to dream big. Be overwhelmed with the possibilities of what can become a reality, but don't get paralyzed by all the choices. Believe that anything is possible, and then figure out how to make that happen. The above quote from Zig Ziglar highlights the fact that setting a goal is a crucial step toward its achievement. When you define your goals clearly, you've already taken a significant stride forward.

Having big end goals is important. That being said, be sure to keep your more immediate goals in the realm of reasonable reality. You can adjust them as many times as you need to along the way, raising the bar as you go. The more realistic your immediate goals are, the more likely you are to meet them. Conversely, the more unreasonable your goals are, the more likely it is that you will fail.

What is it you want to do? What is your ultimate goal? And what intermediate goals will get you there?

At RE/MAX, our initial end goal was to become the best real estate network in the world. We were going to accomplish this by recruiting five people a month for five years. When you know what you want to accomplish, it becomes much easier to achieve.

CREATING ABC PRIORITIES

I've always loved aviation, whether it's flying my own plane or attempting to navigate a hot-air balloon around the globe. Several years ago, I read a book called *Have You Filed Your Flight Plan? Leadership: Destination and Direction* by Erick J. Burton. The premise of the book is that goal setting is a lot like a pilot filing a flight plan before taking off. No commercial airplane pilot can leave the ground without first submitting a plan that includes their destination and direction. The pilot establishes waypoints, meaning the areas they will fly over, and notes them in the plan so their course can easily be plotted and tracked by the FAA.

Many years ago, pilots would use paper maps to chart their courses. Today, it's all done by computer. Digital preflight planning tools not only generate a map with a graphic of your flight path, they also come with overlays that show terrain, real-time weather conditions, potential obstacles, and the various airports en route to guide you in the cockpit. If you put the plane on autopilot and encounter heavy winds, the system will automatically course correct for you.

Planning your flight, in our case, is a metaphor for planning your goals and staying on course. Unfortunately, most people plan a two-week vacation better than they plan their career. And there's actually a good reason for that: When you plan a vacation, you understand that there's a finite amount of time. You know you have only fourteen days to do what you want to do. Once you pick a destination and book a hotel and rental car, your efforts become focused on the sites to see, the places to eat, and the activities to engage in. You have to prioritize so you can do all the things you want to do, because who knows when you might get the chance to return to this destination?

When most people come back to the office, they feel as if they have unlimited time. They're not under a deadline the way they were in their travels. They go to work with no strategy. They have no plan. No goals. They collect a paycheck, and they go home. So the planning process, which includes establishing goals and setting up systems, never gets done by the majority of people in the workforce today.

I've spent six decades setting goals for myself and teaching others how to do the same. In the late 1970s, I taught a goal-setting training program for several years that changed a lot of people's lives. While creating the course, we asked brokers and agents to keep a daily log for seven days. We wanted them to write down every single thing they did from the time they woke up in the morning until they turned out the lights at the end of the day. We thought it was important to know what time they went to the office, how many showings they had, how many listing appointments, and how much time they spent at lunch, at the gym, and running errands—everything. When they turned in these logs, we coded their responses by their income. Whether they were a 100 percent commission agent making $100,000 a year or an agent making $30,000 a year, we sorted their work activities through a system called ABC Priorities. A activities made you money, B activities led you to the money, and C activities were necessary evils. In the case of our real estate agents, activities categorized as As included showing a house or talking to a prospect face-to-face about buying or selling a property. Activities categorized as Bs included doing administrative work, writing an ad, cold-calling, and so on. And, finally, activities categorized as Cs included putting gas in the car, getting it washed, going to the grocery store, picking up the dry cleaning, and the rest of the mundane tasks we do as humans.

What we found was that agents who made less money spent about 20 percent of their time doing A activities, whereas top producers spent 80 percent of their time on those same activities. The top producers didn't have a spare moment to go to weekly sales meetings. They were too busy showing and selling properties. The ABC principle pointed out that everybody put in an eight-to-ten-hour workday six or seven days a week, but the people who made the most money focused most of their time on doing the things that made them money. When they were doing A activities, they were making an average of $400 an hour. When they were doing C activities, they were making zero. Once we had this information, we taught our agents to create to-do lists at night for the next day. We wanted them to put an A, B, or C in front of the items on their lists so they could prioritize what was important to them. Some people always started with the Cs. Why? They're easy, and you can quickly tick them off the list. It made them feel as though they were working hard and being productive. But they never got to the As or Bs. The top producers always focused on the As. They would delegate the Cs to someone else if they had to.

Once we started teaching this method, people could see where their time was being spent and what the return on that time was. It taught them how to make the best and most productive use of their day. If you could make $400 an hour selling property, why would you ever stop to mow your lawn? If you were a top producer at that time, you could hire people for six dollars an hour to take measurements, photograph the property, and do the necessary legwork to get it listed on the MLS (Multiple Listings Service) while you spent your time walking people through homes, pointing out all the features, negotiating contracts, closing sales, and bringing home the income.

To further assist agents in making the most of their time, we introduced the "team concept" under the RE/MAX system. The first person added to the teams in the '70s was an administrative assistant. If you couldn't afford a full-time assistant, you could form a team and share one with several other agents. Each agent could use the assistant for a specified period of time, and they would all split the cost.

Once we started teaching agents that they were the rainmakers, the team concept really took off. An agent could spend the same amount of time selling an $800,000 home as they did selling a $100,000 home and make a lot more money in commission, so the more experienced agents started focusing on the bigger sales. Because they didn't want to be bothered with smaller sales, they would pass that business off to other agents in the office, take a referral fee, and focus on their more significant listings. This raised the bar for everyone on the team as each leveled up their game.

In this whole goal-setting process, it's important not to confuse a goal with a desire. A goal and a desire are two related but distinct concepts: A goal is a specific and measurable objective that you aim to achieve within a set timeframe. It's a result or outcome that you actively work toward. For example, you may say, "My goal is to lose ten pounds within the next three months by exercising regularly and following a healthy diet."

Goals are often concrete, actionable, and well-defined. They provide direction and focus, helping you prioritize tasks and make progress toward achieving a particular outcome. Goals are typically based on specific actions, milestones, or accomplishments that you can aim at.

A desire, by contrast, is a strong feeling or wish for something that you'd like to have or experience. It's a more subjective, emotional longing or aspiration.

Desires are often broader and less specific than goals. They represent your preferences, dreams, and hopes. Desires may not have clear action plans or timelines associated with them. They reflect what you want in a more general sense, without necessarily outlining the specific steps needed to achieve them. An example may be, "I desire to travel the world and explore different cultures and destinations."

Yet both goals and desires play a role in shaping our ambitions and driving our actions and decisions. A company that's poised for success will have a clear set of consistently updated goals to help it achieve its objective. For this reason, we'll talk about goal setting here as a precise description of what your business will achieve within a specific timeframe.

When it comes to effective goal setting, the following are several key pillars that can help guide you toward success.

Ten Pillars of Effective Goal Setting:

1. Clarity: Set clear and specific objectives, timelines, and measurable targets that allow you to track your progress.

2. Alignment: Ensure that your goals align with your values, passions, and long-term vision. When your goals are in keeping with your core beliefs and aspirations, you're more likely to stay motivated and committed.

3. Realism: Set goals that are challenging yet attainable. Consider your current resources, skills, and constraints. Unrealistic goals can lead to frustration and de-motivation, while achievable goals provide a sense of progress and accomplishment.

4. Focus: Prioritize your goals and concentrate your efforts on a few key objectives at a time. Avoid spreading yourself too thin by setting too many goals simultaneously. Concentrated focus allows for better allocation of resources and increases your chances of success.

5. Measurability: Establish clear metrics and milestones to track your progress. Define specific criteria for success and regularly evaluate your performance against these metrics. Measuring progress keeps you accountable and allows for adjustments along the way.

6 Timeliness: Set deadlines and establish a timeline for achieving your goals. Breaking down long-term goals into shorter-term milestones maintains momentum. Time-bound goals also create a sense of urgency, provide structure, and help you allocate resources effectively.

7 Accountability: Hold yourself accountable for your goals. Share your goals with others who can support and encourage you. Consider finding an accountability partner or joining a group that shares similar objectives to stay motivated and committed.

8 Flexibility: Remain adaptable and open to adjustments as you progress toward your goals. Circumstances may change, and unforeseen obstacles may arise. Being flexible allows you to modify your approach, pivot when necessary, and seize new opportunities.

9 Actionability: Take consistent action toward your goals. Create a plan by breaking those goals down into actionable steps. Proactively work toward your goals to make regular progress, and adjust your strategies as needed.

10 Reflection and Evaluation: Regularly review and reflect on your goals. Assess your progress, identify what's working and what needs adjustment, and learn from any setbacks or challenges. Regular evaluation allows for continuous improvement and keeps you aligned with your objectives.

By incorporating these pillars into your goal-setting process, you can increase your chances of success, maintain motivation, and make steady progress toward achieving your desired outcomes.

Unharvested Ideas Are Worthless!

By the way, before something ever becomes a desire or a goal, it's a seedling of an idea. Harvesting your ideas requires diligence and, like anything worthwhile, a process. I use the following five steps whenever I want to turn a big idea into a dream and ultimately a business.

1. Write the idea down and get the words right.
2. Connect the idea to other ideas to expand it to its full capacity.
3. Test the idea to ensure that it's viable.
4. Incubate the idea.
5. Call it a dream and share it.

CREATING YOUR VISION AND MISSION STATEMENTS

Once you've come up with a business idea, it's time to articulate its purpose by putting it in writing. A vision statement in business is a concise and inspiring declaration that outlines the desired future state or long-term aspirations of the organization. It paints a compelling picture of what the company aims to achieve or become in the future. A well-crafted vision statement serves as a compass for the organization, providing direction and inspiration for ongoing strategic decision-making and goal setting.

For instance, the Walt Disney Company's vision statement is "To make people happy." This short yet powerful statement captures the essence of the company's vision and the emotional impact it aims to create through its entertainment and experiences.

Google's is "To provide access to the world's information in one click."

Tesla's is "To create the world's most compelling car company of the twenty-first century by driving the world's transition to electric vehicles."

Starbucks's is "To establish Starbucks as the premier purveyor of the finest coffee in the world, while maintaining our uncompromising principles while we grow."

And at RE/MAX, our vision statement is "RE/MAX will always be the right place for real estate entrepreneurs who want a combination of independence, support, and unique competitive advantages—and the right choice for customers who understand the benefits of having someone like that working on their behalf."

An effective vision statement looks forward. It articulates the impact the company wants to make in the *long run*. It should inspire and motivate employees, stakeholders, and customers; evoke enthusiasm and a sense of purpose; and rally people around a common goal. A vision statement should be easy to understand, memorable, and consistent with the company's core values and fundamental beliefs.

While specific goals and strategies may change over time, a vision statement typically remains constant. It provides a guiding light for the organization's journey, even as the business evolves and adapts to new challenges and opportunities.

A mission statement, by contrast, describes the *present-day* activities and values of the company. It's a short and powerful declaration that communicates the fundamental reason for the company's existence. It establishes what the company does, how it does it, and, often, why it does it. It details its target market or audience, articulates its competitive edge, and makes clear its values and goals. It should provide clarity and direction for employees, customers, investors, and other stakeholders, helping them understand the company's objectives and what it stands for.

Here are examples of mission statements from the companies previously mentioned:

Disney: “To entertain, inform, and inspire people around the globe through the power of unparalleled storytelling, reflecting the iconic brands, creative minds, and innovative technologies that make ours the world’s premier entertainment company.”

Google: “To organize the world’s information and make it universally accessible and useful.”

Tesla: “To accelerate the advent of sustainable transport by bringing compelling mass-market electric cars to market as soon as possible.”

Starbucks: “To inspire and nurture the human spirit—one person, one cup, and one neighborhood at a time.”

RE/MAX: “To be the worldwide real estate leader, achieving our goals by helping others achieve theirs. Everybody wins.”

Once you have clear vision and mission statements, you’re ready to speak about your company in meaningful and effective ways to both existing and prospective stakeholders.

YOUR ELEVATOR PITCH

An elevator pitch is a concise and compelling summary of a product, service, business idea, or individual’s skills and qualifications. It’s called an “elevator pitch” because it should be succinct enough to deliver within the duration of an elevator ride, typically somewhere between thirty seconds and two minutes. The purpose of an elevator pitch is to quickly and effectively communicate the essence of what you or your business offers in a way that captures the listener’s attention and leaves a memorable impression. It’s often used at networking events, business meetings, job interviews, or any situation in which you have a brief opportunity to make a persuasive impact. Think about the people you’ve seen on *Shark Tank*. When they come out to pitch their business ideas, their description must be clear, concise, and engaging from the word go.

A well-crafted elevator pitch should include an opening that’s strong and engaging enough to grab the listener’s attention. This can be a thought-provoking question, a surprising statistic, or a compelling statement related to your product, service, or expertise. Next, it should succinctly describe the problem or challenge that your product or service addresses, highlighting the pain points or needs of your target audience. Then, it should present your solution or value proposition by explaining how your product, service, or expertise solves the problem. Focus on the unique and compelling way it does so. Detail the benefits and advantages it brings. Differentiate yourself or your business from competitors by highlighting what sets you apart. Emphasize the unique features, qualities, or expertise that make your offering or skills valuable and desirable. End your elevator pitch with a clear and brief call to action. This could be a request for a follow-up meeting, an invitation to visit your website, or a request for their contact information. Make it easy for the listener to take the next step.

It's crucial to practice your elevator pitch to ensure a confident and smooth delivery. Refine and reiterate your pitch based on feedback and the specific context in which you'll be using it. Remember, the goal of an elevator pitch is to capture the listener's interest and make them want to know more. It should be concise, compelling, and tailored to your target audience. By effectively conveying your value proposition and leaving a lasting impression, an elevator pitch can open doors to further conversations, opportunities, and business connections.

EXERCISE:

If you were going to explain your business to me in a couple of sentences, what would you say? ______________________________

____

____

____

____

____

With an understanding of what constitutes success and how to frame the goals, vision, and mission of your company (or your idea for one), you're ready for this next step.

WRITING A BUSINESS PLAN

A business plan is a comprehensive document that outlines the goals, strategies, and purposes for a business venture. It serves as a road map for the organization, providing guidance and direction for the company's operations, growth, and financial success. While the specific content and structure of a business plan may vary depending on the industry, the size of the business, and the intended audience, the overall purpose is to provide a comprehensive and strategic guide for the business's success. Think of it as your architectural plan for building a house.

A well-crafted business plan communicates the vision, mission, and objectives of the business and demonstrates how it will achieve its goals. The plan helps entrepreneurs and business owners clarify their business concept, identify target markets, and develop strategies to achieve a competitive advantage. It outlines the steps and resources required to turn the business idea into a viable and successful venture.

A business plan is often necessary when seeking funding from investors, lenders, or venture capitalists. It provides potential investors with an overview of the business, its market potential, and its financial projections, helping the investors assess the business's feasibility and potential return on investment.

A comprehensive business plan also serves as a communication tool within the organization, ensuring that all stakeholders—including management, employees, and partners—have a shared understanding of the business's goals, strategies, and operational plans. It helps align everyone's efforts toward a common vision.

And, finally, a business plan provides a benchmark against which the company's performance can be measured. By setting specific goals, objectives, and key performance indicators (KPIs), the plan enables the business to track progress, evaluate results, and make informed decisions to stay on target. This might include an analysis of potential risks and challenges that the business may face. By identifying these risks, the plan allows the company to develop strategies and contingency plans that effectively respond to or mitigate such challenges.

Key components typically found in a business plan include:

1. Executive Summary: An overview of the business plan, highlighting key points.
2. Company Description: Detailed information about the business, its products and services, target market, and unique value proposition.
3. Market Analysis: Research and analysis of the target market, competitors, and industry trends.
4. Marketing and Sales Strategy: Plans for promoting and selling the products and services, including pricing, distribution, and promotional activities.
5. Operations and Management: Detailed information about the organizational structure, key personnel, and operational processes.
6. Product or Service Line: A detailed description of the company offerings, including features and benefits, and how they address customer needs.
7. Marketing and Sales Strategy: Plans for marketing and an approach to sales, including target market segments, positioning, pricing strategy, distribution channels, promotional activities, sales forecasts, customer acquisition strategies, and ongoing customer relationship management plans.

7 Marketing and Sales Strategy: Plans for marketing and an approach to sales, including target market segments, positioning, pricing strategy, distribution channels, promotional activities, sales forecasts, customer acquisition strategies, and ongoing customer relationship management plans.

8 Funding Request and Financial Projections: A clear statement of the amount you're seeking if you're pursuing funding, the purpose of the funds, and how they will be used. Include detailed financial projections, supporting income statements, balance sheets, cash flow statements, and key financial indicators. Also note assumptions and provide a break-even analysis.

9 Implementation Plan: A timeline and action plan outlining how the business will execute its strategies and achieve its goals.

10 Risk Analysis: The identification and assessment of potential risks and challenges that could affect your business, including legal, financial, operational, and market risks. Consider strategies for mitigating those risks and how you plan to handle contingencies.

Remember, in addition to being well structured, concise, and tailored to your specific business, your plan should convey a clear and compelling vision, demonstrate market viability, and provide a road map for achieving your stated business goals.

Like today's digital preflight planning tools, there are business plan templates you can purchase or find online. Once you've completed your business plan, you're good to go. There's no telling how far or high you can soar!

2

Entrepreneurship

Howard Stevenson, the esteemed professor emeritus at Harvard University, has said, "Entrepreneurship is the relentless pursuit of opportunity without regard to resources currently controlled." It's a wonderful statement, because it emphasizes the one thing entrepreneurs have in common: We're all *doers*. With or without money, we have an idea and the burning drive to see it to fruition. Why and how we do it is the subject of this chapter.

DO IT BECAUSE YOU LOVE IT

There are those who do it for the money,
those who do it because it's easy . . . and
those who do it because they love it.
—Anonymous

I never cared about making money. What I always placed a high value on was *doing better, being better, and helping the little guys like me thrive.* Even though I enjoyed real estate, early on I wasn't driven by a deep desire to be a real estate agent. I eventually got my real estate license to save the commission on houses I bought and flipped in my late teens and early twenties. At the time, though, I had no intention of making real estate my career.

When I was nineteen years old and in the military, I was making $99 a month. Since I was married, I lived off base. My rent was $98 a month, and yet I still insisted that my wife not work. I'll admit that that was a terrible mistake, but back then I let my macho pride get the better of me, adamantly believing I was man enough to provide for my family. Looking back, it would have been much easier on us if she had gone to work. Instead, I held three part-time jobs to make ends meet. I delivered over a thousand newspapers to 7-Eleven and Circle K locations. I had five hundred homes on my newspaper route, which was in Tucson, Arizona. I'd throw newspapers on driveways from two in the morning until six, seven days a week. I did that for eighteen months without a day off. Even if I took a couple of vacation days from the military, I still delivered those papers. I worked myself to the point of total exhaustion. Then one day I fell asleep at the wheel and hit a car head-on. Fortunately, no one was hurt, but my boss demanded that I take a week to catch up on my sleep.

My second job was working at a theater, and my third was at a local filling station. Between the three, I brought home around $500 a month.

Now, at the time, there was an FHA/VA property that came up for sale. (FHA/VA are home loans from the Federal Housing Administration and Veterans Affairs that come with benefits to help people who qualify. These benefits include very attractive loan terms and lower down payment requirements and appealing interest rates. The asking price on this particular house was $10,400. It had been remodeled and even had a swimming pool, but it needed some work. The mortgage was $99 a month. We figured we were already covering that in rent, so why not own our home? We spent the next six months fixing it up, and then we flipped it, making $5,000 on the sale.

The inspiration behind my real estate flipping had sparked in high school, around age sixteen. That's when I first read *Think and Grow Rich* by Napoleon Hill.

I'm not sure any other book I've read throughout my life has impacted me more significantly. Many business leaders I know and respect say the same thing. I'm not aware of another work that has resulted in more entrepreneurial success stories. I must have read it fifty or more times over the years, and each time, I took away something new. The amount of information Hill was able to collect and share from some of the most outstanding entrepreneurs in history is staggering. Their willingness to impart their knowledge and wisdom is second only to being the beneficiary of it. Remarkably, the book was written in the 1930s, and it still holds up today. In many ways, it's as relevant now as it was then, especially as we stare down the barrel of economic uncertainty in similar ways people did when Hill first wrote the book. If you haven't read it yet, do. It will change your mindset in immeasurable ways. And I promise you, it will impact your path as an entrepreneur.

The title might imply that the book is about making money, but it isn't. It's more about taking charge of your thoughts and fate. You are ultimately in control of the path you walk, the choices you make along the way, and, therefore, the outcome. I'll refer to the lessons of *Think and Grow Rich* throughout this book because I believe they're critically important. My biggest takeaway was a simple one: Whatever the mind can think, you can achieve. If you can dream it, you can do it. And I believe that to be true.

The second book that inspired me to get into the real estate flipping game was *How I Turned $1,000 into a Million in Real Estate in My Spare Time* by William Nickerson. It's one of the best and most practical guides on how to make money in real estate with little money down. While the specific details on prices and costs might be outdated, the general premise is still valuable and can help anyone find financial security in real estate.

Nickerson wasn't cut out for college. At least, not at first. While he enrolled at Fresno State as a freshman, he dropped out later that year to travel. He loved to hike, and spent the next three years living as a nomad. He visited several countries, from Peru to Singapore, working on merchant ships to get from country to country. Eventually, he returned to the US and reenrolled at Fresno State, where he earned a degree in English and psychology.

Before joining the Pacific Telephone and Telegraph Company, he became a supervisor for a hosiery company working in sales and staff development. He began buying distressed properties in the mid-1930s. He would purchase a home for $1,000 down. In his spare time, he'd fix it up and rent it out. Pleased with the financial return, he would do it again and again, until one day he owned a thousand properties—mostly apartment complexes with twenty to thirty units, as well as several homes. By this time, his net worth was in the millions, so he quit his job at Pacific Telephone. Excited by his success, he wanted to share what he'd learned, so he wrote his book and became a speaker, traveling the country and earning appearance fees all along the way. The book taught me everything I needed to know as an eighteen-year-old kid who was about to serve in Vietnam. I wanted to become incredibly rich, and I would do it by buying, selling, and flipping houses. My goal was to own twenty-one single-family homes by the time I was twenty-one years old.

Before I left for Vietnam, I was assigned to Davis-Monthan Air Force Base in Tucson, but when I returned, I was reassigned to an Air Force ROTC detachment in Tempe, Arizona. It's incredible what a mischievous and innovative young man can do when he sets his mind to something. I got creative right away and started buying houses. They weren't expensive homes. Each one cost around $10,000. Still, I scraped, begged, and borrowed to make it happen. I even convinced sellers to carry the mortgage, let me take it over, and use the homes as rental units. I'd collect the rent and make monthly payments to the seller as if they were the bank. It took a lot of courage and confidence to look those sellers in the eye and convince them I could do this. I believed I could, and then figured out a way to make it happen.

Eventually, getting my real estate license to save on paying commissions made sense. My percentage of the fees wasn't much, maybe $300 or $400 per transaction, but it was something, and enough to squirrel away and put toward buying another property. I then went to work for Ed Thirkhill Realty, a local real estate company with eight or nine offices in and around Phoenix. Ed was my boss and was a nice-enough guy. He was just like all the other real estate brokers at the time, primarily white men in their fifties or older. There were very few women, and most of them worked as support staff in the offices, not as Realtors. The guys had retired from other jobs and were working in real estate for additional income to live on. At the time, the average Realtor made around $5,000 a year. The job was straight commission, so you got paid only when you sold a home. I was already flipping houses, so I thought I'd give it a try.

When I applied for a part-time job as an agent, no one asked about my qualifications. Agents were a dime a dozen. No one cared a bit whether I had experience or not. As soon as I said I wanted to be a Realtor, they said, "You're in. Sign here." There wasn't much training. You were just thrown into the ocean to see if you could swim. If you wanted leads, you went around local neighborhoods, knocked on doors, and asked if anyone wanted to sell their house.

I drove all over Phoenix that summer in my Volkswagen Beetle, with a cracked windshield and no air-conditioning. I'd show up to a prospective seller's home with my military haircut, looking like a fresh-faced kid—because I was. I was in my early twenties, directly out of the military, and had no formal training or experience other than flipping a few properties for myself. I felt more like a Fuller Brush salesman than a Realtor. People were kind, but they usually let me know I was one of several agents they were interviewing. And because of the way I looked, most people just saw me as a kid. So, they never called. Not once. No one would give me a deal.

I hung my license with that agency for six months without making a single sale or getting a listing. I worked hard and read as much about real estate as I could. I tried to role-play with my wife to build my confidence, but nothing seemed to help. There was no training program and no assistance with marketing or advertising. It was a setup for failure. So, I did something I wasn't accustomed to—I quit. I walked into my manager's office, gave him my notice, and packed my belongings in a brown cardboard box. My manager watched my every move to make sure I didn't steal anything from the company on my way out. I took only what was mine—a stapler, pencils, and a few personal items.

"I didn't think you'd make it," my manager said as I placed the last items in the box.

"Then why would you hire me?" I asked.

"Son, we hire anyone who walks through that door. It's like throwing shit against the wall. One in ten throws sticks," he responded.

That could have been the end of my real estate career, but it wasn't. Doubt me, and I will prove you wrong. I left that office more determined than ever to succeed. The next day, I paid twenty dollars to attend an all-day seminar with Dave Stone, the Tom Ferry or Brian Buffini of that time. Twenty dollars was a lot of money to me. I figured that if I paid it, I was going to listen to every word Dave spoke. I sat in the front row and took copious notes. I'll tell you this—Dave Stone was one smooth talker. He spoke about handling objections with a silver tongue and convinced us there was no objection we couldn't overcome. He presented with ease and confidence, practically preaching like we were in church. During every break, I'd jump up, walk over, and grab Dave's hand to shake it. "Mr. Stone, that was wonderful. If I could say things like you do, I could become successful."

"How long have you been trying?" he asked.

"Six months," I said.

"How many sales and listings have you had?"

"None . . . yet," I replied.

"You ought to quit," he said with great purpose.

"I did. Yesterday, but not today. I'm going to make it," I said.

And then the strangest thing happened. Dave agreed to be my mentor. He didn't want to, but I persuaded him with the intensity of my desire. Okay, maybe I begged him, but eventually he gave in and agreed to do weekly coaching calls with me. He took me under his wing, had me buy books, take courses, and follow curricula. He helped give me the tools that would change the direction of my life.

Not long after that, I was picking up a carton of milk at the grocery store. There was a young Hispanic girl there with her father. She might have been eighteen or twenty years old. Her father was much older and didn't speak English well. Through my limited understanding of Spanish, I could tell they were talking about selling their house. I stopped, turned, and asked the young lady, "Are you talking about selling a house?"

"Yes, my father is moving to Albuquerque," she said. "Our home is in pretty bad shape, so we're trying to figure out what to do."

"Well, your dad needs me. I'm a Realtor, and I specialize in distressed property," I explained. It wasn't a lie because of my experience with flipping houses. I looked over at her father and said, "Señor, do you know how much a commission is?"

"*No comprendo*," he said as he shook his head.

"Do you know what title insurance is?" I asked.

"*No comprendo*."

I turned back to his daughter and said, "Ma'am, he needs me. I can get this done for you." I was being sincere, and sure, maybe a little bit desperate, but they didn't know that.

She asked if I would follow them home to see the property. I agreed.

When I got there, it was in disrepair. Still, I listed it for $10,500. In today's numbers, that would be a $200,000 home. In real estate, we used to tour properties every Tuesday. Once I had the listing in hand and it went up on the MLS, I stopped at two real estate companies with my new listing and said, "I need to make a couple of copies of this brand-new listing. Mind if I use your copier?" I could have made copies anywhere, but I wanted to let these other agents know I had a fixer-upper that was going to go fast. At the time, many investors were buying distressed properties to fix and sell. I was desperate for approval, and after six months in the business, I finally had a listing. That night I had two full-price offers. I sold the property in an hour.

As I lay in bed with my wife the next morning, I turned to her and said, "Let me explain to you that you're sleeping with one fine Realtor. One hundred percent of my properties were sold at full price in one hour or less." And I meant it. My wife was almost as proud of me as I was.

Later that morning, I took the young girl I'd met the day before to look at houses to buy with her fiancé. I sold them a house that day. Later that afternoon, their best friend and his wife went out with me to look at homes too. I also sold them a house that day. There were two more referrals the next day. After six months of no business whatsoever, I sold five houses in forty-eight hours.

What was the difference between the first six months and those two days?

I was still driving the same old beater with no air-conditioning during the summer, in Phoenix heat. But now I had something I didn't have before: *confidence.*

It was amazing.

After that, I became a Dave Stone groupie. I adored the guy.

I began to throw myself into the business. I read every book about real estate, business, and management I could get my hands on. I also started attending conferences and seminars to help me learn and grow so I could live up to my greatest potential.

Every commission check was bigger than my military salary. But even more important, every family I sold a house to bear-hugged me, shook my hand, and thanked me because they never believed they could buy a home. I gave them hope, confidence, and the belief that they were worthy too.

I was off and running, and the rest is history. What started off as a hobby became my career after all—and I never looked back. I beat every local sales record along the way. I was still serving in the military full-time, but I had been bitten by the real estate bug—and I was becoming an entrepreneur too, as I kept flipping houses. It didn't take long before I made well over $100,000 a year. My majors and captains were making only $20,000. They outranked me, but I outearned them. That didn't seem right, so I started an investment club where the guys could put in a few thousand dollars and watch it grow. Nobody made less than 280 percent over three or four years. With returns like that, the word was out, and it didn't take long for everyone to want to do business with me. I was no longer just a real estate agent or a sergeant. I was doing what I loved—helping others thrive. Not only was I was rolling in the money but everybody around me was profiting too.

By 1971, my career was flourishing. That's when I moved to Denver and went to work for VanSchaack. The real estate industry wasn't as big then as it is today. There were fewer than a dozen large brokers with two hundred agents or more nationwide. VanSchaack was one of those, with more than three hundred agents and a reputation as one of the best firms to work for. It was well-run, professional, and successful. At the time, VanSchaack was the number one realty company in town. They had the most market share, the best listings, and the top talent in the area. It meant something to work for them. It was prestigious and sophisticated. The agents who worked there were college graduates, well-dressed and polished. To be seen as a VanSchaack man meant you were making great money, married with children, and living the dream. You owned a beautiful home, drove a nice car, and lived the country-club life. While I worked for VanSchaack, it would be a stretch to say I was ever one of those guys. By this time, I was married with three kids, and that's pretty much where the similarities stopped. I was a college dropout and lacked the sophistication and polish of those other guys. However, I had one trait no one could ignore: my ability to sell real estate. I did it better than just about anyone else. I was unconventional and didn't always follow protocol, but I sold like no other.

My boss was Jack Bradbury. He was the epitome of a VanSchaack man—smart, sophisticated, and well liked. I admired him and, in many ways, wanted to become like him. I think Jack tolerated me because I brought in a lot of income for the company. But I'm not so sure he liked everything I did or how I showed up from time to time. He wouldn't call me out or complain, though, because I always delivered. In many ways, he allowed me to be my authentic self.

The idea for what would become RE/MAX had been swirling around in my head for some time. But now, it wasn't only beginning to take shape as more than just a good idea; it was becoming a fire in my belly, a dream I had to pursue. I hoped Jack would embrace the idea and help me make it a reality. He listened to me and even seemed to understand what I was trying to do, but he said no. He couldn't wrap his arms around my radical vision.

RE/MAX was innovative from the very beginning. Our commission concept revolutionized the industry. However, we weren't the first to offer it. I believe it was Savage Realty in Calgary, Alberta, Canada, that introduced the 100 percent commission idea around 1947. The first company to make it work, though, was Realty Executives in Phoenix. I actually worked there for four or five months early in my career, but I realized even then that Realty Executives had some significant flaws in their system. They had no training program, no corporate relocation, no referral system, and no technology to speak of. It was primarily a brokerage where freelance agents hung their licenses. It was more of a co-op than a top-tier agency like VanSchaack. By contrast, if you were an agent at VanSchaack, you came in with the largest market share in the city, had brand recognition, bought your signs at a significant discount, and shared in group advertising.

One thing I understood, no matter where I had worked over the years, was that almost every firm operated under the same business model. With the exception of Realty Executives, they all paid 50 percent commission to their agents. The more money I made selling, the more I realized I was handing over half of my income to my broker despite my doing all the work. None of the agencies I'd been at did a whole lot to deserve half of my hard-earned money. And Realty Executives didn't do enough to earn the fee I paid them either. I had been questioning the industry's approach for some time. Why had no one done anything different?

I wondered what would happen if the independence offered by a Realty Executives–type experience was combined with the support of a VanSchaack experience. What if agents could have all they needed to be successful and earn their full commissions? That's how I explained my idea to Jack that day. I thought my logic was compelling and my plan was so well thought-out it couldn't possibly fail. I wanted to go national—hell, international—and become the biggest real estate network in the world. I just needed the right systems in place, and I could sell that dream to anyone.

I knew real estate agents were motivated by money, but they also wanted opportunities to succeed and grow. They aimed to build wealth and create a better life for themselves and their families. To get there, most of the agents working in the business, especially in the early 1970s, couldn't do that themselves. They lacked the tools to succeed and the independence to create this type of opportunity. They needed training, mentoring, and motivation. That's where I could make a difference, or so I thought. I couldn't imagine why any real estate agent wouldn't want to work for the best and most prestigious firm, or why they wouldn't be willing to work harder to receive 100 percent of their commission. And I couldn't imagine that a firm offering such an opportunity wouldn't become the world's largest, most powerful real estate agency.

I saw so many ways to improve upon what both Realty Executives and VanSchaack offered. So when Jack declined, I was surprised. Maybe he was too set in his ways. Maybe he had become complacent in an already complacent business. Or perhaps he just didn't believe in the potential of what I wanted to do. Maybe he lacked the desire to pursue the life of an entrepreneur. He was doing just fine and saw no reason to shake the tree. Me? I was still a kid in my twenties. I had nothing but time, energy, and determination to chase my dream. I had great admiration for Jack. He was the consummate professional, the most incredible example of what a refined real estate broker should be. I, on the other hand, was young, naïve, and brash. I was averaging home sales in the $30,000–$40,000 range, and he was selling $500,000 homes. At the time, I aspired to reach his level of success, but I knew I wasn't doing it at the country club or on the golf course. At least, not then.

I left his office that day feeling frustrated but resolved to keep pushing ahead. Despite several more attempts to persuade some of the others at VanSchaack to join forces with me, no one said yes. Some even laughed in my face, saying it would never work. Whenever I heard no, I shrugged my shoulders and thought, *You're wrong.*

Eventually, in January 1973, I gave my notice and left to follow my dream and build my own company.

I called Dave Stone and asked for his help to start the business. I needed his experience, knowledge, and leadership to get this promising new company off the ground. He told me his consulting fee and I said, "Great." Within days, I flew out to see him, and he and I created a thick book, about two hundred pages long, laying out the company plan. The problem was, he had concluded that the concept would never work. He qualified that, however, by saying that if I did some very specific things, it *might* come to fruition. He laid those things out in the last twenty pages, and that became my bible for building the company.

Off I went.

So RE/MAX started as a combination of Realty Executives' 100 percent commission concept with some of the attributes I thought made VanSchaack such a success. I had essentially created a hybrid. From January 30, 1973, which was our first day in business, we offered a formal training program for our agents. It helped a lot, especially because we didn't start with top producers; we began with novices and made them into top producers. Once we were able to do that, the other leading agents in the industry wanted to join us. If we could take rookies and help them earn top dollar, imagine what we could do with experienced agents. Three or four years later, we had statistical proof that our agents were making three to five times what the average agent was making—and we did it through innovation. We borrowed the aspects of the business that were making VanSchaack so successful and eliminated whatever they were doing wrong, such as not hiring women in sales positions. To me, that was crazy. And we continued to refine our model over time in the many ways discussed throughout this book.

All this proves that innovation isn't always a brand-new idea; it can often be a new way of approaching an old idea.

FOUNDING RE/MAX

When I quit VanSchaack, I knew I was going to start a real estate company, but I didn't know what we were going to call it yet. Several people reached out to me the morning after, offering me sales management positions and such. A group of guys even approached me about starting a residential division for their land development company. I met with them and fell in love with the idea. They offered to make me an equal partner in all their businesses, including whatever business I started. They weren't very liquid, but they offered to loan me $50,000. They said they'd add another $450,000 to one of their projects as well. Like an idiot, I said, "That sounds good."

The arrangement immediately fell apart. They didn't have the cash. They said we could go to a bank and borrow the money; however, they wanted me to sign for the loan. It felt wrong on every level, so I passed. The world is full of sharks. You've got to be adept and either learn to swim in that sea or get eaten alive.

We founded the company with the simple notion of giving the very best real estate agents a full slate of support services and 100 percent of the commission they earned instead of the 50/50 split they usually retained at the time. The idea was to build a company where great people could pull together to do great things. We planned to franchise, offering brokers the opportunity to become business owners. We named the company RE/MAX because nobody wanted to call it Dave Liniger Realty, myself included. It felt too egotistical. We wanted the emphasis to be on the sales associates' name when they were selling, not the company name. All the real estate companies at the time plastered their name everywhere. They didn't care about the agents. To us, the agents were the people creating and building our book of business.

We came up with Real Estate Maximums based on the "maximums" we would offer. For instance, we would provide *maximum* service for the customer; we would have full-time people conducting *maximum* recruiting for the broker; and we would assure *maximum* commission for the agent. Everybody wins, right? That was the idea, anyway.

We shortened the name from Real Estate Maximums to RE MAX. But then we thought people might think that there was a Mr. or Mrs. Remax, and we'd appear to be just like all the other companies named after their founders. In 1972, Exxon was unveiled as the new, unified brand name for all former Enco and Esso outlets. They also designed a new logo they had tested linguistically, psychologically, and for design potential. Exxon settled on a rectangular logo using red lettering and blue trim on a white background. The new name was short, consisting of only five letters—just like our name. That's when we came up with the idea of adding a slash to our name and said, "How about RE/MAX?"

And so, the company name was born. And our first slogan for the company became "Everybody wins!"

Once we had the name figured out, we needed a logo. We decided on a red, white, and blue sign. It was so simple. We were all Vietnam vets, so it felt patriotic and right.

While several companies attempted to go national through franchising, including ERA, Red Carpet Realty, and Century 21, most were still relatively small operations working in their local markets. Because we had ambitions for RE/MAX to someday go worldwide, we began looking deeper into the business models of these companies, as well as those of other businesses utilizing franchising, to assess where we could improve on what they were doing to gain a competitive edge. Our idea to give agents 100 percent commission was one of those ways, but it wasn't the only one. Sure, we understood that giving agents more money meant that they would be able to have better lives, and that was important. However, we somehow knew it wouldn't be enough to sustain us and differentiate us from the competition. We had to figure out something that would make us so different that it would turn the business upside down. That's when we realized RE/MAX wouldn't be in the real estate business as much as it would be in the real estate *agent* business. Our customer wasn't the home buyer or seller, as it was for all other real estate companies before us; no, our customer was the agent helping those people achieve their dream. That was a pretty big distinction. If we could pull that off, we knew we'd be able to disrupt the business in ways that would change the rules of the game.

At the time, every leader in the industry told me my business platform would never work. They said the financial model defied how things were done. They warned me that I would be driven out before I could ever get it off the ground. They were certain the company would never survive.

OPENING DAY

On our first day in business as RE/MAX, I sat down with Gail Main, who, as many of you know, was my first hire in the company before she became president in 1979. Together we went through the MLS book for Denver. This was in the early 1970s, so nothing was electronic. There was an actual book of active listings. The MLS book was divided by sections, and the homes listed in each were ranked from lowest to highest in price. There were something like twenty-five sections for all of metropolitan Denver. Gail and I took each section and counted the number of active listings by company. The number one company had around 30 percent. The number two company had about 20 percent. The rest of the companies, which were in the thousands, collectively made up the remaining 50 percent. Some had only two listings or fewer. Intrigued by this, Gail and I continued the practice of counting the listings in the MLS books by company on a quarterly basis. At the time, RE/MAX was at the bottom of the rankings. Dead last. Within three months, we had moved up from two thousandth to two hundredth. Three months after that, we were in the top one hundred. And within nine months of opening our doors, we were in the top ten. Every quarter, we were knocking out our competition, pushing them lower on the list as we made our climb. At every sales meeting we made sure our people knew these statistics too. They made copies of each quarterly report and took them to their listing presentations, where they could proclaim that while we may have looked small, we were definitely growing. A lot of people were showing interest in joining us too. As we recruited agents with their own listings, we climbed farther up the list. Our charge against the rest of the real estate world was to become number one. It was an exciting time, one that required so much innovation, creativity, perseverance, and stamina.

Previously I mentioned that persistence is incredibly important in any endeavor. The first time I really comprehended this was early in the RE/MAX years when the industry reaction to our concept was less than favorable. In fact, it was pretty brutal. Agents didn't really give a damn. They thought, *If it works, I'll come to work for you. But I need to wait and see.* I suppose I understood this; however, those were the agents I didn't want. They were set in their ways, while we were out to become disruptors. Even with time, some people would never welcome our concept. In fact, they sometimes got aggressive about it. Let me explain.

When we were starting out, I drove to Colorado Springs, about a fifty-minute drive from our office. There I went door-to-door to one hundred real estate brokerages and set up appointments to personally pitch the RE/MAX concept. Some people were nice and wanted to hear what we had to say, while others weren't as welcoming. One individual was an ex-military guy who was angry from hello. Every time I opened my mouth to tell him a little bit about our company, he'd stop me and say, "I don't care. I don't want to hear about it." I kept trying to overcome his objections, saying he could, at the very least, learn about what was happening in the industry. Finally, he said, "Okay, show me." He sat there with his arms crossed as I spoke. He never once looked at our audiovisual presentation. He just stared at the wall until I was done with my fifteen-minute spiel.

"I told you I wasn't interested. Now get the hell out of my office," he said. "And if I ever catch you trying to recruit one of my agents, I'm going to claw your balls off." From that day forward, I referred to this gentleman as Claude Balls.

The owners of many other agencies railed against us too, from the smallest to the biggest in the United States. They thought what we were doing was outrageous. They said our concept was evil and that our rent-a-desk idea would never work. Some claimed we were nothing more than a rent-a-desk operation that let anyone work for us, taking their check just for being there. They were putting out the word that we didn't care about our agents. But that wasn't true. From day one, our people were the heart and soul of RE/MAX, and we knew it. Without them, we'd have no business, no company at all.

Occasionally, we would get a nibble on the line when a broker showed some interest. In fact, during the same week I encountered Claude Balls, we had another appointment with a very reputable and well-liked broker who had twenty-five or so agents. I can't recall his name, but I will never forget our exchange. I had initially pitched him over the phone. He liked what he heard enough to invite us to his sales meeting to present our concept to his people. I told him that wasn't a great idea because I was going to attempt to recruit his sales associates if I showed up.

"You're opening the henhouse and letting the fox walk right in before you know whether or not you want to buy a franchise," I said.

"Trust me, Dave, I'm not going to buy a franchise, but I really want you to come and explain your concept to my agents," he told me.

And so I did.

It took two and a half hours to make our pitch. When we were through, the agents seemed very enthusiastic and excited by what they'd heard. Before leaving, I shook hands with every one of them and said, "I'll be back in touch."

The owner walked me out to my car, which I thought was a little peculiar. When I asked him why he'd let me talk to his people that morning, he said, "This isn't public knowledge, but I have terminal cancer. I'm going to die within the next ninety days. I'm trying to find the best place for my agents. It doesn't work for me to buy a franchise, but I think your concept is right on the money. Maybe one of the agents will want in. I'm encouraging you to stay in touch with them because I think what you're doing is the way of the future in real estate."

After countless beatdowns and rejections, I had finally gotten the response I'd been looking for. I was saddened by the circumstances but happy I could help this man's agents and progress our concept at the same time. An experience like this can change your perspective on life, and certainly on the viability of your business. He didn't see us as a threat because he knew he was dying. He was concerned about the welfare of his people over his own well-being. That's great leadership. In the end, about fifteen of his agents ended up coming over. The moral of the story is simple: It doesn't matter how many times you strike out. To hit a home run, you've got to keep swinging.

But, sadly, so many people do give up. The turnover rate in the real estate industry is very high and getting worse, though it hasn't changed much for RE/MAX in all the years I've been in business. In fact, it was especially low during our first few years. The reason for the high industry turnover rate is because many companies will hire anyone, whether they're cut out for the job or not. There are approximately 1.6 million Realtors in the country, and about 20 percent of them do 80 percent of the business. I probably would have quit at some point if I'd stayed a traditional real estate broker. And people would have understood too. They likely would have said, "Geez, Dave, you started your business at the wrong time. It wasn't your fault." After all, there were many years when it was hard for all of us. The economy turned in the early to mid-1970s. Who could have predicted the oil embargo or the fact that the country would go into a recession just as we opened our business? It often felt like the world was against us. But as it happened, we didn't go the traditional real estate route. I started a novel real estate business with the aim of seeing to it that agents were well supported and could also earn their full commission. After so many people questioned our business sense, called us stupid, and accused us of being crooked, it would have been easy to turn tail and run. But remember, God hates a coward—and we were no cowards. We didn't take kindly to all the naysayers. We understood that haters are going to hate. There's not much you can do about that. The more successful you become, the more they're going to despise you. So, we used their vitriol as fuel. The more people said we were going to fail, the more we stood firm. We thought, *By God, you're going to have to put us in our graves to get us out of this business. We will never quit. You'll have to kill us first.* We were out to prove that our concept would work, and ultimately, we did.

Once we were managing hundreds and then thousands of RE/MAX real estate agents, we discovered that most of them were just as spirited and entrepreneurial as we were. We came to respect that kind of grit, hard work, perseverance, optimism, and self-belief. These are the traits it takes to start and successfully run your own business.

If you dream of starting a business or are new to one, you've likely heard the statistics that, on average, 50 percent of small businesses fail within the first five years, and 90 percent of startups fail within ten years. While this may not be very encouraging when you're venturing out on your own, it's important to remember that failure isn't always the end of the story for an entrepreneur. The first few years of RE/MAX were an absolute disaster. Some of the trouble was self-made, and some was industry-made.

As I've mentioned, RE/MAX transformed the way the real estate industry compensated its salespeople right out of the gate. Before we came along, brokers divided their commissions with their agents on what was basically a 50/50 split. We disrupted the norm by posing the question, "Why give up half your commission?" To be more specific, we proposed that agents work in a co-op with us and keep almost all their commission for themselves. I say "almost all" because they paid a pro rata share of the office costs. The situation was very much like a group of attorneys, architects, doctors, or dentists who share their office space and a reception area. Each pays their share of the overhead but keeps what they generate for themselves. It's far less expensive to do that than to start a one- or two-person shop with nobody else around to help you grow your business. But as we built a little momentum, the powers that be in real estate were very much against our strategy. They understood that if we succeeded, they would also have to pay their agents far more than the 50 percent commission they were currently offering. The entire management of the industry tried to drive us out of business.

Fortunately, I wasn't deterred by what other people thought. I'm the kind of man who isn't afraid to roll up his sleeves and do whatever it takes to create his own success. My critics didn't scare me any more than hard work did. No job was beneath me, especially in the early years. I spent plenty of long nights stuffing envelopes, polishing presentations, and hand-folding thousands of flyers. I look back at those grassroots beginnings and smile at the memory of my fearlessness and diligence, especially in the face of the many challenges that came my way. Even so, I knew we were onto an industry-disrupting idea. If we could hang on long enough, I believed we could change how real estate was done worldwide.

There will always come a time when radical ideas, changing technology, or necessary shifts in strategy have the potential to disrupt. This is true in every industry. Amazon, Google, Meta, Uber, and Tesla are all great examples of companies that changed how we shop, learn, communicate, and drive. It wasn't easy; there were many challenges over the years. You see, when you've been an entrepreneur as long as I have, you learn that business is full of cycles. Especially real estate. Some years are up, others down. The good and the great among us are separated by how we navigate the lean years—and believe me, there were many times when I didn't know how we would make payroll, let alone how I would put food on the table for my own family.

Fifty years later, though, RE/MAX has more than 140,000 agents and 9,000 offices in 110 countries worldwide. There isn't a lot in this world that makes me happier than having fun with my friends and colleagues—except, perhaps, knowing that we've somehow impacted their lives.

WHAT IS A STARTUP?

As a startup, RE/MAX was an example of a newly established business venture or company that aimed to develop a unique product, service, or technology in a scalable and innovative manner. Startups are typically characterized by their high potential for growth, often targeting large market opportunities or disruptive solutions. It's not easy to launch a startup. In 2021, I looked at 200 investment opportunities over a year and a half and turned down 190 of them in less than five minutes of reading about the company. Even after going in depth with the few I found intriguing enough to take a meeting with, I came up with only two that I was interested in buying. One was a good concept. The other I passed on because I knew I couldn't work with the founder. You can supplement the talent of a founder with additional people, but it's difficult, because the business is the founder's dream. If they don't have the right mix of drive, ambition, love, and passion for the job, it will never work.

A 2019 report from Startup Genome, a policy advisory and research firm, states that only one in twelve entrepreneurs succeeds in building a successful business. Why is there such a high failure rate with startups? For the most part, during their ideation phase, they haven't yet reached their growth stage, nor have they even determined product fit.

If you're in a startup phase, bear in mind that the first year or two will be much more difficult than the next two or three. If you anticipate that going in, you'll be far ahead of the game. The Navy SEALs have a saying: "The only easy day was yesterday, because there are no easy days." But once you're up and running, you're more likely to be educated and trained and to have momentum, money, and profits. You can hire better people who can do a better job for you—maybe even a better job than you can do yourself. Then it becomes a much easier game.

Here are ten features commonly associated with startups. Not all startups will exhibit each of these features, and the characteristics can vary depending on the industry, business model, and stage of development, but these attributes tend to be in play with startups and their unique approach to business.

10 Features of a Startup

1 Innovation: Startups often introduce novel ideas, products, or technologies to the market. They seek to provide innovative solutions or improve existing ones, aiming to differentiate themselves from established companies by solving specific problems or meeting unmet needs.

2 Scalability: Startups pursue rapid growth and scalability. They aim to expand their operations and customer base quickly, usually leveraging technology and efficient business models to achieve exponential growth.

3 High Risk: Startups operate in an environment of uncertainty and face significant risks. Their success is often subject to market dynamics, competition, and other factors, making risk management and adaptability crucial.

4 Limited Resources: Startups typically operate with limited financial resources, personnel, and infrastructure, requiring them to be resourceful and make strategic decisions to maximize their impact.

5 External Funding: Many startups seek external funding from venture capitalists or angel investors to fuel their growth. These investors provide capital in exchange for equity or ownership stakes, thus enabling startups to accelerate their expansion plans.

6 Agility: Startups often adopt agile methodologies and lean principles, emphasizing iterative development, rapid prototyping, and customer feedback. They aim to build, measure, and learn quickly to refine their products and strategies through continuous improvement.

7 Disruption: Startups may aim to disrupt existing industries or markets by introducing new business models, technologies, or approaches. They often challenge traditional incumbents by offering more efficient, affordable, or convenient solutions.

8 Innovation: The startup culture encourages entrepreneurship, experimentation, creativity, and a willingness to take risks. It values agility, adaptability, and a "fail-fast" mindset—recognizing that failures can lead to valuable insights and eventual success—along with autonomy, initiative, and a drive to disrupt established norms.

9 Customer Care: Startups are customer-centric. They prioritize understanding and satisfying customer needs. They actively seek feedback, engage with early adopters, and iterate based on customer insights to create products or services that resonate with their target market.

10 Adaptability: Startups are often nimble and adaptable, capable of quickly responding to market feedback, adjusting their strategies, and pivoting their business models if necessary. They are willing to experiment and learn from failures to achieve long-term success.

Don't be intimidated by what you don't know. That can be your greatest strength and ensure that you do things differently from everyone else.

—Sara Blakely, founder of Spanx

YOU DON'T KNOW WHAT YOU DON'T KNOW

Many factors contribute to the success of a startup business, but one of the most important is the entrepreneur themselves. *Does this person possess the skill set and traits to create a product or opportunity customers are willing to pay a profitable price for?*

People often think of entrepreneurs as enterprising people with great business ideas and the courage and tenacity to take action in pursuit of their dreams. "Entrepreneur" comes from a thirteenth-century French verb, *entreprendre*, meaning "to do something" or "to undertake." Its original meaning had nothing to do with business. It wasn't until the sixteenth century that "entrepreneur" was used to refer to someone undertaking a business venture. And by 1852, it further evolved to mean a business manager.

I wasn't born wealthy, and certainly didn't come from a long line of successful business leaders. Many of the most extraordinary founders came from humble beginnings and bootstrapped their way up the ladder. I also know entrepreneurs who inherited their companies but aren't instinctively entrepreneurs. I believe entrepreneurs are made and not born. And without a doubt, not all business leaders are entrepreneurs—but more on that later. According to a recent study by the US Census Bureau and two MIT professors, "the most successful entrepreneurs tend to be middle-aged, even in the tech sector." Researchers compiled a list of 2.7 million company founders who hired at least one employee between 2007 and 2014. The study found that the startup founders of the most successful tech companies were, on average, forty-five years old when they launched their businesses. In general terms, a fifty-year-old entrepreneur was almost twice as likely to start an extremely successful company as a thirty-year-old.

Even more surprising, a sixty-year-old startup founder was three times as likely to establish a successful startup as a thirty-year-old startup founder, and was 1.7 times as likely to found a startup that *wound up in the top 0.1 percent of all companies.*

While many opinions exist on what makes an entrepreneur, no single personality profile guarantees success. However, certain characteristics and skills are essential when starting any new business, including curiosity, adaptability, comfort with failure, persistence, innovation, and long-term focus. Despite a turbulent first few years, RE/MAX survived and began to grow exponentially, making it the iconic brand it is today. Our refusal to quit kept us going through all the obstacles and struggles. With my military background, I understood that once you got into a fight, you never quit. That was my attitude. And it paid off.

10 Traits of an Entrepreneur

1 Recognizes Opportunity: Entrepreneurs possess a keen eye for identifying opportunities in the market or gaps in existing offerings. They're often forward-thinking and can envision new possibilities that others may overlook.

2 Takes Risks: Entrepreneurship inherently involves taking calculated risks. Entrepreneurs are willing to invest their time, effort, and resources into ventures that have an uncertain outcome with the expectation of achieving long-term success.

3 Innovates and Creates: Entrepreneurs thrive on innovation and creativity. They develop novel ideas, products, or services, or find unique ways to improve existing ones, aiming to differentiate themselves in the market.

4 Organizes and Allocates Resources: Entrepreneurs assemble and organize the necessary resources, including capital, human talent, and technology, to bring their ideas to fruition. They leverage these resources effectively to launch and grow their ventures.

5 Proactively Initiates: Entrepreneurs are self-starters. They actively pursue their goals, overcome challenges, and drive their ventures forward. They are motivated by a sense of ownership and the desire to make a meaningful impact.

6 Demonstrates Persistence and Resilience: Entrepreneurship often involves setbacks and obstacles. Successful entrepreneurs stick with it, embracing failures as learning opportunities and bouncing back from setbacks to continue their pursuit of success.

7 Creates Value: Entrepreneurs aim to create value for customers, employees, and stakeholders. They strive to meet the needs of their target market by offering innovative products, services, or solutions that solve problems or fulfill desires.

8 Displays Vision and Leadership: Entrepreneurs have clear visions for their ventures and possess strong leadership skills. They inspire and motivate their teams, effectively communicate their ideas, and guide their companies toward achieving their goals.

9 Adapts and Remains Flexible: Entrepreneurs operate in dynamic environments and need to be adaptable. They're open to feedback and willing to pivot their strategies or adjust their business models to respond to market changes and customer demands.

10 Makes an Impact and Leaves a Legacy: Entrepreneurs often aspire to create lasting impact and leave positive legacies. They may seek to make a difference in their industry, contribute to social causes, or generate economic growth and employment opportunities.

I think that without owning something—over an extended period of time, like a few years—where you have the chance to take responsibility for your recommendations, where you have to see your recommendations through all action stages and accumulate scar tissue for the mistakes, and pick yourself up off the ground and dust yourself off, you learn a fraction of what you can.

—Bill Gates

SOME THINGS YOU CAN'T TEACH

Throughout the years, I've discovered that there are many things you can teach about business, and some things that are just inherent. You either have some qualities or you don't. However, it's possible to adopt the habits of an entrepreneur. For example, successful entrepreneurs are curious. This curiosity allows them to continue to seek new opportunities. They ask thought-provoking questions and consistently seek new pathways. In addition to their deep interest, they understand structured experimentation. They test ideas to see if they will work so they can validate those ideas and their potential. As business constantly changes, an entrepreneur expects the unexpected and then adapts.

When Covid shut down so many businesses, entrepreneurs found ways to pivot and create new opportunities despite the circumstances. That was precisely what happened with Daddy's Chicken Shack, a company we invested in and now own. When Covid closed the doors of their restaurant, the owners quickly created a delicious take-out menu, which helped the business evolve to where it is today. Entrepreneurs find ways to keep their businesses moving forward, regardless of unexpected changes that happen along the way. Sometimes, this requires making difficult decisions and standing by those choices, whether right or wrong. Being decisive requires confidence that you're moving in the right direction. And if, for some reason, things don't work out, confidence is often what enables you to course correct.

An effective entrepreneur recognizes their strengths and weaknesses. As I said in the opening of this book, *I* didn't build RE/MAX—certainly not alone. A *team* always contributed to the company's success from the ground up. As we grew, so did our team. We were like-minded enough but willing to challenge and push one another to expand our vision and to achieve our goals.

Starting your own business requires a willingness to take risks. So many things can and will go wrong along the way. But the most accomplished entrepreneurs will balance the risks and rewards to benefit the upside. Sometimes those choices will pay off, and other times they won't—and that's okay, because failure is a part of success. In fact, it's a big piece of the equation.

As an entrepreneur, having a comfort level with failing means you can expect it and therefore prepare for it. Instead of allowing failure to hold them back, entrepreneurs use it as motivation and fuel to adapt, shift direction, and move forward anyway. Persistence is a real difference maker. The willingness to plow through, learn from mistakes, continue to ask questions, and persist are all indicators of a committed entrepreneur.

When we launched RE/MAX, we understood we were taking an existing business model—a well-established norm—and significantly improving upon it. Anyone can adopt an innovative mindset by cultivating their strategic thinking skills. Doing so positions your venture for success. While the early stages of launching a business are critical, growing it to sustainability is where all the fun lives. Some of the most incredible opportunities we encountered came long after we launched RE/MAX. It's important to remember that being an entrepreneur isn't about how you start—it's about how you finish. It's a long-term play that will likely lead to long-term success.

A true entrepreneur also possesses what experts refer to as the *entrepreneurial spirit.* You aren't necessarily born with this; it's developed, cultivated, and refined with time and experience. It's an attitude and an approach to thinking that actively seeks change rather than adapting to the status quo. It's a way of thinking that promotes critical questions, innovation, service, and continuous improvement.

> ***An entrepreneurial spirit is a way of approaching situations where you feel empowered, motivated, and capable of taking things into your own hands.***
> **—Sara Sutton Fell, CEO and founder of FlexJobs**

Someone with an entrepreneurial spirit has the passion, drive, and commitment to build something extraordinary from the ground up. Why is passion so important in business? Whether it's business-driven or not, when you speak to someone with a passion for a subject, their enthusiasm is contagious. Even if you would typically find the topic boring, when someone presents it with complete conviction, it's usually captivating. Passionate people are generally very well-versed in their subject. Theirs is a trait we've always looked for when hiring a team member or backing an entrepreneur's new venture. Passion manifests as a willingness to do whatever it takes to achieve lofty goals. For the passionate person, there are no tasks too big or too small; there are merely things that need to get done.

By nature, an entrepreneur is optimistic. Those with this mindset don't spend much time contemplating what *can't* be done. It's quite the opposite. They're constantly thinking about how to get it done. These people can't help themselves. They aren't afraid to go against norms or public opinion in the pursuit of disruption and change for the better. Challenges and obstacles are just solutions waiting to be discovered. *Impossible* is simply not a word in their vocabulary.

Entrepreneurs are risk-takers, but they aren't blind risk-takers. Their actions are thoughtful and calculated. They're typically willing to lose by trying. When starting a business, there are no guarantees of success. The first couple of years will test you in every way. Regardless of the outcome, your ability to persevere through those challenges will significantly determine your level of achievement. Staying flexible, open-minded, and willing to adapt in unfamiliar territory will serve you and your business well.

As an investor, I've spent years listening to aspiring entrepreneurs share their ideas for the next big business. I take note of what they tell me and always ask, "So, how's it going?" I can't tell you how often they say "I haven't started yet" or "I don't know how to launch." Ideas are meaningless unless they're acted on. Sometimes things work out, and sometimes they don't, and that's okay. Every failure is a lesson about what not to do. I've had more failures than successes. Each taught me something I took into my next decision. However, I consistently executed my ideas. I was always willing to take the hit if it wasn't the right path, just as I was always willing to accept the accolades when it turned out to be the right direction. Circumstances are irrelevant. Just do it. Be intentional. Be decisive. And be willing to fail. Remember, you must be fearless to be limitless.

You don't necessarily have to work in business to possess the entrepreneurial spirit. It's more of a mindset. Those with an entrepreneurial spirit are consistent and proactive, and they work toward their dreams. They create opportunities for themselves and others. They're perpetual learners who experiment, apply, share, and partner. Every experience is valuable. Whenever I hired brokers, I could always tell those who wanted to run their own businesses and those who merely intended to work for those people. Both are necessary for business. There's a difference between an individual who supports company goals and someone looking to create their own endeavor.

10 Traits of an Entrepreneurial Spirit

1. Has Passion and Purpose
2. Has Ambition and Is Opportunistic
3. Is a Dreamer, Thinker, and Doer
4. Is a Natural Leader
5. Is Someone Who Takes Action
6. Has Vision and Foresight
7. Inspires Others
8. Is Not Afraid of Failure
9. Takes Calculated Risks
10. Is Always Learning and Growing

Being a good entrepreneur is more about the way you conduct yourself as a leader than it is about just being a person who runs their own business. Since change is always a factor in startups, how you respond to it and initiate it often says a lot about your entrepreneurial abilities and potential.

Well-known management consultant and author Peter Drucker said, "An entrepreneur always searches for change, responds to it, and exploits it as an opportunity." Drucker is revered for his disruptive ways of thinking about business management. He was the grandfather of management theory, influencing the operations of countless organizations around the globe. He also created one of the first MBA programs in 1971 at Claremont College in California. Of particular interest to Drucker was the practice of business ethics and morals. He originated four theories on management that became the gold standard for many.

His first is the Theory of MBO (Management by Objectives). Drucker believed MBOs help balance the objectives of the employee with those of the company. His idea is simple: If employees have a say in creating the standards for doing their job, they'll be more likely to meet those standards.

His second theory involved the application of the SMART method. He posited that, in order for an objective to be valid, it had to be Specific, Measurable, Achievable, Realistic, and Time-related. Today, the acronym SMART reminds us to check that the objectives we set meet those criteria.

Third, his Knowledge Worker Theory advanced the idea that we've been shifting from a managerial economy to an entrepreneurial one in which workers are increasingly thinkers as well as doers who seek training and further development. These workers are highly productive and creative. Because of their ability to solve complex problems, they're capable of introducing unique ideas, products, and services into society.

Finally, Drucker believed there were significant benefits to the decentralization of management. He observed many leaders attempting to take on every aspect of running their companies as shows of power or control, believing they were the only people who could get the job done. By contrast, Drucker asserted that management needs to delegate tasks, not only to be more productive but also to empower employees.

Today, many large companies support a work culture that fosters enthusiasm, vision, and problem-solving skills that are essential to entrepreneurial success. You don't have to be the owner or founder of a company to be considered an entrepreneur. Remember, entrepreneurship is a mindset, not a title. A collaborative study conducted by the online learning academy Future Workplace and the freelancing platform Upwork found that 90 percent of professionals thought of an entrepreneur as "someone who sees opportunities and pursues them" rather than "someone who starts a company." In fact, 58 percent of millennials consider themselves entrepreneurs. This suggests that, given the right environment, every employee can be an entrepreneur.

All of this points to the fact that companies should welcome, encourage, and pay for innovative thinking on the job. 3M has a guideline that researchers can spend 15 percent of their time working on independent ideas unapproved by management, sometimes known as "skunk-works projects." Post-it Notes were developed that way. And Salesforce has a top innovator program in product marketing that encourages novel ideas, which are then introduced to and celebrated with the rest of the team twice a year. When a group generates ideas, it creates camaraderie, healthy competition, and an incentive to innovate. Frequently, it's your competition that teaches you the most.

ENTREPRENEURS READ A LOT . . . AND OFTEN

Earlier in this book, I talked a little about my reading habits and how the books I read have significantly influenced every aspect of my life. I'm not alone in this habit. I heard a story about Warren Buffett being asked his secret to success, and he responded by saying he read five hundred pages of a book every day, because that's how gaining knowledge works. He added, "It builds up, like compound interest. All of you can do it, but I guarantee not many of you will do it." I've also heard that when Buffett began his investing career, he read between six hundred and one thousand pages daily. Think about that for a minute. He must have spent the bulk of his day reading everything he could get his hands on—and he still does, devoting about 80 percent of each day to reading. Other entrepreneurs who read a lot include Bill Gates, who tackles about fifty books a year, and Mark Cuban, who spends about three hours a day reading. When Elon Musk was asked how he learned to build rockets, he responded, "I read books." And Mark Zuckerberg resolved to read a book every two weeks.

A study of 1,200 wealthy people found that they all have reading as a pastime in common, and they primarily read books to educate more than to entertain. Without a doubt, books are the gateway to learning and knowledge. According to Tom Corley, author of *Rich Habits: The Daily Success Habits of Wealthy Individuals*, rich people read for self-improvement, education, and success. Many of those books are biographies and autobiographies of other successful people, which they turn to in order to learn lessons, gain insights, and be inspired. The point is, you should never stop learning. Reading has been a crucial part of my success, and it can be a crucial part of yours too. (By the way, I'm very happy you chose to read *this* book.)

THE CHALLENGES FOR WOMEN ENTREPRENEURS

The only thing I can think of that's harder than being an entrepreneur is being a woman entrepreneur. It's widely acknowledged that women entrepreneurs often face unique challenges and barriers when starting and growing their businesses. In 2021, there were only forty-seven women CEOs in the Fortune 500. In 2023, there are now fifty-two, representing slightly more than 10 percent of the CEOs on the list. Twenty-five percent of those women became CEOs in the past year. This is a positive sign that many companies are finally recognizing the value in diverse leadership. Companies such as General Motors, CVS, Lululemon, and Sketchers are now led by women.

Because women are still far from reaching equity in the leadership ranks, it's important to spotlight diverse executives, but I certainly hope there will soon come a day when we can simply rank the world's "most powerful," knowing that women and people of color will naturally be all over that list.

Geoff Colvin of *Fortune* recently reported that the criteria for CEOs have changed; vulnerability, humility, and self-awareness are now among the characteristics a first-time CEO must cultivate and exhibit. This seems promising for up-and-coming women CEOs and entrepreneurs. So too is a study from Boston Consulting Group, which found that women delivered higher revenue—twice as much per dollar of investment—than men. Because of that, BCG believes that investing in women-owned companies is a great idea. Despite this good news, there's still a lot of work to be done to achieve equity and parity for all in business.

Several factors continue to contribute to the difficulty women entrepreneurs experience. Of course, there are and always have been gender biases and stereotypes when it comes to women in business. These can be more pronounced in certain male-dominated industries and sectors, making it harder for women to gain entry and thrive in those fields. There are also the age-old assumptions about women's ability to balance work and family, as they often bear a greater burden of caregiving and household responsibilities than men—assumptions exacerbated by the extreme circumstances of the pandemic. Such assumptions and prejudices may affect how women are perceived, their access to resources, and how seriously they may be taken in certain business settings.

Women have always been an integral part of the success of RE/MAX, and make up 65 percent of our people in the US. I also really admire and want to support women entrepreneurs, especially when others don't. That's why it's so important to address these issues here, particularly the difficulty in accessing funding for women's enterprises. Multiple studies have shown that venture capital firms and investors tend to invest disproportionately in male-led businesses, making it harder for women to secure the necessary capital to start or scale their companies. It's even more challenging for African American women entrepreneurs. According to *Fortune*, companies led by Black women consistently received less than 1 percent of all capital funding. According to Project Diane, a biennial report on the state of Black and Latinx women founders by the organization digitalundivided, in 2018 there were only thirty-four Black women founders who had raised more than $1 million in venture capital. By 2021, that number had nearly tripled, with ninety-three female entrepreneurs of color raising $1 million or more. One of the reasons for the uptick in funding for women of color in 2021 was the optics of supporting Black and brown female entrepreneurs in the wake of George Floyd's murder. Unfortunately, this goodwill outreach and support didn't last. According to Crunchbase, in 2022 there was a 45 percent decrease in funding for Black entrepreneurs due to changing market conditions.

Sadly, for many female founders, the only way to keep their businesses up and running is to rely on their assets, maxing out their credit cards and turning to alternative lenders who charge high interest rates to get the funding their businesses need. While this is one way to keep a business afloat, they also tend to be terribly disadvantageous to women-owned businesses.

But financing isn't the only big challenge to tackle. To really hit your stride in business, it's important to network and find people who will mentor you along the way. This is especially true for women entrepreneurs. Unfortunately, enlisting mentors has been problematic for women for two reasons. First, traditional business networks and mentorship programs are often male dominated; and second, the underrepresentation of women in entrepreneurship has resulted in a scarcity of female role models who can mentor the sheer number of aspiring women entrepreneurs. But the good news is that all of this is changing. Because women are, by nature, more collaborative and empathetic, they're finding other women on their entrepreneurial journeys and helping one another out. There are many groups that provide both online and in-person resources, as the list below indicates.

Resources for Women Entrepreneurs

National Association of Women Business Owners (NAWBO)

NAWBO has more than forty years of experience helping women found and run their own businesses. The organization is supported by dues, has chapters across the United States, and represents women in all industries.

Local NAWBO chapters work as networking and support locations, giving women entrepreneurs access to others in their areas. The statewide and national organizations participate in government work, advocating for needs and causes relevant to women business owners.

Ladies Who Launch

Ladies Who Launch provides educational tools to women entrepreneurs so they can get started in business and keep progressing on the right path. On their free website, ladieswholaunch.org, women can find templates to help them create business plans, along with sample legal documents, contracts, and more.

The website also offers premium options for those who need more advanced tools. Videos offering tips and inspiration are available. Women who are just starting out, or those who are in more isolated settings, may find these resources invaluable.

Female Entrepreneur Association

One of the largest global communities for women entrepreneurs, this organization founded by Carrie Green, author of the bestselling book *She Means Business*, offers weekly videos, a magazine, training, and connections to their five thousand members.

SCORE

Part of the Small Business Administration, SCORE is well-known for its ability to connect mentors and volunteers with entrepreneurs. Mentors are a huge factor in the ongoing success of women in the entrepreneurial field, and connecting with those who've faced similar challenges is particularly beneficial. While SCORE works with entrepreneurs across demographics, they have many resources aimed specifically at helping women business owners.

Women's Venture Fund

While the Women's Venture Fund offers training, educational resources, and more to women business owners in the New York City metro area, one of their more important offerings is assistance in acquiring small business loans, as women traditionally face institutional bias when applying for loan funding.

SBA Women's Business Centers

The SBA supports and sustains a network of more than one hundred Women's Business Centers throughout the United States and its territories. The organization's goal is to help women level the playing field in entrepreneurship by providing counseling and training to women who want to establish, grow, and expand their businesses.

National Women's Business Council

The National Women's Business Council is a nonpartisan federal advisory council that offers independent advice and counsel to Congress, the president, and the Small Business Administration on economic issues that affect women entrepreneurs. The chair of the organization is appointed by the president, and the chief executives are split between political parties.

The ultimate mission of these organizations is to create a more inclusive entrepreneurial ecosystem where all people and ideas can flourish. When the body of entrepreneurs is large and diverse, more innovative services and products can be provided—and that improves and enhances the overall quality and enjoyment of life for us all.

3

The Lasting Influence of Ernest Shackleton

There are many important business lessons to be learned from sources outside of business. For example, history, literature, and theater are full of valuable takeaways and insights about motivating people, living with integrity, and being a good citizen.

From the moment I read the book *Endurance* by Alfred Lansing, I became a great admirer of the explorer Sir Ernest Shackleton. His story resonated with me for many reasons, though mostly because it reflected my own experiences of persevering through good times and challenging ones, and always battling against the odds while building RE/MAX. For years, I've repeated stories of Shackleton's heroic Antarctic expeditions, especially the Imperial Trans-Antarctic Expedition from 1914 to 1917. On that particular endeavor, he attempted to cross Antarctica via the South Pole. His ship, the *Endurance*, was a barquentine, three-masted vessel. He received a grant from the British government equivalent to more than $1.3 million in today's currency. Reportedly, five thousand or more sailors applied to be members of his twenty-seven-man crew. That's how exciting the quest was expected to be. The ship set sail, leaving Buenos Aires on October 26, 1914, and stopped at Grytviken, a whaling station on

South Georgia Island. But as it sailed through the Antarctic Ocean, more than 1,200 miles from civilization, the ship became trapped in ice.

At first, Shackleton and his men thought it would be safe to stay on board. They had plenty of food and supplies, but as ten months slowly passed, the ice surrounding the vessel grew thicker. On October 27, 1915, extreme pressure rippled across the ice and destroyed the *Endurance*. The ship's stern was lifted straight out of the water, and its rudder and keel were completely torn off. Freezing water rushed in. Shackleton hurriedly warned his men that they needed to get off the ship before it sank, or they would all surely die. He had spent the prior ten months preparing for this moment, and the hour of reckoning had finally arrived. Shackleton was a cautious leader, someone who would never ask his men to do anything he wasn't willing to do himself. He was also a quick thinker who could pivot easily when he had to—the kind of person you want around when the going gets tough.

It wasn't the first time Shackleton had faced incredible hardship. On his 1907–9 expedition, Shackleton and his crew, including Frank Wild, Jameson Adams, and Eric Marshall, set out to discover a route to the South Pole. They were within ninety-seven miles of reaching their goal when Shackleton decided to turn back. He had enough food to get him and his men there, but he knew they didn't have enough to return safely. They were already exhausted, cold, and hungry. Shackleton wouldn't jeopardize their lives, despite being so close to their destination. He put the safety of his colleagues ahead of any notoriety they were likely to receive had they accomplished their feat. Most explorers of the day craved fame and fortune, and whenever one died in pursuit of his dream, he was worshiped as a hero and a martyr. But that didn't sway Shackleton. While he too wanted fame and fortune, living to enjoy it was of even greater importance.

Finding himself again in peril in impassably icy waters, Shackleton remained cool, calm, and collected. He knew that if he panicked, his men would too. He also knew that allowing them to wallow in their misery or to contemplate their fate would create a toxic environment. So, he made it clear that pessimism and dissent would not be tolerated.

His message was simple: Stay safe to survive. As a master crisis-management leader, Shackleton encouraged everyone to talk through their options. He involved the entire team in the decision to disembark and set up tents on the ice floe, where they were bound to be stuck indefinitely. Some of his men were seasoned sailors, but others, including young scientists, an artist, and even a stowaway, had no experience.

There was no way to radio for help, so they understood that no one was coming for them. Twenty-five days later, the team watched as the last remains of the *Endurance* sank to the bottom of the sea. The only things they were able to salvage from the wreckage were the meager lifeboats.

They spent the next twenty-two months in the freezing cold, enduring conditions so inhumane that they were nearly impossible to survive. It's been said they could hear the water freezing around them. While they had some rations, they ultimately took to eating penguins and seals to survive.

Shackleton instinctively understood the importance of teamwork and an inclusive leadership style. Most men want to lead with authority, as generals do in the army. Interestingly, Shackleton had grown up surrounded by sisters, and their influence could be seen in the way he chose to lead throughout his career. Women managers, as I've said before, tend to be both inclusive and empathetic. They're generally consensus builders and are good at balancing the demands of all the outside forces that pull at them, including children, home, and caretaking responsibilities. Women are also more likely to consider everyone's interests in their decision-making process, which results in team members feeling as if they've had a say in the outcome. Shackleton learned these skills from his sisters as a young man and then adapted them to his work, making him truly successful and well-known for his exceptional leadership abilities under the most extreme circumstances.

Shackleton also consistently revised and reset his goals, especially as circumstances changed, as they often did. Although the initial goal of the expedition was to reach the South Pole, the new goal was simply to survive. Shackleton kept his focus on that for his own sake, but even more so for the sake of his men. Their mission now was truly a matter of life and death.

Many challenges come with managing or leading during trying times. Given the circumstances, Shackleton did everything he could to avoid conflict. He wouldn't allow the men to spend more than one week in the same tent with the same people in order to avoid unnecessary disputes. He treated everyone fairly, refused to play favorites, and went out of his way to care for anyone who was struggling. He asked the men to keep journals as a way of purging their emotions and diverting their attention from the dire situation they were in. To stay connected, he made it a point to visit each tent, checking on his fellow explorers and ensuring that they were in good spirits. Shackleton did this daily, whether there was fair weather or a blizzard underway. He would sit with two or three men at a time and talk with them, asking how they were doing. He'd also remind them to make notes in their daily diaries. He showed empathy and understanding for what they were going through, offering a sympathetic ear or shoulder to lean on—all traits he attributed to being raised by his sisters. Above all, he encouraged his men to believe they could get through this.

He also emphasized their shared brotherhood and the value of loyalty. He was extremely committed to his men and expected them to be committed in return. As a result, the men displayed incredible kindness to one another. They shared their rations, and if one man dropped his, another would fill half of the empty cup with his own food.

As time passed, Shackleton realized that he and his men would perish if he didn't take action. On April 9, 1916, he decided to order his crew into the three lifeboats they had salvaged, and together they set sail toward Elephant Island, a small, uninhabited isle that he calculated to be five days away. He tasked the ship's captain, Frank Worsley, to navigate their course. Once again, the men endured unimaginable conditions. After leaving the ice floes, they weren't prepared for the rough seas. They lacked food and suitable clothing, which resulted in several of the crew getting frostbite. Against all odds, they found the island. They were finally on land, but still a long way from home.

As soon as the men were settled, Shackleton and two others, Frank Worsley and Harry McNish, set sail once again in one of the lifeboats. They were intent on returning to the South Georgia whaling station, 720 miles away, which they had departed from nearly a year and a half earlier. Shackleton packed four weeks' worth of supplies, refusing to take more from the men he left behind. He understood the risks involved in this voyage and knew that if they didn't find South Georgia Island in four weeks, his men would surely die. Miraculously, he made it in just about three weeks. Unfortunately, the three men were at death's door. They were weak, tired, and hungry. Worse, their boat landed on the wrong side of the island. Rather than setting sail again, they slowly walked thirty-two miles, traversing the jagged, uncharted mountains that separated them from the other side of the island. After walking for a day and a half, they finally reached the whaling station on May 20.

Within a day or two of their arrival, Shackleton was already planning his return to Elephant Island so he could rescue his men.

It would take four tries before he was successful. But he refused to give up, and he was finally reunited with his team on August 30, 1916. With a warrior's perseverance, and by the grace of God, they all survived.

When Shackleton's crew was finally rescued, every single man wrote about what a great leader he was. Many reported that they admired Shackleton for putting their welfare above his own.

The first time I read Shackleton's story was around 1999. By then, I understood what adversity, survival, stamina, persistence, and the importance of great camaraderie meant, as all of them applied to building RE/MAX. Each played a definitive role in creating our success. You could say each was the subject of a valuable lesson I learned at the College of Hard Knocks. You see, the first three years RE/MAX was in business were a total disaster. The headwinds were incredibly tough back then. But having spent some time in the United States Air Force fighting in Vietnam, I learned to never quit. No matter how hard things got, you had to find a way to keep pushing through.

Fierce determination and focus are required for any company to succeed. The ability to navigate challenges and unforeseeable obstacles is also mandatory. From the start, I was confronted with situations I didn't expect and wasn't prepared to handle. In our early days I partnered with the Weydert Group, land developers from Denver. At the time, I thought I was giving our little startup real estate company the type of financial infusion we would need to grow. Unfortunately, the economy fell on hard times, and as a result, so did Weydert. Their development projects all went bankrupt. And when that happened, I lost my financial backing. But, even worse, because I was partnered with Weydert when they filed for bankruptcy, I had to assume a share of their debt. It was, at first, a debilitating blow. I was already sinking, and now I was sure our ship would go under for good. Then the unimaginable happened.

From the day we opened our doors, there had been a terrible backlash from other members of the real estate community over our 100 percent commission business model, as I mentioned previously. But unbeknownst to us, the situation was worse than we had anticipated. Anonymous letters were being sent to various government agencies calling our ethics and business practices into question. We were accused of making fraudulent FHA and VA loans, which was absurd, since we weren't a mortgage company. We weren't funding *any* types of loans. We were a real estate company that sold homes. I didn't have any money to hire attorneys, so I personally took each and every accusation on, using my knowledge of the real estate business to refute the claims. The FBI investigated the bogus allegations and quickly backed off when they realized there was no merit to them. That, however, didn't stop the government from coming after us through a different route. The Securities and Exchange Commission (SEC) decided to look into us for fraudulent stock offerings, despite the fact that we had never issued a single share of stock outside of the founders' shares. The Colorado real estate commission jumped on the bandwagon, searching for any reason to shut us down. They ultimately reprimanded us for inappropriate accounting. Why? They found one extra dollar in a RE/MAX trust account. Yes, you read that correctly: *One dollar* was left over when the bank didn't issue a stop payment fee for a lost cashier's check.

While all those stories went public, no specific details about the outcomes were reported. But by then, the damage had been done. The public perception of our company had been tainted in ways we never could have expected. And none of the claims were true. Still, we were deeply in debt due to several mistakes I had made. When we couldn't meet payroll, I refused to take a salary. When that no longer covered our needs, Gail also refused her paycheck, and several other top executives followed our lead. I lived off my credit cards for two years, which is never a good idea, as it tanked my credit and only added more to my already enormous amount of debt. Eventually, we couldn't pay our bills, both business and personal. And that's when creditors began coming after us, including the IRS, who threatened to padlock our doors for nonpayment of taxes. At the time, I didn't realize the IRS could shut you down. I thought they were like any other creditor that you could put off for as long as you needed to. Naïve? You bet.

I wasn't sure how we would survive the mounting bills and pressures. But I did know I had no intention of filing for bankruptcy. That simply wasn't an option. Gail saw the writing on the wall and understood that I wasn't cut out to do everything. She had a plan, and it was a good one. We were both selling real estate at the time and using our commission checks to keep the company afloat. Given the reality of our situation, Gail calmly explained that the only way we could save the company was for me to concentrate on selling and recruiting. She would handle everything else, including our creditors. She knew she would get a lot further communicating with them than I would, and because of that, she could work through those debts. Her thinking was simple: If she could get our financial situation under control, I would be able to focus on growing the company. And she was right. While my approach at the time may have been more aggressive and combative, hers was graceful and endearing, which was far more effective. She was open, believable, and full of integrity, making her much better equipped to resolve the issues and gain the trust of the people we owed money to. By doing this, she was able to create monthly payment plans we could stick to, while I sold the dream of RE/MAX.

Relieved by our newfound division of labor, and free from thinking about giving up and folding shop, we intensified our efforts to become the biggest and most powerful real estate company in the business. Now that we were undeterred, those obstacles and challenges became opportunities. I began recruiting agents from other companies with the promise of a better business model, more money, and the autonomy to run their own business. We had a renewed sense of possibility and energy and were moving in the right direction. We held nothing back. I felt like I was leading the charge, willing to fight for my people and defend the things we believed in. I was moving ahead with confidence and conviction. In many ways, I thought I was born to lead under these kinds of intense conditions, making split-second decisions. That's why I loved the way Shackleton acted with unwavering strength and stamina—why I found his relentless focus and creative ingenuity in meeting and overcoming challenges so powerful and relatable. He never gave up. By surviving, he accomplished so much more than he initially set out to do. And his example inspires me to this day.

I believe some people are born leaders, and there's no doubt Shackleton was one of them. He was also a regular guy with feet of clay, as the idiom goes, meaning he had flaws. In addition to being quite the explorer, he was a known womanizer, a drunk, and a hell-raiser. But none of those traits got in the way of his extraordinary leadership skills. There are some things you can't learn in a classroom. Instinct and empathy are great examples. There's no doubt Shackleton was concerned about his team's chances of survival, but he never let it show. A good leader's composure can sometimes be the difference between life and death, as it was in this case. Shackleton had great instincts and was remarkably effective. I was so influenced by his ways that I created a course around his leadership principles. I taught it at ninety-plus RE/MAX locations, where it became one of the most well-received seminars I'd ever done.

SHACKLETON'S 4 LEADERSHIP PRINCIPLES

Shackleton operated under four primary leadership principles. While countless lessons and practices can be garnered from his leadership style, these four principles were critical to his becoming a truly effective leader—and they're just as powerful in our time as they were in Shackleton's. The four principles are:

1. Creating Optimism
2. Building Morale
3. Communicating Effectively
4. Leading by Example

Let's look at how each of these can impact your business and leadership skills.

CREATING OPTIMISM (PARTICULARLY *REALISTIC* OPTIMISM)

Optimism is true moral courage.

—Ernest Shackleton

From my point of view, the quality that defined Shackleton above all others was his optimism. His ability to provide hope throughout his and his crew's uniquely harrowing experience kept everyone alive. Leaders in today's organizations are also tasked with creating and maintaining a positive and optimistic environment as a means of ensuring success.

Optimism isn't just about whether you see the cup as half full, nor is it simply positive thinking, the denial of problems, or the conviction that everything happens for the best. *Realistic* Optimism is something more active than that. Optimism involves a confident drive to continually better oneself and one's circumstances. It's a particular style in which you acknowledge and explain to yourself the events that are happening and then choose the specific actions you'll take in response.

Shackleton was aware of the severity of his circumstances, yet he was consistent in his belief that he would get his men home alive. He always assumed their situation was temporary. Despite the challenging environment and living conditions, he regularly reminded everyone that they would someday return home. And, most important, in the process of instilling this hope, he searched for solutions to ensure a positive outcome.

Shackleton recognized the power of optimism and understood it to be the source of tremendous courage. He insisted his crew follow his example by maintaining a hopeful outlook too. He closely monitored his men and kept a watch on anyone who was beginning to doubt their fate so they wouldn't have a negative impact on the rest of the group. And while there were excruciatingly challenging days, weeks, and months, he faced each new circumstance and challenge as an adventure, not an obstacle.

Another example of how Realistic Optimism can profoundly affect the outcome of the most daunting circumstances is found in the book *Man's Search for Meaning* by Viktor Frankl. The story of Frankl's survival while being held captive by the Nazis is unforgettable. Although the book is a difficult and emotional read, it's highly impactful. Frankl was an Austrian psychiatrist and neurologist who lived in Vienna during the early days of World War II. Before he was captured and shipped to the first of four concentration camps, Frankl had been working on a thesis about human motivation. He set out to challenge Abraham Maslow's hierarchy of needs, which stated that you won't find wholeness until your basic needs are met. Frankl managed to hide his research papers in the lining of his overcoat when German soldiers picked him up. He prayed they wouldn't find them, but unfortunately, when he arrived at the concentration camp, the guards took his things, including his coat. As a result, he lost all his work. But he hadn't lost the impact his research and writing had upon his mindset. His belief in his thesis undoubtedly saved his life. He held on to the idea that finding meaning in life, no matter how dire or difficult the situation may be, leads to transcendence and, therefore, survival.

Frankl was known to always be present; he lived totally in the moment. Even in captivity, where his basic human needs were clearly not being met, he still found purpose in each and every day. Believing he would survive—that someday he would be free—kept him alive.

The same can be said for many friends of mine who fought in Vietnam and were held at Hỏa Lò Prison, famously known as the Hanoi Hilton. That was where several American soldiers, including Vice Admiral James Stockdale, Congressman Sam Johnson, and the late Senator John McCain, were interned during the war. Although many American soldiers died there, these men all survived.

Stockdale was a pilot who was shot down on September 9, 1965, and sent to the prison. While there, he was tortured, denied medical attention, kept in a windowless cell, and locked in leg irons at night. He was held captive for almost eight years, yet he never gave up hope.

Jim Collins interviewed Stockdale while writing *Good to Great: Why Some Companies Make the Leap . . . and Others Don't.* He wanted to understand what it takes to fully accept a hopeless situation and not despair in the face of certain death.

"I never lost faith in the end of the story. I never doubted not only that I would get out but also that I would prevail in the end and turn the experience into the defining event of my life, which in retrospect, I would not trade," Stockdale told him.

After hearing Stockdale describe why he refused to give up hope and how he stayed optimistic throughout his captivity, Collins then asked about those who didn't make it out alive.

"Oh, that's easy," he replied. "The optimists. They were the ones who said: 'We're going to be out by Christmas.' And Christmas would come, and Christmas would go. Then they'd say: 'We're going to be out by Easter.' And Easter would come, and Easter would go. And then Thanksgiving, and then it would be Christmas again. And they died of a broken heart." (Frankl describes an almost identical phenomenon among some of his fellow prisoners in *Man's Search for Meaning*.)

Stockdale then went on to share the lesson of being *too* optimistic. "You must never confuse faith that you will prevail in the end—which you can never afford to lose—with the discipline to confront the most brutal facts of your current reality, whatever they might be."

Interestingly, when Stockdale mentions faith, he isn't referring to blind optimism. He's referencing faith in one's own ability to persevere in the face of an unfavorable reality.

From this conversation and through the various other insights Stockdale shared, Collins identified what he calls the Stockdale Paradox. The paradox posits that to survive a difficult situation *you must balance optimism with a realistic assessment of your current reality*, whatever that situation may be. Greatness demands optimism, but not in the face of obvious disaster. Many of those who managed to survive in the face of horrific odds understood this. They had the ability to accept brutal facts and see things as they were and not how they wished them to be.

Stockdale and Frankl were two ordinary men who were put in extraordinary circumstances. What set them apart from others who didn't survive was their unique combination of naturally protective traits, which provided a psychological buffer to the trauma they experienced. Not everyone has these traits, but resilient leaders inherently possess this mindset and inspire their team to follow their lead, just as Shackleton did with his men.

Remember that while optimism is a crucial tool in the entrepreneurial kit (especially when it comes to motivating employees), it can lead to disaster if administered too liberally.

> ***What we want is not blind optimism but flexible optimism—optimism with its eyes open. We must be able to use pessimism's keen sense of reality when we need it, but without having to dwell in its dark shadows. The benefits of this kind of optimism are, I believe, without limit.***
>
> **—Martin E. P. Seligman, PhD**

So, you might be asking yourself why I'm leading you to a better understanding of optimism. After all, this is a business book, not a self-help book, right? Well, yes and no. Research has shown that optimism is related to success in all sorts of areas, including work, sports, politics, and health.

Many years ago, Metropolitan Life used an assessment of optimistic attitude to select and hire salespeople, which saved them millions of dollars in the cost of personnel selection. Those highest on the optimism scale outsold their coworkers in their first year by 27 percent, and by an even more significant margin in the years following. When American Express Financial Advisors pilot-tested optimism training, they increased sales enough in the first three months to persuade them to make it a standard part of their training program.

One of the most debated questions in business is tangentially related to the issue of optimism. The question revolves around whether success comes by design or default. Another way to frame the default part of the question might be to ask, "Do some people just get lucky? Do they get a break? Are they born into wealth? Do they inherit success? Or do they happen to be in the right place at the right time?" Jeff Bezos and Bill Gates both claim that luck played a role in their success. And yet there are those, such as Steve Jobs, who say they planned for success. I know that's how I see the path to success. I planned for it and then put in the effort to achieve it. Jack Dorsey, the founder of Twitter (now called X) and Square, once tweeted, "Success is never an accident." And I tend to agree with that. Of course, there are some who believe you create luck through hard work and ingenuity, and that is undoubtedly the case with Bezos and Gates. But whether you think success comes from design or default, both impact how you act and, therefore, your level of success.

Peter Thiel, a cofounder of PayPal and the first outside investor in Facebook (now called Meta), describes two kinds of optimism in business: "Definite Optimism" and "Indefinite Optimism." A definite optimist is someone who believes the future will be better as a result of planning and effort. Definite optimism creates a better world. It engenders disruption and change. For centuries, definite optimism dominated the way inventors, scientists, and entrepreneurs thought, but today that's no longer the case.

The indefinite optimist believes the future will be better but suggests that this is the result of chance more than planning and effort. Instead of building new things, indefinite optimists prefer to rearrange existing things instead of innovating. Think of it this way: Private equity companies make money by buying other companies and restructuring them. This is certainly one way of doing business, and it's fairly common today. But it won't get you from where you are now to where you want to be. Remember my favorite definition of success? It's doing what you want, when you want, where you want, and with whom you want to do it. That doesn't come by chance. That can be achieved only by planning and then executing.

10 CHARACTERISTICS OF THE REALISTIC OPTIMIST

1 They Have Selective Focus: Whereas the pessimist sees problems, the optimist sees challenges. Optimists primarily focus on inducing constructive activity.

2 They Set Realistic Goals and Standards: Realistic Optimists don't try to be perfect. They ask themselves how realistic their goal is given the current conditions and strive to *improve*, not to achieve perfection.

3 They View Events in Proportion: Optimists have a way of keeping difficult events and circumstances in perspective. When faced with a challenge, they're somehow able to reframe any situation by approaching it with a level head and a creative, problem-solving attitude.

4 They Emphasize the Positive: Realistic Optimists make a concerted effort to commend both their own and other people's successes. When given a compliment, they can simply say "Thank you." The ability to confidently acknowledge compliments and rewards helps them appreciate the efforts that have gotten them to where they are today.

5 They Have a Sense of Humor: Humor—not taking oneself too seriously and allowing for moments of levity and laughter—is an important trait of Realistic Optimism.

6 They Are Rational: The Realistic Optimist does his or her best to see reality as it is rather than how he or she wants it to be. They apply reason to find ways to assess and achieve goals. Blind, wistful optimism, by contrast, is irrational optimism.

7 They Are Driven by Self-Improvement: Realistic Optimists recognize the possibilities for continuing growth and self-improvement. They believe that to remain the same leads to inertia and falling behind in today's fast-paced world.

8 They Are Experimental: Realistic Optimism requires more than a belief that things will improve; it requires actively searching for and creating novel approaches. The optimist evaluates each idea and method on its face, and is quick to try new approaches that appear to offer advantages.

9 They Take Personal Responsibility: Realistic Optimism requires understanding the part we play in bringing about the results we want. The optimist realizes that goals can be reliably achieved only through personal effort.

10 They Select and Create Their Environment: Realistic Optimists are immediately attracted to people and surroundings that inspire and support others, and not those that discourage, distract, or undermine. Optimists surround themselves not only with those who agree with them but also with those who constructively criticize their goals and methods.

BUILDING MORALE

The next leadership principle Shackleton relied upon was a very practical one. He understood that he needed to keep his team's morale high, or they would lose hope for survival. To do this, he established an orderly routine that kept everyone productive and performing meaningful work. He made it abundantly clear that their well-being always came first. He also created a sense of community and camaraderie among the men by encouraging them to work together.

When you think about it, the way Shackleton built the morale of his crew is exactly how a good leader would in any business environment today. A happy and engaged staff is an effective staff. Gauging morale is a measurement of job satisfaction and commitment. Very often, morale is raised or lowered by a combination of factors, including salary, job security, team members, management, leadership, and more. When confidence is high, sales are up, turnover is down, customers are satisfied, and employees are more willing and eager to innovate and create.

High company morale has a direct impact on productivity and profit. As numerous studies indicate, a happy team can increase profitability by more than 20 percent.

In Shackleton's case, the stakes and rewards were, of course, significantly higher than an increased percentage of profit. An optimistic, productive team working in harmony to survive was a team more likely to make it home alive.

COMMUNICATING EFFECTIVELY

One of the greatest methods for creating and boosting morale is *strong communication.* Shackleton understood this as well. He wasn't just willing to speak honestly and openly to his men; he was also ready to listen to them, hear their concerns, contemplate their ideas, and actively implement those innovations. Everyone wants to feel seen and heard, especially in the workplace. It doesn't matter if you're the boss or the janitor—or, in Shackleton's case, the captain or the ship's steward. No one in the chain of command wants to feel invalidated or invisible. When communication breaks down, so does the team and their prospects for success.

I also cannot overstate the value of recognition when it comes to keeping morale high. By visiting each team member in their tents, Shackleton was letting every one of his people know that their day-to-day contributions toward keeping one another alive mattered. When was the last time you spoke with your employees one-on-one and acknowledged their contributions to your team's success?

LEADING BY EXAMPLE

With or without a ship to command, Shackleton proved capable of navigating any circumstance. It was his leader*ship* and even his entrepreneur*ship*—the brave way he engineered a path to safety for all his men when none seemed to exist—that served him better than any physical vessel could have.

The reason I love teaching about Shackleton is simple. As a business leader, you will always be faced with challenges. Good leaders must be able to navigate during stable times and uncertain ones. They must also be willing to take risks when the stakes are much greater than expected. How you respond will dictate the outcome. It will influence your team's performance and, ultimately, the future of your business. I also like sharing Shackleton's story because it illustrates that a good leader is, in many ways, responsible for other people's lives, security, income, and dedication—and the best way to influence those things is to lead with integrity and humanity.

4

Leadership

> ***Leaders are not born. They are made with effort and hard work.***
>
> **—Vince Lombardi**

Sir Ernest Shackleton wasn't the only explorer whose story fascinated me. In the early 1910s, Norwegian explorer Roald Amundsen and English explorer Robert Falcon Scott independently set out on a race to be the first to reach the South Pole. Although their quests began around the same time, they started several hundred miles apart in different areas of Antarctica.

The situation was an interesting matchup of leadership styles. For Scott, if the weather was good, he pushed on and attempted to achieve twenty-five miles a day. If the weather was terrible, his group stayed in their tents and didn't advance at all. Amundsen was the complete opposite. Rain or shine, he and his men made their goal each day. And when the weather was nice, they prioritized stopping, pitching their tents, and taking a casual afternoon to eat and regain strength.

As it turned out, Amundsen won, but both men and their teams reached their destination because they had learned a lot from various life challenges and other expeditions before theirs. The point is: Nobody is born a leader, as legendary football coach Vince Lombardi understood. Leadership comes from a lifetime of accumulated experience.

And experience comes in many forms. If you go to college and get a marketing or management degree, you'll have a big head start over someone without those credentials. However, that's being book smart; it isn't being people smart. I would rather hire a C student who was the quarterback of the football team, because that's a leadership position. During the four years he studied at college and earned his degree, that student also gained valuable expertise by guiding his team. Outstanding leadership comes down to how you influence, control, and encourage your team, and that's learned through exposure to different circumstances. Again, leaders aren't born; they're made every day through education and experience.

The reality is that many people with strong capabilities and potential take their foot off the gas when they become leaders because they think they've already made it to the top of the mountain. One thing I learned many years ago is that there's always another mountain to climb and a higher peak to summit. In other words, more experiences await. What you did yesterday is in the past. The critical question is, what will you accomplish today? You must have the drive and motivation to accumulate new experiences every day.

In his book *Peter Drucker on the Profession of Management*, the widely respected business consultant and author wrote, "Executives spend more time on managing people and making people decisions than on anything else—and they should. No other decisions are so long-lasting in their consequences or so difficult to make."

I believe this with all my heart. Being a leader isn't just about having power and control; it's about ensuring that those you lead are cared for and supported. A lot of companies like to refer to their employees as family. Everyone in the company is a part of that family, so if you're a low performer or not meeting your quotas, it's no issue at all, because, well, you're family. And because you're family, you'll overlook the obvious, like a favorite uncle who has a little too much to drink and tells off-color jokes during the holidays. Oh, that's just Uncle Joe, it's no big deal, he's family. Well, you get it.

Now consider a football team. In general, that team depends on their leaders. One of the most important leaders is the quarterback. If he's a good quarterback, he has a strong arm and can call the right plays. As long as he's connecting and the team is winning, everyone is happy. When he starts to lose his arm and can no longer throw like he used to, that quarterback starts to let the team down. When that happens, the team loses its winning spirit. The camaraderie starts to go bad, and the team begins to fall apart. It's a tough decision for a coach to replace the quarterback, but that's the game. That's being a team. You have to lead a team from a place of strength. If the leader is weak, the team suffers. Sometimes you just have to let go of the old and bring in something new. You can have team accomplishments with family values, but your team is not your family.

Here's what I mean. Let's say the quarterback's wife is diagnosed with cancer. All the other players and their wives will likely step up to help support her through her journey. They might bring her meals or offer to drive her to appointments, especially if the husbands are off playing a game somewhere. That is an example of a team exhibiting family values—values the team leader likely modeled. But the leader's primary role is to set the expectation of team *performance*. Never construe the role of team leader as anything other than that.

While the early days after establishing RE/MAX were frustrating for Gail and me, that's when we shaped our team leadership style. As I've said, we struggled—a lot. We made so many mistakes that we knew we had a choice to make. We could blame our early challenges on the economy, the real estate market, and the Realtors trying to put us out of business. We could just throw our hands in the air and give up, or we could accept the challenges as they were and find a way to succeed. There's a saying that resonated with me from the very first time I heard it: "When you point your finger to blame somebody else, there are three fingers pointing back at you." Good point. So, we acknowledged what went wrong and refused to quit.

This was a very humble moment in our lives. By 1974, just a year after we opened our doors, Gail and I had eight offices and eight managers who were ten to twenty years older than we were, and all of them had far more experience. We decided to tap into that experience. We asked our associates, "What did you like best about the company you used to work for? What did you dislike the most? What do you like best about RE/MAX? What do you dislike the most about our organization?" Then I would bare my soul, saying, "Help us be the leaders you want us to become."

One by one, our associates in the trenches gave us advice, and we continued to seek their experienced wisdom for the next fifty years. This really helped us become the leaders our brokers and agents deserved. Their insights and our willingness to listen pulled the company back from the brink of failure. RE/MAX also survived because we had enough personal courage to say, "We're screwing this damn thing up. Everyone's after us. How do we address this?" It was a team effort. True leadership involves many traits, but empathy, compassion, and a willingness to put the needs of others first are essential.

LOOKING OUT FOR THE TEAM

Leadership is not about being in charge. It is about taking care of those in your charge.
—Simon Sinek

Many years ago, I falsely believed that my employees and officers loved me enough that they would never leave the company. It was a terrible mistake. I also overlooked the fact that many of them were incompetent. It wasn't until sometime around 2001, after thirty-eight years in business, that I came to this realization. Just because I worked with a bookkeeper during my first year in business, would it necessarily make sense for that person to become the CFO of a company with a presence in 120 countries? No.

It's critical to consider where the bookkeeper will fit when you recognize that they'll never become the CFO. If you don't have the personal courage to help them move out of that position and into another—or to a different company—it does a lot of damage. When you have incompetent individuals, you actually end up hurting three groups of people. First, you hurt the employees themselves, because you've already pigeonholed them. You've decided that they don't have growth potential, even if you've already promoted them too far. They're living in purgatory, and you don't have the fortitude to fire them. If you handle them the right way, offering them several months of coaching, and they still can't do what the role requires, it's a wake-up call for their next job interview.

The second group of people you hurt are the employees they supervise. They'll look at you and say, "You own the company. Why is this person still here?"

Finally, the third group you hurt is yourself and your shareholders, because you failed to get rid of a C player and replace them with an A player.

I eventually gathered the courage to let people go after taking a hiring-and-firing seminar. I came home and told Gail, "Four of our officers haven't kept up the company. They're tired and burned out." I went on to admit that it was my fault. I didn't have the guts to hurt my friends' feelings. But I had to introduce some changes, which required making difficult decisions. Gail and I worked on a script, which we practiced by role-playing. I considered every possible objection, figured out how to stay firm, and became comfortable with the language I would need to use to execute my decision. I brought each officer in one at a time. I started by saying, "I consider your friendship incredibly important to me, and I love the contributions you've made to our company. But to be honest with you, the company has moved past your abilities. No matter how much I've tried to help you in the last couple of years, it isn't working. So I have two choices for you today. The first choice is I will fire you and give you two weeks' severance. Or you can resign, and in addition to receiving one year of severance, Human Resources will help you with outplacement and assist you in getting a new job."

Inevitably, the arguments I anticipated came.

"That's not fair. I work really hard. You should see what I do."

I would interrupt and say, "No, excuse me. Out of respect for our friendship, I love you. You're my friend. I hope you'll still be my friend tomorrow. My decision has been made. You have to choose right now. You can either take two weeks of severance, cuss me out, and say I'm a miserable bastard, or you can say you decided to resign, get a year of severance, and walk out the door with your head held high. Do you want option number one or option number two?"

All four took the year of severance. Not one of them was my friend the next day. I never spoke to any of them again. That's okay. I did what had to be done, and we allowed them to leave with their dignity.

I should have done it ten years earlier. But I didn't.

A few days later, I was in a stall in the men's restroom with the door closed when two individuals came in and stood at the urinals. They didn't know I was in there. One of the guys said, "Jeez, Dave must be bummed. Thirty-eight years and nobody has ever resigned. And then four people resign on the same day."

The other guy turned to him and said, "Do you really think they resigned?"

The next day, we had a companywide meeting in which we operated as if nothing had happened. It was no secret that those employees were gone. At the end of the session, we opened it up to questions, as always. One team member stood up and asked, "What the hell did so-and-so have on you that you didn't fire him ten years ago?"

I looked at him and said, "I was a coward. I traveled with these people one-hundred-plus days a year. I've been to their weddings. I've been to their family funerals. I've been to their kids' weddings. This is a close-knit family. I didn't have the personal courage to tell them they don't work well with us anymore and are harming themselves, the other employees, and our company. I finally grew enough courage to face up to that and do the right thing."

The room was completely quiet.

The team member looked at me and said, "Got it."

With that, I established my flaws, vulnerability, and leadership in one exchange.

Your responsibility as a leader is to lead. To be effective, you must find the courage to do so. You can't just be a yes-man or yes-woman and tolerate incompetence. It's not an easy job. But it's a good job. Some people will never be suited for it, while others will thrive.

A dictionary definition of leadership includes being in a position of governance or control over people or an organization. True leadership digs deeper into the nuances of what it means to be in charge. When you're running a business, you're leading *people*, and that means you must develop people skills on top of your business know-how.

The greatest leader is not necessarily the one who does the greatest things. He is the one that gets the people to do the greatest things.

—Ronald Reagan

To be an effective leader, you must consistently interact with your staff, colleagues, and clients to achieve your goals. Great leaders don't force collaboration—they invite it. As Apple's Steve Jobs famously said, "Leadership is about inspiring others to accomplish what they thought they couldn't do, whereas management is about persuading people to do what they never wanted to do."

A strong leader has developed skills that help guide others to reach their collective goals. Leadership qualities are traits that every outstanding leader shares, whether they're an executive in the C-suite or a team leader on the sales floor. These skills aren't tied to your job title, pay, or role. They're not even tied to your personality. They're a set of values and beliefs that anyone at any level can adopt.

There are no *laws* for being a good leader either. There are, however, some common traits you can cultivate, as you'll see in the pages to come.

LEADING BY EXAMPLE

To me, the best leadership is taught by example. Throughout the years, I've learned critical habits of leadership and management from some of the most exceptional authorities in the world. The notion of leading by example has taken on increased importance for today's business leaders. Employees at all levels look to their supervisors, managers, and senior executives to act as role models and exhibit effective leadership behaviors worthy of emulation.

Historically speaking, Ernest Shackleton was an exemplary role model and mentor for his crew members. He was ever vigilant about his role as a leader and took every opportunity to demonstrate behaviors he wished his men to exhibit. They looked to him in moments of illness, strife, despair, self-doubt, and celebration.

Shackleton remained fair and structured as a leader but didn't rule hierarchically. His inclusive leadership style stood in stark contrast to the more traditional top-to-bottom style that was prevalent at the time. Class, rank, and status always played roles in leadership during Shackleton's time at sea, yet he made everyone feel like an essential team member. He was cautious about chastising anyone in public. If he had an issue with one of his men, he spoke to them privately and focused on fixing the problems over punishing his people. And he made it a point to praise his crew members easily, publicly, and often. Finally, he looked for opportunities to create pleasant surprises and celebrations, even while stranded in the middle of nowhere. He inherently understood that this would keep his team optimistic and motivated to keep going.

There have also been many modern-day leaders I've admired. Each one showed me through their actions and their words how to be a better leader for my company and my team.

For instance, Darren Hardy has been a key influence on me regarding the art of leadership. I think he possesses the most extraordinary leadership mind of our generation.

Another person I seriously admire is Jack Welch, who's also considered one of the most exceptional leaders of his time. He worked as the CEO of General Electric for twenty years (1981–2001). During his tenure, Welch turned what most people saw as a light bulb company that also made appliances into a diversified international conglomerate that entered the arenas of finance, entertainment, renewable energy, and more. Through Welch's gruff and definitive decision-making, which included massive layoffs and cost-cutting, GE's revenues grew, and its stock price soared. The skills that propelled Welch from young manager in 1960 to CEO in 1981 took decades to develop.

He grew the company and its revenue by slashing costs and reducing labor. At first, people saw him as something like the Terminator. But soon, people began to see the benefits of his decision-making and strategy.

In today's world, Welch's leadership style may be considered hard-edged. And while that might be true, he practiced many principles that greatly inspired me over the years.

Welch believed that excellent leaders must get their "people decisions" right. He thought effective hiring was brutally difficult but also one of the most essential skills to develop. While at GE, he estimated that he spent more than half his time getting the right people in the right places and then helping them grow. Welch was passionate about building the company's team and didn't delegate the hiring. Instead, he inserted himself into the process and was involved in final decisions, especially on key hires. Welch also had an inherent understanding of when to let someone go. He ripped off the Band-Aid fast and firmly. He was decisive and encouraged remarkable honesty, almost always to the point of being blunt. In his book *Winning*, Welch said that a lack of candor is "a killer that blocks smart ideas, fast action, and good people from contributing all the stuff they've got." Welch became an investor, a board member, an educator, and a leadership consultant in retirement. He taught the principles of critical hiring and firing, explaining that managers could easily be judged by their own people's decisions.

A leader is one who knows the way,
goes the way, and shows the way.
—John C. Maxwell

I've observed certain traits in the great leaders who came before me. What follows are the ten I think of as the most important.

1. GREAT LEADERS SELL HOPE

The most effective leaders promote a strong sense of hope among their team members. In fact, hope is the number one trait that motivates people to follow a leader. Presidents run on hope. Martin Luther King spread a message of hope—hope that we can do better, be better, and live a better life. Hope is vital to those who feel that they haven't gotten the brass ring or who don't have the benefits of wealth and success. Politicians, business leaders—you name it—are all selling hope. Hope that they can bring the change that will make a difference. Hope that they will turn their companies around. Hope that they will take their organizations to the next level, that they will give women equality, that they will provide minorities with equality, that we can have a better world. Hope is the number one message all successful business leaders must embrace and prove they can deliver.

So, what is hope?

Hope is a positive and optimistic state of mind characterized by a belief in the possibility of a better future. It's an emotional and mental attitude that motivates individuals to look forward to positive outcomes, even in challenging or uncertain circumstances.

Hope involves having confidence in one's abilities and having a sense of purpose or direction. It's often accompanied by a desire and willingness to take action and work toward specific goals and outcomes.

Hope can provide individuals with a sense of resilience, allowing them to maintain optimism and perseverance in the face of obstacles or setbacks. It can serve as a source of inspiration and motivation, helping people overcome adversity and continue to move forward.

Furthermore, hope isn't limited to personal aspirations; it can also extend to collective or societal contexts. It can fuel social movements, inspire communities to work together for positive change, and create a shared vision of a better future.

Hope is a powerful and essential human emotion that can bring personal growth and a sense of purpose. It plays a crucial role in helping individuals navigate challenges, overcome obstacles, and maintain a positive outlook on life.

Hopeful leaders are visionaries who drive progress toward success.

2. GREAT LEADERS HAVE INTEGRITY AND GOOD ETHICS

Another trait people look for in leaders is integrity. They expect their leaders to model strong ethical behavior. Herb Kelleher, cofounder of Southwest Airlines, was a great example of someone who led with integrity and uncompromising ethics. He created a culture that inspired people to come to work with passion and to be fully engaged. Herb was frequently voted the best CEO in the airline industry. He was a pioneer and an innovator, if not a disruptor. His leadership showed that it was possible to love people, have fun, and make money all at the same time. He believed you could run a business, treat your people like family, and make it fun in the process. He once said, "I'd rather have a company bound by love than a company bound by fear."

I remember watching a speech of his in which he declared, "It's important to understand the customer is not always right. To take the side of the customer over your employee when the customer is wrong . . . is wrong." Here's what he meant: If an angry customer who drank too much on a flight blames the flight attendant for an incident that ensued, it's okay to throw the drunk off. Kelleher empowered his entire staff, from the pilot to the crew, to remove unruly passengers and, in some cases, to let them know they were no longer welcome on Southwest Airlines. Standing by his team went a long way with his employees. Showing them respect earned their respect in return.

I love that the word "integrity" has the word "grit" in it. Integrity means that when choosing between what's convenient and what's right, you do what's right even though it may challenge you in unexpected ways. The right way inevitably yields better results than taking the path of least resistance. Here's one thing I learned very early in my career: Success can come and go, but integrity lasts forever. Integrity is about doing the right thing in all circumstances, even when no one is looking. It takes courage to execute regardless of the consequences. While it can take years to build your reputation, it takes only a second to lose it. And once you lose your reputation as someone with integrity, it's nearly impossible to get it back.

Integrity is an often-overlooked trait, but it's one of the most important for any leader to possess. We live in a world where some people stretch the truth about things, especially regarding their qualifications for a job. They'll overpromise and underdeliver when it comes to profitability and valuations. They'll play hooky from work. You name it, I've seen it happen. Each time someone does something like this, they hurt you, your business, and your customers. Regardless of their justifications, the act and the results prove their lack of integrity. We all know people who lack integrity yet operate as if they have it. In the end, there's a price to pay for that behavior. When trust is lost, good luck recovering it.

Look, integrity isn't something you can pretend to have. You may be able to fake it until you make it for a while, but that doesn't last long. I've always believed that you must act successful to be successful and you must exude confidence to build confidence in others, but you cannot fake who you are for very long. People want to work for somebody who's genuine. They'll accept your policies if they buy into your values. They will also accept your weaknesses. Hell, it's weaknesses that make us human.

When I think about integrity, an interaction with General Norman Schwarzkopf comes to mind. I met the general when I was in the military. Upon the announcement of his retirement in 1991, I sent him a letter. I told him I'd listened to him speak on military matters and felt he had a lot of wisdom to share. I thought he should consider going on a speaking tour to talk about the war. After we'd corresponded for a while, he said he'd love to, but he didn't know how to get started. I explained that he needed a quality speaker bureau behind him and suggested that he contact Washington Speakers Bureau, whom we'd used for many years to book speakers for our company retreats. I offered to give him a reference, because I knew he'd be excellent. I was so convinced that I also extended an opportunity for him to speak to us at the Fox Theater in Atlanta as his inaugural speech. He graciously accepted.

At the time, he was still under Secret Service protection, so the FBI, the Atlanta police, bomb-sniffing dogs, and snipers all had to be present too. After his arrival in an armored car, I stood with him backstage, behind the curtain. An inflatable helicopter that looked like the ones used in Iraq was set on the dark stage. On the screen above the stage, we played a clip of Barbara Walters interviewing him. The audience heard the general tell her, "When the plan came together, we knew that we would strike at exactly one minute after midnight. We gathered around as a group in the command tent, knowing we were going to put tens of thousands of our soldiers in harm's way. We put on my favorite record, 'God Bless the USA,' we said a prayer for our team, and we went to war."

It just so happened that country music singer-songwriter Lee Greenwood owned two RE/MAX offices at the time. Knowing that this unofficial anthem would play while we introduced General Schwarzkopf to the audience, I asked Lee if he would come to Atlanta and sing it for us. Of course, he said he'd be honored. Lee stepped onto the stage. The spotlight hit only him, so the helicopter still wasn't visible. When he began to sing "God Bless the USA," I could see tears in the corners of General Schwarzkopf's eyes.

When Lee finished, the audience erupted in applause, and he moved to the side of the stage. Several RE/MAX headquarters staff, who were ex-military, stood in uniform beside the helicopter. Then the helicopter lights came on and the massive fans we'd positioned in the far reaches of the hall caused the blade overhead to spin, nearly blowing the doors off the room. It was so believable that, to this day, people swear we landed a helicopter on that stage. Then the god mic came on: "Ladies and gentlemen, General Schwarzkopf." He walked out and completely wowed the audience.

When the general finished, he came backstage, where I stood ready to congratulate him.

"Sir, your speakers bureau contract said that you would do a maximum of six photos," I said. "I've had my picture taken with you before, but I've got a couple dozen people here that are ex-military."

Before I could go any further, General Schwarzkopf stopped me and said, "For the money you're paying me for a one-hour speech, bring your entire convention in. My flight doesn't leave until four."

That's integrity. *That's* doing the right thing, even when you don't have to, or when no one else is looking. To be certain, "boss watching" is real, and it never stops.

As a leader, you set the stage. Everyone has their eyes on you—how you dress, act, what time you come into the office, what time you leave. Most of all, they're watching for signs of integrity and strong ethics. People are always looking at the boss's behavior. If you go into the office on the weekend, everyone knows. If you wear a suit and tie or a dress, others will take note and self-select to either match your image and move up or leave your company accordingly. People love to imitate what the boss is doing. As a leader, you set the pace regarding ethics, work, appearance, and attitude.

At RE/MAX, we treat everybody fairly, but that doesn't necessarily mean we treat everyone *equally*. For example, I make numerous personal calls and videos at the request of our franchisees. Some are as simple as a franchisee calling to say they know an eighty-six-year-old World War II veteran who would welcome a call from me wishing him a happy birthday. That's not time-consuming and is a fairly simple task. Another broker might request that I attend their sales meeting and do a photo opportunity with their agents in celebration of their twentieth anniversary with RE/MAX. The reality is, I probably wouldn't say yes to that because of time and distance; it just wouldn't make sense. But I would agree to record a short video that they could play at their meeting. Now, that being said, if the biggest broker in the system with numerous franchises asked me to do the same thing, I'd have to make the trip. Due to limitations on my time, I must be very selective. I certainly wish I could say yes to every request, but it just doesn't make sense. Everyone in our network is an important member of our team. We try to treat everyone fairly, but it doesn't mean we're always able to treat them the same. I will always choose to do the things that have the biggest impact, and when I can't fulfill a request, I'll still go out of my way to make sure there's an alternative solution that keeps everyone happy.

Make no mistake—integrity is a fundamental trait of effective leadership. Leaders with integrity are trusted, respected, and admired. They foster a culture of trust, accountability, and ethical conduct within their organizations. They inspire loyalty and commitment from their team members, leading to higher levels of engagement and organizational success. Loyalty, by the way, is a two-way street. Many leaders think it only works one way: "You must be loyal to me." Yeah, that's not really how it works.

3. GREAT LEADERS ARE FAIR AND RESPONSIBLE TO THEIR STAKEHOLDERS

There are often multiple stakeholders to whom leaders must be fair and responsible. At RE/MAX, one such group is our public shareholders, who have invested in us and therefore have financial expectations of the company. Another group of stakeholders are our employees. They want to work for a company that will continue to progress and present opportunities for promotion. They want proper training and to know they're valued and will have the necessary support to move up to the next level. Our franchisees are yet another group of stakeholders. Many have invested their life savings to be a franchise outlet for us. Our agents are stakeholders as well. They pay us fees and work in the trenches to make our operation function well. Our suppliers are our stakeholders too. For example, only five companies in the United States are designated to produce our signs. We could have fifty companies making signs for us, but fifty companies each doing very little business isn't as fair as five companies doing a lot of business with us. Five is the ideal number, because if we had only one company making those signs, they likely wouldn't care as much about our account because they wouldn't be competing with anyone else to keep our business. Suppliers depend on this enterprise to fuel their success. And the list goes on.

A good leader is aware of all the stakeholders. They must have a keen understanding of how to balance the potential conflicts between them, which is a constant prospect. A franchisee may say they want to be with a big-name franchisor in the market, yet they may not want other franchisees competing to take away their business. You must balance how many franchisees are enough or how few are too little. It's about taking care of your stakeholders, whoever they may be.

And, of course, there are times when being fair and responsible to your stakeholders means eliminating those who aren't going to make it. It's unfair when someone who fails to meet the minimum standards reaps the same benefits as someone who runs an outstanding office with one hundred agents who are consistently paying revenues and growing market share. To claim the benefits of being a franchisee, it must be a two-way street. The franchisor will help make the franchisee profitable, but the franchisee must deliver their end of the bargain to help build market share. At RE/MAX, a franchisee who fails doesn't get to live off those who are giving

100 percent to the job. If they're failing, they don't get renewed. We never worry about the prospect of losing that market because one of our successful franchises will likely buy that territory and add it to their portfolio.

When individuals and organizations demonstrate their commitment to responsible stakeholder management, they build trust, foster positive relationships, and contribute to the well-being and success of all the stakeholders involved. It's clear to see why it's such a valued trait.

4. GREAT LEADERS SHOW VULNERABILITY

I recently heard a story about a CEO who took over at a large advertising agency two weeks before the lockdown in 2020. He had three thousand employees to look after while navigating uncharted waters. To make matters worse, he had a vicious bout of anxiety. He was new to his position and wanted to exude confidence in his leadership abilities, but he was frozen by his angst. After giving it some thought, he wrote an email explaining how he felt. He allowed himself to be vulnerable and raw. Much to his surprise, his email was embraced with empathy and understanding. It created a connection, because many of his team members felt the same way. Instead of putting up a front, he was genuine and honest, and in the process, he won the respect of his team. God hates a coward, and so do I. Likewise, people hate a winner who wins too often.

Several years ago, Gail and I were honored by the Colorado Golf Association. While we're incredibly successful businesspeople and very generous philanthropists, I am, by all definitions, a terrible golfer. I took up the game when I was around fifty years old. I'm not tall and angular. I'm a squat, short, heavyset guy. No matter how often I practiced, I would never become a professional golfer. Never. It wasn't going to happen. When Gail and I were given the award, total a car or two, break a rib, or get hurt in some way, you never think about wrecking again. You just drive. You drive for miles and miles, repeating the task at hand. The more you drive, the more confident you become.

There's a reason most leaders don't start leading when they're in their early twenties. It's because they have no experience. And experience leads to true confidence.

Another truth that applies to confidence is that in life and business, you don't get to win at everything. As a leader, you can find one or two things you're good at and work hard at them. Equally, it's okay to acknowledge that you're not accomplished in other areas. People respect that. Showing that you know what your strengths are, and what they're not, is never a weakness, especially when you surround yourself with people who make up for any deficits. I don't believe anyone at RE/MAX ever thought of me as weak. I had a lot of bravado, confidence, charisma, and chutzpah. You could stand me up against a dragon, and I'd still tell the dragon, "I will kill you," and they would believe it. If you're not confident about your own abilities and the abilities of those around you, your customer isn't going to be confident. Your team won't be confident either. Leadership starts at the top. You set the tone. People are inherently intuitive. They know when you're timid and unsure, just as they understand when you're self-assured.

If you've ever observed or participated in equine therapy, you'll know what I mean. People who participate in this form of therapy engage in activities such as grooming, feeding, and leading a horse (all while being supervised by a mental health professional). Because horses are incredibly attuned animals, they know when you're afraid of them. But if you walk straight up to the horse and take charge, i will be comfortable with you asserting yourself in that way. If y don't show confidence, regardless of how bad things are, everyb in your organization is likely to fail along with you.

it wasn't really for my golf game so much as it was for our golf c
Sanctuary, and the more than $100 million we raised for cha
there. I stood before the audience and casually said, "Well, I'm pro
ably the only seventeen-handicap golfer that has ever been induct
into your Hall of Fame. This is really weird."

Of course, the room roared with laughter. I was serious, though
We weren't inducted because we were good golfers. We were inducted
for being good people who used our golf course to raise money for
important causes.

When leaders lead with vulnerability, they create a space for authenticity, trust, and growth. The resulting benefits include improved relationships, enhanced communication, and a more inclusive and innovative work environment.

It's important to note that leading with vulnerability doesn't mean sharing everything indiscriminately or being excessively self-disclosing. It's about finding the right balance and discernment in sharing personal experiences, emotions, and challenges to create a supportive and empowering environment.

5. GREAT LEADERS HAVE CONFIDENCE

For years, I've heard that courage comes from confidence and confidence comes from experience. The military proved that to me repeatedly, especially during basic training. Drill instructors make you crawl under barbed wire on your belly with your gun in your arms as live rounds are fired above you. You've got to keep your head down so you don't get hit by the machine gun bullets screaming past within inches of your body. They make you do this so that the first time you're in combat, you've already gone through the motions *and* the feelings. You've got the knowledge that you've lived through this before.

When I drove in NASCAR races, the first few times I was on a superspeedway going 200 mph, it was scary as could be. Once you

There have been countless times when confidence served me well, but one particular instance comes to mind. As RE/MAX became increasingly successful and agents flocked to our company, many local boards of Realtors reacted defensively. They tried to throw me out of their associations, claiming that our company violated Article 24 of the Code of Ethics. Now, Article 24 states, "Thou shall not solicit agents from another broker." But real estate franchising was a business model that was bound to undermine that rule. We were the first company to explicitly ask real estate agents why they would split their commissions with their brokers. Once we offered them 100 percent of their commissions, all bets were off.

The various boards' reactions to us threatened our business, and I took it personally. I sat in on several board hearings without an attorney present. I was frustrated and angry. When I was finally allowed to speak, I threw down the gauntlet that would force the entire industry into a reluctant change.

"I want you to know that what you're doing here today hinders free commerce," I said. "That's antitrust activity, and anybody who violates antitrust goes to jail. I didn't fight in Vietnam to listen to you tell me I can't offer your agent another job at a higher wage. I'm going to file criminal charges against you, and I refuse to participate any further in these meetings, because doing so makes me a co-conspirator in your price-fixing activities."

When I finished, I left the room. I wasn't making idle threats. The National Association of Realtors (NAR) and several local boards of Realtors had recently faced antitrust actions by the federal government for fixing commission rates. The practice was standard in the industry, more as a matter of understanding than as a conspiracy. However, the threat of criminal charges made everyone in that room nervous. I didn't hesitate to seize that opportunity and prey on those fears. My strategy worked. In response, the NAR changed Article 24 to take away any antitrust implications. I won a significant battle without spending a dollar on an attorney. In truth, I didn't have the money. What I did have was confidence—lots of it.

I say this next part with great humility, so bear that in mind as I continue my thoughts on confidence. I've mentioned before that I fall on the short side when it comes to height. When I grew up, the jocks and the star athletes were big, studly guys. The cheerleaders couldn't get enough of them. Every day I thought, *I'm as big, bad, and tough as all those guys.* I didn't want to take crap from anyone. Maybe it was a bit of a Napoleon complex, but it certainly shaped who I became. I don't give a damn how big you are, I'm going to take you on, and then I'll kick your ass. If you beat me, it was indeed a good fight. But I'll come back tomorrow and never stop until I win. That's how confident and determined I am.

Historically, leaders are tall. In fact, almost every president of the United States has been over six feet. George Washington was six foot two, while the average size of his soldiers was five foot four. Great leaders have a big, powerful presence. In the military, it's called command presence. If you walk onto a battlefield, you can usually tell who's in command without looking for the star on their helmet. If you lead from the front, you're a commander who will be respected by the people working for you. Developing a command presence is critical to being an effective leader. But having a command presence isn't the same as being a leader. Here's what I mean. I remember a time in Vietnam when I stood on the field with mortars and rockets whizzing toward us. I had binoculars with night vision, so I could see pretty clearly. My senior master sergeant and captain were with me. I was smoking a cigar, calm as could be, while most of the guys in our battalion had their heads tucked between their legs and their butts sticking out of the dugout, scared to death. The three of us were standing in the middle of the madness, talking about it. To be clear, we were as terrified as any of those guys in the foxholes, but they never knew it.

Our commanding officers were incredibly confident, despite the surroundings. Their strength set the tone for how we needed to respond. Their actions dictated ours. *That's* command presence. Command presence sets the tone; leadership is about the direction and follow-through that comes next. When I stood beside them, I was looking at the situation like this: if the mortar hit us, we would die anyway. If it struck near the foxhole, the guys there were dead too. The guys in the foxhole needed to see their leaders in the thick of things. And when they did, they started coming out from under their cover. The same holds true when it comes to business. If you panic, your team will too. If you lead with a command presence, they'll feel confident and follow you anywhere.

One final word on confidence: It should be balanced with humility and a willingness to learn from others. It shouldn't be mistaken for arrogance or stubbornness. A confident leader acknowledges their limitations, seeks feedback, and continuously works on personal and professional growth. Overall, being a confident leader means inspiring others, making effective decisions, fostering innovation, and building trust and credibility. Confident leadership creates an environment in which individuals and teams can thrive, resulting in higher performance and increased success.

6. GREAT LEADERS HAVE STRONG COMMUNICATION AND LISTENING SKILLS

Communicating effectively is critical in any relationship, personal or business. When it comes to leadership, strong and effective communication can be the difference between profit and loss, winning and losing, and surviving or dying. Returning to one of my favorite examples of strong leadership, Ernest Shackleton knew to constantly check in with each of his crew members. He used that time to monitor their morale, receive input on important decisions, evaluate each person's current health and well-being, and inform them of any change in strategy or plans.

It isn't enough to be able to articulate a vision and a strategy. The most impactful and effective leaders must also keep the lines of communication open, especially during times of great change.

Leaders inspire positive change by empowering others to work toward shared goals. Communication is a leader's most powerful tool for doing so. The best leaders are skilled at listening to and communicating with a wide range of people in different positions and locations, with varying personalities. The success of your business strategy is directly affected by the quality and effectiveness of communication among the leaders throughout your organization.

Several years ago, sixteen thousand Southwest Airlines employees bought a full-page ad in *USA Today* to express their gratitude to Herb Kelleher for Boss's Day. When asked why they did this, the people unanimously said he was an incredible listener. They explained that when Herb was with you, he was always fully engaged. He made you feel as if you were the most important person in the room—and to him, you were. He showed genuine interest in his people, asked about their families, celebrated their successes, and empathized with their failures. He loved his people as people, not just as employees. This was one of the many secrets that led to his great success. And it's so easy!

I learned long ago that we have two ears and one mouth. How do you expect to learn anything if you're always talking? Your job as a leader is to listen and gather facts. You must harness information to be able to make good decisions. If all you're doing is talking and posturing about how smart you are, nobody will respect you for it. Some will say they do, but it won't be true. Asking people what they think and listening to their responses, ideas, opinions, solutions, and so on makes them feel valued, seen, and heard. Guide, advise, and then ask for their insights to solve whatever problem you're grappling with.

Good communication skills empower leaders to convey their vision, build relationships, motivate their teams, resolve conflicts, enhance productivity, manage change, and represent their organizations effectively. By mastering effective communication, leaders can create a positive and productive work environment and drive their teams toward success.

7. GREAT LEADERS ARE FEARLESS

Fearlessness built RE/MAX. In fact, it's gotten me through every challenge I've faced in both business and life.

And I've had plenty of inspiration in that regard. There have been many fearless leaders throughout history who've made significant impacts in various fields.

Mahatma Gandhi was a fearless leader who led India to independence from British rule through peaceful civil disobedience. He fearlessly challenged the oppressive colonial regime and inspired millions with his principles of truth, nonviolence, and social justice.

Nelson Mandela was a courageous leader who fought against apartheid in South Africa. Despite being imprisoned for twenty-seven years, he remained steadfast in his commitment to equality, justice, and reconciliation. After his release, Mandela became the first democratically elected president of South Africa and worked toward a peaceful transition and dismantling of apartheid.

Malala Yousafzai is a Pakistani activist for female education and the youngest Nobel Prize laureate. Despite facing threats and a near-fatal attack by the Taliban, she fearlessly advocated for girls' right to education and continues to be a global advocate for children's rights.

Winston Churchill was the prime minister of the United Kingdom during World War II and was known for his fearless leadership through one of the most challenging times in history.

These are just a few examples, though there are many others in different fields and contexts who've made significant contributions to society.

When you do the right thing, you earn people's trust. That applies not only to political leadership but also to anyone who deals with customers. And it definitely applies in our business. Over the years, I've learned the many benefits of being a fearless leader.

It's important to note, though, that being a fearless leader doesn't mean being reckless, and it especially doesn't mean disregarding the opinions and concerns of others. A truly fearless leader combines fearlessness with empathy, open-mindedness, and a willingness to listen and learn from others.

8. GREAT LEADERS CREATE AN ENVIRONMENT IN WHICH YOU CAN BECOME SUCCESSFUL

For years, I used to give a speech at RE/MAX in which I conveyed the concept of a great leader as someone who creates an environment where people can become as successful as they want to be. Now, let me clarify something: I didn't say that you create an environment where people are motivated to do something in particular. I said that you create an environment where people can achieve what *they* want to achieve. One individual might want to make $250,000 a year, while another might want more time to spend with loved ones or to play golf. Everyone has different goals, especially in real estate.

For a long time, I didn't understand why I couldn't motivate everyone at the company to be all they could possibly be. Then one day it occurred to me that I was looking at this from my point of view instead of theirs. The epiphany came at a time when I least expected it.

In October 1983, Gail and I were in Canada for a RE/MAX International conference. RE/MAX was only ten years old at the time and was growing fast. We were quickly becoming one of the most powerful real estate brands in the world. Gail and I were fully committed to our company, making sacrifices to realize our dreams. We were on the road five days a week, sometimes longer, selling new franchises while strengthening and expanding our relationships with existing territories. We were both workaholics who found more satisfaction helping others reach their career goals than we did almost anything else, except caring for each other. Gail and I were engaged to be married the following month. We were on top of the world, at the top of the real estate game, and about to top that joy off with the start of a new life together when the unthinkable happened.

We were at the Deerhurst Resort in Huntsville, Ontario, not far from Toronto. During our stay, Frank Polzer, who co-owned RE/MAX for all of Eastern Canada, invited Gail, me, and a mutual friend, Randy Lerum, to visit his cabin on a nearby lake. We'd have to travel by seaplane to get there. Although Gail and I were both trained pilots, she had never been on a seaplane before, so she was very excited to make the quick fifteen-minute trip from our resort to Frank's vacation home. I decided not to go because I had some business dealings I wanted to attend to with colleagues who were waiting for me inside the resort.

It isn't the clearest day, nor are the conditions perfect for flying, I thought as I stood on the dock to watch their plane take off. To my trained eye, something seemed odd as the seaplane struggled to ascend into the air. It appeared heavy and climbed a little too slowly for my comfort. As it cleared the trees in the distance, I turned to walk back to the resort but had a bad feeling as I made my way up the path.

The plane landed safely at the lake, where Gail and Frank took a quick tour before boarding for their return trip. This time, however, as the plane began to accelerate for takeoff, it simply couldn't get off the ground fast enough. It was headed toward the edge of the lake, where it surely wouldn't clear the trees and the power lines in front of it.

When Frank's plane didn't return to the resort, I began to worry. I called the local police stations to see if anyone had heard about an accident involving a small aircraft. In my gut, I already knew the answer, but it didn't hit me until someone confirmed the worst.

"There has been a plane crash, sir. Some of the passengers are dead. We don't have any more information at this time," I heard an officer say over the phone.

The pilot was killed on impact, but rescue workers and Good Samaritans from the lakeside community who saw the crash were able to pull Gail, Randy, and Frank from the wreckage. Frank and Randy were badly hurt, but they weren't in critical condition. Gail wasn't as lucky. Her injuries were so concerning that the paramedics wanted her immediately transported to Sunnybrook Hospital in Toronto, a facility that specialized in severe trauma cases.

I raced to be by her side. By the time I got to Sunnybrook, Gail was in a coma. The doctors told me that she wasn't likely to survive, and if she did, she might never walk again due to the brain injuries she'd sustained. I've never been the kind of man who accepts defeat with grace, and I surely wasn't about to then. That kind of dire prognosis was simply not an option. I knew Gail had the strength to not only survive this ordeal but find a way to walk again someday.

In the military, I had never left a man behind, and I wasn't about to start. This was the kind of philosophy the military ingrained in me, and it's been a part of my vernacular ever since I served. Soldiers are trained to move through hell and high water to the extent that's possible to make sure they bring their comrades back with them. The truth is, sometimes people do get left behind—but not on my watch, and certainly not the woman I loved.

Although Gail suffered a traumatic brain injury, partial paralysis on the left side of her body, and several shattered bones, I was committed to helping her get through this. I did everything I could to keep her strength up, her motivation high, and her morale bolstered so she would never think about giving up her fight.

When we were able to, we made arrangements to transfer Gail back to Denver, where she started her long and tough road to recovery at Craig Hospital. Gail has no memory of the accident. To this day she wears a brace on her left arm to keep her muscles from constricting and another brace on her left leg to support her foot.

Right after the accident, she spent two months in a coma and four or five months at a spinal rehab center after that. Brain-injured people think differently than those of us without injury. When Gail regained consciousness, I gave her a terrarium to brighten her room and her spirits. It was in a giant brandy-snifter-shaped glass container. The terrarium had all kinds of plants and a porcelain toadstool. I watered that terrarium every day, and when I couldn't be in the hospital, the nurses watered it. None of us had a green thumb. Six months later, although the plants themselves were beautiful, I could see that the dirt had grown green mold. I was concerned about it, so I went out and bought her a new one. When I returned, I explained that the old terrarium was getting yucky. Since she was in a hospital setting, I wanted things to look as pretty as possible for her. I explained that we should throw the old one out.

At the time, her mental capacity was probably that of a ten-year-old child. She couldn't process what I was saying through the eyes of the adult that she was. She immediately voiced her objection: She didn't want to throw the terrarium away. It had been with her every day, and it was one of her favorite things. I tried to convince her that the mold made it look unattractive, but she couldn't understand why this vital part of her life, which had been by her bedside the whole time she had been recovering, was now being thrown away. Again, I tried to reason with her using logic. I said, "I'll tell you what we ought to do. Take the new one. It's beautiful and fresh. I'll take the old one home and save the plants for you. They need to be repotted. You'll have lots of plants in your house that came from that terrarium."

Gail finally acquiesced. And here's where that epiphany comes in: I soon noticed that, for nearly a year, the plants in the terrarium never grew past the open top of the glass container they were in. The container's shape constricted them. Once I replanted them, some eventually grew to be fifteen feet tall. The lesson I learned from that was life-changing. People in the wrong environment have a glass ceiling that prevents them from living up to their greatest potential because they can't get out from under those restrictions.

I started talking about this concept in my speeches. I explained that one's mentality can keep them stuck in an environment where they believe they've done all they can achieve. I then explained the benefits of breaking out. Then, and only then, can a person grow and thrive.

This concept wasn't new. When RE/MAX first launched, that was the idea behind the agents keeping their full commission. It wasn't about getting paid more. It was about being in charge of your life. And when you control your life, you can work as much or as little as you want. You can promote yourself as often as you wish. People quickly realized they were in business for themselves, which took away the ceiling. Once we did away with the idea of a boss holding you back, our people were free to fly. And a lot of people flew like birds!

This understanding was important as I matured into a successful businessperson. If you have a business with employees, it's an absolute must that, as a leader, you provide an environment in which your people have the ability to achieve the highest level of success they want. And if that isn't high enough for your company, you can promote them to another company. I've mentored so many people over the years, plucking them from their prior positions and introducing them to a workplace where they could grow to their highest potential.

Adam Contos is one such example. He was a police officer when I met him. He reported to a superior officer who commanded what he could and couldn't do. Once I brought Adam over to RE/MAX, he gained more and more freedom, proving himself in various parts of the company. He ultimately became CEO and director of RE/MAX Holdings, Inc. He has since stepped down, and today he and I are partners at Area 15 Ventures, an investment company focused on franchising companies and high-growth small businesses. Adam is also a business school professor teaching other aspiring business leaders. There is nothing holding Adam back from doing all that he wants to do.

Yet another example comes to mind. When we bought Port of Subs, the Nevada-based sandwich quick service restaurant chain (QSR) in 2023, the owner had been there for more than fifty years. He opened one or two stores annually and closed one every three or four years. Eventually, he grew the company to 135 franchised locations. He built the network he wanted by being involved with every franchisee. He wanted to know their names and their families, and it was important for him to closely oversee the operations of his business. The two of us had entirely different approaches to how we ran our franchises. That's not to say that one is better than the other; however, when we bought his company, we were going to march forward with the same methodology that grew RE/MAX into the largest real estate company in the world. His restaurant owners wanted to make more money, which meant they wanted to be able to open more than one shop. We were all for that. They were unbelievably delighted when we bought the company. Our leadership style was the opposite of what they'd been used to.

Three senior officers—the founder and his two daughters—were retiring from management. Healy Mendicino, the executive vice president, was one senior officer we desperately needed to help us make a smooth transition. She had been with the company for twenty years. She's an amazing woman who's very charismatic, very smart, and well-liked by everybody. When I met her, it quickly became obvious to me that she would make an excellent CEO. For years, she'd had no freedom or room to grow. That's all changed now. She's teaching us about the submarine sandwich business, and we're allowing her to do it without anyone standing in her way. Not only is she free to fly but she's free to soar. Her future has never looked brighter.

Our job as a leader isn't about getting everything we can from somebody. It's about creating an environment in which people can achieve as much as they want. Think of it this way: Have you ever gotten onstage or given a speech? Chances are, the first talk you gave wasn't great. But if you kept doing it for a year or two, you probably became much more comfortable. And when you grow comfortable, you become devoted to speechmaking and want to hear the applause, so you try new things. Some new things work, and some don't. You quickly learn what to do and what not to do. Eventually, you become a great platform speaker. That education and growth comes from gaining self-esteem and confidence, but more important, it comes from not limiting your opportunities. It comes from having the freedom to fly.

In leading this way, you create an environment that nurtures success, motivates your team, and drives positive outcomes. Remember that leadership is an ongoing process; continuous improvement and adaptability are crucial to sustaining a thriving environment.

9. GREAT LEADERS ACCEPT CRITICISM AND LEARN FROM MISTAKES

Effective leaders are not only willing to take criticism, they also welcome it, regardless of where or whom it comes from. Many years ago, I was out having drinks with some people after I'd given a seminar. It was June 25, 1976, a date I'll never forget, because I learned one of my most valuable business lessons that day. We went to a bar, sat around, and told a bunch of funny stories that night. As we riffed and egged each other on, I made a particularly off-color comment. I had no idea that what I'd said was insensitive and offensive, but it was. Deeply. I was just trying to be funny. Later that night, a few of the fellas came over to me and let me know that they found my comment unkind and insulting. And they were right. If I had tried, even for a moment, to defend myself, it would only have made things worse. So I listened, and when they were through speaking their piece, I nodded and said, "You're right. I was wrong. I made a mistake." While my intentions were good, my execution was less than stellar.

I learned an important lesson that night: Take the criticism.

It's not easy to do, whether you're the boss or a team member, but it will make you a better leader. It's much easier to become defensive, make excuses, and push the responsibility off on others. This won't serve you well. Trust me—I've made enough mistakes throughout the years to know.

In my early career, I was known to lose my temper quite a bit. I eventually learned that wasn't how to get people to do what you want. The more matter-of-fact, logical, and reasoned you are, the easier it will be to take emotion out of your decisions. It just works better. So I learned to become patient and keep my mouth shut. If there was a disaster, I stayed calm by reminding myself to slow down, speak clearly, start organizing the best approach to resolve the issue, and only then take action. I'm so different today from the way I was thirty or forty years ago. Some might say it's maturity. I like to think of it as an evolution—the process of becoming who and what you are.

I've found that anger typically clouds your judgment, but there are some times when it can serve you well. Twenty or so years ago, we were at the MGM Grand in Las Vegas for a RE/MAX event. We had a fun night with six thousand agents and brokers who paid for tickets to enjoy dinner, entertainment, and cocktails.

At large events, it's difficult for Gail and me to eat with others because so many people approach us that we never get a bite of food. Besides, it's a banquet; it's about the people who are there, not about us. So we sit back, eat our meal beforehand in another location, and then join the group. Now, on that particular night, the event was slated to start at 7:00 p.m. Outside the room, thousands of people stood waiting to get in. As we approached, I thought, *What is going on?* I went to the front of the line, about one hundred yards away, and saw that they had two ticket takers at a single door. Now, there were eighteen separate entrance doors, and the hotel had only two people handling one door. At this pace, the event would be over before the last person was permitted into the room.

I approached hotel security and asked them to explain what was happening.

"If they don't have a ticket and a wristband, they're stealing from you. We won't allow it," one of the security guards said.

I was furious at his response. My face must've been red, and I felt as if steam were coming from my ears. I looked at the guard and said quite firmly, "Open the doors and let every person in right now!"

"Who are you to talk to me like that?" he said.

"I own the company. I'm paying the bill. Now do it!" I quickly retorted.

Was I worried about twenty people taking advantage of me for a free meal, or was I worried about upsetting the six thousand people in that line who'd paid me my living? Well, they got those doors open real fast. The RE/MAX people applauded as they walked past me.

"Give 'em hell, Dave!" I heard someone say as he went by.

There's a time for anger and a time to stay calm. Perhaps I should've handled that differently, but those agents talked about that moment for weeks. So, in retrospect, I think it all worked out.

Look—as a leader, you're like an actor on a stage. Once you have the skill set, the leader in you takes over. That's leadership. It's a mystery. It's not a science, it's an art.

In his book *Start with a Win*, Adam Contos wrote that as a leader, there are three sentences you can never say:

I don't know.

It's not my fault.

Nobody told me.

That's it. If you're the CEO or the leader of your company, those words should be banned from your vocabulary. You have to take ownership and responsibility for the outcomes of everything that happens in your company. There is simply no excuse for ignorance. If you find yourself in that trap, believe me, you won't have the respect of your team. You've got to be humble and say, "My bad. My fault."

In 2023, I gave a speech at the fiftieth-anniversary conference of RE/MAX. In that speech, I refrained from using the word "I" unless it was to say "I made a mistake" or "I did this wrong" or "I learned from this experience" or "I want to tell you how proud I am of you." Other than that, I used the word "we." Because as cliché as it sounds, there is no "I" in "team." To effectively lead your team, you must be a team player. You must get down in the trenches and roll up your sleeves with a "no job is too big or too small" mindset. You must credit everybody as a group—your "we." This is done by saying things like, "We've accomplished so much together." Finally, if I used the word "you" in that speech, it was directed to the audience. "Every good idea this company has comes from you." And I meant it.

Every person in that audience, and those who couldn't be there that day, had collectively spent billions of dollars on building our company's image. RE/MAX is *their* company, *their* accomplishment.

We.

Yours.

Us.

These are three of the most powerful words you can use as a leader.

Accepting criticism as a leader is essential for personal growth, fostering a positive work environment, and improving overall effectiveness. It often builds trust, improves decision-making, strengthens relationships, enhances emotional intelligence, fosters continuous improvement, boosts employee engagement and satisfaction, drives better performance and results, helps you serve as a role model for others, and promotes adaptability and innovation. By embracing criticism, leaders create a culture of open communication and learning, benefiting themselves and their teams.

10. GREAT LEADERS ARE RESILIENT

Resilience can be defined as the ability to adapt, recover, and bounce back from adversity, challenges, or stressful situations. It's the capacity to withstand and navigate difficulties, setbacks, or traumatic events while maintaining emotional, mental, and physical well-being. It involves having a flexible mindset and the facility to cope effectively with and recover from challenging situations. It doesn't imply that a person is immune to or unaffected by difficulties but instead that they can successfully work around and grow from them. A resilient leader possesses these abilities, especially to adapt, persevere, and maintain a positive outlook in the face of the most trying circumstances.

Resilience isn't a fixed trait but a set of skills that can be developed and strengthened over time. It plays a crucial role in being able to rebound and move on successfully.

If I could go back in time and offer young Dave some advice on leadership, I'd tell him, "It's not everything you think it's going to be." When you have the responsibility for other people's careers and lives in your hands, you must figure out how you'll fulfill that responsibility. If you're happy and optimistic, that shows, and it impacts everyone. If you're having a bad day, that also rubs off on the people around you. If you encounter significant challenges, you need to face them with a smile and know that you'll make it through whatever it is you're dealing with.

I lived through eight recessions during my time at RE/MAX, including the one we're currently in (as of late 2023). I've endured interest rates as high as 17 percent for an FHA loan. It didn't really matter. We made it. We're still here. In fact, we always came out stronger because we adapted. People get by. And so do many companies, if they're under solid leadership. It's about knowing you've been there, done that, and it's going to be okay. It's also understanding that change is constant.

LEARNING FROM ADVERSITY LEADS TO GREATER RESILIENCE

It is not the strongest of the species that survives, nor the most intelligent that survives. It is the one that is the most adaptable to change, that lives within the means available and works cooperatively against common threats.

—Charles Darwin

Malcolm Gladwell, a bestselling author and journalist, explored the concept of adversity as an advantage in his book *David and Goliath: Underdogs, Misfits, and the Art of Battling Giants*. In this book, Gladwell challenges the conventional understanding of disadvantage and adversity, arguing that they can often serve as catalysts for growth and success. He suggests that people who face obstacles are forced to develop unique strengths and skills in response to their circumstances, fueling resilience, fierce determination, and extreme creativity. Gladwell argues that this ultimately gives them an advantage over those who haven't faced similar difficulties.

I agree with Gladwell's hypothesis. Everything I learned in business and life, I've discovered through trial and error (or from reading about other people's trials, errors, and experiences in books). In fact, my strong work ethic and discipline developed while I was growing up on a farm in the Midwest. Not doing the work wasn't an option, unless I wanted to risk the wrath of my parents. This and my training in the military set me up to handle just about anything that ever came my way. It allowed me to bounce back from my multitude of mistakes and failures.

But if we are to accept that trial and error is a part of our growth, then we must accept that all humans are fallible in some way, even the exceptional ones. Let me explain what I mean.

I asked Dave Stone to speak at our first annual RE/MAX convention about a year or so after we launched. We were hosting it at the Thunderbird Inn on the Strip in Las Vegas. It was a real dump, but it was all we could afford. Dave showed up but didn't check into the room I'd arranged for him. He told me not to waste any money on him. He was heading to the Hilton, where they put him up in a suite because he's a big gambler and had a line of credit there. I was so offended and hurt. Dave was someone I looked up to and greatly admired. He assured me he'd be back at the Thunderbird in time to give his speech, which was fantastic. Everyone loved him—so much so that I decided he needed to come to Denver to help build our training program.

When he arrived, I mentioned to Dave that I wanted to take him to dinner.

"Sorry, no. I don't do dinner with my clients," he said.

Once again, I felt offended and hurt. Curious, I asked why.

"You'll feel differently about me tomorrow," he said, very matter-of-fact.

"I think you're a god—you're the greatest thing in the world," I shot back. And I genuinely felt that way.

Dave shook his head as if he were disappointed and said, "Okay, let's go to dinner."

Later that night, we met at the Sawmill, a casual restaurant in Denver. He ordered a twenty-dollar bottle of wine, which didn't seem crazy to me. And then he said something I've never forgotten.

"I'll teach you a lesson I don't ever want you to forget."

When the bill came, I paid for dinner. We decided to send our wives home and stay for another drink. But that drink led us to another bar, where we partied until two in the morning. I sat back and watched this man, my mentor, the smoothest and smartest guy I knew, get sloppy. I didn't think it bothered me until the next morning when Dave showed up to our office and we were both hungover. "Well, do you feel differently about me today?" he asked.

I did.

"That was an expensive lesson for you, but you don't think I'm a god anymore, do you?"

And I didn't. I realized that Dave was a regular man who had extraordinary talent.

"Please don't ever forget that lesson," he said.

That night out totally changed how I thought about him. The next day, he disappeared. We couldn't find him anywhere. His wife couldn't track him down either. Three weeks later, they found Dave at a fishing camp in Minnesota with three guides, drunk as skunks. His wife put him in rehab, but he could never fully give up the booze. Eventually, it killed him.

I loved that guy, and I was disappointed in how things ended. But then I realized that no matter how much money we have, we're all just people dealing with our own stuff. I'm no better than anyone, and no one is any better than me. As a result, I've spent my life loving and accepting people for who they are, not for who I want them to be. And I took the lessons I learned throughout my years working with Dave wherever I went. I spent forty-plus years on the road, doing seminars 250 days a year. And I rarely went to dinner with the people I worked with because I didn't want to change how they viewed me. Lesson learned.

Over the years, RE/MAX events proved to be learning grounds for me on many levels. Hosting that first convention with twenty-six agents was awkward at best. Thirty years later, I was hosting conventions with fifteen thousand agents. Both were huge undertakings in their own way. It wasn't an overnight change. We learned to do it step-by-step. I would go to conventions held by other companies, such as Amway and Mary Kay, to see how they hosted theirs. I observed them closely, took copious notes, and educated myself, reflecting on what I liked and didn't like. Those companies put on great conventions with lots of music, talent, and enthusiasm. I even made my way to some major competitors' conventions to check out what they were saying and doing to inspire their people. I was trying to emulate other leaders. There was a lot of trial and error as I refined my own style. I've often joked that throughout my life, I've never read a manual. Some might say it's because I'm a man, and we don't read manuals. The truth of the matter is that I learn best through experiences and self-education. And I definitely learned the most about our business during those days when our company was small. While I've never been one to stop and ask for directions, I'll admit that once GPS came along, I got lost a lot less than I used to.

The College of Hard Knocks provides a hell of an education. The problem is that it isn't a good education if you haven't endured some pain. Somebody has to knock you on your butt so you can bounce back stronger, smarter, and wiser. That's resilience.

Truly resilient leaders inspire and empower their teams to navigate adversity, maintain motivation, and achieve success. They create a culture of support and guidance so individuals and teams can thrive even in challenging circumstances.

Building resilience as a leader requires conscious effort and ongoing practice. It requires consistency, self-reflection, and a willingness to adapt and grow. By strengthening your resilience, you'll be better able to navigate yourself and your team through whatever challenges inevitably come your way.

10 Traits to Grow as a Leader

1 Hopeful leaders are often persistent. They stay committed to their vision and goals, even in the face of obstacles or setbacks. They inspire others to keep pushing forward and maintain a sense of optimism and determination.

2 Leaders with integrity are often authentic. They're true to themselves. They don't pretend to be someone they're not. They act consistently with their values, beliefs, and personality. They inspire trust through their genuine nature.

3 Leaders who are responsible to stakeholders are often long-term thinkers. They consider the future impact, not just the near-term impact, of decisions and actions on stakeholders' well-being and sustainability. They take into account the consequences for *all* stakeholders over time.

4 Leaders who show vulnerability often promote healthy conflict resolution. When leaders are open and vulnerable, they create an environment where conflicts can be addressed openly and constructively, leading to better resolutions and stronger relationships.

5 Leaders who are confident are often effective decision-makers. They're more decisive in their decision-making. They trust their judgment, weigh options efficiently, and make informed choices, leading to more effective and timely decisions.

6 Leaders who are good communicators often empower others. Leaders who communicate well actively involve their team members, seeking their input and valuing their opinions. This creates a sense of ownership, leading to higher levels of employee engagement, commitment, and growth.

7 Leaders who are fearless often embrace change and innovation. A fearless leader creates an environment in which people feel safe to express themselves, explore new possibilities, and think outside the box. It's easy to get stuck in a rut, especially if your business is booming. It's much harder to be open to and embrace change. One thing I know for sure is that the only thing in life and business that stays the same is change. That's why a fearless leader is unafraid to challenge the status quo and explore new ideas, technologies, and strategies. By encouraging a culture of innovation and embracing change, they position their business to adapt and thrive in dynamic and competitive markets.

8 Leaders who create an environment in which you can succeed are often good collaborators. They emphasize the importance of teamwork. They encourage cross-functional cooperation and foster a sense of camaraderie that promotes well-being, respect, and inclusivity. Ultimately, they create an environment in which everyone feels valued and respected.

9 Leaders who accept criticism are often emotionally intelligent and raise the emotional quotient (EQ) of those around them. Those who can manage their emotions, actively listen, and respond constructively to criticism have an EQ that positively impacts their relationships and influence as a leader. When leaders listen openly to feedback, it models how to trust, respect, and engage in open dialogue with others, leading to stronger working relationships.

10 Resilient leaders are often continuous learners. They cultivate a self-improvement mindset. They stay curious, seek new knowledge and skills, and adapt to changing circumstances. What's more, they embrace challenges as opportunities to expand their expertise.

TO BE A GREAT LEADER, BE WILLING TO BET ON YOURSELF

People often ask me how my leadership has changed over time. I always say that two things happened. First, I had to grow with the company; second, I had to acknowledge that I would be left behind if I didn't. I had to be bold and challenge myself to do things—*many* things—I'd never done before, from planning conventions to building our satellite television network. I had to learn and earn my confidence and experience. Any entrepreneur who started in their early twenties would probably tell you the same thing. Thankfully, I had Gail by my side. And I had a team I could trust. For the most part, my managers were all fifteen to twenty years older than me, so I could sit down with them and say, "This isn't working. How can we solve this problem?" I wanted to know what I was doing right, but even more important, I needed to know what I was doing wrong so

I could fix it. I was like a sponge, soaking up everything they had to say. If you sincerely care, you'll want to solve the problem, especially if you created it. You can't let your ego and pride get in the way of learning what you don't know.

I also learned, as the motivational speaker Jim Rohn says, that we are an average of the five people we spend the most time with. You must pick your associates carefully, because they will make or break you. We know this is true when it comes to our kids. We cringe when they're spending time with the wrong group of friends. The same holds true for adults. If you're around negative people, you'll be negative. If you want to lose weight, spend time with a healthy crowd, because you will either fail at or imitate whatever they're doing. If they're not out drinking cocktails every night, chances are you won't be either. Surrounding yourself with the people you want to be like is sometimes tricky, but getting there is worth the effort. The older I've become, the wiser this advice proves to be.

What I know for sure is that Gail and I are footnotes in the history of RE/MAX. We were lucky enough to be the founders, so we couldn't get fired. That's a pretty enviable position to be in. After my bout with an MRSA infection in 2012, which you can read about in my book *My Next Step: An Extraordinary Journey of Healing and Hope*, the long-term effects impacted my physical abilities. For the first time in my career, I decided to build a succession plan. As it turned out, I could hire younger, faster, more intelligent people to grow the company in ways I might not have done had I remained CEO. It was much better to become the chairman of the board, where I could mentor others and help them grow to their highest potential. My secret was simple: I hired better than myself. And I succeeded. It's equally important to remember that when you build a company, you aren't building a financial statement or an arsenal of cash. You're not building a network of thousands of retail locations. You're changing people's lives by building personal relationships with individuals who will say "I respect you" when you've earned that honor and who will think *I thank God we met* when you die.

Gail and I receive hundreds of letters a year, some three or four pages long, from people thanking us for giving them a life they never expected to live. Knowing we've had a hand in that—in creating wealth for others while passing on our wisdom and experiences—means more to us than anything. To hear someone tell you they respect you, well, I'd have to say that's the ultimate definition of outstanding leadership.

5

Management

I once heard someone describe management as a lot like golf. You can find infinite tips on becoming a better golfer, and just as many on how to be a great manager. The problems start when you try to keep all those tips and rules in your head and use them at the same time, creating what is often known in golf and business as "analysis paralysis." Those who successfully manage their teams make it look easy—as if it's second nature. Just like Phil Mickelson's seemingly effortless swing.

There are, of course, many different ways to manage. When I was starting in business, I adhered to the old autocratic way, which was through command and control. That's the "I give the orders, and you do what I tell you to do" approach. Interestingly, I was only that way at headquarters. I was more democratic with my entrepreneurial broker owners, which was a real dichotomy.

As I became more experienced, I learned to have a pretty thick skin and not take criticism from those on my team personally. If someone was complaining, they probably had a reason. And, often, the reason was me. For example, we used to have a regional meeting every sixty to ninety days at RE/MAX. I'd travel around the country, stopping in each territory where all the regional directors would gather. Since I chaired most of those meetings, whenever someone came up with a good suggestion, I'd say, "Great idea. I'll handle that for you." And I meant it in the moment. However, I said it enough times with no follow-through that an older regional director approached me and said, "Dave, don't say you'll handle something if you're not going to do it. You're always promising but never keeping your word."

I must admit that at first I was quite offended. I thought of myself as a man of my word. But this regional director shared four or five occasions when I was supposed to do something and I didn't. He was right. At the time, I was so busy that the minute I opened my mouth, whatever I said I would do died right there on the vine. I never kept track of my promises because I was always on to the next crisis. I was embarrassed, and truthfully, my feelings were a little hurt by this man's candor. Then it dawned on me that if I had an employee who was consistently overpromising and underdelivering, that person would no longer be an employee. It had long been a motto at RE/MAX to underpromise and overdeliver. And here was an example of me doing the exact opposite. My inaction wasn't serving the business one bit.

When I realized the error of my ways, I suggested that we memorialize our meetings with minutes. I also created a to-do list and wrote down who was responsible for each item. When we opened the next meeting, we recapped that to-do list. This became a regular practice. This simple shift in how I operated totally changed my personal productivity and allowed the group to hold me accountable. It also changed my reputation and relationship with my team for the better.

In my latter years at RE/MAX, my approach to management evolved quite a bit. It became more inclusive. It took a lifetime of experiences to realize what works, what turns people on, and what motivates them. I remained in a "take a central role" position only if I was running a meeting or seminar. Even then, everyone had a voice. I adapted my management style, often wearing several hats, depending on the circumstances. Eventually, that helped me figure out what worked best for our company.

Several years ago, a former Navy SEAL joined RE/MAX as a real estate agent. After about four months, he quit. He didn't leave for lack of production. He stopped because he didn't want to be in business by himself. He wanted to be a member of a team. He said, "In the SEALs, our team was our family." SEALs operate as eight-member squads. If they plan a mission, everyone has an equal say in what will happen. When they debrief, they all sit down and discuss what went wrong. He made a valid point—one I've never forgotten. This also impacted how I wanted to manage going forward.

WHAT GOOGLE DISCOVERED ABOUT GOOD MANAGERS

In late 2008 and early 2009, researchers at Google launched Project Oxygen to explore what constitutes a great manager. Their goal was to devise something that would ultimately impact the future of the company more than their next product or algorithm. They wanted to create a better manager.

Project Oxygen started with some general assumptions. The team at Google believed that people leave a company for one of three reasons, and sometimes a combination of them. First, they don't feel connected to the company's mission or sense that their work matters. Second, they don't like or respect their coworkers. And third, they have a terrible boss. At Google, the latter proved to be the most significant variable. Because the company conducted quarterly performance reviews instead of annual ones, they could see huge swings in the overall ratings employees gave their bosses. Managers had more impact on employees' performance and how they felt about their job than any other factor. The general belief was that their best managers had teams that performed better, were happier, and therefore stayed with the company. It raised the question, "What if every manager was that good?" To answer that question, they needed to discern what made their managers good in the first place.

Project Oxygen analyzed more than ten thousand observations about Google's managers across more than one hundred variables. They took into account past performance reviews, feedback surveys, and nominations for top-manager awards. They correlated phrases, words, praise, and complaints. Then they coded the comments to look for patterns. Next, they interviewed the managers to collect additional data and looked for evidence that supported their theories. Once they had all that information, they coded and synthesized those results into a four-hundred-page document they rolled out to their managers to utilize.

Initially, they came up with eight habits of effective Google managers. Though they weren't exactly groundbreaking, the resulting list proved to be highly predictive of team outcomes, including turnover, satisfaction, and performance. The research team at Google then added two more traits, and when they did, they found that the higher a manager scored on these two new behaviors, the better the outcomes were for their teams. They were more likely to stay at Google, gave higher subsequent satisfaction scores on employee surveys, and were better performers overall.

In conducting their research, Google discovered that what employees valued most were bosses who were approachable, made time for one-on-one meetings, and helped guide them through their problems by asking a lot of questions, thereby inviting them to find their own solutions instead having answers dictated to them. They also valued a boss who was interested in employees' lives and careers. Until then, Google had always emphasized that the best managers, especially those on the engineering side, needed to be as technically expert as those who worked for them, or better. It turned out that

Google understands this, and its intensive study reminds us that it's essential to listen to the messages your business is conveying to you.

TURNING A MANAGEMENT DECISION AROUND

Several years ago, I got the yearning to buy a Harley-Davidson dealership in Colorado. At the time, a buddy of mine who was a Marine in Vietnam was the general manager of a dealership in Colorado Springs. I tried to buy that one, but the owner and I couldn't agree on a price, so we walked away. But this friend and I were brothers in arms, and I admired him so much that I called him one day and told him I was getting involved in drilling oil wells in Oklahoma.

"You know anything about oil wells?" I asked him.

"No, but I can learn," he said.

"Well, hell, let's go. Let's build us a business and go drill some oil wells."

And we did. We drilled about two hundred wells, starting with no knowledge at all. Lo and behold, we made it work. We ended up selling our interest at the top of the market, with oil around one hundred dollars a barrel. We made a lot of money on that deal, and my buddy got a great severance package.

Not long after we sold the business, I called him and said, "I still think about motorcycle shops."

"Indian just got bought by Polaris. They went bankrupt three times," he casually mentioned.

Indian motorcycles had a history as good as Harley-Davidson, so I was intrigued, especially knowing that an established company like Polaris had invested money in them.

"Let's start a dealership," I said.

We couldn't find a space we liked, so we bought an existing motorcycle store and added the Indian brand. We quickly acquired another store carrying BMW and Triumph, and then two more that was the least important thing. What their employees want was an accessible manager they could connect with.

Once Google began teaching these traits, it quickly paid of They saw a significant improvement in the quality of their managers Google came away from Project Oxygen with a greater understanding of why good managers matter. For Google, the ten behaviors that make a great manager are as follows.

10 Highly Effective Manager Traits According to Project Oxygen

The study found that a great Google manager:

1. Is a good coach.
2. Empowers the team and doesn't micromanage.
3. Shows concern for the success and well-being of the team and is inclusive.
4. Is productive and results-oriented.
5. Is a good communicator who listens and shares information.
6. Discusses performance and supports career development.
7. Has a clear vision and strategy for the team.
8. Has critical technical skills to help advise the team.
9. Collaborates across Google.
10. Is a strong decision-maker.

Now it's time to determine what makes a great manager in your organization. Every business will tell you its secrets if you let it.

where we sold only Harley-Davidson. We subsequently drove those stores into the ground. A lot had changed since this friend had last managed a dealership. We didn't know how to oversee today's workforce, nor did we understand the value of using social media for digital marketing. All we knew was an old-school way of doing business: command and control. Do this, do that, don't do this, don't do that. It didn't work at all. We also underpaid our general sales managers, making the common mistake of watching the bottom line so closely that we had no choice but to hire unqualified people to run the stores. One of my favorite sayings about wages is, "If you pay peanuts, you get monkeys." And that's precisely what we had done. We and our management style were outdated. We went from the second-largest Harley dealership in the state to number seven in two years.

I loved this guy, so it was hard for me to be tough on him, but it was apparent we weren't the right team for the job. So, I called several Harley dealers in the region and began to ask about Janet Cooke. Janet was the regional director for Harley-Davidson. Since most people who owned or managed the dealerships were older white men, I wasn't sure what to expect. Everyone I called said, "She's brilliant. The smartest person I've ever met."

I found that very interesting. Sometimes the best man for the job is a woman. And Janet was the answer to our prayers.

Janet is a beautiful, petite woman with a sparkly, charismatic personality. She's always cheerful. And she drove a bike at 200 mph at Daytona, which made her fearless and my kind of person. I'd driven a race car as fast, but I had a roll cage and a fire suit for protection. Janet was the solution. We knew it. Now all I had to do was convince her. We called and begged her to show us how to change our marketing plans. There was simply no one better to help us turn things around. Sadly, she said no. Then one day, out of the blue, Janet called and asked if we could get together for lunch.

"Sure. Del Frisco's, tomorrow, 11:30. I'll be there," I responded.

I showed up to lunch and immediately said, "Let's have a drink."

"I don't drink at lunch," she said.

"Well, you're going to drink at this one, and here's why." I proceeded to tell Janet that I knew she was there to take me to the woodshed and paddle my backside for driving the Harley-Davidson brand from second to seventh. I knew we had an outstanding brand, and we'd totally messed up. I fully expected her to give me an ultimatum to straighten up our act or they would cancel our dealership franchise.

I could see Janet was taken aback by my brutal honesty. But I understood her position. At the time, RE/MAX had eight thousand franchises, and if we had someone who'd driven the brand down as we did with the motorcycle store, I would terminate them.

"And so I understand why you're here," I said. "However, if you're going to terminate us, you're not going to do that while I'm sober, so have a drink."

Janet ordered a glass of wine, and I continued to speak.

I laid out five things we knew we were doing wrong. I continued down my list until Janet stopped me and said, "Well, you've got this all figured out. So, what are you going to do about it?"

I knew I had to change the team, and as hard as that might have been on a personal level, it was the right decision for the business. I never wanted to hurt my friend's feelings, so I planned to offer him a very generous severance package. Next, I planned to bring in a new CEO. I had already chosen that person. I told Janet we would fire all our sales and general managers. It was time to wipe the slate clean and rebuild the business by going after and hiring the best team, paying them top wages, and offering every reason for them to join us.

Janet leaned in and said, "Well, Dave, that sounds great. Just one question—who is the CEO you're hiring?"

"You," I said, and then I stayed quiet.

She was clearly surprised by my selection.

"I've been with Harley for eighteen years. I'm not quitting," she firmly replied.

"Yes, you are. You're quitting them today. It's done. Get over it."

"You don't even know what I make," she told me. But before Janet could say another word, I quickly said, "Yes, I do. And my opening salvo is to double your salary starting tomorrow."

Her eyes widened. It was a considerable number, but I wanted the best in the state, and I was more than willing to put my money where my mouth was. Being brilliant and confident, Janet asked about profit sharing, vacation time, and other benefits. And I was willing to give her a three-year guarantee in writing. I gave her everything she asked for. Her job would be turning our company around. I promised that as CEO, she was free to run the company as she saw fit and that I would never interfere with any decision she made. I was busy watching over eight thousand real estate offices around the world. I didn't have time to get caught up in four motorcycle stores.

"I have to talk to my husband," Janet explained.

"I'm not hiring your husband, Janet. I'm hiring you. I need an answer now."

But Janet insisted on speaking to her husband before giving me her answer. I had to respect that decision, so I gave her until 8:00 p.m. that night to get back to me.

I sincerely appreciated her willingness to stand up to me. It was one of the traits I knew would make her an incredibly successful CEO. And I admired her commitment to her family. Either way, it was a fun lunch that I hoped would pay off for both of us.

Ultimately, she took the job, and we've been in the most spectacular business marriage ever since. We love each other. We share our thoughts and opinions, and we respect one another. Within the first quarter of her coming on board, we went from a loss in all four dealerships to turning a profit. Five years later, we're booking record profits, and she's riding high.

To me, many people can be managers, especially when good systems and processes are in place. Those systems act like a blueprint for running a business. Whereas leadership must be inspirational, management is more about following the rules and checking the boxes. If you're like Janet and you have a combination of both qualities, meaning you possess strong leadership skills and you can implement sound management practices too, well, that's money in the bank.

THE BLURRED LINE BETWEEN LEADERSHIP AND MANAGEMENT

There can be some confusion when it comes to differentiating management from leadership, and for good reason. In many ways, there's a lot of crossover. Here's how I distinguish the two. It isn't a perfect separation, but this is how I see it: Leaders figure out the secret sauce—what makes a team gel, how they can move forward in the right direction, and how each individual can feel like they're an essential part of the team. Managers execute that strategy day in and day out. Leaders care for the stakeholders, while management keeps those stakeholders happily doing what they're supposed to be doing. They keep the wheels turning. And in totality, they each contribute to the team's overall success. Think of it like the military: There can be leadership at every level. Although the noncommissioned officers make the military work, the overarching leadership comes from the officers.

TIME MANAGEMENT

It's worth noting here that there's one skill that *all* leaders, managers, and team members in an organization must learn to succeed: time management. It can be a struggle for a lot of people. The busier you get—especially if you're running your own business—the more critical it is to allocate your time, as it's a precious commodity. How we spend time matters, and it impacts *everything*. If you're spread too thin, you won't accomplish anything, especially your goals.

Interruptions and distractions—usually in the form of emails, texts, and calls—can eat up most people's working hours, keeping them from completing their most important tasks. Many years ago, I read *The Power of Focus: How to Hit Your Business, Personal and Financial Targets with Confidence and Certainty* by Jack Canfield, Mark Victor Hansen, and Les Hewitt, which described the "Four Ds of Time Management," and I have never forgotten them. If you find yourself struggling to take charge of your time, consider applying this genius productivity strategy to your routine.

The Four Ds of Time Management

To start, create a document segmented into four quadrants. Each quadrant should represent one of the four Ds. Then, before responding to any requests, emails, or calls, ask yourself which of the quadrants each belongs in. This system works for prioritizing just about anything.

Quadrant #1: Do

These are the tasks that require your action, now—meaning you must act on them. The task must move you closer to your goals to qualify for this quadrant. Before deciding to do anything, though, I like to use David Allen's two-minute rule, which is: If it can be done in two minutes, just do it. Otherwise, categorizing and reviewing the task will take longer than finishing it in the moment. Allen says there are many times when you'll be faced with tasks in this quadrant that will take more time. These might include working on a proposal, creating a pitch deck, and so on. Obviously, they can't be done in two minutes, but it's always a great idea to knock off the smaller, less time-consuming tasks from your to-do list whenever you find windows of time. It will put you in a productive frame of mind when you tackle bigger tasks.

Quadrant #2: Delay

These tasks are important but not urgent. Placing them in this quadrant is a way of saying "not now" instead of saying "never." It is *not* an excuse to procrastinate; putting it in this quadrant means you *will* get to it. Perhaps it's a new project you want to take on, but not right now. It could be something as simple as answering an email that requires some time and thought, or it may be something that's pressing, though not quite urgent—at least not to you. Don't create false emergencies for yourself. Is it really a fire, or does it just appear like one?

I make time at the end of every week to get to my delayed tasks. I make it a goal not to have them carry over into the following week's action items. Also, when you choose to postpone a task, you may also consider if it's one you should dump instead.

Quadrant #3: Dump

While I refer to this quadrant as "dump," many in the business world label it "delete." It's the same thing, and obviously the easiest of the four Ds to implement. It's a black-and-white decision. Once it has been made, you don't have to do anything else except take it off your list of things to do. When deciding to let something go, I often ask myself if it will matter in sixty days. If it won't, it's a dump, plain and simple.

Quadrant #4: Delegate

When running your business, many things must be done daily, but you shouldn't be the only one doing them. The key is to have managers and staff who can do things on your behalf while meeting your standards and expectations. In general, if someone else can do the task at least 75 percent as well as you can, then delegate it. If you're not used to delegating, this may be challenging at first, especially when the results aren't what they would be if you had done it yourself. This doesn't mean you shouldn't delegate. You must. It's a great way to leverage your day. Again, how do you want to spend your time?

To delegate effectively, create a plan as if you were a coach with a playbook, and then execute it by breaking it down step-by-step so everyone is clear about the expected outcome. This makes the results less dependent on who's doing the task. Delegate across departments, to your peers, and even upward when it applies. If you don't have anyone to delegate to, find someone and start training them. In the meantime, outsource it if you can!

WHAT DISNEY TAUGHT ME ABOUT MANAGEMENT

Several years ago, I took seven officers from RE/MAX to the Disney Institute for a five-day course on marketing and management based on the concepts that have made the Disney resorts so successful. I'd seen the curriculum and gone through the paperwork, and I thought it would be helpful to our team. When we registered, I mentioned that eight of us were attending and that I wanted us to sit and work together throughout the course. They told me that was against their policies. They wanted us to spread out and interact with the other attendees. As it turned out, about 75 percent of the participants were government workers.

The instructor shared that the one area Disney had the most trouble with was laundry. Orlando can be brutally hot in the summer months, making laundry a grueling job. It also paid minimum wage, and their employees spoke thirty-seven different languages. Between the working conditions, cultural diversity, and pay, their turnover rate was 90 percent every ninety days. It was a very tough situation to navigate.

Management couldn't give the staff more money because they were unionized. So, they asked for ideas from their employees. Naturally, the employees were terrified to offer their opinions, fearing that they would be fired if their concepts didn't work. Over time, however, management won their confidence and devised a simple, inexpensive, and effective solution. They made powdered flavoring available for ice water so the employees could stay hydrated throughout the workday. They occasionally offered free ice cream bars in the afternoons too. Doing this resolved the challenge and brought the turnover rate to about 10 percent. It was such an easy solution, conceived and implemented with the cooperation of every team member. Good management is often a collaborative effort. It involves actively listening to the people affected by your policies and procedures.

We were so impressed with the Disney Institute course that we brought their business instructors to RE/MAX to do a weeklong course for 250 of our employees.

Whether you're a leader or a manager, continuing your education is critical to your success. Over the years whenever we walked into a classroom, auditorium, or seminar, we always sat in the front row, in the seats closest to the instructor or speaker, taking copious notes. It didn't matter what the subject was; we knew there was always something we could learn. And so can you. If you think you know everything, I assure you, you don't.

Many years ago, I was the keynote speaker for a group of Marriott executives. About four hundred had flown in from around the world for the meeting. Sitting in the front row and taking notes was none other than Bill Marriott. I loved seeing him so engaged. You might say we're kindred souls, because I would have done the same thing if it were Bill giving the speech at one of my conferences. I got to talking to one of his men, Roger Dow, who shared that Bill was always the first one in the conference room, ready to listen and learn. I've never forgotten that. Knowing this habit inspired me to adopt it myself. You'd be wise to do so as well.

MANAGING IN A CRISIS

Both a leader's and a manager's mettle can be put to the test in a crisis. That's when continued education can help. In 2007, when we saw early signs the real estate industry was collapsing and homes were going into foreclosure, we knew we had to pivot so our people could survive the crisis. I heard from a longtime RE/MAX associate who lived in Paradise Valley, Arizona. Before the crisis, she hadn't sold a home for less than $1 million in the prior ten years. When she called, she said there hadn't been a single million-dollar sale in Paradise Valley in almost six months. Her only way to survive the worsening market conditions was to pick up foreclosures and short sales. She took a course on how to master that and was now selling ten $100,000 homes to get to the $1 million mark she had been used to. She worked a lot harder but was getting it done and staying alive.

In real estate, a situation in which a homeowner sells their property for less than the outstanding mortgage balance is called a "short sale." It typically occurs when the homeowner is facing financial difficulties and can't keep up with mortgage payments, and the current market value of the property is less than the amount owed on the mortgage. In a short sale, the homeowner must obtain approval from their mortgage lender to sell the property at a loss. The lender agrees to accept the proceeds from the sale as a full settlement of the mortgage debt, even though it falls short of the total amount owed. This allows the homeowner to avoid foreclosure and its potentially severe consequences. Short sales involve a complex process that requires cooperation among the homeowner, the lender, and any other lienholders on the property. The homeowner typically needs to demonstrate financial hardship and provide documentation to support their inability to continue making mortgage payments.

For buyers, short sales can offer opportunities to purchase properties at reduced prices. Still, they often involve lengthy negotiation periods and uncertainties due to the lender's involvement. It's advisable for both buyers and sellers to consult with real estate professionals and legal experts experienced in short sales to navigate the complexities and potential risks.

In 2007, though, only seven hundred people in the entire real estate industry had that designation. I knew this would be a good way for our agents to stay afloat, so I reached out to the creator of a course on the subject and invited him to come to Denver to teach it to a small group. If I liked it, I would arrange for ten thousand RE/MAX agents to take the course. We had established the RE/MAX Satellite Network (RSN), and RE/MAX University in 1994 to help educate our affiliates. It would be easy to provide them with this course if I liked it.

I did like the presentation, so we got behind it and offered a two-day course specializing in short sales, eventually making it available to everyone in the company. When we saw what was happening in the market, we provided educational videos and curricula and told our brokers to get as many of their agents certified as fast as they could, because we were going to own the foreclosure market.

At one point, due to our relationship with a large lender, we were handling over 80 percent of their foreclosures. We set up a computer program to geo-target the agents who could sell foreclosed properties. We went to HUD (Department of Housing and Urban Development), FDIC (Federal Deposit Insurance Corporation), Fannie Mae, and Freddie Mac—everywhere we could find foreclosures—and we let them know we had the most certified brokers, all of whom knew how to get it done, and that we'd be happy to do the work for our fair share. While our agents constituted only about 5 percent of the Realtors in the United States at the time, they made up 97 percent of the people with the professional designation to sell foreclosed properties. That gave us a distinct advantage, because we could sell those properties thirty to sixty days faster than anyone else, saving those institutions significant money. *Everyone wins*. That's the idea.

Not only did we push the program hard but we also used it as a recruiting opportunity, because many companies were going broke. We invited the competition to take the course, because we would sell one another's listings and properties anyway. In the process, we picked up not only an unbelievable amount of foreclosure business but also hundreds of real estate agents who came to take our course.

We didn't know much about foreclosures when the market took a downward turn, but we knew that if we wanted to retain our agents, we had to quickly figure out a solution. It's the nature of the game. When you're managing in crisis, you roll with the punches, figure out what to do, and then execute.

10 Effective Ways to Communicate through a Crisis

1. When a crisis strikes, immediately address your staff.
2. Promptly take charge of the situation by offering a plan of action and asking for input and support.
3. Show absolute confidence in a positive outcome.
4. To keep your staff on course, present them with an occasional reality check. Doing this will prevent people from losing their focus or treating the crisis as business as usual.
5. Keep your doubters close to you. Avoid the urge to evade them. If possible, try to win them over and gain their support.
6. Do your best to defuse tense situations. Try to lighten up the mood with some light humor to put people at ease.
7. Ask for advice and information from various sources, but ultimately make decisions based on your best judgment.

8 Allow the people involved in a crisis to participate in the solution, even if it means doling out some work that's less vital.

9 Leaking details early allows plenty of time for the team to get used to a new idea brought about by an unpopular decision.

10 Never lose hope.

MANAGING INDIVIDUAL VERSUS TEAM GOALS

One of the major functions of management is to create an environment in which people on the team can succeed better collectively than they can by themselves—and in which they can also achieve their personal and team goals. When we first started RE/MAX, my aim was for every single agent to be in the 100 percent commission club. I wanted them to make money—a *lot* of money. What I discovered, though, was that different people are satisfied at varying levels of success. We had agents who made $1 million a year and others who made $60,000. Both were happy. I struggled with that for a long time. I couldn't figure out why I couldn't motivate the $60,000 agent to make more money. When I asked them about it, their response was surprising. For the most part, they were achieving their personal goal and were satisfied.

What I learned from this is that, at least in a franchise environment, it's up to everyone to set their own goals. It's not up to anyone else to push someone somewhere they don't want to be. It's tough to motivate someone who likes where they are and isn't inclined to improve. Even if you get a bump in productivity from them, it's likely superficial and won't last. So, over the past five decades, we've created an environment in which people are self-motivated and can achieve what they want. We've offered mentoring and coaching and let people develop and grow personally and professionally at their own pace. We found that with increased confidence, many set new goals for themselves and achieved more than they'd ever dreamed. It takes courage to step outside your comfort zone. Courage, of course, comes from experience, and experience comes from confidence.

There's a saying in the military that goes, "When fatigue steps in, confidence and courage walk out." Tired people, underfed people, and people in stressful situations find it extremely difficult to be courageous. It's easy to sit in a room with no problems and be bold. The reality is that most people just don't have the confidence in themselves to succeed. So, when a manager takes the time to care for their team—and I mean *really* care—that builds confidence. When somebody else believes in you, you grow into that belief.

You set the tone from the top. If you want your people to grow, you must provide a fertile environment for them to bloom in. I had an officer at RE/MAX who wasn't great at public speaking. I thought she was capable but needed time to become confident. She had to take baby steps before she could run. So, I brought her on the road every time I gave a speech. Her job was to introduce me. That's it.

The first time she took the stage, she blew it. She was deeply humiliated. She ran off to the ladies' room and stayed there. When my speech ended, I found her and said, "Let's go have a drink."

"I'm so embarrassed," she said.

"You're still new at this. What did you learn today?" I asked.

"I should have been better prepared. I should have had a script or a note card," she responded.

"Great. Then next time, that's what you'll do. You'll practice and rehearse over and over until you feel comfortable and confident," I said.

Several years later, she was promoted to regional director, and she had to make a speech that night at a big awards banquet. I took her aside before she went on stage and said, "I have to tell you something. All my officers are so proud of your accomplishments. You're talented, charismatic, and just as confident as you can be. This is your day. You've been working toward this for years. Knock it out of the park."

And she did.

She stood up there, smiled, and gave a rousing speech. In fact, the room gave her a standing ovation. It was perfect. After numerous failures, she'd finally built up her confidence.

In the book *How to Win Friends and Influence People*, Dale Carnegie explained that there are two things people can't give to themselves: personal attention and appreciation. No matter how successful we are, we all need someone to say, "I appreciate you. I love you. You're great at what you do." Those are the things that make people believe—not just think—that they're worthwhile. When you lead a company or manage a team, this is part of the job. You must lead and manage by example. When you heap earned praise on people, they feel good about themselves. We made this a point at RE/MAX. It's part of the culture we created to celebrate our wins and our people. By doing this, we found that people stepped into their success.

KNOW YOUR NET PROMOTOR SCORE

Several years ago, we did an experiment at RE/MAX that involved asking our agents one question. On a scale of 1 to 10, with 10 being the highest rating, how likely were they to recommend us to a friend or family? We were curious about agent loyalty and satisfaction.

If they answered with a 9 or a 10, they were extremely satisfied. Those people were our promoters. If they gave us a 6, 7, or 8, they didn't count because they couldn't care less. If we received a 1, 2, 3, 4, or 5, those people were dissatisfied and were our detractors. When we had all our scores, we subtracted the total number of detractors from the total number of promoters to get our Net Promoter Score (NPS).

One study compared two airlines, Southwest and United. At the time, Southwest had a net promoter score of 62, which is very good. United had a score of 2. They flew the same planes, had the same unions, and paid the same rates to their flight attendants and pilots. They also flew to the same city hubs and had comparable discount systems and customer loyalty programs. The people who flew Southwest relayed that they liked the flight attendants. They were younger and happier. They weren't burned out or just punching the clock, waiting to retire. Unfortunately, things weren't as good at United. When we took the test, our score at RE/MAX was a 72, which put us alongside some of the very best companies in the United States, including Apple and Microsoft. According to the tally instructions, scores could range between +100 percent or –100 percent. At the time, we had four thousand brokers in our network. Two hundred of them scored less than zero. We also had several hundred who scored in the top percentile, and a few who received that coveted perfect 10.

After we gathered the data, we asked a follow-up question about why people answered the way they did. About half sent responses. The team in Anchorage, Alaska, which scored the highest, sent in comments such as "We have the greatest broker in the world. She loves us" and "We have a family operation and are provided with all the services and support we need." Occasionally, responders added, "Our fees are too high, but you get what you pay for."

The answers from agents in the offices that scored the lowest reflected one common challenge: "Our broker doesn't care about me. If I ask for help and training, he says go to your computer and sign in to the RE/MAX training program." One specific responder said that his broker wouldn't help him with an appraisal problem. He summarized his experience this way: "I just rent a desk in his office and it's my problem, not his."

It was evident that we had two very different management styles within the same company, within the same network, and sometimes within the same city. We knew we had a problem that had to be fixed.

So, we sat down with the broker owners and went through the results individually. It was either "Congratulations, you're the best of the best! We love you, and here's what your agents had to say" or "You're not performing, and here's what your agents think of you." Of course, those who tested poorly always blamed it on RE/MAX International, claiming we were the problem and that their agents loved them. The comments told a different story.

What this information indicated was this: No matter how good the brand is, people *join companies* and *leave managers*.

What Is Your Management Style?

Simply put, a management style is how one gets an individual, a group, a meeting, a project, or a company to reach its goals.

A person's management style can depend on many factors, including the type of business they have, their specific set of goals, and the people around them. Each management approach has its pros and cons. If you understand different management styles, you can create and implement the guidelines best suited for yourself and your company. This will lead to more engaged employees, lower turnover, and greater productivity.

Bear in mind, there isn't a one-size-fits-all approach. In fact, the most effective managers use different management styles to support their needs and goals at different times. They adjust their approach based on various factors and on meeting their target goals. Both internal and external factors can impact their strategies.

Examples of internal factors include the company's organization and corporate culture, policies, priorities, employee engagement, and staff skill levels. External factors may include employment laws, the economy, competitors, suppliers, and customers. While these factors are outside the company's control, they impact managers and their employees.

When hiring, knowing a potential employee's management style is essential. According to a Gallup poll, companies fail to choose the right candidate for management 82 percent of the time. The same study showed that managers have a substantial bearing on employee engagement, turnover, productivity, and other factors that can positively or negatively affect business. That's why asking the right questions about management style is critical when hiring or when deciding upon your own style.

To correctly identify your management style, you need to understand who you are. That means knowing your temperament, your character traits, the types of employees you have, and the business you're in.

10 Factors to Consider When Deciding Your Management Style

1. The volume of work to complete.
2. How fast you need it done.
3. What industry you're in.
4. The company culture.
5. Your personality type.
6. Your management qualities.
7. Your team.
8. Your company goals.
9. Your attitude.
10. The personalities of those you're managing.

Any management style that's incompatible with your people, project, or situation can produce less-than-ideal results. Leaders who default to one management mode without questioning their methods are usually less effective. As I've said before, simply asking "How can I improve?" is a good start to being a great manager. On any given project, you should also ask if you and your team have the right tools to meet the demands. If not, further your and their education by arranging for additional management training.

And don't be shy about asking for constructive feedback from your direct reports, peers, or more senior leadership. The most successful managers remain flexible, open, and mindful. They have a desire to master multiple management styles, and you should too.

THE 10 MOST COMMON MANAGEMENT STYLES

The various management styles listed below are among the most common for organizing and leading a team.

You'll remember that my original management style was autocratic. I was a command-and-control guy with the employees at headquarters, but more of a democratic guy with my entrepreneurial agents and brokers. Today, I'd say I'm more inclusive, but it took me a lifetime to figure this out. This is why I say that while leaders display certain tendencies, over time their leadership styles may evolve or vary in different contexts or during different periods of their careers. Management styles aren't static; leaders must adapt their approaches based on circumstances and organizational needs. Here are ten of the most common management styles:

Autocratic Management

Autocratic managers centralize the decision-making authority and exercise strict control over their subordinates. Their organizational structure is typically hierarchical, with a clear chain of command. The manager occupies the top position, while the employees have limited autonomy or decision-making power. Sometimes this style is referred to as the top-down approach. While this management style was quite popular in the past, it's no longer considered ideal or effective. In my early management days, I would often coerce people into doing things *my* way, which wasn't always the right way. I quickly noticed that this wasn't the best approach for our fledgling company. It separated me from the others in a way that didn't always work as well as I wanted. Why? Because communication under an autocratic leader or manager often goes in only one direction—from the boss to the employee. Employees don't feel valued or heard. They feel dictated to, and that wasn't the type of environment I was trying to build. Despite its drawbacks, this style can be effective in certain situations, especially when there's a crisis or a need to make quick decisions, but it must be selectively used, as it can lead to low morale, a lack of employee motivation, and limited opportunities for personal growth and development. It's generally less conducive to fostering a positive and collaborative work environment. Many organizations today favor more participatory and democratic management styles that encourage employee engagement and empowerment. There have been notable business leaders who exhibited autocratic tendencies, however. Here are a few examples:

Steve Jobs, the cofounder, former chairman, and CEO of Apple Inc., was known for his strong personality and autocratic leadership style. He had a reputation for being demanding, highly focused, and involved in every aspect of the company's operations, driving innovation and creating groundbreaking products. He was highly involved in the decision-making process, often making key product and design choices without extensive input from his team. His attention to detail and insistence on perfection contributed to Apple's success, but also created a challenging work environment.

Elon Musk, the CEO of Tesla; founder, CEO, and chief technology officer of SpaceX; and owner, chairman, and CTO of X Corp., among other entities, has also been described as an autocratic leader. He's known for his hands-on approach, making critical decisions and driving projects forward with minimal input from others. Musk's ambitious goals and high expectations have been credited with pushing boundaries and achieving remarkable advancements, but have also led to intense work environments.

Rupert Murdoch, the media mogul, chair of Fox Corporation, and executive chairman of News Corporation, is known for centralized decision-making and tight control over his media empire. He's made critical strategic decisions and exercised significant influence over the editorial content of his publications. As an autocratic leader, Murdoch has been praised for his ability to steer his companies and criticized for potential biases in media coverage.

Henry Ford, the founder of Ford Motor Company, was recognized for his hands-on approach to management, tight control of production processes, and centralized decision-making, which enabled mass production and revolutionized the automobile industry. Ford's focus on efficiency and standardization played a pivotal role in the advancement of automotive engineering, but also led to limited employee autonomy.

Jack Welch, the former CEO of General Electric, was known for his results-oriented and authoritative leadership style. He implemented a strict performance-based culture, making tough decisions that led to the transformation of GE into a global conglomerate. He set high performance expectations and implemented a rigorous management system known as "rank and yank," in which employees were ranked and the lowest performers were let go. Welch's autocratic approach was credited with driving GE's financial success, but also generated criticism for its potential negative impact on employee morale.

Akio Toyoda, chairman of the board at Toyota Motor Corporation, has employed an autocratic leadership style to drive the company's growth and success. He has been personally involved in making strategic decisions and implementing changes to enhance Toyota's competitiveness.

Democratic Management

Democratic managers are known for their inclusive and participatory style. They involve team members in decision-making and value their input. They encourage employees to offer feedback through open communication and collaboration and seek consensus whenever possible. Doing this helps employees feel valued and heard. A democratic manager is ultimately responsible for the outcome. As I've mentioned, over time I became less autocratic and more democratic in my approach to our team. This shift significantly enhanced our results, but there was still room for improvement.

Here are a few examples of business leaders who have embraced democratic leadership:

Sundar Pichai, the CEO of Google and Alphabet Inc., is often recognized for his democratic style. He fosters a culture of open communication and encourages employees to share their ideas and opinions. Pichai values transparency and seeks input from various stakeholders to make informed decisions.

Mary Barra, the chair and CEO of General Motors, actively promotes employee engagement, seeking input from those at all levels of the organization. Barra encourages collaboration and teamwork, fostering an environment that values diverse perspectives and ideas.

Paul Polman, the former CEO of Unilever, was known for prioritizing sustainability and encouraging employee involvement in decision-making. Polman believed in the importance of shared values and collaboration to achieve long-term success.

Howard Schultz, the former CEO of Starbucks, believed in empowering his employees, actively seeking their input, and involving them in decision-making. Schultz fostered a culture of inclusivity and collaboration within the company.

Anne Mulcahy, the former chairperson and CEO of Xerox Corporation, focused on building relationships and engaging employees in decision-making. Mulcahy believed in the power of teamwork and collaboration to drive organizational success.

Ben Cohen and Jerry Greenfield, the founders of Ben & Jerry's Homemade Holdings, Inc., also practiced democratic leadership. They encouraged employee participation, sought input from all levels of the organization, and maintained these practices even as the company grew. In addition, they actively prioritized social responsibility.

Laissez-Faire Management

Laissez-faire managers monitor their team's activities but are entirely hands-off. They expect their team members to perform on their own. Providing a high level of autonomy to their team members gives them the freedom to make decisions and complete tasks independently, with little guidance or supervision. There is a trust-but-verify approach in place. While laissez-faire management can be effective in specific contexts, it may not be suitable for all businesses or leadership scenarios, as it requires a high level of employee self-motivation and accountability.

Here are a few examples of business leaders who've been associated with a laissez-faire management approach:

Ingvar Kamprad, the founder of IKEA, was known for his hands-off management style. He believed in hiring competent individuals, giving them the freedom to make decisions, and fostering a culture of autonomy and innovation within the company.

Warren Buffett, the chairman and CEO of Berkshire Hathaway, has been described as a laissez-faire leader. He trusts his managers and gives them considerable autonomy to run their businesses. Buffett values long-term thinking, and his approach allows leaders within his conglomerate to make independent decisions.

Ricardo Semler, the former CEO and majority owner of Semco Partners, is a well-known advocate of a laissez-faire management style. He implemented a radical form of workplace democracy, allowing employees to set their schedules, choose their managers, and make essential decisions collectively.

Sergey Brin and Larry Page, the cofounders of Google (now Alphabet Inc.), have been known to embrace a laissez-faire management style as well. They created a culture that values employee freedom, creativity, and innovation, allowing Google's employees to spend a significant portion of their time pursuing projects of personal interest.

Transformational Management

Transformational managers inspire and motivate their team members by setting a clear vision and high expectations. Their primary focus is on creating an environment that supports innovation. They push employees in a positive way; in return, employees feel motivated and strive to improve their overall team performance. Transformational managers inspire and motivate their teams to achieve extraordinary results. They encourage creativity, innovation, personal growth, and a sense of purpose. They often lead by example and develop strong relationships with their followers.

Here are some examples of business leaders who've been associated with transformational management:

Jeff Bezos, the founder and former CEO of Amazon, is often recognized for his transformational leadership style. He has been known to challenge the status quo, encourage experimentation and risk-taking, and drive innovation within the company. Bezos's vision and ability to inspire his employees have played crucial roles in Amazon's extraordinary growth and success.

Satya Nadella, the chairman and CEO of Microsoft, has precipitated a cultural transformation within Microsoft, emphasizing collaboration, empathy, and innovation. He has inspired a growth mindset and a sense of purpose among his employees, driving Microsoft's resurgence as a technology powerhouse.

Tim Cook, the CEO of Apple Inc., has demonstrated transformational leadership and management since taking over from Steve Jobs. He has emphasized values such as inclusivity, environmental sustainability, and employee well-being. Cook's ability to inspire and motivate his teams has been instrumental in Apple's continued success and growth.

Transactional Management

Transactional managers focus on setting clear goals and establishing structured systems and processes. They emphasize adherence to rules and policies. Their management style focuses on maintaining stability and achieving desired outcomes through rewards, punishments, and clear expectations.

This management style is most common among sales teams. It's effective when setting targets and goals. However, it isn't a good fit for an organization that values creativity and innovation. While it's not as commonly associated with long-term organizational change as transformational leadership, some business leaders have utilized transactional management effectively in specific contexts. Here are a few examples:

Alan Mulally, the former president and CEO of Ford Motor Company, is known for his transactional management style. He implemented a comprehensive management system called "One Ford," emphasizing clear goals, accountability, and performance-based incentives. Mulally used data-driven metrics to monitor progress and align the organization with common objectives.

Carlos Ghosn, the former CEO of Nissan and Renault, implemented a performance-based culture known as "Ghosnism," which involved setting ambitious targets, holding managers accountable for results, and providing financial rewards for meeting objectives. Ghosn's approach aimed to turn around struggling organizations and improve performance.

Larry Ellison, the cofounder, chairman of the board, and chief technology officer of Oracle Corporation, emphasized individual accountability, set high performance expectations, and rewarded employees based on their contributions. Ellison fostered a competitive environment where results were valued and recognized.

Robert Iger, the CEO of the Walt Disney Company, also incorporated transactional elements into his leadership style. He implemented performance-based incentives and clear goals for executives, thereby aligning their interests with the company's financial success. Through contracts and compensation structures, he ensures accountability and drives desired outcomes.

Jack Welch, the former CEO of GE, who was noted earlier for his autocratic style, also embraced transactional management, illustrating how some leaders utilize or combine multiple management styles. He emphasized performance-based rewards and penalties to drive results and maintain a competitive edge. Incentives such as bonuses or stock options motivated his employees to meet goals. At the same time, his "rank and yank" system, referred to previously, meant that not making goals resulted in punishment or dismissal.

Coaching/Consultive Management

A coaching/consultive management style focuses on developing employees' skills, fostering growth, and providing support. Managers who prefer this style act as mentors and guides, helping team members reach their full potential by sharing feedback, offering resources, and helping them set and achieve goals. They often hold discussions with team members to hear their opinions before finalizing a decision. They prioritize individual growth and improvement. This often leads to higher employee engagement, more substantial problem-solving as a team, and less turnover.

Here are some examples of business leaders associated with a coaching/consultive management style:

Bill Campbell, also known as "The Coach," was a prominent Silicon Valley executive and mentor to many successful leaders, including Steve Jobs, Larry Page, and Eric Schmidt. Campbell prioritized his team members' personal and professional development. He provided guidance, support, and encouragement, helping individuals unlock their potential and achieve their goals.

Eric Schmidt, the former CEO of Google (now Alphabet Inc.), encouraged a culture of learning and growth within the organization. He provided guidance and support to his teams, fostering an environment in which employees could experiment, take risks, and develop their skills.

Ginni Rometty, the former CEO of IBM, has also been associated with a coaching/consultive management style. She prioritized employee development and invested in training and mentoring programs. Rometty believed in building strong relationships with her employees and providing opportunities for growth and advancement.

Servant Management

Servant leadership is a term that was coined in 1970 by Robert K. Greenleaf to describe a method of management that prioritizes the needs of the team. It's based on the premise that when one serves and supports their team, members grow wiser, more capable, and more autonomous. Managers who embrace this style aim to empower and develop their employees. When managers model this behavior, team members learn to serve, support, and collaborate with one another. This practice also extends to how the organization serves its customers and constituents. Servant leader organizations often appeal to younger job seekers because they act on issues that serve the larger good of their communities.

Several prominent business leaders have embraced these principles and significantly impacted their organizations and beyond. Below are a few who've demonstrated that servant leadership can be powerful in driving success, employee satisfaction, and positive social impact within their organizations:

Herb Kelleher, the cofounder and former CEO of Southwest Airlines, practiced servant leadership by putting employees first and creating a culture that emphasized teamwork, employee empowerment, and customer service. Under his leadership, Southwest Airlines became known for its exceptional customer service and employee satisfaction.

Bob Chapman, the chairman and CEO of Barry-Wehmiller, a global manufacturing company, is committed to the well-being of his employees and has implemented a people-centric leadership philosophy called "Truly Human Leadership." Chapman emphasizes trust, empathy, and creating a sense of purpose in the workplace.

Richard Branson, the founder of the Virgin Group, a multinational conglomerate, has exemplified servant leadership by focusing on employee engagement, trust, and empowering his team members.

He encourages a culture of innovation and has created a people-centered work environment across various industries.

Indra Nooyi served as the CEO of PepsiCo. She embraced servant leadership by promoting diversity and inclusivity, investing in employee development, and emphasizing sustainability and social responsibility. Nooyi's leadership style emphasized long-term value creation and stakeholder engagement.

Charismatic Management

As the name implies, these managers possess charismatic qualities and use their charm, vision, and personal magnetism to influence and inspire employees. They often have strong communication skills and can galvanize others through enthusiasm and imagination. They can captivate and motivate their teams, often leading to high levels of loyalty and commitment. Charismatic leaders create a solid following and significantly impact their organizations and industries. They have a lasting impact within and outside their corporate culture because of their ability to connect with people and rally them around a shared purpose.

At RE/MAX, charismatic leadership became the most preferred, dynamic, and essential management style. This is the type of leadership I ultimately embraced, not only for myself but also for our team. I looked for managers who were considered charismatic, perhaps not in the traditional sense but in the sense that they possessed the traits I knew would work exceptionally well in our culture. I sought high-energy, action-oriented, connected, and committed people with an intense focus on drive. These were the best people to cultivate the culture we wanted at RE/MAX and to create the growth I envisioned for the company.

Here are a few examples of other business leaders who've been associated with a charismatic management style:

Oprah Winfrey, media mogul, talk show host, producer, actor, author, and philanthropist, is known for her charismatic leadership style. She has a powerful presence and has inspired millions through her various endeavors. Winfrey's charisma and ability to connect with others have made her a highly influential figure in the business world and in the world at large.

Anita Roddick, the late founder of the Body Shop, was also seen as a charismatic leader. She was passionate about ethical business practices and sustainability, and her magnetic personality helped her inspire employees and build a loyal customer base. Roddick's solid beliefs and ability to communicate her vision effectively contributed to the success of the Body Shop.

Angela Ahrendts, former senior vice president of retail at Apple Inc., brought a strong sense of style and luxury retail experience to Apple, which transformed the company's retail operations. Ahrendts's ability to connect with people and inspire a customer-focused culture made her a charismatic figure within the organization.

Tony Hsieh, the late CEO of Zappos, was known for his commitment to delivering exceptional customer service. He built a unique company culture focused on happiness and employee empowerment. Hsieh's enthusiasm and dedication to creating a positive workplace environment made him a charismatic leader in the e-commerce industry.

Situational Management

Situational managers adapt their management style based on their team's specific circumstances and needs. They analyze the situation, assess the capabilities of their team members, and adjust their approach accordingly. Also known as situational leadership, this approach emphasizes the importance of adapting one's management style based on the specific situation and the needs of the individuals being led. It recognizes that there is no one-size-fits-all approach, and that successful leaders must be flexible and responsive to their team members' varying needs and capabilities. The concept was first introduced by leadership theorists Paul Hersey and Ken Blanchard in the late 1960s. They proposed that effective leaders should assess their followers' competence and commitment level in a given task or situation and adjust their leadership style accordingly.

Situational managers are highly attuned to their followers' readiness or maturity level and adapt their leadership style to match the situation's needs. By doing so, they can maximize the potential and performance of their team members.

Here are two examples of business leaders who've been associated with situational management:

Doug McMillon, the president and CEO of Walmart Inc., is known to employ situational management principles. He acknowledges the diversity of Walmart's global workforce and adapts his leadership style accordingly. McMillon focuses on building solid relationships with his team members, providing guidance and support while empowering them to make decisions based on their expertise.

Sheryl Sandberg, the former COO of Facebook (now Meta), promotes a collaborative work environment and believes in empowering her team members to take ownership of their work. Sandberg adapts her leadership style based on the unique needs and circumstances of the teams she oversees.

Leaders I've already written about, including Indra Nooyi, Tim Cook, Mary Barra, and Alan Mulally, are also known to demonstrate situational management principles in their approach to leading. They recognize the dynamic nature of business environments and the importance of adapting their style to support their teams' and companies' needs and goals.

Inclusive Management

Inclusive management strives to create an environment in which all individuals can contribute and thrive. It identifies and values diversity in all its forms, including but not limited to race, ethnicity, gender, age, sexual orientation, disability, and cultural background. It is a holistic approach that involves leadership commitment, organizational policies, and fostering a culture of belonging for the benefit of employees and the business's overall success. It actively promotes equity, diversity, and inclusion throughout all levels of an organization, including leadership, decision-making processes, and organizational culture. It acknowledges the importance of diverse perspectives and experiences in driving innovation, creativity, and problem-solving. This management style fosters a sense of ownership among the workforce and leads to increased employee engagement, improved creativity and innovation, enhanced decision-making, higher employee retention rates, and improved organizational performance.

Here are a few examples of notable individuals who are known for leading with inclusive management practices and promoting diversity and inclusion within their organizations:

Roz Brewer, the CEO of Walgreens and Boots Alliance, has been recognized for her commitment to diversity and inclusion. She has prioritized creating an inclusive work environment and driving diversity initiatives within the company.

Brian Chesky, the CEO of Airbnb, has emphasized the importance of diversity and inclusion at Airbnb. Under his leadership, the company has implemented initiatives to combat discrimination and increase representation in their workforce.

Julie Sweet, the CEO of Accenture, is known for her focus on diversity, equity, and inclusion. She has worked toward increasing diversity in leadership positions and has championed initiatives to foster an inclusive culture within the organization.

John Donahoe, the CEO of Nike, has made diversity and inclusion a priority at the company. He has taken steps to increase representation and inclusion within the organization and has been actively involved in addressing issues related to diversity and social justice.

Mellody Hobson, the co-CEO of Ariel Investments, is a prominent business leader and advocate for diversity and inclusion. She has been actively involved in initiatives to promote diversity in corporate leadership and has spoken out about the importance of embracing different perspectives and backgrounds.

There are many other outstanding leaders in business who prioritize inclusivity, diversity, and equality within their organizations. They demonstrate a commitment to creating inclusive cultures that value and leverage the strengths and perspectives of diverse individuals.

Conflict Management

Another area of management that isn't often considered or talked about in business is conflict management. Conflict management refers to identifying, addressing, and resolving conflicts or disagreements that arise within an organization. And believe me, they do arise—often. This type of management involves employing strategies and techniques to handle disputes constructively, minimize negative impacts, and promote positive outcomes. Conflict management is crucial for maintaining a healthy work environment, fostering collaboration, and ensuring the efficient functioning of teams and departments.

The first step in conflict management is identifying the sources and nature of the conflict. This involves actively listening to the parties involved, gathering information, and understanding the underlying issues or differences that have led to it.

Effective communication plays a vital role in conflict management. Encouraging open and honest dialogue between the parties involved allows for the expression of concerns, perspectives, and emotions. In addition to active listening, empathy and a respectful tone are essential in fostering a productive communication environment.

Conflict management aims to find mutually beneficial solutions through collaboration and problem-solving. Bringing the conflicting parties together helps generate ideas, explore alternative perspectives, and find common ground. This approach encourages ownership of and commitment to resolving the conflict.

In situations where conflicts are complex or highly charged, a neutral third party can act as a mediator or facilitator. This individual helps guide the discussion, ensuring fairness and balance, and assists the parties in finding mutually acceptable solutions. Mediation provides an unbiased perspective and helps maintain the focus on resolving the conflict effectively.

Conflict management often involves negotiation and compromise. Parties may need to identify areas of potential agreement and be willing to make concessions to reach acceptable resolutions for all involved. Negotiation skills, flexibility, and a focus on long-term relationship building are crucial in finding mutually satisfactory outcomes.

Having clear policies and procedures in place helps manage conflicts more effectively. These guidelines provide a framework for addressing conflicts and ensuring consistency and fairness. They can also help prevent disputes from escalating by establishing a structured approach to handling disagreements.

Conflict management presents an opportunity for learning and growth. Reflecting on past conflicts, understanding their root causes, and implementing preventive measures can help organizations improve their conflict management practices. Encouraging a culture of continuous learning and providing conflict resolution training can enhance the skills and capabilities of individuals in managing conflicts. I never had any formal training in conflict management, but I did understand one thing very clearly: we all have two ears and one mouth, so we should listen more than we talk.

By constructively managing conflicts, organizations can transform potential sources of tension and disruption into opportunities for growth, innovation, and improved relationships among team members.

I recognize that I've shared a lot of concepts, considerations, and management styles with you in this chapter. Using a real estate metaphor, I've shown you a mix of Colonial, Ranch-Style, Craftsman, Mid-Century Modern, Mediterranean, Spanish, Tudor, Georgian, and Italianate-Style homes. Which appeal to you? Which don't? Remember, you may choose a style for now but eventually outgrow it. I've done that; I guess you could say autocratic management was my starter style. Or you may embrace more than one at a time. I've done that too. My hope is that you'll revisit this chapter often as you evolve and as different circumstances present different management challenges that require different approaches. It's meant to be a robust and ongoing resource for you as you go.

6

Building Your Team

I've spent a lot of time thinking about optimal strategies for putting together the best teams in business. I've done it numerous times over the course of my fifty years as an entrepreneur.

In many instances I've taken cues from sports. I love watching the Denver Broncos and Denver Nuggets. A sports team, like any other business venture, requires an organizational structure, strategic goals and objectives, financial management, marketing and branding, human resources, operations and logistics, and attention to fan engagement and experience.

Through strong management and leadership, the entire team works toward the achievement of a common goal—usually, to win a championship. Take basketball, for example. The star of the team, even if he's immensely talented, cannot take on another team by himself. Stephen Curry is a great dribbler and shooter, but he's short for an NBA player. Rebounding and blocking shots aren't his strengths. He needs the rest of his teammates to win.

Behind any business success you'll find a great team. You can't scale from an idea to actualized success without the help of teammates. A great idea doesn't build a business. People do. When we started RE/MAX, we wanted to create a championship-caliber organization with star players who anchored our team and supporting players who helped our business grow. Of course, we knew we wouldn't be able to recruit the Michael Jordan or Magic Johnson of the real estate world out of the gate, but if we laid the groundwork, established a strong and stable foundation, had the best leadership, and created greater opportunities, I was certain we would eventually get there.

There's a theory that most NBA championship teams take a three-star pillar approach to achieving success, meaning that they have three all-star players at the top of their roster. These three are clearly better than anyone else on the team. Because not every player can be an all-star, the rest of the team's skills need to complement theirs. The Miami Heat perfected this approach with LeBron James, Dwyane Wade, and Chris Bosh. Other teams, such as the Boston Celtics, the Denver Nuggets, and the Cleveland Cavaliers, have done it too. While the three pillars hold up the structure of the team, determining how high a ceiling they can reach, the surrounding talent is able to move around freely to do whatever's necessary on the court to support them.

When I moved to Denver from Phoenix, I had a great record selling real estate, even though I'd only been doing that part-time while I was still in the military. I interviewed at the nine or ten best companies in Denver. By far, the leading company to work for was VanSchaack. They've been around since 1911. During my interview, I told them that I was really looking for a future management position. My goal was to become a branch manager and move up in the company. I was eager to be an all-star there.

"You have to prove yourself," they said.

And so I did.

I worked for eleven months. During that time, I handled part of VanSchaack's training program. I also became president-elect of my board of Realtors. There was no doubt that I'd proven my worth. When I met with the CEO at the end of my first year, I had a long list of accomplishments. “You’re just the kind of young talent we’re looking for,” he said. “We’re going to go places together.”

“I’m on track now to get into management. How long is it going to be?” I asked.

“Well, soon,” he replied.

“How soon?” I asked.

“You know, why don’t you get a few years of experience, and then we can revisit this.”

That wasn’t what he’d told me in my interview. He’d said I was what they were looking for.

“Dave, you’re only twenty-six years old,” he continued. “Almost every man in the company is older than you. And how are they going to feel about your getting promoted over them for a management position?”

In my mind, the answer was clear. If I outproduced them and I was a better manager than they were, what difference did my age make? It didn’t make sense to me, so I pressed him further to say how long he thought it would be before I would be considered. “Are you talking two years, or are you talking five years?” I wanted to know.

“Probably five years or more,” he said.

I was steaming mad. I looked him straight in the eyes and said, “I know exactly how a woman feels when she says, ‘You used me.’ You had no intention of making me a vice president of this company. You just sucked me up, and I gave you all my business.”

I was furious. I stood up to leave. Before I walked out of his office, I turned around and said, “You watch me. I’ll build a company bigger and better than VanSchaack in five years. And I’ll bankrupt you sons of bitches.”

And I did bankrupt them. Twice.

I’ve never forgotten that day and how it made me feel. When I decided to launch my own company, I actually wasn’t looking to get rich. My dream was to better the lives of top producers in the real estate business. Most real estate companies will tell that you their customer is a real estate buyer or seller. From our first day in business, I said, "I'm in the real estate *agent* business. The agent is in the real estate customer business." I wanted to create an ideal environment in which real estate agents could succeed to the level of their wildest expectations and not be hindered in any way by what managers typically wanted from them. We designed the whole program to be different from the existing model.

Remember, in that era, top producers were on a 50/50 commission split. If you made $100,000 in gross commissions, half went to the company. But what was the company providing? What did the agent get for splitting their commission?

If an agent came to work for us, they would get nearly their entire commission, after paying a reasonable fee to work for us and to utilize the shared resources we provided. If they wanted to take a lower commission on a sale to secure a listing, that was their choice. It was their money. It was their company. We were offering freedom and independence. They could run as many or as few ads as they chose. They could make their names as large as they wanted to on the signs. They could personally promote themselves as much as they wanted. We encouraged building their book of business, and we tagged along with support to be a part of that journey.

This was such a different approach.

Top producers would often work for five, six, or seven years before they started their own company. Back then, all you needed was an answering service or machine, a small office, and some money to post ads in the local newspaper saying that you had clientele. Voilà! You were in business for yourself. The barriers to entry were very small. However, when you struck out on your own, you suddenly lost the competitive advantages of being with the biggest and best company in town. You were a nobody trying to compete with the giants. Realistically, you never got the freebies, such as the walk-in customers or the referrals from long-standing clients—the people who would say, "My parents used VanSchaack twenty years ago and told me it was the only real estate agency to use." Of course, those who opened their own small agencies would end up hiring a couple of agents to help them out. Usually, those hires were new agents with very little experience. That meant owners had to take time away from selling real estate to train their agents. This created a vicious cycle that made it a lot more challenging to branch out on their own. I was aware of the conundrum. I began to think about it, a lot. It seemed like an easy decision. We would provide an extraordinary opportunity to earn the highest amount of money in an environment where independent-minded agents could become as successful as they wanted to be. It was up to them to do the work.

When we began hiring at RE/MAX, I was very much against part-timers and beginners, because everyone had to pay us to come to work for us. Nobody got a draw or a salary. Instead, what we offered were real estate maximums: the maximum commission for an agent, the maximum full-time service for the real estate customer, the maximum recruiting and retention bill for the broker owner. We weren't there to exploit anyone. Quite the opposite: We were there to help people at the top of their game earn what they truly deserved.

TEAM MEMBER # 1

The month before we opened RE/MAX, we incorporated. Our first office was a half mile from the makeshift administrative office we'd been using on Belleview Avenue in Denver. It was 1,200 square feet and had two small conference rooms, a manager's office, and ten bullpen-style desks. When I hired Gail as our first employee on January 30, 1973 (the day we've always considered our official Founder's Day), I'd gone to two or three employment agencies. I held face-to-face interviews with twenty-seven people, and she was the twenty-seventh. Gail was college educated, had a marketing degree and a few years' experience working with Ralston Purina, and was moving to Denver with her husband, who had been transferred there for his job. She was smart, confident, and articulate. I was looking for someone who could do the things I couldn't. I had entrepreneurial ambition and smarts, but I lacked experience in areas I knew would need a lot of nurturing. When I met Gail for the first time, I knew she was exceedingly qualified, and she seemed to understand the vision as well as I did. I'm a salesman. I can recruit and train sales agents, but I'm not detail oriented. I needed somebody who could set up bookkeeping systems, find the office space, decorate it, buy the furniture, hire the secretarial and administrative staff, and deal with all the other day-to-day managerial tasks I didn't have any experience in. Knowing that these areas were being handled by someone I respected and trusted, and who had excellent taste and capabilities, allowed me to do what I did best—sell. I traveled nearly 250 days a year selling franchises, training agents, speaking, running marketing campaigns, and focusing on growing the business.

Gail was so effective that, within the first month she was at RE/MAX, I promoted her to vice president of administration. We mutually agreed that my strengths were selling real estate, teaching real estate principles, and leading and managing, while Gail was the brains behind every facet of the day-to-day operations.

It was a perfect relationship between the two of us. I sold, and Gail managed.

There are many qualities and traits to look for in a prospective life partner, but if you're considering running a business together, the most important characteristics are mutual respect, an understanding of your strengths and weaknesses, patience, and a sense of balance—all characteristics we had throughout our RE/MAX expansion, and continue to have to this day.

Our experience was unique.

Gail and I became the perfect duo. Together we were the ultimate power team. When we were struggling financially, she dealt with the bill collectors and held them at bay. If she hadn't done that, I'm certain we would have collapsed. She was also an integral part of the Regional Directors Council, the broker owner councils, and the advertising committees. I would be on the road giving seminars or selling franchises, and she would take charge of the meetings. It was her rightful place. Everybody knew that she was there when I couldn't be, and there was a great deal of comfort in that. I've always believed that the number two person in any position should be fully capable of assuming the number one's role at a moment's notice. We wouldn't have succeeded without Gail. To be certain, A-players are rare, and that made her a unicorn.

Of course, we were both married to other people at the time, so the notion of anything other than a professional relationship was never expected. However, after ten years of working closely with one another, we fell in love. In all our time together, our relationship was never negatively impacted by the growing business. In fact, it was empowered by it. The same could not be said of our first marriages. Almost every one of the officers, including Gail and me, ended up divorced from our first spouses. You could say that we all fell in love with RE/MAX. We created this beautiful thing together. The day-by-day operation was getting bigger all the time, and job satisfaction surely enveloped us. We had created a family environment that was based on trust and close personal relationships among the senior leaders. Our original team, which included me, Gail, Daryl Jesperson, and Bob Fisher, among others, was strong. Our bond and commitment to one another and to our business cost almost all of us something personal during those early years. Even so, the long-term survivability and interconnectedness of the company endured.

I've known many business partners who were married and ended up divorced, most within the first five years of working together. Being in business with your life partner doesn't always pan out, but when it does, believe me, it's a winning combination. At least it was for us. As I said, we'd already established a long-term relationship of mutual respect before we became a family. In our case, we first learned to work well together, and *then* we fell in love. I'll offer this advice about relationships, whether business or personal: There must be give and take, and if you're planning on building an empire together, never assume a dominant or traditional gender role. When we first founded RE/MAX, the man was usually the head of the household, and the woman was the homemaker, but that wasn't the case with us. Gail and I divided our responsibilities and always viewed each other as equal partners. We kept our egos checked and ran the business while also enjoying family life. We wanted a close-knit family, but we never wanted to treat the family business as a dynasty. As our children reached working age, we gave them menial tasks in the company if they wanted to work there, but we never intended to have them take over positions that our VPs, who had been working with us for twenty years, filled.

Sometimes, 1+1 equals more than 2. That's the equation that best describes us. It's magic, and definitely a key ingredient in the secret sauce that led to our global success. We have complementary skills and talents. I credit our massive success to our synergy and our undeniable ambition and grit.

YOU ARE THE AVERAGE OF THE FIVE PEOPLE YOU SPEND TIME WITH

I mentioned Jim Rohn earlier in this book in reference to his quote, "You are the average of the five people you spend the most time with." Why do I think this is worth repeating? The answer is simple: The people you spend the most time with ultimately shape who you are.

Rohn was an entrepreneur, author, and motivational speaker focused on the principles of human behavior that have the greatest impact on performance. His insights and lessons are well worth checking out, especially when it comes to creating success. As he explains, most people underestimate the importance of the company they keep. This is a mistake.

Darren Hardy also explores this notion in his book *The Compound Effect*, writing, "According to research by social psychologist Dr. David McClelland of Harvard, the people you habitually associate with determine as much as 95 percent of your success or failure in life." Now, think about this for a minute, as it has gigantic consequences for the outcome of everything you do. If other people can affect *95 percent* of your success or failure, you can see why it's so important to choose your company wisely. The effects of any negative company you keep will start to compound, which will eventually create roadblocks to reaching your goals.

I firmly believe that you can accelerate your personal growth in whatever direction you desire, so surround yourself with people you admire, especially those who have more experience and wisdom than you do. If they're hardworking, you'll probably imitate that. Common sense dictates that if you want to lose weight, you don't hang around with a bunch of unhealthy, overweight friends. You start running with physically fit friends, because you'll likely start adopting whatever traits and behaviors they exhibit. People are pack animals by nature. We follow what we see and then mimic it.

While growing up, I looked at John Wayne and some other inspirational actors and thought, *Man, that's what I want to be when I grow up.* I didn't want to be a businessman. I didn't want to be a teacher. I didn't want to be a doctor, even though I admired some people in those fields. No, I wanted to be an adventurer. I wanted to scuba dive. I wanted to skydive. I wanted to fly airplanes. So the people who did those things were the people I molded myself after. They were usually the heroes or heroines of the movies, and they were always fearlessly overcoming obstacles.

The first day I landed in Vietnam after a twenty-plus-hour flight from Stateside, I opened the door and looked out onto a tarmac filled with helicopters, jeeps, and tanks, and thought to myself, *I'm John Wayne, and I'm built for this minute.* I was a skinny little guy. I was a young, 120-pound weakling, and yet I wanted to kick ass, save the country, and come home a hero. But I'll tell you that by the last time I came home, I didn't have that attitude anymore. Sometimes, even if you're surrounded by good people, the environment you're in can change you. And the environment of war certainly does that.

But back to Jim Rohn and his thoughts on the subject of our daily influences. I was first introduced to his wisdom when he was a speaker at one of my conventions. Later I bought his CD set, *The Weekend Seminar with Jim Rohn.* I was home recovering from knee-replacement surgery when I decided to listen to what he had to say. I immediately thought he was great. Now, I'm not an especially religious man, but Rohn told a story that I've never forgotten about Jesus and a disciple who came to him and said, "It's time to pay our taxes. The only problem is, we have no money."

"No problem," Jesus said.

Now, the reason Jesus said it was no problem was that he was known to be something of a miracle worker. If you bring a miracle worker a problem, what do you think their answer is going to be?

That's right: *No problem.*

You've got to hang out with people like that. How many miracle workers do you know? In business, I know dozens. You hand these people a problem, and you know what they'll say?

You guessed it.

No problem.

Modern-day miracle workers are people who will do whatever it takes to solve those problems. They'll hire consultants, burn the midnight oil, get up early, look at every possible angle, and eventually find a solution.

Those are the kinds of people I want to be around. And those are the people who helped us build RE/MAX.

According to Rohn, if you aren't intentional about the people you spend your time with, you won't be able to achieve the continuous improvement you're looking for. There's no doubt that there are people who can hold you back, while others help propel you forward. This is why it's so important to be highly selective about the company you keep, as the individuals surrounding us can significantly influence our behavior, mindset, and overall success in life. If you spend your time with four losers, eventually you will become loser number five.

Whether you realize it or not, the people you spend time with impact everything, including your thoughts, beliefs, and actions—or inactions. You may notice that when you spend enough time with certain people, you start to take on their traits, which can influence your attitude, values, and behaviors. If you spend time with positive, ambitious, and motivated individuals, you're more likely to adopt similar qualities. Interacting with people you admire, especially in business, can help you stretch your boundaries. When you surround yourself with knowledgeable, accomplished people, you stand a good chance of learning from their experiences and wisdom. This comes in very handy when starting or running a business.

Another reason to be especially particular about who you spend time with is so you can create a solid support system. When your support system includes individuals who believe in you and your dream, it positively affects your confidence, resilience, and outcomes. A group of us have created a mastermind group we refer to as the Dirty Dozen. We meet twice a year for three or four days.

There's no agenda. It's just a gathering of successful businesspeople sharing everything we know. Each member of our group is someone I respect, admire, and believe has ideas of value to offer. This collaborative experience helps each of us gain incredible perspective and intelligence that positively impacts our work. I highly recommend creating a mastermind group of your own.

Now, it's easy to believe that your best strategy is to spend time with people who are all your cheerleaders. Not so. Of course you want to be around people who support you, but it's equally important to receive constructive feedback so you can continue to grow and flourish. Novices seek positive feedback to validate their work, whereas experts look for negative feedback to explore and uncover areas that may need improvement. So, find someone to join your circle who will be your best critic and will play devil's advocate when necessary. It should be someone who makes you think twice and who pushes you a little harder than others do. You won't regret inviting this person into your world.

While I totally agree with Rohn on this theory, it's important to note that we aren't solely defined by the five people we spend the most time with. People we encounter only once can have a profound impact on us too. Rohn's statement serves as a reminder to be conscious of the company you keep *and* to seek out interactions and relationships that support your personal and professional growth and overall well-being. So spend your time with the people who are already living the life you want to live, those who've been successful in your field, or those you really admire and aspire to be like.

I'd like to leave you with one final thought on this subject. While it's important to know who your five people are, it's equally important to become a respected and admired person yourself. Be one of five people for others. I've found that one of the best ways to learn in life is to teach. Putting yourself out there for others not only benefits you; it can also benefit those you come into contact with.

SOMETIMES A-PLAYERS COME FROM UNEXPECTED PLACES

When it came to hiring, RE/MAX developed a philosophy over the years that was relatively simple: Find people who want the dream as badly as you do, and hire good people with the right attitude, even if there is no position or title waiting for them. We've done this countless times throughout the years. Diane Metz was an agent who worked for Metro Brokers, one of our competitors in Denver that was utterly obsessed with measuring their performance in the market against ours. This comparison only highlighted what was wrong with that company and made it abundantly clear that we were the best place to work. Diane's mother had been a RE/MAX agent, so I'd met Diane a few times at various real estate events. She knew me well enough to reach out, so she did. When she called, I answered the phone as I usually do: "Hi, this is Dave . . ." She must have thought she'd get my secretary or an answering service. She didn't. She got me.

Flustered at first, she said, "Hi, Dave. This is Diane Metz over at Metro Brokers. You don't know me, but . . ."

I stopped her and said, "Of course I know who you are."

Diane explained her predicament. She was frustrated with where she was working and was aware of all the innovative things we were doing at the time, such as launching our own satellite television network that offered extensive training for our agents. She had called to express interest in working with us. I suggested we set up a meeting with two of our vice presidents. She agreed. By all accounts the interview went well, but it took four months for us to bring her on board because we weren't quite sure where to put her or in what role. Diane was relentless in her efforts to get us to make a decision. She wore us down until we had no choice but to hire her. I knew what I was doing from the start. I understood Diane and believed she had the capacity to become a tremendous asset to our company. When we hired her, there was no title or specific job for her, but it became immediately obvious to Diane that she was now part of our team and dream, so she stepped into a role of her own creation beautifully. She found what she could do to add value and did it. The moral of this story is simple: Find people who want the job so badly that they will hunt you down and prove to you their tenacity and commitment.

Adam Contos was another interesting hire. I met Adam for the first time in 1995. At the time, he was a SWAT commander in the Douglas County Sheriff's Department. While building Sanctuary Golf Course, we hired off-duty officers to work part-time patrolling and protecting the property. There was some vandalism on and around the golf course. The property was out in the country with few houses or witnesses around. It was an easy place to come and wreak a little havoc. To get rid of the vandals, I went to the Douglas County Sheriff's Department and said, "I want to start hiring some of your deputy sheriffs to work at night from 7:00 p.m. until 5:00 a.m." The construction crews were getting there at 5:30 and leaving by 6:00, so we'd be covered nearly twenty-four hours a day.

Most cops, especially younger rookies who aren't paid that well, will work off-duty hours at sporting events or provide private security to earn extra money. To hire one of them, you pay the local police department, and then they pay the officer. They take a tiny bit of the fee to help cover overhead, and they give the majority of the money to the officer.

Sanctuary is near my home, so I would often go there around 10:00 p.m. to check things out. I would show up with a dozen donuts, milk and cookies, and sometimes a six-pack of beer. I have an affinity for those who choose law enforcement for their career. During my time in Vietnam, I was temporarily assigned to base duty at an outpost that needed additional guards. I volunteered to be an air police augmentee. Instead of doing any other work on the base, I did air police work, which meant that while others guarded the gates, I did combat in the field. When I came back Stateside and was established in my real estate business, I went to the county sheriff's office and volunteered to become a reserve officer. I've been one for more than forty years now. You see, I like the camaraderie of the individuals who are involved. I also like a change of pace, as you can probably tell from all my activities outside of selling real estate. I suppose being around guys like Adam and the others who worked off-duty at Sanctuary meant something more to me.

We usually had one or two off-duty officers working every night. I would sit there, visit with them, have a cup of coffee in the dark, and just talk shop. We all became friends.

One night I asked Adam, "Do you like to shoot?"

Of course he said yes.

"Well, I brought some guns. We have to patrol the place anyway. Let's go shoot some porcupines," I suggested with a sheepish grin.

Now, before you jump all over me about cruelty to animals, you should know that porcupines are hell on trees. They eat a ring of bark around their trunks, which kills them. When we built the course, we saved more than two hundred pine trees—some of them thirty to forty feet high—by replanting them. That was very expensive to do, so letting those little critters kill them was not acceptable.

That night started a tremendous friendship. I got to know Adam and learned that he'd dropped out of college twice. He then joined the United States Marines, where he learned the meaning of extreme discipline and found a cause. His goal at that time was to be in law enforcement.

When Adam was on duty, he would sometimes invite me on ride-alongs. I loved it. While we were patrolling, I watched how he behaved. Adam wasn't just a police officer on the beat. As I said, he was a SWAT commander. I analyzed his every move, and I knew there was something extraordinary about this man. In my gut, I understood that he had the ability to succeed in anything he wanted to do, but I especially believed that he would excel in business. Sometimes, when he would finish a radio transmission with another officer, he would say, "Hey, when you get a second, call my cell."

When they did, Adam would talk to them for a while, calm and clearheaded even if he wasn't delivering the best news. Curious, I asked him one time why he had the officers call him.

"There are two hundred officers listening on a radio transmission. I had to tell him he screwed up, but I wasn't about to discipline him and have two hundred other cops judging his rookie mistake." It was that kind of sensitivity that got my attention.

I also observed how safety conscious he was. In general, SWAT guys are pretty gung ho. They often have a "let's go knock down some doors and kick some ass" mentality. It was Adam's responsibility to bring the men and women on his SWAT team home uninjured. You do that through proper leadership, management, and preparation. Before any mission, he would sit down with his team. Everybody would have input on what they should be doing. Everybody had a chance to voice their opinion. Most special forces do this. It's quite inclusive. And when the event is done, everybody participates in a debrief—a free flow of information about what went right and what went wrong. No one is mean to each other in these recaps. The discussion is always centered around how they could do better next time. I watched how he led those discussions and, again, I was impressed. Adam gave every person a chance to express their fears, concerns, and thoughts. As a result, he built a cohesive team, and that's what you must do in business. After spending several months observing Adam, I was convinced that he could apply that skill to a business environment. He and I spoke about his future a lot. As strongly as I felt about his potential, Adam needed to feel that shifting away from law enforcement and into business was right for him too. As we became better acquainted and closer friends, there was no doubt we were on the same page.

The way I observed Adam in the field was a very common practice at RE/MAX. It wasn't unusual for us to intentionally pair new or prospective hires with senior leaders, whether in a taxi, during a golf game, or over dinner, without them realizing that we were watching their every move. Look, if someone cheats on the golf course, they can't be trusted in business. We wanted to know our people, who they really were. For the most part, those encounters were scripted, structured, and designed to maximize the learning experience and create stronger and more productive employees. The senior leaders assessed what they saw, discussed new information, probed for weaknesses, and created developmental plans. It would become clear who needed new challenges, coaching, or even some informal mentoring. Nurturing our young leaders in this way helped them to become their best and most successful selves. We were always pushing people to believe they were better than they thought they were.

Adam was inherently entrepreneurial, even when he started as a cop. He had a police supply internet store that sold leather goods, holsters, and other items cops needed. He naturally had that mindset, and that's how he ended up with us.

I went to the local sheriff and said, "I'm never going to take a man from you, but I'm telling you, he's the real deal, and he could be very successful if you let me give him a chance."

Thankfully, the sheriff gave me his blessing. I hired Adam to come work for RE/MAX. Adam is one of the most coachable people. He took more action than almost anybody I've ever worked with. Sure, there have been others, but mostly I speak to people, give them advice, mentor them, and they still do whatever they want to do even if it's not working for them. That wasn't the case with Adam.

I've often spoken at meetings about how hard it is to motivate someone to do something. Most of our motivation comes from within, and that typically comes from the environment you grew up in. From the time you first open your eyes all the way through adolescence, you're either building confidence or losing it. Some people are driven to succeed. Some people have grit. And there are those who will try something and give up after only two attempts, while others will look at the problem and still be working on it two days later. They won't stop until they get it done. For some, it's heredity. But for most people, environmental influences have molded them into the kind of person they are.

There are a few incredible, talented people who are somehow naturally molded to persist in whatever they do. They know how to focus and achieve greatness. For them, it comes from within. But for all the rest, it's drawn out and nurtured by others. I had a strong mother who was very encouraging and didn't put me down if I made a mistake. She would encourage me by saying, "That's a mistake, but we'll get over that. I believe in you. You're going to do great things." The more people believe in you and the more you're aware of their belief in you, the more fully you develop your abilities. I think it's a learned trait, but it's a subtle aspect of learning. It's so subtle that you don't even realize you're learning something. I believed in Adam that way.

Adam joined RE/MAX in 2004, working with franchisees and agents in the Mountain States Region. Through his dedication and perseverance, he steadily rose through our senior leadership ranks until, in 2017, he was named co-CEO, and ultimately CEO in 2019. To earn the position, our board insisted that he get an MBA, which he did in between his responsibilities with our company and the police force, where he still volunteered. When he was faced with this proposition, Adam sat down with his family and explained that sacrifices would need to be made if he agreed to get his master's. He knew his family time would be limited, that Little League games and dance recitals would likely be hard to juggle. With their blessing, he took the next eighteen months and dedicated himself to doing what was required for the job. His approach to leading high-performance teams with us remained the same as when he was running his SWAT team. His goal was always to break down barriers, blow up conventional thinking, and help as many people as possible achieve success. That way of thinking fit right in at RE/MAX, and it certainly earned my respect. Under his leadership, RE/MAX explored new and innovative ways to improve our company's position in the marketplace. He led the acquisitions of booj, an award-winning, Colorado-based web design and technology company, and the Gadberry Group, a data science company, both of which offered new building blocks in the RE/MAX quest to become the worldwide leader in real estate technology.

HUNTERS AND FARMERS

Now that we've discussed the process of filling leadership roles within your company, it's time to turn your attention to hiring salespeople. That process is unlike the hiring process for any other position. When building a sales team, there are two types of employees we look for. First, there are the hunters. They're always eager to go out and make the deal. They're extroverts who want to do nothing but sell. Hunters might cold-call, send emails, or do social selling and prospecting to break into new accounts. Their goal is converting leads into customers and driving new growth. While they're outgoing, happy-go-lucky people, they're incredibly skilled at tracking a lead and making the kill. When they bring the deal back, they throw it on their broker's desk, saying, "Take care of this. I'm going out to get another deal." Thank goodness for hunters, because you've got to have them to be successful. They work very independently and like to do their own thing.

Then there are the farmers. They're relationship builders. Farmers generate revenue by cultivating and expanding opportunities with existing customers. This can be done through upselling current products, cross-selling new products, or expanding into new divisions or regions.

A farmer's goals are to increase sales and grow their customer base. Farmers typically engage in a lot of networking activities. They may attend meetings or industry events where customers are likely to be. When they're trying to do business with someone, they're in it for the long term, creating programs that may have them working together on a daily or weekly basis for many years. They're very nurturing. These are the people who are willing to plow the ground, plant the seed, fertilize it, water it, and then harvest the crops year after year.

As a startup, you need hunters *and* farmers. There are some people who are absolutely not cut out for sales. Different personalities thrive in either a hunter or a farmer role. Today, most organizations need people in both roles to successfully drive revenue. It ultimately depends on your industry, business model, and team dynamics. When you run a synchronized hunter-farmer sales model, you'll see significant growth with new customers while retaining the ones you've already closed. You can't retain deals that aren't closed, and you can't close deals if your best customers exit out the back door. So, both roles are essential to your company's success.

Recently, we had a regional owner who wasn't a very likable person. Even after making many sales, his brokers hated him. But they loved RE/MAX, so they didn't leave. I found another regional owner who was a young, handsome, ex–professional football player. He was known for being very courageous on the playing field, but for whatever reason, he couldn't close a sale in real estate. I had to shut down his operation because he couldn't muster the same courage off the field as he once had on it. He could tackle another player and never think twice, but he was too scared to call a real estate office and talk about a franchise opportunity.

Good salespeople often get a bad rap. People don't fully understand their skill set. They're frequently told that a really great salesman shouldn't get into management or leadership. I find that to be absolute nonsense. A really great salesman works on referrals. When people love working with you, they'll always tell their friends, "Buy a house from Dave; he'll really treat you right." It's for that very reason that I believe good salespeople can make great leaders. They're already people oriented, and they're also service oriented. They return calls, show up on time, and turn down deals when they know something about them is wrong. They create loyalty and trust by being honest. These are all great traits in a leader.

FIVE GENERATIONS IN THE WORKFORCE TODAY

I believe it was Darren Hardy who first discussed with me the fact that there are currently five generations in the workplace. He'd spent a great deal of time studying the various generations, and he communicated how significant and different each of them was and how important it is for a leader to serve all five generations to be effective.

This is a very unusual phenomenon, and it got me thinking about how the world we live in now is so different from the one I started out in. I struggled in my early career because I failed at getting an advanced education. I believe that would have made the trail I took so much easier. But the fact that I failed was neither good nor bad. I still found a way to be successful. I just took the hard way.

If you want to be an entrepreneur today, one path is to go to college, get an MBA, and work someplace to build experience before you cash out and try to be in business for yourself. While that may give you a leg up on some other people, it's not a guarantee of success. There are a lot of people, myself included, who didn't take that route. More and more people are choosing not to go to college today. Perhaps higher education isn't where they shine, or it's become too expensive. Many young people are deterred by the prospect of having to pay back astronomical student loans. And some of those who did attend college during the pandemic years felt that learning via Zoom meant they got less than they paid for. Those who opt not to go to college, for whatever reason, get their degrees at the College of Hard Knocks, and there is no shame in that.

Over the years, Gail and I were both awarded two honorary PhDs from Colorado State University and the University of Colorado. Both were doctorates in humane letters. Gail and I had both been lecturers at both universities, speaking on business, entrepreneurial studies, and leadership. While we were thrilled and grateful to receive these degrees, I struggled with the idea of anyone referring to me as Dr. Liniger. Why? I'm not really a doctor. I had the title but not the education. When I voiced this to the people at the universities granting me these honors, I was put in my place both times. The heads of each college explained that I was unanimously voted to receive the doctorate because of my business experience. They valued my fifty years of field-acquired knowledge as much as they valued their ten or twelve years of formal education. I was taken aback for sure. To this day, though, the only time I use the title Dr. Liniger is when I lecture at colleges.

Because of my history, when I'm hiring, I couldn't care less if someone graduated from Wharton, Princeton, Harvard, or community college. It makes no difference to me if you were magna cum laude or pulled straight Cs. I want to know what else you did in college. Did you play a sport? Were you on the debate team? Did you start a small business? Did you travel? Life experiences are equal to learned experiences. While I value reading books, I happen to gain so much more from other experiences.

But one of the reasons I believe we've grown more disconnected generationally these days is that five distinct groups, with vastly different life experiences that extend well beyond such considerations as education, are now working side by side. These groups include traditionalists (sometimes called matures or the silent generation), baby boomers, Gen Xers, millennials (also sometimes known as Gen Y, though they aren't really the same), and, finally, Gen Z. For the first time in American history, we're managing these various groups in the workplace *together.* I will later expand these distinctions beyond birth years, discussing them in terms of type of worker, but for now, I'll stick to the standard definitions of who makes up the workforce today.

The five generations in the workplace today include:

Traditionalists–born between 1927 and 1946
Baby boomers–born between 1947 and 1964
Generation X–born between 1965 and 1980
Millennials–born between 1981 and 2000
Generation Z–born between 2001 and 2020

*Note: Dates used to define each generation vary among sources. Some of your employees' experiences may be more reflective of a preceding or succeeding generation.

While there are still some actively working traditionalists, including myself, the bulk of the workforce is composed of the remaining four categories, with the largest generation currently being millennials. Many think the government or the census bureau came up with these terms. The reality is that these generations have been named by "experts" in the field who've made these labels stick through their research—research, by the way, that's skewed one way or another by key political, economic, and social factors that tend to define the behaviors of a demographic cohort. This leads to some common misconceptions about who makes up these groups. For example, confusion exists around Gen Y and millennials, depending on the year of birth used to define those generations. There are several different ways research teams have decided on those dates. Take a look at the following to see what I mean.

Research Team	**Preferred Name of Generation**	**Year Dates**
William Strauss and Neil Howe	Millennials	1982–2004
Ad Age	Generation Y	1981–1994
Pew Research	Millennials	1981–1996
Gen HQ	Generation Y	1977–1995

With different sources offering different definitions, the expert with the most significant reach usually wins the name game. For the purposes of this book, however, I'll refer to millennials (not Gen Y) as those who were born between 1981 and 2000. They are, to my mind, the generation born before the September 11 terrorist attacks, the 2003 invasion of Iraq, and the Great Recession. I'm sharing this information because it differs from the views of others, comes from my experiences and observations, and will be necessary to keep in mind as I continue to discuss the various generations in this and upcoming chapters.

Putting differences about dates aside for the moment, I've learned over the course of my fifty-plus years in business how to manage each generation as they came up the ranks. Doing so required three things: patience, an open mind, and a willingness to learn from each group. They all brought something significant to building RE/MAX. As our business changed, so did our team. I didn't know a lot when I started the company, but I knew enough to develop talented people regardless of their age. They learned from me, and I learned from them.

THE BOOM IN AGE DIVERSITY

For some entrepreneurs and managers, overseeing multiple generations can be a challenge. But it doesn't need to be, especially if you understand the value of each group and their different expectations, communication styles, and points of view. Learning to manage the distinctive characteristics of each generation can bring tremendous benefits to employers and their teams by fostering their individual strengths and, as a result, becoming more competitive in the marketplace. By studying the work habits of each generation, you'll be more prepared to anticipate their needs and, therefore, the advantages they bring to your company.

Let's take a look at each generation and talk about their strengths and concerns in the workplace. But before we do that, think for a moment about the last time you attended a family reunion or gathering. Who was there? Were there multiple generations, such as your grandparents, maybe your great-grandparents, aunts, uncles, cousins, and so on? I know when I get together with my family, there's a lot of boisterous dialogue. Sometimes we agree, and other times we can go at it pretty hard to make our point. A few members of my family might stay quiet in the wings, but others insist on having their say. Each generation in the room has a point of view, and all of them matter, because they provide insights into everyone's life—how they act, what they believe, what they stand for, and what they're against.

If you sit back and listen, you'll learn a lot.

The same holds true in a healthy working environment where the leadership strives to build strong team interactions and dynamics.

Traditionalists

The oldest generation still working today is my generation—the traditionalist or silent generation.

Traditionalists grew up with the impression that each new generation should be better off than the last. Many of us saw our parents experience significant unemployment and poverty, so we felt lucky to come of age in an era when jobs were more plentiful. Traditionalists have seen, heard, and done a lot during their working years. We acquired wisdom from decades of ingenuity, drive, hard work, and tough economic times. We have knowledge and expertise that can benefit any organization and its workforce.

We did not, however, have modern technology or many of the conveniences younger generations take for granted today. Most traditionalists are like me: We never really got comfortable with technology, even if we use it. And to be certain, we tend to think that nothing beats the value of face-to-face interactions, especially when building business relationships. While social media may be a good thing for most, I never felt that I had the time to dedicate to it. Even now, I know it's essential, but in my mind, I have bigger and better things pulling at me every day.

If you can leverage the knowledge of the traditionalists and tap into their skill sets to train and mentor the younger generations coming up the ranks, your company and team will reap the rewards.

Baby Boomers

Aside from the traditionalists, the baby boomers have been working the longest. They also entered the workforce wanting to do better than their parents and have years of experience and knowledge to share. They want their opinions and know-how to benefit others, and above all, they want their coworkers to value what they have to say. This generation comes from the school of thought that the more hours you work, the better the results. They believe that a good work ethic is critical to success. They were and still are willing to sacrifice personally to achieve their professional goals. A 2016 study published in the *Journal of Marriage and Family* showed that dads in the 1960s spent about sixteen minutes a day with their kids. Moving up the ladder of success was and still is a priority for them. It's said that they live to work. Baby boomers are team players. They know it takes a village, and will go out of their way to create the right team around them, especially if it means that they'll be recognized in the form of promotions or raises.

Gen X

The Gen X demographic is sandwiched between baby boomers and millennials. They were shaped by the advancement of technology, especially the use of personal computers. They're generally more educated than their predecessors, viewed as hardworking self-starters, and don't necessarily want to be supervised. They're usually financially responsible, if not a bit conservative. They entered the workforce with a work-to-live mentality instead of the boomer live-to-work ethic. They've also experienced both upswings and downswings in the economy, which undoubtedly impacted their career choices, successes, and failures.

Millennials

As mentioned earlier, millennials represent the largest generation in the workforce. Many came into careers during a recession, which no doubt influenced their trajectory. The internet revolutionized everything, making email, texts, and direct messaging standard methods of communication, even when they're in the same room. Some might say they do this to be efficient, and that may be true, but I still contend that there's nothing more personal than meeting with someone face-to-face. When it comes to millennials, research shows that they're the most family-oriented generation in the last fifty years.

Instead of outearning their predecessors, they've emphasized being better parents, having a better quality of life, and creating a better balance between work and play. That's not to say they don't have a solid work ethic. They do. But sometimes they get a bad rap as being lazy and entitled. I don't think that's necessarily true. I believe millennials have figured out a way to be just as productive in less time. In part, I believe that they're motivated to attain a better quality of life because they typically grew up in homes with two working parents, were kept busy as children, and therefore have a keen understanding of how to get things done. It may not be conventional, but it's efficient, and it offers more free time to keep their work and personal lives stable.

Gen Z

The Gen Zs have never known a world without technology. They've grown up connected and have a perpetual "on" switch. Information is literally in the palms of their hands at all times, making it easy to know everything without knowing much of anything. This constant access to information and technology, whether at home or in the classroom as they grew up, has created an incredibly tech-savvy generation. While there are a lot of benefits to that, there have also been some drawbacks, especially in behavior and lifestyle. This generation has grown up lonelier and more disconnected from each other, despite being digitally connected all the time. They communicate primarily through their devices. And while that might be normal to them, it can prove to be frustrating to members of the other four generations they work with.

Gen Zs watched their parents struggle during the economic downturn in 2007 and 2008, with many losing their jobs, homes, and savings. Witnessing this created a generation desirous of job stability. They tend to be willing to stay in one position or one company

and exhibit a commitment to their job and family. This generation is also highly concerned with social responsibility and diversity. They love to be mentored and coached, and enjoy learning from older generations. They also have a strong desire to be collaborative. They look to their management to create and foster situations that will help them learn and grow.

So now that you have a brief understanding of the generations making up the workforce today, what exactly does this all mean? In short, an aging population and more years of working are shaping the labor market. The newer generations are challenging existing models. They're shaking up old habits while creating better, more efficient methods. In addition, the constant improvements in technology and the digital universe make it crucial to stay current. If you don't learn to effectively manage each generation, you'll find yourself constantly putting out personnel fires. Knowing who makes up your team and understanding their points of view will help you create a thriving workplace and build the strongest possible business. As your company grows, so too will your team. This, of course, means that you'll constantly need to adapt as your workforce changes and welcomes newer generations.

THE GREAT RESIGNATION

Speaking of changes, a recent dynamic has profoundly affected the way *all* the generations are experiencing work today. "The Great Resignation" is a term that gained popularity in 2021. It was first used by Professor Anthony Klotz of Texas A&M to describe a significant wave of employees voluntarily leaving their jobs in various industries and sectors. The phenomenon was driven by individuals seeking new opportunities, career changes, or improvements in work-life balance. In fact, the nation's quit rate reached a twenty-year high in November 2021, with mid-career employees and those

in the technology and healthcare industries having the highest rates of resignation.

There are several factors that contributed to the Great Resignation, including the Covid-19 pandemic, which prompted people to reassess their priorities and reevaluate their career choices. A Pew Research Center survey found that low pay, a lack of opportunity for advancement, and feeling disrespected at work were at the top of the list for people who decided to make a change. The impact of remote work, health concerns, and reconsideration of personal values also led to individuals seeking more fulfilling and flexible work arrangements.

In general, people were feeling burned out, especially those who had significant challenges and increased workloads during that time. Long hours, blurred boundaries between work and personal life, and heightened stress levels also contributed to that burnout. As a result, a lot of people began seeking positions that offered greater flexibility and well-being.

The disruption caused by the pandemic gave people a lot of time to reflect on their career paths and aspirations. There was a great deal of uncertainty and mass layoffs at the onset of the pandemic. Those who remained gainfully employed stayed put out of necessity. Those who had more leeway and financial freedom had the capacity to move on if they wanted to. Many had already been considering career changes, pursuing entrepreneurial endeavors, or exploring new industries that aligned with their passions and values, and many started to think about these alternatives as a result of the drastic changes we all faced.

While experts believed the pandemic would decimate the economy, the recovery following the pandemic actually resulted in increased job openings and a demand for skilled workers. Most of the people who quit then are now employed somewhere else with better pay, more opportunities for advancement, and better work-life

harmony. This has increased individuals' confidence about leaving their current jobs to seek greater opportunities.

As employees were evaluating their careers, managers were left to navigate the effects of people leaving their jobs. They faced challenges in retaining talent and attracting new employees. Organizations needed to adapt their strategies to address changing workforce expectations and create work environments that supported employee well-being, growth, and engagement. How we organize work will likely never be the same as it was pre-pandemic. The old one-size-fits-all approach has given way to a new way of thinking that creates more supportive work settings and asynchronous work organization. Some companies found that remote working was equally productive and actually more cost effective, so they now permit employees to stay remote or to fill hybrid roles combining in-person and remote working.

While the office was the gathering ground for employees prior to the pandemic, many companies have now chosen to close their physical offices altogether.

Not all industries and occupations experienced the effects of the Great Resignation, but the concept still highlights the shifting dynamics of the labor market and the increasing emphasis on work-life balance, purpose-driven careers, and employee well-being. The current work environment calls for *self-leadership*, where employees are not only willing but able to take on more responsibility so they may ultimately thrive. To effectively manage this, a company must select the right talent, hiring individuals who are capable of working independently while also remaining highly productive. This involves creating a culture of individualized working conditions while also establishing mandatory guidelines that cannot be compromised. This is the new normal, and it ought to create a scenario in which *everyone wins*. Plenty of research on the efficacy of in-person versus virtual teams clearly shows that both perform better when there's clarity regarding roles, tasks, systems, and expectations, especially virtual teams. The companies that have made it a priority to hire dedicated, dependable, and performance-oriented individuals have found the transition to more flexible and future-oriented work much easier.

The Principle of Mutual Enrichment

The ideal relationship in business is one in which all parties benefit from the association—not just one person but *all* people. If you enter management in this era of age diversity with your eyes and ears open, you'll discover that one generation might bring years of hands-on experience while others are more adept at streamlining work through their understanding of technology. Millennials and Gen Z are exceptionally well-versed in the technological world because they're "digital natives"—the only generations who've grown up with it from birth. They don't know any other way.

Wise business leaders will implement programs within their organizations to take advantage of diversity in age, experience, and knowledge. More than twenty years ago, Louis Schweitzer, then CEO of Groupe Renault, tasked top-ranking executives in the company with learning new technologies by partnering up with younger, more tech-savvy employees. He called this "reverse tutoring," and it proved extremely valuable.

Adapting isn't the responsibility of one generation over another. The entire organization needs to modify its work habits, expectations, and opinions to succeed. Because millennials currently make up the largest portion of the workforce (and will continue to do so for years to come), they will likely have to make a lot of adjustments along the way. The good news is that studies show most workers today know their positions will progress and evolve, so leading with this reality in mind will come as no surprise to them. Focusing on a "we" over a "me" mentality is what will get you and your team where you want to be. Create an environment that welcomes and reinforces purpose, commonalities, and goals. And those goals shouldn't all be driven by profit or pay; think about opportunities, room for advancement, and growth potential. Grow your people first, and your business will grow too.

MAKING EVEN SMARTER HIRING DECISIONS

When I first met Darren Hardy, he had already achieved a great level of success. He quit Century 21 to come work for RE/MAX, becoming our agent of the year in California. Eventually, he left the real estate business and bought a couple of cable television channels and focused their programming on motivation and success. He also brought *Success* magazine back from bankruptcy, published a few hundred issues, and made it profitable. While he was publishing the magazine, he had the opportunity to interview two hundred of the most successful businesspeople in the country. He digitized the best quotes from those interviews and ended up with an unbelievable encyclopedia of business concepts. He's an excellent presenter who tells it like it is. I liked him from the day we met, and, more important, I greatly respect him.

One of the lessons Darren espouses is the importance of building an A team made up of A players, meaning they're all self-starters, have a good work ethic, are genuine, and are well liked. B players contribute to the company. They're the workers who carry out the tasks that A players delegate. C players, on the other hand, are there to hold down a job but aren't terribly engaged. There's a lot of turnover among these people. In most companies, about 10 percent of all employees make up A players, 30 to 40 percent are B players, and the rest are C players, so it's important to know who is who.

A players don't want to play with C players. They're hard chargers who are seriously committed to getting the job done, and when hiring, they look for other A players. B players don't want to hire A players because they're intimidated by them or worried that they might take their jobs in six months. B players will hire either B or C players. This is part of being human; we all want to survive.

If you looked at one hundred people within a company, you would find that 5 to 10 percent are A players, 10 percent are B players, and the rest are C players. The least-engaged employees make up the largest part of your workforce. They're pushing paper and collecting a paycheck. This isn't a good way to grow your team or your business.

We hired more C players when we started than I care to admit. When you recruit, you always try to find people who are similar to you, or whom you believe are similar. But the worst thing a salesman can do is hire another salesman to run a territory. Their skill set is selling, not managing. Hiring the wrong person to run a territory often means that they're likely to make mistakes in hiring salespeople to report to them. Two of the biggest mistakes are not interviewing thoroughly enough and not checking credentials or referrals. There were instances when we hired people who told us they had numerous contacts, that their people would follow them wherever they went, or that they could sell ten franchises with their eyes closed, yet they never sold one. The bigger the ego, the harder the fall—or at least that's how it appeared to us.

Hiring A players actually saves you money in the long run. When you hire an A player, they're free. Even if you pay them $300,000 a year, they're free. Why? Because they're going to bring you $1 million a year in revenue.

For many years before we wised up, we tried to take a marginally talented person and make them into a leader. That's a very hard thing to do. In fact, it's nearly impossible. So, on average, we ended up turning over our first crop of regional owners twice in a ten-year span. They just couldn't get the job done. They didn't work hard enough, and rarely—if ever—met their quotas early. They were complacent and felt that there was enough profit in the business without their having to put in real effort.

That mentality didn't last long with us.

Eventually, we got it right, making smarter hiring decisions and doing our due diligence before selling franchises to prospective franchisees. In the last thirty-plus years of business, we've assembled an incredible group of regional owners, but we had to go through a lot of them to get to the real winners—the ones who embraced the concept and made it work. It would have been much easier to do this sooner if I hadn't been under financial pressure to take a check—any check, from whoever would write it. I could have sat back and said no to ten people while I waited for the one good one—that A player—to join our team.

Sometimes entrepreneurs make decisions out of desperation, from lack of patience, or lack of experience. When you hire people this way, all you're doing is spinning your wheels. You never end up with A players, and you'll eventually have to remove those bad hires from the company. You're in survival mode, and everyone has to find their own way to ride out the mistakes you're making. We got through those tough times with pure perseverance. Taking back a master franchise is an extraordinarily difficult task, not to mention an expensive one, and it always ended up in litigation. It was a hard way to learn a lesson.

SOMETIMES THE BEST MAN FOR THE JOB IS A WOMAN

I want every little girl who's been told she is bossy to be told again she has leadership skills.

—Sheryl Sandberg

Some of the smartest, most effective people I've worked with are women.

From the day I hired Gail, and every day since, I've wanted only the best in the business to work with us. If those we hired were successful at selling homes, people would see our company as successful too. We knew the business would flourish if we kept our agents and customers happy. I was convinced that the most accomplished agents would be intrigued and attracted to our company because of our unique commission structure, which was infinitely better than the usual 50/50 split. So very early on, I placed a small ad in the *Denver Post* that read, "Realtors, why split your commission? Join RE/MAX." The ad went on to explain our concept in greater detail.

I knew the ad would be controversial with other brokerages, mainly because I was targeting competitors' agents, and that was a no-no. Okay, it probably happened all the time, but likely over a meal or behind closed doors. But I wanted to shake things up in an industry that had been asleep at the wheel for quite some time, and I also wanted to attract A players. I thought the ad would do that.

My plan worked—sort of. The ad generated over a thousand calls, not all of them good. About one hundred threatened to run us out of town, tar and feather us, or bankrupt the company. The other nine hundred were from real estate agents asking how our scheme would work. That resulted in several hundred interviews, most of which were busts. They weren't the candidates we were looking for. In the end, however, I hired four people. Why only four? They were the only ones who said yes—and they were also the only ones who saw the impact our company could have on the industry. They were the people who realized that their greatest potential was ahead of them. It wasn't their experience, their intelligence, or their drive that got my attention. It was their hunger—a passion to improve the quality of their lives and to be a part of something new and different.

There was one more reason I offered positions to them. Interestingly, three of the four people were women. While this might not sound unusual today, it was downright radical at the time. In the 1950s and '60s, women were nonexistent in real estate. It was an old white man's business. Back then, most agents didn't start in real estate—either the commercial or residential kind—when they were in their twenties or thirties like they do today. There was no salary, and most people couldn't afford to wait six months to make their first deal. They would have lived hand to mouth. Accepting an all-commission wage was risky. As a result, the business predominantly attracted retired teachers, retired civil servants, retired military, and others who had twenty or thirty years' experience doing something else. This started to change a little in the 1960s, when the early baby boomers, born after 1946, turned twenty years old. In that era, women married at seventeen or eighteen, and many found themselves divorced single moms a few years later. They needed to work, so they became office support staff—mainly bookkeepers. They weren't agents yet. In fact, when I worked at VanSchaack in the early seventies, all three hundred agents were men. It was the same for the next biggest competitor.

What's more, when I first started selling real estate in 1966, women couldn't qualify for a mortgage on their own. The banks worried that they might get pregnant and wouldn't be able to repay their loans. Even if they had a husband and worked, their income would count only if they had a letter from a doctor verifying that they were on birth control and weren't planning on having children for five to ten years. Sadly, that's the way business was done back then. Sure, there may have been some sneaky ways to work around that caveat, but it existed, and it made things terribly difficult for women. By the late sixties, however, women began seeking their freedom, and suddenly they were allowed to buy homes without a man to personally guarantee the loan. They could finally get credit cards on their own. And there was a plethora of college-educated women looking for work. All those factors helped create the perfect storm for the real estate industry. After all, who understood the importance of a home to families better than women?

By 1970, there were an unbelievable number of women coming into the real estate business. The all-male companies hated them. They thought of them as part-time housewives who weren't serious about the business. Companies like VanSchaack and others openly said, "We don't hire women in sales positions. They can be bookkeepers or paralegals or receptionists, but they're not going to be in sales." It was very prejudicial—and it wasn't just women who were being discriminated against. People of color didn't exist in the real estate industry then either.

I couldn't hire men from the top two companies because they laughed at me, and the women who wanted to be agents couldn't work at the top companies—so we ended up building our company with women.

The fact that women couldn't break the glass ceiling at the top real estate companies back then seemed like a huge mistake to me. Women are perfectly suited for the job. Let's be honest: It's women who usually decide on the big family purchases, including homes. If the house wasn't the right fit, especially in those days, there was a near zero chance that the husband would prevail and make the purchase. A woman looks at a house through a completely different lens from the one a man looks through. Men talk concrete, siding, and windows; women look at the layout, the functionality, the number of stairs, or the benefit of having a washing machine on the same floor as the bedrooms. They understand the importance of good schools and access to daycare and parks. Women who started as part-time agents began making money and quickly wanted to work full-time. Women who didn't need money but wanted independence also flooded the workforce, and by the time I founded RE/MAX, many talented and eager women were looking to join our team. And we were more than willing to welcome them with open arms. Besides, I've always believed that women have and show more empathy than men. They connect with their clients' needs and readily close sales. So, yes, I was thrilled to add women to our sales team.

During our first year in business, we hired twenty-one new agents. We doubled that number to forty-two the following year. By our third year in business, our agent count was up to eighty-four. We had 134 in our fourth year, and 289 by the end of 1977. After five years in business, our agents were about 70 to 75 percent female, and we became the top real estate company in the entire state. Our women were damn serious about their business. They had to pay their bills just like everybody else.

By then, our sales records proved we were number one in income per agent, transaction size per agent, total transaction volume, and total transaction size volume. After we'd beaten out the two top companies, two hundred men who had worked for exclusively male companies quit to join our merry band of ladies, who had easily kicked their butts.

We created a company of driven, hardworking producers who were committed to their business. They were all career-minded men and women seeking and achieving great success. Eventually, the novelty of women working in real estate faded as RE/MAX proved the value of how good women could be in the business. We gave women the opportunity and the forum to shatter that elusive glass ceiling in our industry by shepherding them from clerical positions to their rightful roles as agents. And, eventually, many became franchisees, owning their own businesses.

That slow and steady growth eventually led us to expand our team worldwide. It wasn't an accident—at least, I didn't think so. But if it was, it was a happy one that paid off for everyone.

For years I've preached that the best man for the job is a woman, and I mean it. RE/MAX always kept women at the forefront of our business. In a world where women found it difficult to make as much money as men, real estate was a business in which women often made more.

Gail always found innovative ways to ensure that the women in our company knew they were valued. She started a tradition she called Ladies' Day to recognize the contributions of women, especially those working in our back office. Eventually, we expanded our acknowledgment of women's importance to our company and industry by creating programs focusing on themes critical to women's lives, including safety, health, and self-protection.

Today, there are approximately 1.6 million Realtors, roughly 66 percent of whom are women. And every year, there are women agents who are raped and never report the crime because they're humiliated. There are also a lot of muggings, robberies, and even murders.

Many years ago, there were a number of instances that hit too close to home. One of our female employees was raped, and two others were physically beaten by their spouses. We saw to it that these women got the help they needed, including getting them out of their abusive conditions and into shelters and hospitals and arranging for legal assistance, counseling, and care. On another occasion, one of our agent's clients was raped in a vacant home. Walking into an empty home and encountering danger is every real estate agent's nightmare, but especially female agents.

Concerned about these very real threats, we asked Adam Contos to help us develop a safety awareness program for all of our agents, but especially for the women at RE/MAX. This wasn't a self-defense course so much as it was lessons on how to stay safe. A lot of the measures he taught are now universally practiced in the real estate industry. Everyone was incredibly grateful for this course, which had nothing to do with real estate and everything to do with making our people a priority.

There are more women graduating from college today, working in positions from tech to medicine and, yes, real estate. They're physicians and nurses, lawyers and paralegals, entrepreneurs and CEOs, and so on.

Over the fifty-plus years RE/MAX has been in business, 65 percent of our sales force in the United States has been women. Fifty percent of our officers at headquarters are women. Sixty percent of our board of directors are women. And throughout our five decades, we've had five CEOs, two of whom are women whose combined tenure spanned roughly twenty years.

What we've observed, and what studies have proven, is that women tend to be more inclusive in their leadership style, which has greatly influenced the way businesses are led, especially in America. As you'll recall from Chapter Five, for many years, the most popular leadership style in corporate America was autocratic. It mirrored the military style, in which a general says, "You'll do it my way," and the colonels below him execute his strategy by saying the same thing to those below them in the chain of command, passing the message on to the captains, majors, and sergeants. It's what's referred to as top-down command.

People hate this method of leadership because they have no say in how their business is run. They're treated like soldiers or worker bees who have to follow the rules, with no chance to challenge the norm, even if they have better ideas. The military has adapted over the years, especially regarding special forces. The Green Berets, Delta Force, and Navy SEALs operate in small teams, each with a leader and a second-in-command. Every team member has multiple skills, assuring, for example, that if a full-time medic is injured or killed in action, there's always another member of the team who has medical training and can cover that loss. Special forces exemplify the concept of high-performance teams, which plan together, execute together, and analyze together. Unless there's an emergency, they will sit and brainstorm before they take on any task, discussing the target, strategizing, asking for opinions and ideas, and creating a plan. Every person has the right to voice their concerns. It's not disrespectful; it's what helps keep them alive. Their survival depends on this inclusive attitude and willingness to hear everyone's input. Once they have their game plan, they execute it as a team.

I found that once the first shot was fired in battle, nothing went the way we planned. Managing through the unexpected—and teaching others how to do so—helps create a stronger team. Special forces teams always have after-action discussions, which are meant to be constructive, not demeaning or critical. They're opportunities to download and review what went right and what went wrong. The conversation is an exercise meant to make things better for next time, so the same mistakes aren't repeated.

This kind of inclusive attitude is essential for today's leaders, and women seem to have a natural instinct for this style. It's as if they're the business equivalent of special forces leaders. The size of your business, by the way, is irrelevant. The smaller the business, the easier it is to be inclusive. But larger companies must work diligently to be inclusive too.

There is, of course, a difference between inclusion and diversity. With five generations working today and the workforce comprising more than 50 percent minorities, it's critical that you understand that difference. The two are interconnected but not interchangeable. Diversity is about having representation in your business from a variety of groups, and inclusion is about integrating them and making them all feel essential to the team effort.

When we started RE/MAX in 1973, our mission statement called for hiring and supporting everyone in our community. We didn't care about race, gender, or sexual preference. We didn't care about what culture you came from or your nationality; if we hired you, you became a part of our organization. That wasn't the norm in 1973. Returning to the military analogy, if you're in a foxhole and the enemy is shooting at you, I can tell you from personal experience that you don't give a damn whether the person next to you is a man or a woman, gay or straight, Jewish or Catholic, Black, brown, or yellow. You're all brothers- and sisters-in-arms. When you're fighting for your life, you're fighting to come home. Everyone bleeds red.

Thankfully, racial equality has improved over the years. It may not be perfect, but we've come a long way. When I served in Vietnam, we had Black and brown lieutenants, captains, and majors. We all worked together and loved one another. And by God, we would die together if we had to.

At RE/MAX, we've always been inclusive and diverse. Our company celebrated Christmas, Hanukkah, and Kwanzaa during the holiday season out of respect for the different practices and beliefs of our team. During our holiday party, we always made it a point to ask team members who celebrated those holidays to say a few words to the rest of the group, explaining their various traditions and how they celebrated.

When our company officers had a gathering, we encouraged them to include the accounting team, the back office staff, and those who keep our business running. We fostered mutual respect in every way we could. Women in leadership positions helped cement such inclusion.

Finally, and sadly, there continue to be disparities and inequalities that exist in employment opportunities, wages, promotions, and overall treatment among genders. Globally, women tend to earn less than men for similar work. Women are often underrepresented in leadership positions, including executive and board roles. This disparity can be attributed to gender bias, limited access to mentorship and sponsorship, work-life balance challenges, and systemic barriers.

Women also face obstacles in career progression and promotion compared to their male counterparts. Unconscious bias, stereotypes, and limited opportunities for skill development and training often impede women's advancement. Governments, organizations, and advocacy groups are working to achieve gender equity and parity in the workplace through policy changes, awareness campaigns, and diversity initiatives, but we still have a long way to go to reach this goal.

If you want something said, ask a man. If you want something done, ask a woman.
—Margaret Thatcher

10 Traits That Make Women Such Strong Leaders and Entrepreneurs

While I contend that women are often better leaders and entrepreneurs than men, it's important to note that the traits and capabilities that make a successful entrepreneur are not inherently tied to gender. Both men and women can excel in entrepreneurship, and success depends on individual skills, experiences, and circumstances. However, it's worth recognizing the unique strengths that women often bring to the entrepreneurial landscape. Here are ten reasons why women can be exceptional entrepreneurs:

1 Strong Relationship Building: Women tend to excel in relationship building and collaboration, which are vital for networking, team building, and fostering partnerships. Their ability to connect and empathize with others allows them to develop and maintain strong professional relationships.

2. Multitasking and Time Management: Women often possess strong multitasking and time management skills. They're accustomed to juggling multiple responsibilities and can effectively prioritize tasks, making them adept at managing the various demands of running a business.

3. Effective Communication: Women are known for their strong communication skills, including active listening and empathy. These qualities enable them to understand customer needs, negotiate effectively, and build strong relationships with stakeholders.

4. Problem-Solving and Creativity: Women entrepreneurs bring unique perspectives and approaches to problem-solving. Their diverse experiences and perspectives can lead to innovative solutions and creative approaches.

5. Perseverance and Resilience: Women have shown resilience and perseverance in the face of adversity. These qualities are essential in entrepreneurship, in which setbacks and obstacles are common. Women often demonstrate the ability to bounce back, learn from failures, and keep pushing forward.

6. Customer Focus: Women tend to have a customer-centric approach. They're attentive to customer needs, preferences, and feedback, which helps them develop products or services that resonate with their target market.

7. Inclusive Leadership: Women entrepreneurs often embrace inclusive leadership styles that value diverse perspectives and promote collaboration. They create environments in which team members feel valued and empowered, leading to increased employee satisfaction and productivity.

8 Flexibility and Adaptability: Women are often flexible in their approach to business. They can quickly adjust strategies, pivot when necessary, and respond to changing market dynamics, which are crucial skills in today's fast-paced and evolving business landscape.

9 Emotional Intelligence: Women often possess high emotional intelligence, which allows them to understand and manage their emotions and those of others. Emotional intelligence facilitates effective leadership, team building, and conflict resolution.

10 Social-Impact Orientation: Women entrepreneurs frequently have a strong sense of social responsibility and a desire to make a positive impact. They're often motivated to address societal challenges and contribute to their communities, leading to socially conscious and sustainable business practices.

Emphasizing the unique qualities and perspectives that women entrepreneurs contribute can help foster a more inclusive and supportive business ecosystem, though it's important to celebrate and recognize the diverse talents and strengths all individuals bring to entrepreneurship, regardless of gender.

BEST HIRING PRACTICES IN FAST-CHANGING TIMES

Certainly, some of the changes we've discussed in this chapter, from the rise of women in leadership positions to the entrance of a fifth generation to the workforce—and even the Great Resignation to some extent—have been a long time coming. But there are other changes that feel more sudden. For example, some businesses today are struggling to fill job openings. If yours is one of them, it's important to know that you're not alone. The job market has changed significantly over the past couple of years, and it can be challenging to keep up. The Covid-19 pandemic has created some hurdles when it comes to hiring. Jobs that were once easily filled, such as service-sector positions in restaurants, retail, and hospitality, face a lack of applicants. Some industries that have historically paid low wages now have a difficult time filling those roles, as millions of workers look for higher or more stable wages in other industries.

A recent CareerPlug study found that the number of new jobs posted through the service increased by 49 percent in 2021, but the number of applicants decreased by 30 percent. The study also showed that 55 percent of workers desired to increase their pay, and of those workers, 67 percent reported interest in exploring new industries.

These findings contain both good news and bad for employers. Simply put, people want to work, but only for companies that promise increased pay and security. In-N-Out, for instance, successfully hired and expanded throughout the pandemic and beyond, because they offer higher-than-average pay and have used that fact as a recruiting tool for years. To stay competitive, other fast-food companies are now following suit. They believe higher wages create higher productivity and lower turnover. The businesses that are thriving are those that have changed their hiring practices to match our changing times.

As discussed earlier, in sectors of the market where people have been able to work remotely, most don't want to return to the office, or at least not full-time. One benefit of this is that job seekers aren't limited by their geographic location. If you can offer a remote position, your pool of candidates is multiplied—and many employers are doing just that.

Job openings increased across all disciplines in 2022, and as a result, hiring strategies that were effective before the pandemic may not work as well today. To address this, I suggest personalizing your engagement with prospective candidates. A good way to do this is to search their social media channels to see what interests they have outside of work. Do they coach their child's Little League team? Do they volunteer? Let them know your company values flexibility and balance, and make any necessary changes to assure that flexibility, as that has become very important to most job seekers.

If you want to hire effectively, start bringing in people who share your passion and fit the dynamic you've created within your organization. Interview for culture before competency. Find out what's important to this person before you assess what they can do for you. Everyone puts their best foot forward in an interview, which sometimes masks a potential employee's authentic self. What do they care about? Who are they? What are their values? Once you've got a clear understanding, you can move on to deciding whether they're properly qualified to do the job.

Make sure you look for people who are goal oriented and have the complementary skill sets to accomplish the tasks they'll undertake. The *Harvard Business Review* conducted a survey to explore what's holding people back from applying for certain jobs. Most people, especially women, feel like the job qualifications are out of reach. With so many available openings, people tend to gravitate toward opportunities where they believe they have a higher probability of being hired. The best advice I can offer to employers facing a shortage of applicants is to be flexible in your requirements.

An interview scoring matrix, also known as an interview evaluation form or a scoring rubric, is a tool that provides a structured framework for evaluating and comparing candidate responses based on specific criteria during the interview process. A scoring matrix typically includes a set of predetermined evaluation criteria or competencies that are relevant to the position being filled. These criteria may vary depending on the organization and the nature of the role, but often include factors such as technical skills, communication ability, problem-solving capability, teamwork, leadership potential, and cultural fit.

Here's an example of how an interview scoring matrix might be structured:

Criteria:	Rating Scale:
Technical Skills	1–5
Communication	1–5
Problem-Solving	1–5
Teamwork	1–5
Leadership	1–5
Cultural Fit	1–5

Each criterion is assigned a numerical rating scale, such as 1 to 5 or 1 to 10, with corresponding descriptors that indicate levels of proficiency or performance. The interviewer uses this scale to rate each candidate's responses or behaviors during the interview. After the interview, these scores are tallied to provide an overall assessment of the candidate's performance. It's not necessarily the score that matters most; it's the conversation that comes from discussing the lowest scores. This allows you to dive in deeper to figure out whether the candidate is a good fit.

By using an interview scoring matrix, organizations can establish a more systematic and objective evaluation process, making it easier to compare candidates, track their performance, and make informed hiring decisions based on the collected data. It's an excellent and extremely effective tool, but unfortunately, very few companies use it.

It used to be common practice to stretch out the hiring process over the course of several months as you did whatever due diligence was necessary and continued to interview other candidates for the position, especially if you were filling an executive-level role. Today, if your process takes too long, you'll likely lose a good candidate to a competitor. If you find someone you like, hire them. Remember the story of Diane Metz? We weren't exactly sure what her role or responsibilities would be when we hired her, but I knew we didn't want her working anywhere else. Another strategy to use here is "pipelining," which is the practice of building a pool of potential candidates before a position opens. This requires ongoing conversations to give these people reasons to join your company when you finally have an offer to extend.

Finally, it's important to understand what job seekers are looking for. As discussed earlier, most people want flexibility and the option to work from home at least some of the time. Limeade, a company that tracks employee well-being, did a study showing that 40 percent of employees left jobs in 2021 due to burnout, inflexibility, a lack of appreciation or recognition, or discrimination. This makes managers who have compassion and emotional intelligence more important than ever.

Again, there is no one-size-fits-all answer when it comes to building your team. The better you understand and adapt to the changing dynamics in the workplace, the more likely it is that you'll attract, engage, and hire an all-star team of purpose-aligned, performance-proven people.

10 Strategies to Effectively Hire and Retain Employees

1. Hire people who share your core values and vision.
2. Hire people who want to grow with you.
3. Give people a sense of purpose in their work.
4. Help people improve and grow.

5. Help people achieve their goals and dreams.
6. Create a path for advancement.
7. Nurture relationships with employees.
8. Implement transparent and equitable policies around hiring, pay, promotions, and terminations.
9. Always be transparent.
10. Be flexible.

CREATING YOUR COMPANY CULTURE

One of the main functions of a great leader is to create an environment in which the individuals on the team can collectively succeed better than they would by themselves. In doing so, everyone can achieve their personal and professional goals. As I said earlier, when we first started RE/MAX, I wanted every single agent to be in the 100 percent club—which was made up of individuals in the company who were making at least $100,000 a year. Back in 1973, that was a lot of money. But over the years, I discovered that we had agents making $1,000,000 a year and agents making $60,000 a year, and both were happy. I couldn't understand why the $60,000-a-year agents didn't work harder. When I talked to them, those who were older explained that they were ready to slow down a bit. They'd made more money in the past, but they were satisfied with where they were now. They also made it clear that I had no right to tell any agent how much money they should be making. If they were happy and achieving their goals, who was I to push them toward somewhere they didn't want to be? This was a good point, so we chose to create an environment in which people who were self-motivated could achieve what they wanted to achieve, with no pressure and no demands.

Company culture is an important part of any business, and it can be as unique as the business owners who create it. The most successful companies are grounded in the reasons that moved their founders to create them. Back in Chapter One, we talked about defining your purpose and creating your mission statement. Successful company cultures are grounded in that mission and those core values. Workplace culture includes how employees work together as a result of the policies, procedures, and decision-making processes that exist within the company. Company culture also sets expectations. When a company's culture is aligned with its mission, its chances of success are increased. According to research by Deloitte, 94 percent of executives and 88 percent of employees believe that a distinct corporate culture is important for any business to achieve success.

As a storyteller, I learned the importance of creating your narrative a long time ago. This is especially true in business. You know who else figured out the value of a great story?

Netflix.

Their first foray into original scripted programming was a show called *House of Cards*. At the time, *House of Cards* was considered risky for many reasons. Unlike most traditional TV shows, which film a pilot, get network funding, and then produce and release episodes one at a time over the course of a season, Netflix released all thirteen episodes of the first season of *House of Cards* at once. This created the binge-watching phenomenon that transformed TV viewing for the entire world. This didn't happen by accident. Netflix was willing to take a risk despite the data that the traditional networks lived by. Their research showed that people were hungry for great stories and would give their rapt attention for hours and hours at a time if the story was good enough. If you've found the right story, you'll talk about it—everywhere. You'll post about it on Facebook, X, Snapchat, Instagram, and other platforms. You'll tell your friends, your colleagues, and anyone else you engage with, and you'll do so with great passion. Try to imagine people talking about your company the way they talk about *Game of Thrones* or *Billions*.

It's very important to let job seekers know that your company is a great place to work and that you care about your employees. The more passion and excitement you show when sharing about what it's like to work at your company, the more you'll entice prospective employees. And the best reviews come from the people who work for you: Employee testimonials are very effective.

Companies that are named one of the Best Places to Work generally achieve success. They tend to have strong, positive corporate cultures that help employees feel empowered to perform to their highest potential. For example, Alphabet Inc. (Google) is renowned for its positive and innovative corporate culture. It emphasizes a supportive and inclusive work environment that encourages creativity, collaboration, and personal growth. The company also offers numerous perks to its employees, such as flexible work arrangements, on-site amenities, and a focus on work-life balance. Zappos is another company with a strong corporate culture. It prioritizes employee happiness and satisfaction through its "Delivering Happiness" approach. Zappos fosters a positive and fun workplace, focusing on core values, employee empowerment, and a strong orientation toward customer service. Patagonia is renowned for its commitment to environmental sustainability and social responsibility. It has a strong company culture rooted in values such as environmental activism, work-life balance, and employee well-being and actively encourages its employees to pursue their passions while supporting initiatives aligned with their values.

A strong corporate culture is one of the best ways to entice potential employees. People want to work for a company with a good reputation, and a positive culture will always attract the type of talent you're seeking—people who want to make your company their next home, not just a pit stop.

A positive corporate culture also fosters a sense of employee loyalty. Employees are more apt to stay in their positions when they feel valued and treated right. Employers who invest in the well-being of their people create an environment of happy and dedicated employees. Numerous studies have shown that a positive company culture is linked to higher rates of productivity. When employees feel inspired and motivated, they perform at higher levels.

It's important to understand what motivates your employees and what matters to them most. If you're creating a company culture for the first time or reworking an existing one, make sure you go right to the source and ask your employees how they feel. If they aren't happy, try to find the reasons why. Perhaps they feel that their opinions aren't valued or that they don't have the tools or resources they need to effectively perform their work. Would they like additional training? How is their relationship with their managers? You can harvest a lot of information when you ask the right questions. Once you have that information, you can evaluate what's working and what isn't and begin to create a company culture that resonates with your employees' wants and needs.

Public perception is also critically important. More than half of all job seekers won't apply for a job if they see negative reviews about a company on sites like Glassdoor and Indeed. If your business isn't a great place to work, dissatisfied employees past and present will tell everyone they know, helping you develop a negative reputation that can cost you applicants.

Your business will only be as good as the people who work for it. When you take care of your people, your people will take care of your business. Nurturing a positive work environment and company culture will help you hire and retain people who look forward to coming to work and who will take great pride in what they do. Creating a fantastic company culture takes time and a lot of tweaking along the way, but if you get it right, you'll build an exciting environment that will make your company a coveted place to work.

7

Franchising

ALWAYS SELLING THE DREAM

From the start, we had a singular mission at RE/MAX: We were going to revolutionize the real estate industry. And we would do it statewide, nationwide, and then globally. If you're going to dream, dare to dream big—and always be so enthusiastic that your excitement becomes contagious.

In our early days, we had to sell people on our vision. There wasn't much else to show prospective brokers and agents, so we did our best to create a clear picture of who we were and where we believed we could go. We also brought in some key employees who added their insight to the equation. Bob Fisher and Daryl Jesperson (Fish and Jes, as we called them) were two of those people. They were old college roommates who joined RE/MAX at the same time in 1973 as real estate agents. Before coming to RE/MAX, Fish was with Denver-based Gates Rubber, for whom he traveled nationwide, expanding their business. He knew how to sell, and would surely become a top agent. Jes was a former officer in the US Navy. He'd exhibited tremendous leadership potential throughout his naval career, and we thought that would translate well at our company.

In October 1975, a young man from Kansas City named Dennis Curtain reached out to us. Dennis had been working for a small, family-run real estate business and was quickly promoted to branch manager at one of their offices. At the time, Kansas City was a competitive market for real estate, and the firm where he was working offered good training and was making a name for itself. As he began to succeed, he found himself getting antsy. He started looking for a better business model that would help him make more money. He'd read an article in the local paper about a firm called Real Estate 100. Like RE/MAX, they were offering 100 percent commissions. The founder had actually come to Denver to talk to me about selling him a franchise. He milked us for a lot of information, but in the end, I decided not to sell to him because I didn't like the guy. The article gave us our due for establishing the model, which must have intrigued Dennis because he reached out to me directly to explore what it might be like to work with RE/MAX. He and Jim Donaldson, his boss's son, wanted to come see me. I picked them up at the airport (Stapleton at the time) and drove them to our small office. We began to negotiate almost immediately, but to no avail. We weren't able to come to terms.

Six months later, despite the country being in the midst of a recession, RE/MAX had continued to grow due to our unwavering focus on top-line growth and commitment to sharing our dream. As Dennis tells the story, he hadn't been able to shake the vision we'd shared with him when he and Jim came to visit the first time, so he ended up calling me again. By this time, he'd left the firm he'd been working with and wanted to know if I would be willing to sell him a franchise. I wasn't exactly sure how we could do that, since we hadn't yet transitioned from selling licenses at the time, but I said yes and told him to come to Denver with his checkbook in hand. Within hours, he'd bought the first RE/MAX franchise. (By the way, our first franchise agreement was a two-page document.

Today, it has evolved into a 180-page tome.) After Dennis signed it, he spent the rest of the day training with me and a few others. That night, I asked him to come to dinner at Gail's house. At the end of the evening, I pulled him aside and handed him back his check. He was stunned. I explained that I couldn't take it. At first Dennis thought he'd done something wrong and that I was backing out, but that wasn't the case.

Within two years of launching RE/MAX, we'd managed to open eight offices, but I was deep in debt. Although it was short-term debt, it was choking us, and I was worried that we were about to lose everything. Creditors were all over us, and we weren't able to pay our bills. It just didn't feel right under the circumstances to take his money.

"You go ahead and open up Dennis Curtain Realty. I'll teach you everything I know about the RE/MAX commission concept, and we'll walk out of this thing as friends," I said.

"What are you going to do?" he asked.

I explained that we had a sales meeting in the morning, and I was going to tell everyone it was over. I was going to do whatever I could to protect their commissions, but I knew that would be hard to pull off. Much to my surprise, Dennis insisted on being there. He didn't feel right about giving up on RE/MAX—not yet, anyway.

I told Dennis more about what had been happening. "Man, this is terrible," I said. "I've got to tell you what's going on behind the scenes."

The week before, a con man named Trenton Parker had approached us. I didn't know that he was a con man at the time. He was well-dressed and a very smooth talker. We were broke and looking for money. When he came to us, he said, "I represent some investors, and we know that you're in debt. I can arrange a long-term loan because I think you're making a profit." I said, "Yeah, we're actually paying down our debt." And he said, "Well, let's take a look at your books."

So I agreed.

That's when the proposition went from being a long-term loan to a loan with some stock interest. Then the death threats began. Yes, death threats. It turned out that the people we were dealing with were part of the Smaldone family, the well-known Colorado crime family with ties to the Mafia. They threatened to kill Gail, me, and my wife and kids. Being a Vietnam vet, I didn't give a damn about their threats. I knew how to defend myself, and wasn't afraid to act if I had to.

"Come give it a try," I said boldly.

On Columbus Day, we got a phone call, which I recorded on tape. Not only did the person on the other end make death threats, he shared some other information meant to scare me. He said, "Thank God it's Columbus Day. The courts are closed. We've paid a federal judge fifty thousand dollars in cash, and he's going to take you out of your own company tomorrow morning at nine. Just make it easier on yourself. Sign the company over right now."

Like hell I would. I told them where they could go.

Do you know what the definition of diplomacy is? It's the ability to tell somebody to go to hell and make them look forward to the trip.

The next morning, two Douglas County sheriffs walked into the office around 9:15 and said, "Is Mr. Liniger here?" I looked at them stone-faced and said, "I'll have to see if he's come in today."

Just then, the phone rang. I picked it up, and it was a reporter from the *Denver Business Journal*. "Would you like to comment on the fact that you and Gail have been thrown out of RE/MAX and the company's been turned over to the Smaldone crime family?"

"What? You can't be serious," I said.

I called the attorneys who were representing us and asked them to tell the Smaldones to stay the hell away from us. I explained that there were cops in our office with restraining orders against Gail and me.

"What do we do?" I asked.

One of our attorneys said, very quietly, "Walk into Gail's office, tell her to get her purse, grab the checkbook, and run."

And that's exactly what we did.

We headed straight to the attorneys' office.

"This isn't possible," they said. They'd listened to my recording of the death threats and the attempted extortion and immediately went to see the judge, who happened to be in trial. They handed the bailiff a note that read, "This is an emergency. We must talk to the judge."

The judge was very angry. Even so, he recessed his trial, went back to his chambers, and said, "What's going on here?"

"Your Honor, why did you take Liniger and Main out of their own company?"

"Well, they were served, and they were supposed to show up for this restraining hearing, but nobody from their side came. So I had to."

"Your Honor, we represent Liniger and Main. And we've talked to the Smaldones' attorney. You've been lied to. They were never served at all." Our attorney insisted he was telling the truth. And then he said, "Oh, by the way, what did you do with the fifty thousand dollars in cash?"

"What are you talking about?" The judge appeared to be confused.

That's when our lawyer played the tape recording for him that said the judge had been given $50,000 in cash to make this happen.

The judge sent US Marshals to throw the Douglas County sheriffs out of our office. Next, they tracked down the Smaldones' attorney. They brought him in that afternoon in handcuffs. He stood in front of the judge, and I was standing right there to watch.

The judge was angry. "You're crooked and sleazy. I'm going to disbar you. I'm putting you in jail for ten years," he said.

This other attorney looked at the judge, looked at me, and then his eyes rolled back in his head and he dropped dead of a heart attack.

I got one of them!

Even though everything was finally cleared up in court, the press was already on the story, and I knew the headlines would be bad. This was humiliating. We had some damage control to do, so we called a special quarterly sales meeting of all seventy-seven of our agents.

"It's going to be a 6:00 a.m. breakfast meeting where we'll be making a big announcement," I told everyone.

Gail, Dennis, and I got there at 5:30, stuck our quarters in the newspaper vending machine, took all the newspapers out, and threw them in the dumpster so nobody would see them before we had the meeting.

The seventy-seven agents were waiting for me that morning. I stood in the front of the room, took a deep breath, and began to speak. I knew I was about to let down every single person there. Each of them had trusted us enough to come on the ride, and now I was telling them that we'd had a good run, but it didn't work. I had to admit both failure and defeat. My vulnerability was raw and very real. I felt sick and sorry.

"I just don't know how to save our company. If any of you wants to leave, I'll give your listings to you. The only thing I ask is that you pay your final bill to me, because I need to pay down the debt. Even if we can't make it, I'm not going to file for bankruptcy."

People had a lot of questions, and they were coming at me fast and furious. One of our earliest backers, Grant Goodson, stood up and said he'd known me for a few years and thought I was a good man. He insisted that RE/MAX was a great concept and believed wholeheartedly that it would work. "This is the Mafia trying to take over a future gigantic company," Grant said, "and they think they can steal it. And Dave will never quit. Gail will never quit. And I'm standing beside them."

He believed in Gail and me and vowed to stay by our side. Another guy, who had been an Episcopal minister at one time, also stood up and said, "You know what? I'm not going to quit. Where else can you go and have this kind of entertainment every single quarter?"

One by one, the people in that room stood up and followed Grant's lead, insisting that they weren't ready to throw in the towel. And then, finally, Dennis stood up. No one knew who he was at the time.

"I just bought the first RE/MAX franchise. Dave Liniger handed me back my check last night. He said now that I was connected to RE/MAX, they'd come after me too. I'm not sure what kind of organization you've built here, but I know it's a good thing." Dennis reached into his pocket, pulled out his check and handed it to me. "Here. You need this money for legal fees. I'm your first franchisee. Now, boss, I'm here to the end with you."

And he's still with us to this day.

After those votes of confidence, the consensus in the room was that people were going to ride this out with us. We were in it together. Someone yelled, "Screw it! You go save the business; we're going to sell real estate. We're not leaving you now. Let's beat the bastards."

Hearing this from people we'd known since day one, and from someone like Dennis who had just come on board, helped Gail, Fish, Jes, and I go to battle. The camaraderie and loyalty in that room was palpable, and it's what drove us even harder. Within forty-eight hours, we were able to reach out to all our creditors and persuade them not only that we weren't going down but that we were going to thrive. I couldn't help but think about Ernest Shackleton that day and how I never understood the meaning of his words "By endurance, we conquer" better than I did in that moment.

As we worked through the financial mess we were in, Dennis came back to Denver for more training, and we started working with him and his partners to teach them the RE/MAX way. On breaks, we would go to Gail's house or mine to eat, but then it was always right back to work. How were we going to grow our company?

The decision to become a franchisor was easy, but the execution was a little more challenging. After we sold the first franchise to Dennis, a second in 1976 to another party in Washington, DC, and a third later that year in Calgary, Alberta, Canada, we decided to test the idea in Colorado Springs as well. Fish and I drove the seventy miles from Denver every day to make our pitch to potential franchisees. For the most part, it wasn't going well. We couldn't figure out what had changed. One day on the way back to Denver, Fish was pulled over for speeding. He wasn't happy about that, or the fact that we had cold-called 125 brokerages and not one showed any interest. There had to be a solution.

"If we can't sell these guys franchises, I'll buy one!" Fish said. I wasn't sure if he was just blowing off steam or if he meant it, but I liked the way it sounded.

Unbeknownst to me, Fish and Jes had been brainstorming with Gordon Schick and Ollie Winters. They were all buddies who were with our company and were always trying to devise ways for us to make the business better. The challenge we faced was that many of those who were interested in becoming franchisees were successful businesspeople, but they weren't brokers. A broker's license is necessary to run a real estate office in Colorado. While these businesspeople might have had the money to buy a franchise, they didn't have enough to open an office that had a broker as well.

In December 1976, a solution presented itself. Eight of our top managers, including Fish and Jes, came to our office Christmas luncheon, where they told Gail and me that they wanted to buy a franchise too. They saw themselves as the missing piece to the prospective buyer's puzzle. All eight were brokers, so if they could put together enough money to buy the Colorado Springs franchise, they could partner with the buyer, who didn't have a broker's license.

I thought it was a great idea. And then I asked the money question: "How are you going to pay for the franchises?"

They couldn't.

So I suggested they figure out an equitable price per office and that Gail and I would sign it sight unseen. I trusted them and knew they would be fair. I slid a yellow legal pad across the table, and then Gail and I went to lunch. If they wanted to, they could have put one dollar down and we would have agreed.

When we returned to the office, the eight managers were ecstatic. I never looked at the details they wrote down. I took the pen from the table, signed the paper, folded it up, and placed it inside my jacket pocket.

Later that night, as we all attended the agent holiday party, they approached me and asked if I had read what they'd written. I hadn't. I could tell they were eager for me to see the results of their deliberation, so I took that piece of paper out of my pocket, opened it, and smiled. They had placed a higher value on the eight offices than we would ever have asked for. Gail and I thanked them, and then we all had a drink together and cried, because everything we'd worked so hard for was no longer ours alone. That was a tough moment for us, albeit one that eventually turned the page. You see, the eight managers had bought those offices on sweat equity and were willing to work for free for two years until they paid off the debt. As they grew the business, they gave us money every month to pay down what remained of the balance. The only condition was that they wanted to run their own business; what they built was for them, not us. I liked these guys. They were solid, and I could tell they would be committed to our dream, so I said yes.

I began to type up the purchase agreement right there and then. As I tapped on the keys, I paused, looked up, and said, "You know the Boulder market pretty well. Would you be interested in buying that too?" Later that night we found ourselves at a local bar, where we expanded their territory until Jes, Fish, and Schick had purchased franchises from Colorado (excluding Denver) to New Mexico. Our final deal was scribbled on the back of a cocktail napkin and sealed with a signature and a handshake. I knew they would succeed, and when they did, others would come on board as franchisees to help us build the dream.

One day, Fish came to Gail and me and suggested that he and Jes work for RE/MAX to sell franchises for our company in addition to running the franchises they'd acquired from us. He asked if we would allow them to hit the road and expand our business throughout the country. While I appreciated what I heard, it wasn't their experience that got me to say yes. It was their enthusiasm and confidence. The only problem? I didn't have the money to pay them a salary.

All our agents worked on straight commission. Gail and I had cut our salaries way back, and we were barely drawing paychecks at the time. Every dollar we made went right back into the business. I explained my predicament to Fish and Jes and offered them 50 percent of whatever they earned licensing and selling franchises. It was a risky plan, but they were eager to use their talents in a way that would grow our company more significantly. They had fire in their bellies, and the expansion idea sounded like a lot of fun.

We appreciated self-starters with a "go for it" attitude, and we fully embraced those who saw opportunities and took the initiative to take advantage of them. Why? They made our dream their dream. There isn't a better formula for creating success or a more powerful and productive work environment. When your team is happy, it shows. In fact, it radiates everywhere, especially when a company has good leadership. If your people respect and admire their management, they'll be inspired to go the extra mile. When your words and actions match, people will take notice.

As we grew our business, we noticed that the brokers who joined our company all shared one common intention: They were dissatisfied with the real estate industry as it was and wanted to prove there was a better way. To the best of my knowledge, few, if any, companies were offering what we were offering at that time. Not only did that make people want to join us, but it also made them want to stay. And they worked hard, mainly because they saw how much effort and determination those of us at the top possessed. I put in seven days a week, twelve hours a day or more. There were some days when I'd get to the office at 5:00 a.m. and not leave until midnight. Others followed suit. It felt as if the only limitations were those we put on ourselves. And for most of us, we believed the *sky* was the limit.

Fish and Jess were two of those believers. So, in 1977, they literally took their show on the road to franchise the RE/MAX brand to interested parties. They rented a motor home and drove all over the country, sharing our story, telling people why we were a better place to work. When Betty and Dick Hegner, who lived in Illinois, acquired a license from them, the Illinois state securities commission found out about it and knocked on our door. They claimed we were selling franchises and not licenses. At the time, there were no federal laws about selling franchises, but Illinois and California had enacted state laws that regulated franchising in their states. As a result, Illinois insisted that we stop immediately. We thought that was absurd. Even so, we were given the option to pay a fine, go to jail, stay out of Illinois, or register as a franchising organization and keep doing what we were doing.

It wasn't a difficult decision. We would become a franchisor.

Over the next few years, Jes and Fish opened nine offices. They hired talented, top-tier managers and made them partners. They were able to pay for their franchises by 1977, a little over a year after we shook hands. One thing became clear to all of us: The system would work as long as there were other franchisees. Without the others, they were just a group of offices owned by these guys. For the system to benefit one of us, it had to benefit all of us. That was the underlying meaning of *everyone wins*.

So, to help the company protect its investment, the guys set out to sell regional franchises as well as individual franchises. By 1977, we had sold a mix of 110 franchises around the country. One of the proudest moments of my career at RE/MAX was when Jack Bradbury circled back and asked to join our company as a franchisee. You'll recall that Jack was my former boss at VanSchaack and the first person I ever pitched the idea of RE/MAX to.

Things were going great—so well, in fact, that we knew it was time to improve our level of organization and provide training so every agent had the resources they needed to succeed.

Red Carpet Realty was based in Walnut Creek, California, and was founded in 1966. They were the first real estate company to franchise. Century 21 and a dozen others started franchising too, and the franchising wave really got going around the time we founded the company. By 1978, 178 franchisors were exhibiting at the National Association of Realtors' annual convention and trade show. All the franchise salespeople were running around telling everyone they would be out of business in five years if they didn't buy *their* franchises. Each would claim that their company was offering a ground-floor opportunity and was destined to become the biggest in the business.

Clearly, 178 companies were never going to survive. Some were bigger than others, but everyone was making the same claim—that within five years, 80 percent of the business would be handled by franchisors. It never happened. The original 178 eventually shrank to about eight or nine companies, including RE/MAX.

A HISTORY OF FRANCHISING

The concept of franchising is fairly straightforward. It's when a "franchisor," or brand owner, licenses the use of its brand, product, service, systems, and/or other intellectual property to a "franchisee," or investor, to allow both parties to expand their businesses. To obtain these rights and benefits, the franchisee pays specific fees to the franchisor and agrees to comply with certain obligations, which are typically set out in a franchise agreement.

There are many theories about when the concept of franchising began. During the Middle Ages, European monarchs allowed noblemen and the church to manage lands that belonged to the Crown. Their primary objective was to protect the land and collect taxes. Occasionally, those nobles permitted local farmers to use a plot of land, and the farmers paid them a royalty for this use.

By the mid-1850s, Isaac M. Singer was busy manufacturing commercial sewing machines, but the demand for them was so great that he needed to raise more capital to mass-produce the machines, and he also needed help distributing them. His solution was to sell licenses to people who would, in turn, sell his sewing machines to the public. The fees the franchisees paid to Singer enabled him to keep production going, and the volume of machines he was able to manufacture, along with the training he provided, enabled the franchisees to increase sales, benefiting everyone. This is often cited as the first franchise business in the United States.

Licensing quickly became commonplace for growing businesses, including Coca-Cola, which was the biggest franchisor in the world for many years. After World War II, as the need for new goods and services increased, franchising really began to take off. By the 1950s and '60s, franchises were a big and profitable business model. One company that made great use of franchising was McDonald's. Much of what I knew about McDonald's I learned from reading articles on the company's success and Ray Kroc's posthumous 1987 book *Grinding It Out: The Making of McDonald's.* In 1939, Kroc came across a multimixer that blended six milkshakes at the same time, and became a distributor of the machine. He made some adjustments to the mixer and demonstrated how you could put a paper cup inside a metal sleeve, hold it under the mixer head while making a shake, and then slip the cup out and hand it to the customer the minute the shake was done. He peddled this concept from store to store, going to soda shops, drive-ins, and anywhere else he could find that served milkshakes.

During that time, Kroc heard about Richard and Maurice McDonald, better known as Dick and Mac McDonald. The brothers had a restaurant in San Bernardino, California, called McDonald's Bar-B-Q. They had bought eight of his machines, and in 1954, Kroc flew to California to meet them. As a result of that visit, he became the restaurant's first franchise agent, selling his first franchise to himself. He opened a location in Des Plaines, Illinois, in 1955, when he was fifty-two years old. From the beginning, he saw opportunity, calling his new restaurant "the first in the McDonald's system." The McDonald's operating system required franchisees to follow the core McDonald's principles of quality, service, cleanliness, and value. Ray Kroc worked to build a restaurant chain that would be famous for providing food of consistently high quality via uniform methods of preparation. He wanted to serve food that tasted the same no matter where you purchased it.

To accomplish this, he carved his own path. He persuaded franchisees and suppliers to buy into his vision of working for themselves, but also together with McDonald's. He promoted the slogan, "In business for yourself, but not by yourself." His philosophy was based on the simple principle of a three-legged stool: one leg represented McDonald's franchisees; the second represented McDonald's suppliers; and the third represented McDonald's employees. The franchise, just like the stool, was only as strong as the three legs it stood upon.

By 1961, the McDonald brothers and Kroc were no longer seeing eye to eye on the expansion of the company. His ambitions and their goals had ceased to align, and Kroc took his entire life savings and bought the brothers out for $2.7 million. It was a risk, but one he thought was well worth taking. Within a few years of that agreement, Kroc had sold five hundred franchised McDonald's restaurants across the country—and today, approximately 80 percent of all McDonald's locations worldwide are franchises.

When Kroc took over McDonald's in 1961, he created a training program at a new franchise in Elk Grove Village, Illinois, that he later named Hamburger University. This was a place where franchisees could learn the specific methods of running a successful McDonald's restaurant. The team at Hamburger U did extensive research to develop innovative cooking, freezing, storing, and serving processes. More than 275,000 franchisees, managers, and employees have graduated from the program. When my four kids were teenagers, they all worked at McDonald's, as I believed it would be an excellent learning experience for them. Today, of course, McDonald's is the world's largest hamburger chain, serving sixty-nine million customers a day at thirty-eight thousand locations in one hundred countries.

Ray Kroc died in 1984. At his funeral, he was remembered for many things, but three apply here. First, he was said to be a marvelous storyteller. Second, he knew how to make hamburgers. And third, he knew how to make money. Now, that's my kind of guy!

Fast-forward to the present day, when franchising has spread throughout industries such as convenience stores, food services, transportation, hotels, and so much more. Brands like 7-Eleven,

Hertz, Subway, Marriott, and, yes, RE/MAX are all franchised. Although some of these companies have been around for years, they continue to grow and evolve, changing with the needs of their customers while becoming global powerhouses. Subway has more than forty-one thousand locations. 7-Eleven has some seventy-one thousand stores in seventeen countries. Interestingly, of the top ten franchises today, just three are unrelated to food. We're proud that RE/MAX is one of them.

When we look at buying a franchise through our company, Area 15 Ventures, we budget around $5 million. We figure that we'll spend $1 million in operating costs, legal costs, trademark costs, franchise disclosure documents, and learning management systems and technology. Despite knowing that our cash flow will be negative, we plan to have the money to expand with and a marketing team that will get us to our goals.

I learned so much from our experience of rolling out RE/MAX as a franchisor. First, until we were well established, we really weren't bankrolled enough. Second, I occasionally sold to people I shouldn't have. Finding qualified buyers is the most important aspect of franchising. Each franchisor has their own criteria, but when we're considering a prospective buyer, we typically look at their previous successes and their background. For instance, somebody who's been a manager in the restaurant business for many years would be a good fit for Daddy's Chicken Shack, while somebody who ran their own real estate office would be terrific for RE/MAX. Today, we're most interested in multiunit managers, because they know how to scale. They're already running several successful businesses, and that's a good thing for us. The more units you own, the more you've proven you're capable of handling the kinds of personnel problems that can arise. A single McDonald's location can employ over one hundred people with a six-month turnover rate that can be as high as 60 to 80 percent, so experience in quick-service restaurants is invaluable.

If I'd done more research and studied harder when we first launched, I would have known better. It wasn't so bad selling to the franchisees, because most of them owned their own offices at one time or another, and they already had established reputations. It was the master franchisors that we were selling to—people who had responsibility for entire states—that turned out to be more problematic. A master franchisor, also known as a sub-franchisor, is a party within a franchise system that holds the rights to develop and sub-franchise the brand and business model within a specified territory or region. The master franchisor acts as an intermediary between the franchisor (the original brand owner, in this case RE/MAX) and sub-franchisees (individuals or entities that operate franchise units in their specific territory). These days, master franchising is primarily used internationally.

When we started master franchising, we would sell an entire state to an entrepreneur who we believed could open fifty RE/MAX offices over the course of ten years. They became the sub-franchisor, and we split the duties of running the state. We would handle international matters for our foreign franchisees, training programs, and trademark actions, while they handled the local needs. This meant that to be cost effective, they had to open a regional office, host broker meetings once a month, provide training sessions for agents on how to work within the RE/MAX system, buy local advertising, and so on. The sub-franchisor was also responsible for selling franchises in their territory and helping the franchisees recruit agents. We set up a system for sharing expenses and fees, the majority of which stayed within the region while a small portion went to us as the national company.

In the beginning, a lot of people wanted to be master franchisors, and for us, those licenses were the easiest things to sell. They were appealing and prestigious, and, if successful, very lucrative. By the time we started selling master franchises in 1977, Century 21 had been selling them for four years. When they went public, they started buying back their master franchises. This was a classic roll-up: They used independent entrepreneurs to grow the business, but once they got to fifty or more franchises—a situation that required professional management more than entrepreneurial guidance—they bought them out. People who'd invested $100,000 to become master franchisors were getting $4 to $5 million paydays. That was big money back then.

Again, this isn't a popular method of working in the United States franchise industry today, but it sure was fun when we launched. I'm glad we did it. If I'd known then what I know now, I might have been a little more selective about who I accepted money from, but I have no regrets.

A Few Facts about Franchising

- There are more than 750,000 franchises in the United States.
- Franchises provide more than eight million jobs nationwide.
- Output from these franchises is approximately $760 billion a year.
- Approximately four hundred new franchisors enter the market every year.
- There are four thousand franchisors in the United States.
- There are 1,400 franchisors in the International Franchise Association (IFA).

ENTREPRENEURIAL SUCCESS THROUGH FRANCHISING

These days, just about every business venture I engage in has to have two elements: The business needs to be scalable and able to franchise. It took years of building the RE/MAX franchise model to get to this valuable understanding. We didn't do it quickly, but we didn't do it without a plan—even if the plan was fluid and not always the one we initially set out with.

The cornerstone of RE/MAX was and still is a slow and steady build. In 1983, several of us gathered around a campfire late one night during a leadership weekend with brokers and company leaders. One of the guys, Sid Syvertson, said: "Dave, one log makes a lousy fire."

I've never forgotten that moment or what Sid said. At first, I wasn't sure what he meant, so I asked him to explain.

"When you have one log and you try to light it, you can't get it to burn. It just smolders. But if you take ten logs, add some kindling, and light it with a single match, you get a terrific bonfire. It does something. You're creating one hundred thousand burning logs, Dave. And that's unstoppable. That's the meaning of RE/MAX."

I was fascinated by his observation. Sid was right. That was what we were trying to do. And when he put it in terms that were easy to understand, everyone got it. That was the RE/MAX strategy, and it was one we could feel proud about. But to Sid's point, you can build a bonfire only with the proper number of logs. Finding those people and nurturing them wasn't easy. It took a lot of patience, perseverance, failure, and stamina.

When we launched RE/MAX, we were aware of the challenges, especially the reality that we wouldn't be able to compete with the big boys, at least not at first. We were operating with limited capital, and they weren't. Other companies were also starting to infiltrate the market, making it harder to recruit top talent and create a name for ourselves.

One of the other big challenges was recruiting potential franchisees, because it was complicated, expensive, and very stressful. We were flying by the seat of our pants. Eventually, though, we hit our stride, and in the process, we generated tremendous brand awareness—something we would get very creative with as our company grew. But more on that later.

While other companies were driven by a "company first" mentality, RE/MAX put the emphasis on our people. We understood that individuals made us, and that individuals also had the power to break us. They drove all our business. They had personal relationships with their clients, and they created a mutually beneficial and loyal relationship with them regardless of where they hung their license. Fortunately, we were relentless with our "promote yourself" strategy. We wanted their name on the door and the signage, not ours. As it turned out, this strategy was a good one. Not only did it promote more business but it also created a happy work environment in which our team felt good about themselves and where they worked.

In 2016, RE/MAX started a second franchise called Motto Mortgage, a network of locally owned and operated mortgage brokerages across the United States. More than two hundred of these franchises are operational now, and another two hundred are in the process of opening.

We'd noticed that our biggest real estate brokers had been around for a long time, and all of them had started their own mortgage companies. They had hundreds of agents and expanded their businesses by opening branch offices. They also saw that there was money to be made in the mortgage title and escrow businesses, and, being big and successful enough and having the cash flow to branch out in this way, they did. We were certainly intrigued. We looked at a mortgage origination platform that essentially provided "a mortgage company in a box" so franchisees could open one right in their own offices. It's a simple, easy-to-follow, step-by-step plan. We designed the systems, signed up the wholesale dealers to take either our mortgage products or theirs to market, and then showed real estate brokers how they could open a mortgage operation in an office that had roughly twenty or twenty-five real estate agents.

To become a mortgage broker, you have to get a mortgage license. You also have to set up an escrow account that coincides with your accounting systems. We set all of that up for them in a training program; the only thing they needed to do was organize an office space expressly for mortgages within their real estate office. This made it convenient for a customer who was already there looking at houses to be qualified for a mortgage. Because it's so systematized, it's had a tremendous success record.

Almost every consumer study shows that consumers want transactions to be as easy as possible. They like the concept of one-stop shopping. Of course, you're never going to pick up all the business your real estate agents can bring to you, because they likely already have their favorite mortgage lenders who've helped them put together deals in the past. But if you say you've got your own mortgage company right across the hall, you can capture part of the business, and that will surely increase the profitability of your overall brokerage business.

Under our model, a franchisee needs to convert 10 to 15 percent of the deals that come through their office to turn a profit. That will cover the cost of the facility and the mortgage lenders and their salaries and commissions, plus add profit to the bottom line. Some offices convert as much as 50 percent. It's the system that makes it work.

If you want to be successful in business, you must have clearly defined systems. A lot of entrepreneurs believe they know all about the business they want to start—and that may be true for some, but for most, it's a rookie mistake. Let's say you want to open a restaurant. The first thing you'll probably do is go out and find a space. You've got your savings, your family's and friends' savings, and voilà!

You believe you're ready to run the restaurant. Now, you might say that opening your own restaurant is less expensive than spending $45,000 out of the gate to buy into a franchise. But in reality, successful franchisors actually help you make money. Why? Because they come with proven systems.

SYSTEMS

Systems are sets of processes, procedures, and methods that work together to achieve specific outcomes and support the overall functioning of the organization. Which systems are necessary to implement in your business depends upon your industry, company size, and unique requirements. While building your system might not sound all that exciting, it's one of the most important steps you must take to build sustainability within your company. You want to create systems that allow your employees to operate as a well-oiled machine, keeping them productive and your company profitable.

I talked earlier in the book about the importance of goal setting. But without a plan, it's difficult to reach your goals. Think of that plan as a system to get you where you want to be. If your goal is to lose ten pounds by Christmas, the system you'll use will likely include eating healthy and exercising five days a week for forty-five minutes to an hour. If you follow that system, you'll achieve your goal. Simple enough, right?

If you set a goal and don't have a system in place that forces you to take the necessary steps to reach that goal, you likely won't achieve it. McDonald's is a great example of a business that systemized everything from how to cook the French fries and flip the burgers to how to make the milkshakes. Ray Kroc not only specified the basket to be used for the fries but also the exact temperature of the oil and the time the fries should be submerged to consistently achieve the same great taste. If you're making a Big Mac, you know exactly how many pickles go on the burger, and how much ketchup too. Anyone can do it. By installing these systems, your Big Mac or chocolate shake will taste the same every time.

When you want to grow from small to big, you have to systematize everything. There's less chance of error and less waste, and the business is poised to run on autopilot. At Daddy's Chicken Shack, we built our own proprietary systems and technology from the ground up. Through our research, and because of Covid, we knew there was a significant shift happening in consumer eating habits. Gen Y, Gen Z, and millennials are either looking for a unique dining experience or picking up food to eat at home. Knowing this, we budgeted for around 60 percent of our business to be takeout. We also learned from Covid that the restaurants suffering the most were the ones with a lot of square footage. In many cases, the kitchen took up anywhere from 15 to 20 percent of the total space, while the rest was used for seating. Daddy's Chicken Shack locations hovered around two thousand square feet, so we decided to create a half-and-half setting, allocating one thousand square feet to the kitchen and another thousand to seating, which means we can accommodate around forty-two people at our tables. We also understood that having a drive-through window would increase our sales by as much as 20 percent. But it's hard to find real estate with that feature, and very challenging to retrofit a space to add it. In addition, driving up to a menu, speaking into a box to order your food, and then inching your way forward in line to pick up your order at a window is an antiquated experience. Knowing this, we decided to create an app that allowed customers to order their food in advance, making our drive-through window pick-up only. The app remembers what you've ordered and your credit card information, so the entire process is streamlined. If you don't have the app, you can order by phone, through Grubhub or Door Dash, or you can go inside, where we have two counters, one for pickup and the other for ordering. Every Daddy's Chicken Shack, with the exception of our original location in Pasadena, California, operates under the same system. (The Pasadena location is walk-up only.)

Before a prospect signs a franchise agreement, most franchisors offer what's called a discovery day, which is an opportunity for the prospective franchisee to come to corporate headquarters and spend the day with the officers of the company. They get to see what a shift is like and how it's performed. They hear about the franchisor's plans and are introduced to everything being offered as part of the deal. This includes learning the technological systems the business operates on, seeing what advertising for the franchise might look like, and becoming acquainted with their area's council of owners. They see what ordering supplies entails and get a better understanding of the training systems. Although the discovery day is brief, it provides the prospect with a very clear picture of what they're buying into and what they can expect going forward.

Systems are essential for most businesses, especially those that you expect to scale. While it's easy to understand the need for restaurants to implement systems, companies such as Merry Maids, the UPS Store, Jiffy Lube, Motto Mortgage, RE/MAX, and countless others utilize systems that include computer, accounting, recruiting, advertising, and back-office support. It's much easier and far less expensive to buy into someone else's system than it is to create your own.

Systems are also very important when it comes to training. Most franchise businesses have a learning management system that usually consists of written manuals and digital presentations staff can watch. The videos are short, usually three to four minutes, and meant to be watched several times during on-the-job training. Daddy's Chicken Shack makes our learning management system available to franchisees when they sign the franchise agreement and pay their fees. We require three to four weeks of on-the-job training for the management and shift leader at each location. It's important that the manager and shift leader understand and know how to do everyone's job, while the person in charge of, say, making sandwiches only needs to know how to make sandwiches. In between shifts, managers are in a classroom learning all the other aspects of managing the business, including becoming acquainted with all HR and employment guidelines and policies. Everything we provide is designed to help the franchisee succeed. If they follow our systems, they've got an excellent chance of doing so.

8 Types of Systems for Business

Here are eight examples of systems that businesses may implement to streamline operations, improve efficiency, and support overall business objectives.

1 Operational Systems are designed to facilitate day-to-day operations and the delivery of products or services. They may include inventory management systems, production systems, quality control systems, supply chain management systems, and customer relationship management (CRM) systems.

2 Financial Systems manage the financial aspects of a business, such as accounting, budgeting, payroll, invoicing, and financial reporting. These systems help track income, expenses, cash flow, and financial performance, ensuring compliance with regulations and enabling effective financial management.

3 Human Resources Systems are responsible for managing various aspects of employee-related processes. They include systems for recruitment and hiring, employee onboarding, performance management, training and development, compensation and benefits administration, employee recordkeeping, and compliance with government regulations.

4 Information Technology (IT) Systems encompass hardware, software, and networks that enable businesses to manage and process information effectively. This includes computer systems, servers, software applications, databases, cybersecurity measures, and communication networks, all of which support data management, communication, and technology infrastructure.

5 Marketing and Sales Systems support their namesake functions, and may include CRM systems, lead generation and management systems, marketing automation systems, analytics and reporting tools, and sales tracking and forecasting systems.

6 Project Management Systems help plan, execute, and monitor projects within a business. They provide tools for project planning, task allocation, resource management, progress tracking, collaboration, and documentation, ensuring that projects are completed efficiently and effectively.

7 Communication and Collaboration Systems facilitate internal and external communication and collaboration, and may include email and messaging systems, video conferencing tools, project management platforms, document sharing and collaboration tools, and intranet or internal communication platforms.

8 Quality Management Systems focus on maintaining and improving product or service quality. They include quality control processes, quality assurance measures, compliance management systems, and continuous improvement methodologies to ensure consistency, customer satisfaction, and adherence to standards and regulations.

BUILD OR BUY

I always love to see the newest generations' contributions to business, particularly in franchising. Over the past fifty years, franchising has evolved into one of the world's most dynamic, transformative business strategies. Franchising is, however, a very complex business. On the surface, it may appear simple: create concepts and authorize others to imitate them. But as mentioned earlier, of the four hundred new franchisors in the US each year, a significant percentage of them fail within the first five years. And they're not alone: *all* startups have a tremendous failure rate. Well over 90 percent of small businesses that are non-franchised independents fail within that same five-year timeframe. Even those that have a solid core business, such as dog groomers, landscapers, and beauticians, may not have a scalable enough model to start a nationwide chain. When you look at small business owners, most are inexperienced, learning the business as they go. It's difficult, and the chances for success are really small. That's why franchising is such a good option to consider.

As an entrepreneur, I've followed my gut and taken risks on several business models, from drilling for oil to breeding Arabian horses. Most have worked out for me—not all, but many. Some I lost interest in; others I didn't see a future in; and some were short-lived because of unexpected health challenges. One thing is for sure: The diversity of my pursuits kept things interesting and prevented me from burning out.

The story of how one particular food franchise was built intrigued me when I entered the arena in the 2020s. I share it here because it's a testament to what can happen when the idea and process are right. Moreover, I'm sharing this story because it's also a testament to what can happen when the process goes wrong.

Fred DeLuca started Subway when he was seventeen years old. He had just graduated from high school and was unsure how he could pay for a college education. He came from a blue-collar family that didn't have the means to help him, so Fred approached a wealthy family friend for some advice. In the back of his mind, he'd hoped this friend would say, "I'll pay for it, and you can pay me back after you graduate." But that's not what this man said; instead, he suggested that Fred pay his way through college by selling sandwiches. He pulled an article from his pocket about a guy who'd opened such a shop in northern New York State and ended up owning thirty-two restaurants in just ten years.

How difficult could it be to open a sub sandwich shop? Fred thought.

"I'll buy half the company," his older friend said, and wrote him a check for $1,000. And the rest is history, as they say. His friend made billions of dollars from his $1,000 investment.

Fred wrote a great book—*Start Small, Finish Big: Fifteen Key Lessons to Start—and Run—Your Own Successful Business*—that focuses on the mindset of the entrepreneur. Early in the process of planning Subway, he discovered that it's actually difficult to make a good sub sandwich. To arrive at the perfect recipe, he and his partner did research by going to several other sub shops, ordering sandwiches, and watching how they were made. Some sliced the roll in half. Some used only a little oil and vinegar on the bread, while others used a lot. There were those who never added lettuce; they just used meat, cheese, and other vegetables. It wasn't rocket science, but it was critical information he needed to know before launching his store. Fred and his partner looked for ways to create a system that would establish both consistency and efficiency. There were hundreds of little steps they needed to work on before establishing what became the best sandwich shop in the business.

Until then, I thought I was the dumbest, luckiest entrepreneur after everything I'd been through. It turns out that DeLuca was ten times dumber and luckier than me, but he figured out how to take a four-hundred-square-foot sandwich shop and turn it into 37,540 locations in more than one hundred countries. For many years, it was the fastest-growing franchise in the world.

Then, in 2016, that all changed. Subway oversaturated the market, allowing new franchises to open in close proximity to previously existing franchises. They gave those franchisors the choice of buying the new location or allowing them to sell to someone else. By doing this, they glutted the market and saw store sales decrease. People will drive two or three miles to get their favorite sub sandwich, but shop oversaturation creates too much competition for too few customers, causing both restaurants to go out of business. Since 2016, Subway has closed more than 6,500 locations domestically, and it was even worse worldwide. Eventually, Subway sold to Roark Capital in 2023 for over $9 billion. In the end, a lot of small entrepreneurs lost everything they had because they were forced to close their shops due to the excessive number of locations.

Loyalty is the responsibility of two parties: The franchisor expects loyalty from the franchisees, and the franchisees deserve an equal amount of loyalty from the franchisor. Oversaturating a market might be fine for the franchisor to maximize their profit, but it isn't fair to the franchisees. Franchisees build the business; it's their success that creates the success of the franchisor. A franchisor shouldn't be allowed to take advantage of the franchisee, and when they attempt to, like Subway did, it often backfires. When you cut the head off, the body dies too, and that's exactly what happened.

After reading a story like Fred DeLuca's, it seems logical to ask, What makes buying a franchise more desirable than building one? Well, there are many reasons, but for most people, it boils down to security. Let's return to the example of McDonald's: Their franchisees succeed because their business is so well systematized. It's nearly impossible for them to fail. McDonald's has not only perfected their product and their ability to deliver consistent quality but they've also invested billions of dollars in advertising, polishing their formula for outreach and replicating their model worldwide. They drive business daily because they're on television, radio, and other outlets. If you buy into a sandwich shop with only three locations, they have no brand awareness, market share, or technology to speak of. Even if they have a good-tasting product, you wouldn't want to bet the house on them.

While there's no sure thing in business, buying a strong franchise allows you to work independently while also enjoying professional guidance. Mistakes will be made, that's for sure, but the franchisor will be right there to help you navigate those challenging times. A good franchise already has excellent systems in place to help you avoid pitfalls and costly mistakes.

Being a franchisee of an established business makes it much easier to get funding than when you're starting from the ground floor. Benefits such as a business plan and financial projections come with the deal too, so not only do you know what to expect, the bank does as well. This is especially important when applying for a loan, because a long, solid history is meaningful to your financial institution.

We've always tried to instill confidence in our franchisees that we'll be there when and if they ever need help. When you run a startup without this type of support, finding someone to mentor you can often be challenging. The only other people who understand what you're experiencing are your competitors, and the likelihood of their helping you is pretty low—so you're forced into figuring almost everything out on your own.

Many small business owners go into their solo ventures with wide eyes and lots of passion. They rarely anticipate the areas that will need attention and expertise to maintain, such as accounting, training, HR, marketing, and so on. No single person can do it all, or at least do it all effectively. This opens you up to making mistakes that you will definitely learn from, but that could easily have been avoided had you been part of a bigger team. By contrast, the support and access franchisors provide can be the difference between succeeding and failing.

Essentially, buying into a franchise allows you to acquire a turnkey business with a proven track record and successful training programs, supply chains, and support. Purchasing an existing, fully operational location allows you to jump in faster than starting from scratch ever could.

When you look at the biggest competitive advantages of franchises—brand awareness, a built-in customer base, systems support, relatively low risk compared to starting a business from scratch, and consistent quality of goods and services you can provide to your patrons—you can see what a great business model it is. As a franchisor, paving the way for others to follow your model is never easy, but if you execute it right, it's worth it for the franchisee to take the leap. At RE/MAX, we were selling the dream of being an entrepreneur with all the resources and strength of a bigger company behind you. The best franchisors create opportunities for startups to enjoy great rewards.

Having said all that, buying a franchise isn't always an ideal fit for some. First, a franchise can be expensive. Depending on the business, the costs can reach as high as $500,000 to $1 million to get up and running—and that doesn't include operational expenses to keep the business going. The franchisor will expect fees and payment for the cost of goods, and may even install mandates.

At RE/MAX, we sell large franchises in major metropolitan areas for $35,000, and smaller franchises in smaller communities for about half that much. Whatever the franchisee spends on office space, furniture, advertising, and staffing are additional costs. There are also monthly fees: Each agent has to pay a fee through the broker for group advertising, including national advertising. Sometimes there's a technology fee that might be four or five hundred dollars per office per month to keep all the systems up and running. Today, RE/MAX is a pure franchisor, with no corporate-owned franchises.

Some franchises, like McDonald's and Chick-fil-A, give you a nearly perfect chance to succeed, while others are risky, especially those that are just starting up. At RE/MAX, we know when a franchise is in trouble because they're no longer paying us. We immediately meet with them to straighten things out. We offer counseling, help with budgeting, and assistance in borrowing money if needed. If, however, their business is failing because of incompetence or because they don't know how to manage even with the tools we provide, we'll shut them down or force them to sell to an adjoining or better broker. With more than ten thousand offices, things like that can happen. We have programs in place that help mitigate any losses for the franchisee and for us. We always want to keep the agents happy, and we'll do whatever we can to ensure that they aren't paying the price if their broker falls short.

We had a situation a few years ago in which a franchisee decided to break his contract. Legally, he couldn't do that, but his response to us was that we could sue him. Either way, he was closing the office and going private. His agents were furious. They didn't want to give up the brand, the national advertising, or the technology. I flew out to meet with the agents and was able to salvage 200 of them out of 204. We opened three offices and offered them to three top agents who wanted to become broker owners. In most cases, these are the franchisees who own the offices. When the original owner went out on his own, he went bankrupt, while we stayed in business and significantly grew those three offices.

This suggests that you've got to do your due diligence before you decide to buy, and like any other strategy, a franchise works best if you follow the blueprint for success that's provided by the franchisor. Even if you're a pillar of perfection, things can sometimes happen that are simply out of your control, so if you want total autonomy, franchising might not be suitable for you. While the franchisee owns their business, they must still follow the trademark guidelines, the quality standards, and the performance metrics set by the franchisors.

Ultimately, those who go the franchise route do so because the model works. It's a stable, tried-and-true business, making it very easy to step into quickly and efficiently.

4 Things All Franchises Must Have to Be Successful

1. Unique product or service
2. Brand and market share
3. Group purchasing
4. Training, systems, and technology

It's important to understand that if you're starting a business from scratch—meaning you aren't buying into an existing business or established franchise—all four essentials for success won't necessarily be available to you on the day you open. The same can be true of fledgling franchises. When McDonald's first launched, they didn't have a brand or market share. They also didn't have the benefit of group buying. What they did have was a simple concept: a counter or window for customers to order food and receive it in a minute or less. The menu was simple, which made the food easy to prepare quickly. Customers could take it with them and leave. In fact, when Ray Kroc was first building the chain, he wouldn't allow picnic tables or seating outside. He didn't allow telephone booths or newspaper stands on the premises either. At the time, hamburger joints were gathering places for teens, but McDonald's didn't want groups of kids hanging around on the property.

They did, however, have clean bathrooms, which were important to mothers with children. As time went by, many of their original mandates were changed to accommodate customer wants and needs, so along came indoor and patio seating, Happy Meals, and playgrounds. As the restaurant evolved, it became increasingly successful. It took time, but they created a recognizable global brand with significant market share.

If you're considering buying a franchise, my best advice is to proceed with caution. Study, do your research, and contemplate every step. It's important to find the best route to achieve whatever vision and goals you've set for yourself. Seek the advice of franchising experts who can act as trusted advisors throughout the process. It takes a strong team to make a franchise work.

There are four paths to franchising. First, you can buy into an existing independent business. This option is most often available when someone is looking to expand, needs money, and/or wants to take some chips off the table. They'll typically offer some percentage of their existing business, selling perhaps half of their interest and sometimes offering the right of first refusal for the other half when they decide to sell the remaining piece.

Second, you can buy into an existing unit of a franchise. For example, if someone who owned a Jack in the Box wanted to retire, it would be very easy for a buyer to enter the franchising world because the seller has the records proving that the restaurant has been profitable.

Third, you can buy a franchise that doesn't exist yet in an area, which is what we're offering with Daddy's Chicken Shack and Port of Subs.

Finally, you may already have a business or an idea that's a good candidate to franchise, and you can become a franchisor.

When vetting a franchise opportunity, assess which path is right for you. Do you want to buy or build? Consider the associated costs of both. If you buy an existing business that's been around for a few years, you'll have all the information you need to make an informed decision, including bank records, taxes, and other financial documentation. If you buy an existing business that you can qualify, meaning it's been successful and makes money, you can look at the financials and see how much money it is making. If you decide to buy a franchise, be aware that it'll take at least three to six months before you start to see positive cash flow. When you're evaluating the business, ask yourself if you'll be able to run it as well or better than its current owner.

Bear in mind that not every business is scalable or viable for franchising. In 2021, I looked at somewhere around two hundred businesses to invest in, and I made only one deal. Just by looking at these businesses' websites and talking to their owners, I knew they would never work. When you start looking at a franchise, you have to pay attention to many things. Ask yourself a lot of questions about the company, their values, who the owners are, and if you're likely to mesh with their systems and standards. Understand the manual, technology, trademarks, training programs, management systems, and products and/or services.

While there are many feasible companies, there are some franchisors out there who are absolute scumbags. There was a sandwich chain that once had thousands of franchised units. I played golf with the owners one time, and that was all it took to sense that they were lying, cheating idiots. Sure enough, the company imploded under the weight of several yearslong lawsuits. As it turned out, they also owned the companies where they bought their napkins, forks, straws, and drinking cups. They were the only vendors their franchisees could buy from, and they jacked up the prices of those goods—which is illegal. Eventually, they had to file for bankruptcy twice and are now down to fewer than two hundred units. So, do your homework and due diligence. You might take it on the chin if you bet on the wrong people.

I always advise listening to your gut and following your intuition. Talk to several franchise owners, which is required by law. A franchisor must give you a list of every franchise in its system that has opened or closed within the prior three years. With regard to Daddy's Chicken Shack, the company is so new that there aren't a multitude of locations yet—but I'm the owner of the company, and my franchising track record holds a lot of weight with anyone considering becoming a franchisee.

KNOW THE ALL-IN COSTS BEFORE SIGNING ANYTHING

George S. Clason's 1926 book *The Richest Man in Babylon* is a classic. While it's a work of fiction, it imparts financial wisdom through a collection of parables about a group of characters living in ancient Babylon, a city known for its great prosperity and wealth. The central character is Arkad, who begins the book as a poor scribe and manages to become the richest man in Babylon. Arkad shares the secrets of his success and his financial principles with his friends and fellow citizens, imparting valuable lessons on personal finance and wealth accumulation. The book's enduring popularity lies in its ability to simplify complex financial concepts into relatable stories and lessons that provide practical advice for building personal wealth. Arkad gives his seven "Cures" to generate wealth and his five "Laws of Gold," which describe how to protect and invest that wealth. Some core aspects of his advice are the concepts of paying yourself first, living within your means, and investing in what you know, and Arkad emphasizes the importance of long-term saving and home ownership. When I first read this book, it made perfect sense. If you haven't already read it, I highly recommend doing so.

It's a wonderful reminder of how important financial literacy is, especially if you're starting or building a business.

If you're contemplating launching a business or presently own one, chances are you're looking for financial freedom, success, and ways to create some level of wealth. Know this in advance: When it comes to starting a new business, nothing costs as little as you think it will, especially in a post-Covid economy. I have a beautiful ranch in northern Colorado, with a lake that's forty-five feet deep, though the lake wasn't always there. It started off as just a stream, mostly from snow melting in the surrounding mountains or from a big rainstorm. To create this lake, we needed to build a dam to hold the water. It took three years of fighting with the Corps of Engineers and the EPA to get permission. There hadn't been a dam built in the state in more than a century. When the first part of the dam was completed, the runoff from the first snowmelt filled it in approximately two weeks.

Then we decided to build a shed so we could store our boats and lawn furniture in the winter. Tough Sheds is a Denver-based company that manufactures such sheds, so I reached out to them to get an estimate. I knew I needed to pour a concrete slab to place it on and that it would require a building permit, so we applied for the permit in February. We didn't get it until May of the following year—fifteen months later! There was no electricity, no plumbing, no water, and no sanitation involved; it was a prefabricated shed on a platform. This was during Covid, so no one was working in their office, but it really shouldn't have taken that long.

This is a personal example to illustrate that nothing is ever going to be as cheap as you think it will be, nor will it get done as fast as you expect it to. Most people create a budget to do a project and are optimistic they will hold to the budget. However, in most cases, this isn't necessarily true. Unexpected costs and delays come up. Throw in inflation, where costs are subject to unforeseen increases, encountering supply chain problems and labor shortages, and you will instantly understand that the budget you set is no longer relevant. This is especially true when starting your own business. As an entrepreneur, you must be ready for whatever challenges come your way.

Now, some franchisors will be quite honest with their franchisees about timeframe and costs. They'll explain the expenses involved in getting started and will be forthcoming about how long it takes for cash flow to come in. Franchising was once the Wild West of business investing, but by the late 1970s, the FTC began requiring all franchisors in the US to disclose certain information to their franchisee candidates via a nationally registered document. This document is now known as a Franchise Disclosure Document (FDD), and it must contain twenty-three standard items, along with the franchise agreement the candidate will eventually sign if both sides agree to move ahead. If you don't receive this document from the franchisor, run for the hills, and whatever you do, do not hand over any money.

An FDD is often a huge and sometimes overwhelming document that provides necessary and valuable information to the franchisee candidate. (Several states have compliance documents that must be attached to the federal document, which can make it even longer.) The specifics of an FDD can vary from company to company, but the overarching structure is always consistent. It should detail who the franchisor is, who its parent company is, and who its predecessors and affiliates are. It should also present all the fees involved in starting and operating the business, such as franchise, royalty, advertising, and technology fees. This information will provide a total investment range so you know exactly what to anticipate. Next, it should explain everything you can expect to receive as a franchisee, the financial opportunity, the health of the franchisor's business, and legal documents inclusive of trademark, patent, and copyright information, as well as any prior declarations of bankruptcy, any current or previous litigation the franchisor has been involved in, and, of course, a copy of the contract to help you make your final decision.

For example, the FDD for Daddy's Chicken Shack itemizes everything and lays out the associated costs. We indicate what you can expect to pay per square foot based on your location, because renting space in Pasadena, California, is a lot more expensive than renting in Omaha, Nebraska. We also offer a range of prices for the kitchen equipment, fixtures, furnishings, and bathrooms, as well as the costs for training, including hotel, airfare, food, and so much more. Successful franchisors who've been around for a while will offer all of these figures without hesitation. Why? It's how the franchisor helps the franchisee get set up for success.

Again, with any franchise, it's important to remember that you have to be prepared to carry the business with little to no income for a period of several months. When we were building out our first two locations for Daddy's Chicken Shack, the only stipulation I had was that they couldn't be in California. I gave the founders a choice among Scottsdale, Arizona; Denver; and Texas. I made a mistake when doing that, because they chose Texas. I knew that Scottsdale had a four-week permitting process, so if we were able to find an existing building that only needed some remodeling, it would have taken a month or so to get the proper permits to start construction. In Houston, however, we were still following up on our permits sixteen months later. We could have had multiple locations by that time if we'd chosen one of the other locations.

FUNDING YOUR BUSINESS

One of the most impactful seminars I ever attended was led by a banking executive who ran a course on how to borrow money. This was in the mid-1970s, when I was broke and owed everyone money, so I needed to find out how to borrow more. At the time, our loans were mostly short term, which put an extraordinary amount of pressure on us. So, six of our officers and I took the course. I remember that the speaker started off the day by saying something I adamantly disagreed with: "What you need to do is change your banker every two to three years. And while you're at it, change your PR and advertising agencies every couple of years too."

Right away, I knew that wasn't me. I'm loyal to the people who helped us get to where we are, and even then, I knew the value of relationships in business. I also knew that when you have a personal relationship with a bank, they know you as a person; you aren't just a financial statement reviewed by a random loan assessor. I raised my hand and asked the executive why he felt this way.

"When you're young and the business is new and you borrow money, a bank committee [the group in charge of approving or denying your loan] will assess everything about you," he said. "If you've borrowed, say, one hundred thousand dollars and paid it back on time, and then borrowed it again, that's great. But if that loan was a stretch in the first place, when you go back and ask for two hundred fifty thousand dollars, that committee will know the original loan was barely approved. Why would they now loan you two and-a-half times as much?"

I have to admit, he had a point. As we grew, banks approached us all the time to win our business. One of the first things they did was try to lure us with a larger credit line. When you have an offer like that in your hand, you can pit your old bank against the potential new one.

As an aside, this presenter was also absolutely right about PR and advertising agencies. I learned very early in the game that both will romance you to land the account, then treat you like their biggest client for a few months, but that quickly wanes. Before you realize what's happening, they're out there hunting for another big client. The longer you stay with somebody, the more they're going to take advantage of you.

I didn't implement this valuable lesson right away, but as we grew, I began to believe in it, and most certainly started teaching it. The point the executive made during the seminar was to keep growing and get away from those people who may doubt you. If you can have a long-term relationship with a bank, that's great. I've had a thirty-year relationship with one of our national banks and a forty-two-year relationship with a local private bank in Colorado where I do all my other business. However, when you start with a local bank, as you get bigger and need to borrow $100 million instead of $1 million, they can't touch it. You have to expand, go to New York, meet money managers, and get ten banks involved to get a bond. RE/MAX is now spread over six or seven banks from Denver to New York. I learned along the way to invite our bankers, private equity teams, investment bankers, and other financial advisors to our conventions. When they come, they see the enthusiasm of the people who are there firsthand. They experience the breadth of the business and hear brokers, franchisees, and agents talk about what it's like to work with RE/MAX. Believe me, they're listening—and the message they consistently hear is, "We love the management at RE/MAX. . . . Dave, Gail, and Adam are the greatest people in the world. . . . We trust them with anything. . . . We're going to stay with this company for the rest of our lives." You can't pay for that kind of endorsement.

I recognize that most people won't need to borrow $100 million or grow their revenue to $1 million, but those who do have a steep learning curve if they're starting from scratch.

By our third year in business at RE/MAX, we were growing at a steady-enough pace that we were considered a decent credit risk. We were paying our bills while paying down our debt. We had grown every single month since opening our doors, so I thought it was time to secure a loan.

I sat with a banker I knew and said, "Look, we're destined to be number one in Colorado. It's inevitable. We've got the quality of agents to carry us there. Our sales are going up, our agent retention is high, and new people are joining us. When I started the company, my business plan was to recruit five people a month for five years. By then, I'll have three hundred agents. We would have enough transactions and volume to be the number one real estate company in the entire state."

And then I stopped talking. I noticed the banker writing something on the back of a white envelope. I looked across the desk and saw the words "Number one real estate company in the state." Believe it or not, he still has that envelope today. He framed it, and it hung on his wall for thirty-plus years until he retired.

I knew right then and there that he was going to approve the loan. And when he did, we kept borrowing.

I was full of confidence and bravado, but I also believed what I was saying to be true. That type of faith in yourself is contagious. If you don't believe you're going to be successful on every level, why would anyone else?

As it turned out, we didn't get those five agents a month that first year, nor did we do so in the second year. But we were growing bigger and bigger, and the more we grew, the easier it became to keep growing. At the end of our fifth year in business, we hadn't gotten to 300 agents; we had 289. But we were number one, just as I'd predicted. That goal had come true because of every word I spoke, every action we took, and every hard-luck challenge that came our way.

When starting a small business, one of the biggest pitfalls aspiring entrepreneurs should avoid is not having enough financial backing. As we've discussed, nothing ever happens as fast as you think it will or costs as little as you hope it will. Financial backing gives you the staying power to live through your mistakes. It enhances your product or service, making it more valuable.

When it comes to borrowing money, there's a philosophy that says, "Borrow everyone else's money, then go try your idea and fail fast. Close it down. Try another business. Fail faster. Sooner or later, one of those ideas is going to work." I'm totally against that way of thinking. The people who loaned us money when we started RE/MAX—whether it was our vendors, small business owners, or the local weekly newspaper—would have gotten really hurt if I hadn't paid them back, if I'd filed bankruptcy, or if I'd left them holding the bag in any way. I was always a man of my word. If I told someone I was going to pay them back, I did. Those actions led to exponential returns. I still marvel at how kind some of our creditors were when they knew we were struggling. We always communicated the truth and assured each one that we weren't giving up, that our company would work. It's amazing what you can accomplish with enthusiasm, confidence, and self-belief.

Securing funding for your business isn't as easy as it once was. Banks aren't going to lend to you unless you've got some really good assets and they know they can get their money back. Plus, rapid hikes in interest rates have put many small businesses in crisis, making the cost of capitalizing extremely high. Even so, when you want to secure financing for your business, there are a variety of ways to borrow money. Start with what you've got and then crowdfund with family and friends. Borrowing from them is the easiest way to raise capital. It's also relatively simple to put a small group of people together to start a business, sharing ownership and contributions based on the percentage amount each invested. Sometimes your employees are a good resource, as they might jump on the opportunity to become owners. Buyer beware, though, as partnerships have a high failure rate.

Banks provide many options for lending that can grow with your company, especially for small businesses. Small business loans come with many advantages, although it's important to know that the terms aren't flexible. You'll borrow a set amount, make monthly payments, and be expected to pay back the loan in a specific timeframe. Interest rates will depend to a great extent on both your personal and business credit scores. While the rates banks offer are generally lower than those for some other funding options, it can be challenging to qualify for those preferred rates. The question lenders will ask you first is how you intend to use the money. Having something in writing, such as a business plan that clearly outlines how the funds will be used and the impact they'll have, will greatly improve your chances of securing a loan.

Securing a business loan can give you a head start launching, as you won't have to wait for the business to become profitable or to begin generating cash flow. Most businesses will occasionally experience cash flow issues; they're particularly common if your business is growing quickly and you need to subsidize more employees, more inventory, additional equipment, or expansion. Securing a loan will help expedite your business's growth without your having to rely on investors or giving up equity. Remember, once you take on investors, they'll own a percentage of your business and your profits. They can also dictate and monitor how you spend their money. As long as your business loan isn't for something specific, such as new equipment, however, there are usually no restrictions on how you use the money.

There are different types of small business loans, and each has its pros and cons. Research each option to know its benefits and drawbacks. If you've got great credit, a Small Business Administration (SBA) loan has some of the most favorable terms. The SBA is one of the most well-known organizations in the United States related to the operations of small businesses. It offers funding options, educational resources, connections to mentors, and more. If you can't qualify for an SBA loan now, once you've established your business, you can go back to the SBA and get a longer-term loan. Most small business loans at banks are guaranteed by the SBA, including the SBA Express Loan for funding up to $350,000 and the SBA 7a Program, which loans up to $5 million. If you seek an SBA loan, however, know that it can take many months to get approved and receive the funds, so if your need is urgent, this might not be an ideal option.

Microloan lenders provide up to $50,000 to startups and small businesses, and often prefer those that are run by women, minorities, and veterans. If you're not seeking a lot of money, this could be a good option, especially if you're just starting out and have no track record.

A term loan is one of the most common options for small businesses. Once the loan is approved, you'll receive the full amount all at once. These loans are similar to loans you would get from the SBA, but often come with less favorable terms.

There are also equipment loans, which are made specifically for purchasing equipment. Unlike other types of loans, business owners can usually qualify for this type of loan, even if they have less-than-good credit, as the equipment serves as collateral.

Applying for a business loan can be a drawn-out process that takes longer than other types of loans. Along with the paperwork, the lender will want to see tax returns and financial statements, profit and loss statements, and a business plan. The lender will base their decision on the company's creditworthiness and whether the company has the ability to pay back the loan. As a result, I've seen people stretch themselves, taking loans from their credit cards, which come with high interest rates. When they do this, they drown themselves in debt that they'll have a difficult time paying off. I absolutely do not encourage you to go this route unless it's an emergency.

If you have good credit, a small business loan actually makes more sense than a personal loan, especially if you've been in business for a while. The lender may ask for some type of collateral in case you fail to make your payments. If you use the business itself as collateral, you risk losing it if you can't make your payments and default on your loan. If your business is new, you may be asked to secure the loan with a personal asset, such as your home. Again, there's risk in using your property as collateral. If you know you'll be able to make the payments, the risk is obviously mitigated, but it's something to be keenly aware of.

Venture capital (VC) and angel investors will primarily be interested in companies that already have track records. Angel investors are wealthy people who are willing to invest in businesses with their own money. VC funds are willing to invest more money than an angel investor but are also risk averse. Both VCs and angel investors expect to receive significant returns, even though they know they'll lose on seven or eight out of every ten investments.

If you're a homeowner, you can get a home equity loan based on the available equity you have. Think of this as a second mortgage: you borrow a specific amount of money to be repaid in installments over a period of anywhere from five to thirty years. The terms are set, including your payment amount and interest rate. By using real estate as collateral, you'll often receive an interest rate that's less than that for other types of loans. About one-third of the houses in the United States are owned free and clear, which means that there are a whole lot of people who've paid their mortgage off, and even more who have several hundreds of thousands of dollars in available equity. If you have that kind of equity and a good business plan, you can likely find a regional bank that will loan you money to get your business started.

Similarly, a home equity line of credit (HELOC) can be especially useful, as you can draw funds from it over several years. Depending on the terms, your payments may only have to cover interest and not principal. Once the draw period expires, however, you'll have to make payments that cover both. Unlike with a home equity loan, a HELOC's terms can change over time, so it's important to know that going in.

Mergers and acquisitions are excellent ways to expand your business. At RE/MAX we have brokers who receive 100 percent marks on their management leadership, while five miles away from their office is a broker who's tired, burned out, and barely hanging on. When we see that happening, we sometimes encourage that broker to consider making a change, explaining before we terminate their deal that they can sell to a stronger broker. We explain that a new broker owner can come in with additional financial resources and may add some features and benefits to the business to make it a little easier. We have lots of franchisees who start with one office and end up with a dozen or more because they acquire faltering offices. That's a function of experience and profitability. The more experience you have, the more profit you make. The more assets you have, the easier it is to borrow against and leverage them to acquire more businesses and make even more money. However, the farther you stray from your core skills and abilities when making acquisitions, the more likely those acquisitions will fail. In other words, when you venture too far outside your technical, managerial, and business experience, you increase the odds that your merger or acquisition will falter or fail altogether.

There are advantages and disadvantages to each of the wide variety of loans that are available. It's up to you to do your homework and determine which loan makes the most sense for you and your needs. I would start by talking to a loan professional at the bank where you do your business banking.

AREA 15 VENTURES

While RE/MAX will always be my favorite business venture, Gail and I have owned twenty-two businesses over the years that have made us extremely proud. Nearly all of them were successful, and so far, I've sold only two. A few years ago, we started a private equity company called Area 15 Ventures, a small operation consisting of Gail; my son, Dave Jr.; Dan Predovich, who was on the RE/MAX board for twenty years; Adam Contos; and me. We founded Area 15 to help small business owners build their companies. Through our subsidiary, Area 15 Franchising, we focus on emerging franchisors in high-growth businesses who require investment to scale their operation and who could benefit from our team's experience in franchising and business.

It was during the pandemic that we came across Daddy's Chicken Shack. The chef, Pace Webb, and her husband and business partner, Chris Georgalas, originally started their company as a high-end caterer in Los Angeles. When Covid hit, it killed their business. Interestingly, in 2018, Pace had been thinking of starting a sandwich shop. She figured her dad could run it while she focused on catering. One of her best recipes was for an Asian-inspired fried chicken sandwich. People went crazy for it. So, Pace and Chris opened a seven-hundred-square-foot space in Pasadena with enough room for only four people to work. There was no bathroom, parking, foot traffic, or indoor dining; it was all takeout. During the lockdown in 2020, Daddy's saw a 200 percent increase in business, doing $1.3 million in sales. That's an astronomical number, and it placed a demand on their small business that they had neither the staff nor the space to meet. Even so, they made it work.

As Pace and Chris researched the costs involved in franchising, they contacted Dr. Ben Litalien. I was well acquainted with Ben; he's a friend who taught a franchising course I'd taken at Georgetown

University. He explained to the couple that it could cost millions of dollars. They couldn't pay that kind of money, but Ben mentioned that he knew an investor who was one of the best in the franchising business. He offered to call and see if I was interested in meeting with them. I was. At that time, Area 15 had just opened. We didn't have phones or fiber optics yet—in fact, we'd barely gotten our furniture moved into our office space. Adam Contos, then the CEO of RE/MAX, had just given his notice to leave and join us.

Adam and I flew to California for a taste test and to meet the founders. We were utterly blown away by what they'd accomplished. I also found Pace to be very charismatic and likable. She comes from a family of entertainers and has a performance-minded attitude. She was a great front person for the business. That was important to me too. As lovely as she is, her husband is equally appealing: handsome, intelligent, and a successful Wall Street executive who got heavily involved in technology. As a result, Daddy's was an early customer of Ordermark (now Nextbite), an online ordering solution that offers integration of third-party delivery providers. By the end of 2018, Daddy's was available on eleven delivery apps and offered native online ordering. Chris had also developed a proprietary application for customers to pick up their food. We thought it was brilliant and wanted to create a prototype immediately. We were so impressed that Area 15 bought 51 percent of their company, and I became Chief Chicken Officer, first franchisor, and a member of their board of directors.

I don't take any investment lightly. I'd done my due diligence on Daddy's Chicken Shack, just as I would for any potential investment. The company is a rock-solid brand with a remarkable foundation for expansion. It checked every box.

Gut feelings have always been important to me, and I had a gut feeling about these two people, their products, and their potential. There was great chemistry, and they had substantial numbers.

If there isn't enough profit—if you can't make enough money from someone buying a franchise—there's no reason to do it.

When it came time to open the first Daddy's Chicken Shack with our participation, we learned that Pace and Chris owned a property about forty miles north of Houston that had been in their family for a hundred years. This family home's proximity to Houston is, of course, why they chose that city for their first franchised location. Because of Covid, supply chain issues, and the aforementioned length of permitting, it took a year longer to complete than we would have liked, but we managed to build and open a 2,400-square-foot location by early 2022. While the store was being built and we were contending with delays, we developed a learning management system for them, utilizing a combination of video and written documents. We also created a system for ordering all their ingredients through Cisco, drafted a boilerplate agreement for future franchisees, and began selling franchises. In that same year, Daddy's opened its second franchise in Texas and signed its seventh regional development deal. As of this writing, Daddy's has inked eight other franchise agreements across California, Oregon, Texas, Colorado, Arizona, Georgia, and Florida, and the brand boasts a total of 120 units in development.

Eventually, our company bought out the founders' share of Daddy's Chicken Shack. We had different visions for the growth of the company, but we parted ways amicably, which doesn't always happen. It's always been important to me to have good endings whenever possible. You never know when your paths may cross again.

In 2023, our company also purchased the Port of Subs chain of sandwich shops. Port of Subs was founded in 1972 by two brothers from New Jersey who opened a modest place in Sparks, Nevada, called the Sub Shop. John Larsen and his family seized the opportunity to purchase an interest in the business and later bought the company in 1975, renaming it Port of Subs. Between 1975 and 1985 the Larsens developed ten company-owned units, but people began approaching them about opening stores in other locations. Port of Subs started franchising in 1985, and as of today, there are more than 135 units in seven Western states.

Ben Litalien initially brought the deal to us. He had been trying to persuade the owner to hire a marketing team and expand the business throughout the United States, and right away we saw a tremendous opportunity. After all, Subway had opened thirty-six thousand stores, Jimmy John's had opened five thousand, and Firehouse had three thousand. Why hadn't Port of Subs scaled like these others? As I mentioned in the leadership chapter, the owner ruled the company with an iron fist. He didn't want franchisees to own more than one store, because he wrongly believed that would give them too much power. As we would later learn, this bothered his owners because it limited their earning potential.

It took a year from the day we first heard about Port of Subs to finalize our deal. To be candid, we hated the name of the business, which was the winner in a naming contest they'd held on the radio. Even so, I'd discovered a long time ago that names don't really make a difference to people. Who knows what RE/MAX means? Don't get me wrong—a strong name can matter, especially with luxury brands, but for most things a name is just a name.

When we closed the sale, we decided to get to know our franchisees better, so we met with them to introduce ourselves and to have a clean transfer of ownership. The owner was there that day, although we wished he hadn't been. We held roundtable discussions and asked vital questions, including "Tell us three things you like most about Port of Subs and three things you dislike most" and so on. This didn't bode well for the owner. The franchisees were angry. For fifty years, there had been only 135 stores, with seventy-five located in

Nevada and the other sixty spread among Arizona, Northern California, and Boise and other parts of Idaho. The franchisees were desperate because they felt constrained. They realized that a national brand with national advertising would drive additional customers to their shops. When we discussed what they liked and disliked, many franchisees said that Port of Subs had grown rapidly, like many of their competitors, but they hadn't reaped the benefits. This must have been difficult for the owner to hear, as he had personal friendships with many of the franchisees.

There was only one other question we posed that day: "What can we do as a company to help you grow?"

Every single franchisee said, "Open more units." They felt as if they were dying on the vine. They had no marketing budget, couldn't advertise on television, and didn't feel that they stood a chance against the big franchisors. Once we explained our method of franchising, they realized that they hadn't had any of those benefits before. It was clear that they wanted them, and we felt they deserved them.

Chick-fil-A has a great corporate culture, a good product, and all the chicken concepts you can imagine. They are by far the most profitable chicken sandwich restaurant, even though they're open only six days a week. They allow you to buy only one franchise, however; they won't let you be a multi-owner. I'm not sure why they limit their franchisees to one unit, but I suspect that it's because they think it's better to have the owner-operator present in a single location than it is for that person to spread their time and attention over several locations. In RE/MAX's case, we've found that multiunit owners are astute businesspeople. We even have one California owner with over a hundred units.

In real estate, by the way, you can be a multiunit owner, but you can represent only one brand due to licensing laws. So, if you're a RE/MAX owner, you can't also own a Century 21 franchise. In any other business, that doesn't apply. It's possible, for instance, to possess thousands of units, including a mix of five hundred Wendy's locations, twenty Jack in the Box restaurants, and fifteen Jiffy Lube units. People like Shaquille O'Neal and Magic Johnson are two great examples of multiunit franchisees.

Owning multiple units tends to be profitable, especially if the brand has been around for a while. Multiunit franchisees, however, must get rid of any unprofitable, poorly managed operations as they become aware of them. It's also important to note that once there's a saturation point in a specific market, opening more units won't work; the new franchises will only cannibalize business from existing owners.

When helping a franchisor scale his or her business, you can always supplement the founder's talent by surrounding them with additional people who make up for what they don't know. Still, it's not easy when a founder lacks certain talents, because it's their dream you're buying. It will never work with them at the helm if they don't have the right mix of drive, ambition, love, and passion for the job. Conversely, the owner/franchisor cannot care more about the business than the individual franchisee does. If the franchisees don't give a damn or decide to go rogue, you're wasting your time with them.

At Port of Subs, we've already started a regional development program that will double or triple the number of franchisees within a very short period of time. We have great expectations for this brand, given all the changes we've implemented and will continue to make and the support we're now offering existing franchisees.

10 Things to Know before Buying a Franchise

When you're considering buying a franchise, it's crucial to have a solid understanding of the key aspects involved. Here are ten critical things to know about buying a franchise:

1. Franchise Model and System: Understand the franchise model and system offered by the franchisor. Familiarize yourself with the franchise's brand, products or services, and operational procedures, and what support is provided by the franchisor.

2. Franchise Fee and Initial Investment: Determine the franchise fee and initial investment required to purchase the franchise, including costs such as equipment, inventory, leasehold improvements, and working capital. Understand the financial obligations and ensure that you have the necessary funds.

3. Franchise Agreement: Review the agreement carefully. This legally binding document outlines the terms and conditions of the franchise relationship, including rights, obligations, fees, royalties, and termination clauses. Seek professional advice if needed to understand the agreement fully.

4. Franchisor's Track Record: Research the franchisor's track record and reputation. Evaluate their history, financial stability, and litigation history, and the success rate of their franchisees. Speak with existing and former franchisees to gain insight into their experiences.

5. Training and Support: Assess the training and support provided by the franchisor. Understand the initial training program, ongoing support, marketing assistance, and operational guidance. Strong franchisors offer comprehensive training and continuing support to help franchisees succeed.

6 Franchisee Responsibilities: Understand your responsibilities as a franchisee. This includes adhering to the franchisor's operational standards, following established procedures, maintaining quality control, and complying with branding and marketing guidelines.

7 Territory and Competition: Investigate the territory rights and exclusivity offered by the franchise. Understand the competition in the area and whether the franchise system has protected territories or market restrictions.

8 Franchisee-Franchisor Relationship: Understand the nature of the relationship between the franchisee and the franchisor. Franchisors typically maintain control over certain aspects of the business, such as branding, marketing, and product/service offerings. Make sure you're comfortable with this level of control.

9 Profitability and Financial Projections: Obtain financial projections and understand the potential profitability of the franchise. Review the franchisor's financial disclosures, including average sales figures and profitability of existing franchise units. Conduct independent research and analysis to validate the financial projections.

10 Exit Strategy: Consider your exit strategy. Understand the terms and conditions for selling the franchise in the future. Determine whether there are any restrictions or limitations on transferring ownership and if the franchisor offers any assistance in the resale process.

It's crucial to conduct thorough due diligence, seek professional advice from attorneys and accountants experienced in franchising, and carefully evaluate all aspects of the franchise opportunity before making a final decision.

THE LINIGER CENTER FOR FRANCHISE STUDIES

By now, you know my wife and I have made a lifelong commitment to learning. There's no greater gift you can give yourself or others than the gift of education. Interestingly, only a few places offer certified college courses teaching franchising, including Georgetown University, which has a certificate course on franchise management. That course is taught by my good friend Ben Litalien, one of a few global franchise experts with broad franchise experience and academic credentials. He's the founder of FranchiseWell, an agency that consults with groups like UPS and IKEA.

Despite how big franchising is, for most people it's something they must research and teach themselves about. Knowing this, we've decided to create certificate courses at the University of Denver teaching franchising. Gail and I established the Liniger Center for Franchise Studies at the Daniels College of Business, one of the best business schools in the western United States, as a new resource for the business community. With fifty-plus years of experience, we wanted to share our knowledge with others. The courses will offer franchisors and franchisees guidance, support, and resources through education, networking, and thought leadership.

When looking to develop our curriculum, Adam Contos, Dave Jr., myself, and two other team members at Area 15 Ventures decided to take Ben's course at Georgetown. Ben brought in seven or eight experts to speak about different areas of business, including mergers and acquisitions, innovation, legal entities, marketing, and other relevant topics. One of the speakers who presented on franchise documents stopped my son in the hallway before his presentation and said he was so nervous about speaking that day because I was going to be in the room. Now, I don't see myself as being all that important. I enjoy admiration but am uncomfortable with it, especially if my presence detracts from the speaker's confidence. This guy had written twenty books and was a well-known lecturer, and he was nervous because of me?

And then he shared with the class that I was his first franchise client. "Mr. Liniger started my career," he said.

Unbeknownst to me, the company this man had worked for was run by Scott Smith, my wing commander in Vietnam. Scott had begged me to sell him the Florida region for RE/MAX. I initially turned him down because he was an attorney, and I worried that he would sue me forever if he didn't make it as a franchisee. Scott did his best to persuade me otherwise. "We're brothers-in-arms," he said. "I promise I can make it work. I'll shake hands with you on it."

So I agreed. Unfortunately, a year later, I had to take the region back from him. It was a big job, and I needed someone with the experience to get it done. When I did, I asked, "Are you going to sue me?"

"Absolutely not. We're still brothers-in-arms. You do, however, need a good franchise attorney, so let me make back some of my money by allowing me to be that guy."

We worked together for fifteen or twenty years, and the speaker in our class that day was one of his first employees. It was just a reminder that you never know who will impact your business, or how.

While I thought the course was good, it helped me think through what we wanted to offer in ours. Classes at the Liniger Center will focus on various areas that are critical to franchising, including different business models, trends, patterns, future directions, financial analysis, real estate considerations, ethical decision-making, and conflict resolution. The center will also research franchising. Our teachers will have vast experience in franchising through various entities. As a member of the IFA Hall of Fame, we can recruit the best of the best to address our students. Our hope is that the center will serve as a place where networking and higher education come together for those seeking a career in franchising. We intend to create a degree program in addition to the certificate program so students can major or minor in franchising.

We've spent more than fifty years watching the amazing things that can happen when entrepreneurs come together, share their experiences, and support one another. The center will be a hub of learning and growth. We're thrilled to help new generations discover the incredible value of franchising and the power of joining forces with like-minded professionals. With the right concept, values, and people, anything is possible.

READ AS MANY BOOKS AS YOU CAN

This chapter only skims the surface of what you need to know about the franchise business. If you're thinking about buying a franchise, look for and read books written by other successful franchise founders. While I knew a lot about franchising from my many years running RE/MAX, I still looked for books that would teach me about the fast-food business when it came time to launch Daddy's Chicken Shack and Port of Subs. Here's a comprehensive list of some of my favorites from my personal library.

The Classics That Are Still Relevant Today

How to Win Friends and Influence People, by Dale Carnegie

Time-tested, rock-solid advice that has carried thousands of people up the ladder of success in their business and personal lives. A classic book that gave birth to the self-help industry, *How to Win Friends and Influence People* is a phenomenal bestseller, having sold more than 15 million copies worldwide and still going strong.

Think and Grow Rich, by Napoleon Hill

Think and Grow Rich has been called the "Granddaddy of All Motivational Literature." It was the first book to boldly ask "What makes a winner?" The man who asked and listened for the answer, Napoleon Hill, is now counted in the top ranks of the world's winners himself.

The Magic of Getting What You Want, by David J. Schwartz

This book explains how to determine personal objectives and learn how to work effectively with others to reach your goals and to achieve greater prosperity, happiness, influence, and personal fulfillment.

The 22 Immutable Laws of Marketing, by Al Ries and Jack Trout

There are laws of nature, so why shouldn't there be laws of marketing? As Al Ries and Jack Trout—the world-renowned marketing consultants and bestselling authors of *Positioning*—note, you can build an impressive airplane, but it will never leave the ground if you ignore the laws of physics, especially gravity. Why then, they ask, shouldn't there also be laws of marketing that must be followed to launch and maintain winning brands?

A Message to Garcia, by Elbert Hubbard

A Message to Garcia, written by legendary author Elbert Hubbard, is widely considered to be one of the one hundred greatest books of all time. This great classic will surely attract a whole new generation of readers. For many, *A Message to Garcia* is required reading (or listening) for various courses and curriculums.

THE BEST BOOKS I'VE EVER READ

The Compound Effect, by Darren Hardy

As the publisher of *Success* magazine for more than twenty-five years, author Darren Hardy has heard it all, seen it all, and tried most of it. This book reveals the core principles that drive success. *The Compound Effect* contains the essence of what every superachiever needs to know, practice, and master to attain extraordinary success.

Atomic Habits, by James Clear

No matter what your goals are, *Atomic Habits* offers a proven framework for improving every day. James Clear, one of the world's leading experts on habit formation, reveals practical strategies that will teach you exactly how to create good habits, break bad ones, and master the tiny behaviors that lead to remarkable results.

The Success Principles, by Jack Canfield

Since its publication a decade ago, Jack Canfield's practical and inspiring guide has helped thousands of people transform themselves for success. In *The Success Principles*, the cocreator of the phenomenally bestselling Chicken Soup for the Soul series helps you get from where you are to where you want to be, teaching you how to increase your confidence, tackle daily challenges, live with passion and purpose, and realize all your ambitions.

Start with a Win, by Adam Contos

In *Start with a Win: Tools and Lessons to Create Personal and Business Success*, Adam Contos, the CEO of RE/MAX Holdings, delivers a powerful exploration of how leaders process information and lead boldly, especially during times of crisis. Packed with the practical lessons Adam learned as the leader of one of the most recognized real estate brands in the world, the book shows you how leaders recognize emotion, chaos, and fear and transform those negatives into opportunity.

Good to Great, by Jim Collins

If you believe that a visionary leader with a strong ego is an essential component of sustained business success, then Jim Collins has a few thousand words for you. His carefully researched book explains that the success of companies that outperform the market for fifteen years in a row comes from selfless leadership, rigorous focus, and a culture of discipline.

Crush It!: Why NOW Is the Time to Cash In on Your Passion, by Gary Vaynerchuk

Do you have a hobby you wish you could indulge in all day? An obsession that keeps you up at night? Now is the perfect time to take that passion and make a living doing what you love. In *Crush It!*, Gary Vaynerchuk shows you how to use the power of the internet to turn your real interests into real businesses.

Start with Why: How Great Leaders Inspire Everyone to Take Action, by Simon Sinek

In 2009, Simon Sinek started a movement to help people become more inspired at work, and inspire their colleagues and customers in turn. Since then, millions have been touched by the power of his ideas, including more than twenty-eight million people who've watched his TED Talk based on *Start with Why*, the third-most popular TED video of all time.

Never Split the Difference: Negotiating as If Your Life Depended on It, by Chris Voss

Never Split the Difference takes you inside the world of high-stakes negotiations and into Voss's head, revealing the skills that helped him and his colleagues succeed where it mattered most: in saving lives. In this practical guide, he shares the nine effective principles, counterintuitive tactics, and strategies that you too can use to become more persuasive in both your professional and personal lives.

The 7 Habits of Highly Effective People: Powerful Lessons in Personal Change, by Stephen R. Covey

One of the most inspiring and impactful books ever written, *The 7 Habits of Highly Effective People* has captivated listeners for nearly three decades. It has transformed the lives of presidents and CEOs, educators and parents, and millions of people of all ages and occupations.

The One Minute Manager, by Ken Blanchard and Spencer Johnson

For decades, *The One Minute Manager* has helped millions achieve more successful professional and personal lives. The principles it lays out are timeless.

The Five Dysfunctions of a Team: A Leadership Fable, by Patrick Lencioni

In keeping with the parable style, Patrick Lencioni begins by telling the fable of a woman who, as CEO of a struggling Silicon Valley firm, took control of a dysfunctional executive committee and helped its members succeed as a team. Succinct yet sympathetic, this guide will be a boon for those struggling with the inherent difficulties of leading a group.

What They Don't Teach You at Harvard Business School: Notes from a Street-Smart Executive, by Mark H. McCormack

Mark McCormack, one of the most successful entrepreneurs in American business, is widely credited as the founder of the modern-day sports marketing industry. This business classic features straight-talking advice that you'll never hear in school.

8

Marketing

When we opened our first RE/MAX office, we bought a gigantic map of Denver that measured four feet by eight feet. We put it on a corkboard so we could push tiny pins with red, yellow, blue, and green heads into it. We started with yellow pins for every address we sold. That first year in business we had twenty-one people who closed around two hundred deals. The second year, we closed four hundred deals, which we indicated with green pins. By the third year in business, we had tripled our sales again, covering the map with blue pins. When we stood back and looked at this giant map, we started to see clusters of pins in specific areas around the city. When we recruited new agents, we would always meet them in the conference room where we kept that corkboard so they could see the incredible number of transactions we were doing. It was one hell of a marketing tool.

MARKETING AND ADVERTISING

Marketing and advertising are related concepts but have distinct roles and purposes within a business's overall strategy. Marketing utilizes various methods, techniques, and activities to understand customer needs and wants and create offerings that deliver value to target customers. Advertising specifically focuses on promotional communication to reach and influence target audiences. Marketing takes a more comprehensive approach, considering all aspects of the customer journey, while advertising is a specific tool used within the marketing framework to promote products, services, or brands.

Marketing includes a range of activities, including market research, pricing, distribution, advertising, sales, and customer relationship management, as well as contributions to product development. These activities are designed to attract, acquire, retain, and satisfy customers by offering products or services that meet their needs and desires. It involves identifying target markets, understanding customer preferences, analyzing competition, and developing effective communication and promotional strategies to reach and influence customers.

While building our dream at RE/MAX, I knew that creating an overwhelming market presence would benefit our entire team of agents and franchisees. The more RE/MAX agents there were in a given area, the more people would know our company. Every For Sale sign, ad, promotional brochure, billboard, and sponsored community event was an advertisement for all the agents in our system. Therefore, the more RE/MAX agents and franchises there were, the more everyone benefitted. I called this approach Premiere Market Presence, or PMP. There were five elements that made up PMP: market share, brand awareness, customer satisfaction, quality agents, and community service. This was our pathway to market dominance.

Marketing isn't limited to traditional advertising methods. In today's digital age, it also includes online marketing, social media marketing, content marketing, email marketing, search engine optimization (SEO), and various other digital channels and strategies. The goal is to create a strong brand presence, establish a competitive edge, and build long-term relationships with customers, which leads to increased sales and business growth.

Without customers and sales, you don't have a company. Virtually every company is selling something to somebody. If you're H&R Block, you're selling tax preparation services. If you're a real estate franchise, you're selling houses or commercial property. If you're a technology company like Apple, you're selling technological tools or goods. If you're a restaurant, you're selling food. But no matter what industry you're in, never forget you're also selling yourself. Most investors invest in people over a concept. They're betting that you're the reason a company will succeed. Even if you have the best product or service in the market and are offering it at a competitive price, it won't matter much if you can't sell it. It's also important to mention that when you're marketing a product, service, or business, you're really selling the experience. If you're selling a Ferrari, one approach is to point out the facts—this is how fast it goes, this is how much it costs, this is how rare it is, and so on. But when you sell facts, you're overlooking emotion. The reality is that all people buy on emotion and then justify that decision with facts, so when a prospective buyer drives a Ferrari and hears the rumble of the engine, feels its power and speed, and gets excited to be sitting in the driver's seat, they're connecting to what they want over what they need. Everything we do, from buying a house to falling in love, is based on emotion, and great marketing recognizes this truth.

When it comes to marketing, a lot of terms get thrown around that have similar but very different meanings based on context. For the purposes of this chapter, when I talk about marketing, I'm going to focus on three aspects:

Marketing Your Business
Marketing Your Concept, Product, or Service
Marketing Yourself

It doesn't matter what type of business you're in; if you want to succeed, you must know who your customer is and how to reach them. Doing this requires a deep understanding of customer behavior, market trends, and competitive landscapes. It involves conducting market research, analyzing data, and applying consumer insight to develop tailored marketing strategies that resonate with a specific audience. By employing innovative and targeted marketing techniques, businesses can effectively communicate the value of their products or services, differentiate themselves from competitors, and drive customer engagement and loyalty.

Of course, there are many ways to reach your customer, but they all entail exploring, creating, and delivering value to meet the needs of a target market. The product or service itself is irrelevant; how you present it and promote it is everything.

My wife and I own several different entities, some of which are non-franchise companies, including Sanctuary Golf Course and a part of LifeSpot, a crisis mitigation system that uses an app to speed response time and improve communication during an emergency. Another company we own and are extremely proud of is Maroon Fire Arabians.

In the summer of 1988, Steve Woolley, one of our vice presidents, invited Gail and me to his home for a barbeque. The house was in a rural area, so Steve could keep his beautiful Arabian mare there. The horse pranced around, snorted, jumped, kicked, and was full of energy. Gail and I loved her spirit. We sipped a few cocktails and watched the sunset, and I noticed that the mare calmed down. The darker it got, the quieter she became. I remember thinking, *This is such a majestic animal. Wouldn't it be fun to own one like that?*

Steve and I got to talking that night, and he told me about the Tom Chauncey Arabian horse sale in Scottsdale, Arizona, which happened every February. He suggested we go down to Phoenix, play a little golf, and see the horses.

I thought Steve's suggestion was outstanding, and at the very least the trip would be an ideal escape from the real estate business for Gail and me. Steve had given me a copy of *Arabian Horse*

Magazine to look through, and I was fascinated. Before going to Scottsdale, I began reading books and subscribing to every publication I could find that focused on these swift and elegant creatures. The periodicals were thick and glossy and filled with beautiful photos of horses that were for sale and breeding. I was amazed by the number of advertisers in their pages. From what I could tell, this was one hell of a business to be in—until the tax rules were revised in 1986, that is. That's when Congress changed the tax law so you could no longer take passive losses on a business you weren't actively involved in. Before that change, syndications of cattle and horses were huge write-offs, just like syndications of rental properties. People could buy a fractional ownership in a stallion for $10 million, take their share of that investment, and depreciate it over three years, giving them a considerable tax benefit. When the government cracked down on that practice, horse prices tumbled.

For some reason, the center of the Arabian horse business was Scottsdale. About twenty major breeders had done exceptionally well there, until the business tanked and most of them eventually went bankrupt. But they were sitting on so much desirable land that the losses they suffered on their horse businesses were made up by the sale of their ranch land to real estate developers.

In February 1989, Gail and I joined Steve and his wife at the Arabian horse sale in Scottsdale, and it was thrilling. We were first-time bidders, full of anticipation and enthusiasm about becoming horse owners. There were eleven auctions over seven days, and at the time, these auctions were pretty fancy. The sellers turned barns and stables into beautiful dining rooms, complete with white tablecloths, fine china, and crystal glasses. They brought in high-profile entertainment to ensure that everyone had a good time. The more expensive the horses were at auction, the nicer the event. Gail and I dabbled in our newfound passion, buying two relatively inexpensive horses at the Legend Sale.

Back then the market was still favorable to the sellers, but as soon as it started going down, Arabians became even more of a passion for us. As with everything I get involved in, I tried to figure out the best way to educate myself. I wanted to know all I could about the horses, the trainers, and the breeders. I especially wanted to know who was honorable and who wasn't. I particularly focused on what to look for in an Arabian horse and what to avoid. Everyone in the business knew who was naughty and who was nice, and they didn't hold that information back. Plenty of trainers would rave about the horses they worked with, failing to mention that they were getting a 15 percent commission on the sale if you bought them. Some were pretty seedy, while others had a stellar reputation.

As I searched for trainers who could teach me the business, one name repeatedly came up: Sheila Varian of Varian Arabians. Sheila was ten or so years older than me and 100 percent a cowgirl. In fact, she was inducted into the Cowgirl Hall of Fame. (Yup, there is such a thing!) When Sheila was sixteen years old, she and her mother went to Poland, bought some breeding horses, and imported them back to the United States. The die was cast after that. Sheila had three big successes in a row, training a trio of very famous and highly productive stallions that all won national championships in the performance arena.

There are two types of Arabians. The first are Halter Arabians, which are kind of skinny. I like to think of them as supermodels walking a runway. They're sleek, pretty, and sexy, and they move with such grace and gusto. There's no muscle to them at all. The second type of Arabians are Performance Arabians, and as the name indicates, they're athletic, high-performance horses. They're the heavier of the two types, but they're all muscle. They have to be strong to meet the demands their riders place on them. Those were the horses I had my eye on.

After a few months of hearing about Sheila, I finally met up with her at the Scottsdale horse sale. I introduced myself and explained that I was trying to get started as a breeder. I mentioned that she'd been recommended by a dozen people and asked if she would show me the ropes.

Fortunately, she agreed, and Gail and I met her time after time at various horse shows, bought her dinner whenever her schedule allowed, and took extensive notes every time she spoke. We must have written two hundred single-spaced pages of notes about judging horses, breeding horses, selecting mares, and so on. Sheila was a wealth of knowledge, and I was her diligent student. She was a true horse trader. You never got a bargain from her; you either paid top dollar or she didn't deal with you. She had the ultimate reputation in the business, and she knew it. But we eventually became close friends, and I did end up buying some horses from her over the years.

I also spoke with others I met along the way, including Don DeLongpré, Gordon Potts, and Richard Petty (not the race-car driver), who graciously advised us and would eventually sell us many good horses. Gordon Potts impressed upon me the importance of learning about and understanding a stallion's strengths and what he was capable of as a sire. Once I knew those strengths, I could gather the mares and secondary stallions that complemented my stallion physically, mentally, and in breeding. While it sounds simple, it isn't. There are so many nuances to becoming a world-class breeder, and I had a lot to absorb.

Being so new to horse breeding, I had no idea what I was doing. Asking just anyone for advice is stupid. If you want to figure out how to get rich, you don't ask someone who's poor; you ask someone who has gotten extremely wealthy. Similarly, if you want to know how to excel in sports, don't ask someone who has never made it to the pros; go to the number one ballplayer you can find and say, "Can you give me some tips?"

The *Think and Grow Rich* formula I read about many years ago was the exact strategy I used when I got into horse breeding. I identified my goals and what I aimed to accomplish. I was specific, knowing I wanted to focus on performance horses. I studied them, found my mastermind group, and learned from each member of that group. Then I stuck to my plan.

I committed to learning as much about breeding Arabians as possible while running RE/MAX and the other businesses I owned. I spent seven or eight hundred hours—and maybe more—studying horses during that first year. I attended horse shows that lasted three or four days, from 7:00 a.m. to 10:00 p.m. every day. Between shows, I spent time in the stables.

Horse shows are elaborate operations. The trainers arrive with truckloads full of stuff. They create a meeting space in front of their temporary stables, hang beautiful drapery, lay down sawdust, and offer a variety of snacks, sodas, and wine. If you want to walk through the stalls, you can; but if you want to see a specific horse, they'll bring it out in front of the stall, where everyone can ooh and ahh at the sight of it. Almost every trainer is an excellent, highly skilled show person. The most prominent trainers will bring thirty to forty horses to a show, and every time a horse wins a ribbon, it goes on the front of its stall. The more ribbons on display, the more business it attracts.

Gail and I returned to Scottsdale a year later to buy better and more expensive horses. And when we did, members of the horse trades started taking notice. When a reporter asked us about our plan, I explained that Gail and I were building a herd of foundation stock with the hope of establishing a major Arabian breeding farm in the future. That writer didn't think much of what I said, however; she practically shrugged us off as two more people coming into the industry with the same ambitions as many others had before, predicting that we'd be out of the business in a few short years.

There's nothing I enjoy more than a challenge, and that writer threw down the gauntlet. To be fair, it wasn't wrong of her to have doubts, because, in general, very few people have the perseverance, patience, and passion to make it in the business. While I didn't care much for her opinion, I never forgot what she said, and used her skepticism to fuel our achievements. As they say, success is the best revenge.

It's been said that becoming a good horse breeder takes a hundred years. Well, I didn't have a hundred years, but I had spent many years building a thriving company and knew that if we approached our Arabian horse business in a similar way, it couldn't fail. We assembled a group of trustworthy and knowledgeable professionals with years of experience in the industry to fast-track our goals. I didn't hesitate about committing; I just dove right in. By the late 1980s, I was seeking advisors I could trust and bringing them into our fold.

While Gail and I had been boarding our horses at various locations around the country, it became clear that we should consolidate our operation in one central place. Sheila introduced us to Tim and Marty Shea, two excellent horse managers and trainers with their own stables in St. Clair, Michigan. I bought a couple of horses at auction and shipped them to Tim and Marty to start training. In the meantime, I started looking for a stallion to breed. I must have looked at more than a hundred and still came up empty-handed. But I knew the bloodlines I wanted and wasn't going to compromise.

Sheila sent Tim a junior stallion named Afire Bey V to train and sell. As with all horses Sheila had a hand in, the letter V was incorporated into the name to signify Sheila's last name. The stallion was a handsome blood bay with impeccable breeding. The only problem with this horse was that he had shin splints. Theoretically, an operation could resolve that ailment, but it could also stop him from becoming a show horse. Even so, Gail and I flew to Michigan on a beautiful September day to meet him. I looked at his pedigree in a video, and it was magic. This was the most charismatic horse I'd ever seen. We instantly fell in love with him and bought him on the spot. We then sat down with Sheila and two or three of her people and asked, "How do we go about establishing a broodmare band around him?" I was looking for mares with the right pedigrees and physical attributes. We knew exactly what his strengths were: he was incredibly beautiful, with lots of motion, and had good size; he was nearly a park horse, which are elite performance horses. Our quest led us back to Sheila, who had the mares I wanted.

While at dinner one evening, I sat beside Sheila and said, "Why don't we cut to the chase? I want to buy three of your mares."

She turned me down flat.

I alluded to paying her more than top dollar, and she still said no, insisting she wouldn't sell them at any price.

They were Sheila's top mares and her foundation bloodstock. She had told me that good breeders don't sell their best horses until there's a proven daughter or son—or several—to replace them. I could see from the look on her face that she wasn't happy with my attempt to take that away from her. It was as if I'd offended her, and maybe I did. But it wasn't my intention.

We ended up buying eighteen mares from other breeders to breed with Afire Bey V. I knew it would be fantastic.

Now, this is when my years of marketing came in very handy. Nobody was buying ads to sell horses at the time, because the business had drastically changed. The glossy magazines I'd read a year earlier were all in financial trouble. So, I purchased an ad on the back cover of *Arabian Horse World*, one of the best magazines in the industry. The ad would run forever—or at least for as long as I wanted it to run. No matter how much they kept raising the price for that space, it was mine. In fact, I kept that back page for twenty-plus years. And as Gail and I bought mares, we began to advertise that they had been bred to our stallion. Suddenly, people began to see this beautiful boy as something special. We sold nearly a hundred breedings that year. When we started selling, we charged around $3,000 to breed. Eventually, we got between $7,500 and $10,000. Over his lifetime, Afire

Bey V ended up being the most successful sire in the Arabian breed, with nearly two thousand breeds before he was retired.

I quickly learned that most backyard breeders have one or two horses and little to no concept of how to breed them. They usually try to raise foals for their daughters or sons to ride in competition. Even so, everybody in the horse world has a dream. I sure did. In 1985, thirty thousand Arabian horses were born in the US, and among them was a national champion we would eventually raise. When people saw that, who do you think they wanted to breed their horse? You guessed it—us.

Sheila was an excellent teacher. Eventually, we had four outstanding trainers and almost two hundred horses at one time. We've been with the Sheas for more than thirty years, and they've been exceptional to work with. We've let them make decisions and have trusted their judgment. They've worked hard every day, building our confidence and friendship. Together we've bred, marketed, and managed the greatest Arabian stallion to ever live—Afire Bey V. And we've written a remarkable success story for our follow-up breeding stallion, National Champion IXL Noble Express+, sire of more than one hundred national winners. We've worked as a team to build Maroon Fire Arabians into what it is today—the home of the finest Arabian English Pleasure Horses in the world.

Our passion turned into quite a business. We had a lot of help getting there, and, of course, it was the extraordinary horses that really made the magic happen. You can build a good business with a solid plan, top advisors, good management, and common sense; you can create clever, consistent promotions and advertising, spend the money, and do everything right—but you can't sell an empty box.

Today, more than thirty years after getting into breeding Arabian horses, we are arguably among the greatest Arabian horse breeders of the last hundred years. While many of our colleagues have given up and gotten out of the business, Gail and I haven't slowed down one bit. We're currently sending the fifth and sixth generations of Maroon Fire Arabian horses into competition and consistently bringing home National Champion rose blankets. In fact, we've become the leading breeders of champions at all the national horse shows.

CREATE A MARKETING PLAN

Whether you're in the business of breeding horses, selling real estate, feeding a hungry nation tasty sandwiches, or any other business of your own making, you'll need a marketing plan. A marketing plan is a strategic document that defines how you'll communicate with your customers and successfully promote your products or services. It's not just a list of things you want to accomplish; a good marketing plan defines who your buyers are, it establishes your product or service, and it identifies what makes you unique. It should also define the outcomes you're seeking. For instance, will your marketing develop a pipeline to repeat customers and generate leads to new ones? It should also explain the strategies you plan to implement to achieve those outcomes. Think of your marketing plan as a road map.

10 Types of Marketing Plans

1 Advertising

2 Branding

3 Content Marketing

4 Customer Acquisition

5 Direct Marketing

6 Public Relations

7 Social Media

8 Retention

9 Reputation Management

10 Crisis Management

If you're launching a business—any business—you must first figure out what unique qualities it has that will help it become successful. Ask yourself: What is my business's competitive advantage against every other player in the same market? How will I stand out? Define your target market, then do the essential research to understand its needs. This might entail user surveys, focus group interviews, and due diligence to determine specific metrics and demographics. It's important to know what other people think about your company, product, or service. Before writing your marketing plan, spend some time talking with employees, customers, shareholders, and colleagues to gauge what they think about your idea and how they feel about your company. This will provide you with a cache of valuable information that you can use in other areas of your business.

When conducting your research, create a list of who you believe your competitors are and how your company stacks up against them. Having a clear understanding of your competition is critical to your business. When we built a marketing plan for Daddy's Chicken Shack, by law we had to provide a list of all our major competitors in the food service chicken business, including Kentucky Fried Chicken, Zaxby's, Raising Cane, Chick-fil-A, Wingstop, and El Pollo Loco, just to name a few. This information is included in our Federal Disclosure Document. When analyzing your competition, do a web search and review their official sites and any news about them. If you want to see how your website compares to theirs, go to Semrush.com or Ahrefs.com to find out how they perform, how many keywords their site ranks for, how many visitors they attract each month, and their authority score. Look for similarities and differences between your metrics and theirs.

When you set out to write your marketing plan, having a clear understanding of your company's strengths and weaknesses (your internal situation) and the opportunities and threats that exist (your external situation) will help you create a visible path to get you where you want to go. This is often referred to as SWOT analysis. It's so important to be honest when you're gathering this information. There's no right or wrong answer—just the facts. These truths will help you form the basis of your marketing plan.

By now you know that I believe in setting goals and objectives and then creating a plan to meet them. The goals section of your marketing plan is strategic and should clearly lay out how you want your business to evolve. Create goals that are specific, measurable, attainable, relevant, and time bound. Your objectives are the tactical milestones you have to hit along the way to achieving your goals.

When creating a marketing strategy, the message you'll ultimately send depends on what you want the market to know about your company, your goods or services, and what you stand for. Your message should be strong enough to persuade a potential customer to buy your product or service. Your message should also relay what makes your company unique and why someone ought to do business with you over your competition. It can take time to find the right message. In today's digital world, you can A/B test your content on social media to see what resonates and why, giving you data that can drive your direction. Make sure to update this information regularly, as marketing goals can change with time. Having a plan allows you to prepare for the unexpected and establish a strong connection between your brand and your customers.

Once you've got all this information, it's time to execute. Your marketing plan should include the tactics you've chosen to use, such as writing blog posts; creating content for social media; generating a newsletter, brochures, flyers, and email blasts; running digital advertising, banner ads, traditional television ads, and print ads; conducting search engine optimization, publicity campaigns, telemarketing campaigns, promotions, contests, and surveys; exhibiting at trade shows; and hosting webinars. There are countless ways to deliver your message and marketing to your customer base, and these are just a few.

Ultimately, your budget will determine your path forward. Assess the cost of each channel you choose to pursue. You may opt to allocate funds to several different pathways or just a few. If your budget doesn't allow for hiring an expensive public relations firm or advertising agency, get creative. Leverage social media platforms to engage with your target audience. Create compelling content, conduct giveaways, and encourage user-generated content. Engage with followers by responding to comments and messages promptly. Collaborate with influencers or micro-influencers who align with your brand values and target audience. They can promote your products or services to their followers, helping you reach a wider audience in an authentic way. Develop high-quality content that provides value to your target audience. In addition to blog posts and articles, post videos, infographics, or podcasts. Share this content on your website, social media platforms, and relevant online communities to establish thought leadership and drive traffic. Word-of-mouth marketing can be a powerful tool in spreading the news about your business, so encourage your existing customers to refer your business to their friends and family by offering incentives or discounts. Support local events, charities, or community initiatives. Sponsor a local sports team or participate in local trade shows or fairs. This can increase your brand visibility within your target community and demonstrate your commitment to your home area. Build an email list of interested prospects and existing customers and regularly conduct outreach to them with valuable content, exclusive offers, or personalized recommendations. Email marketing is cost-effective and allows you to nurture relationships with your audience over time. Encourage your customers to create and share content related to your brand in the form of testimonials, reviews, photos, or videos. Repost and share user-generated content on your social media platforms to showcase customer satisfaction and build social proof. Participate in online communities, industry forums, and relevant social media groups where your target audience hangs out. Provide valuable insights, answer questions, and establish yourself as an expert in your field. This can help build trust and credibility, driving organic interest in your business. And don't forget to develop a rewards program to encourage repeat business. When a company sells something once, it's a sale—but if that customer loves something so much that they buy it again, it's a brand.

Remember, creativity and a deep understanding of your target audience are key to making the most of your marketing strategy, especially if you're on a limited marketing budget. Focus on building meaningful connections, providing value, and leveraging the power of word-of-mouth and digital channels to maximize your marketing efforts.

10 Key Elements of a Marketing Plan

1. Executive Summary
2. Situation Analysis
3. Target Market Definition
4. Marketing Objectives

5 Marketing Strategies

6 Marketing Tactics and Channels

7 Budget Allocation

8 Implementation Plan

9 Measurement and Evaluation Tools

10 Process for Refining Future Marketing Plans

A marketing plan should be dynamic and adaptable, so continuously monitor the effectiveness of your strategies and adjust your approach as necessary to achieve your marketing objectives and drive business growth.

PLAYING WITH YOUR MARKETING FUNNEL

In business, a funnel refers to the process that potential customers go through as they move from being aware of a product or service to becoming a paying customer. The term "funnel" is used because, at each stage, the number of potential customers typically decreases, resembling the shape of a funnel.

At the top of the funnel, potential customers become aware of a product or service through various marketing channels such as advertisements, social media, content marketing, or word-of-mouth. The goal of the marketing at this juncture is to capture the attention of a wide audience and generate initial interest. At this point, customers may actively seek more information, compare options, read reviews, or engage with the brand's content. The marketing then is intended to nurture their interest and provide valuable information to help them evaluate the offering. While potential customers are deliberating over whether the product or service meets their needs, they might request demos, ask for quotes, or seek additional information to help them make informed decisions. The marketing focuses on addressing their concerns, providing clear benefits, and establishing trust to influence their decision in favor of the offering.

In the final stage, potential customers become paying customers by making a purchase, signing up for a subscription, or booking a service. The marketing in this instance is meant to facilitate a smooth and seamless experience, removing any barriers or obstacles that may hinder the purchase.

The funnel concept may vary depending on the industry, business model, and specific marketing and sales strategies employed. Some funnels may include additional stages or variations to accommodate the unique characteristics of a particular business. If you understand the funnel dynamic, you'll be able to optimize each stage of the customer journey, identify potential areas of improvement, and implement effective marketing and sales tactics to guide potential customers through the sale, ultimately increasing the conversion rate and revenue for the business.

I can't recall where I learned the concept of playing with your funnel—a.k.a., experimenting with what works best at each stage of marketing—but over the ten years Gail and I did it, it became one of the hallmarks of our success. If you worked at RE/MAX, you were taught this concept, because I use this model in all my businesses. One of the things it illustrates well is the value of size. For example, if we had sixty thousand agents at RE/MAX, we wouldn't even be able to cover the annual cost of doing business, which might include salary and commissions, benefits, buildings, utilities, and marketing—but if we boosted that number to one hundred forty thousand agents, our marketing funnel would open up so dramatically that we'd be able to cover those costs and make a 50 percent margin. Remember, every For Sale sign, ad, promotional brochure, billboard, and sponsored community event was an advertisement for all the agents in our system, so the more agents we had, the more brand awareness we generated.

Let's say you publish a newsletter. Hypothetically, the overhead might include twenty to thirty writers and researchers, designers, and office personnel. If you charge $300 for an annual electronic subscription, you would need 1,700 customers to break even. You've got an incremental profit of almost $300 pretax for every person over that 1,700 who subscribes to your newsletter. When you have fifty thousand subscribers, your incremental profits go up. Membership businesses—in which customers sign up for an annual subscription—are a revolving letter of credit to make money.

The following graph indicates how this works:

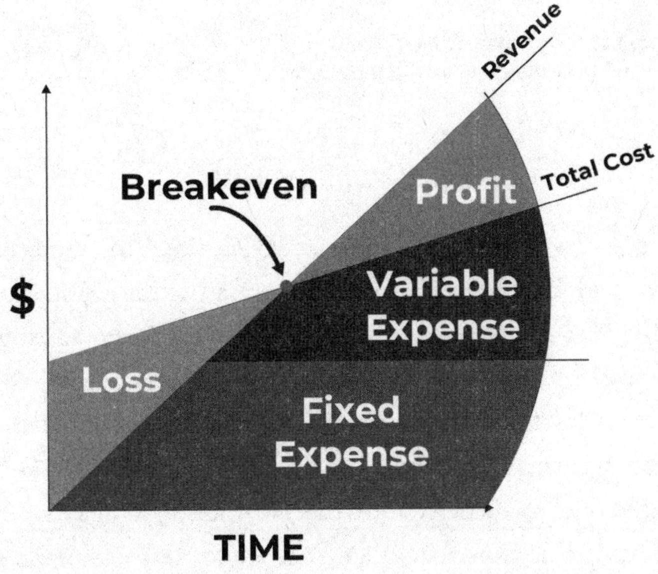

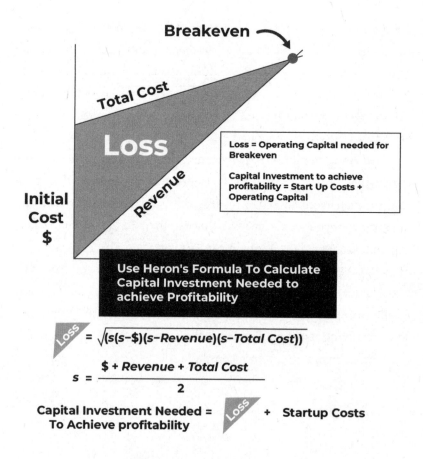

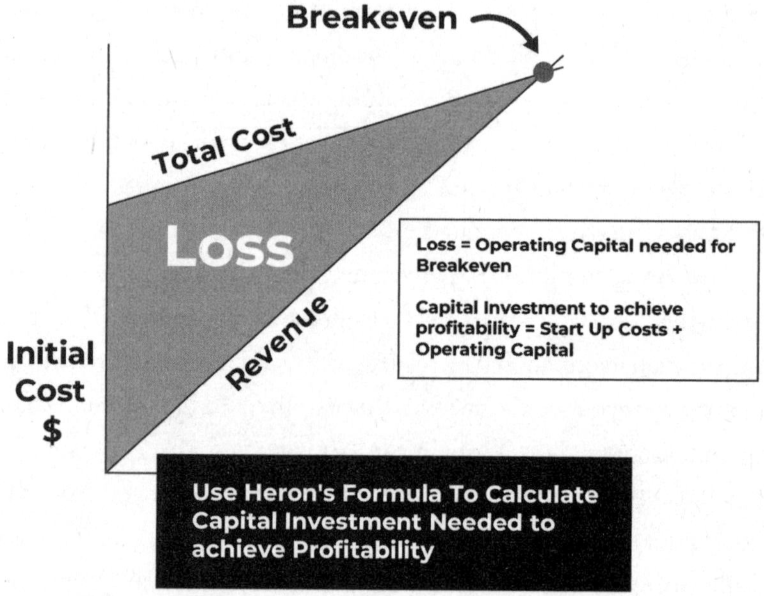

$$\text{Loss} = \sqrt{(s(s-\$)(s-\textit{Revenue})(s-\textit{Total Cost}))}$$

$$s = \frac{\$ + \textit{Revenue} + \textit{Total Cost}}{2}$$

Capital Investment Needed = Loss + Startup Costs
To Achieve profitability

THE POWER OF MORE

We had a very simple philosophy at RE/MAX: The more market share we had, the higher the average earnings of the agents. Around our fifth year in business, many brokers began complaining that there were too many offices, while agents complained that there were too many agents. It took a long time to convince them they were competing with all the agents in the market anyway, and they were better off if 10 percent of the For Sale signs out there were RE/MAX signs. To substantiate this, we looked at our three best regions and analyzed the average number of transactions per agent in those areas for the prior year, not just against the transactions for

RE/MAX agents but against those for *all* agents. We found that we had the most agents and the greatest market share, and despite how competitive this market was, the average earnings and average number of transactions per agent were the highest in the whole company.

At the same time, we had three other regions that weren't doing well. When we looked at them closely, we found that we didn't have very much market penetration in those regions. In Denver, one of the regions with the greatest number of transactions, we had three thousand agents, whereas in Las Vegas, one of the regions with the lowest number of transactions, we had only twenty-five agents. Our test study certainly proved that the power of more worked to build brand awareness *and* sales. As I've always said, most people want to be with the biggest company in town. Why? It comes with competitive advantages that a small company can't provide.

At our Sanctuary Golf Course, we have a clubhouse that sells clothing, hats, balls, and other branded items. But, for reasons I'll explain shortly, there are no members at this club other than Gail and me. Suffice it to say for now that it's an event space, not a typical golf club.

One day I decided I wanted a new set of clubs. Our golf pro said, "Well, why don't you go down to Golfsmith?"

I was surprised by his statement, because I'd thought I would be able to buy them from Sanctuary cheaper. But the pro explained that large retailers sell so much volume all across the country that they're able to sell their clubs for less than we can buy them wholesale. This is called volume purchasing. The cost to the manufacturer of producing a large retailer's order is amortized over a greater number of units, thereby reducing the price they charge the retailer and, in turn, the price the retailer charges the consumer. In the food industry, McDonald's is a great example of a volume purchaser. Did you know that they have agricultural contracts enabling them to buy a farmer's entire potato crop five years in advance? They do this to ensure that they never run out of French fries. They're buying in such bulk that they're getting the very best price they can possibly get. Those savings are passed on to the franchisee, who passes them on to you.

It's the same thing when it comes to advertising. One hamburger joint doesn't have much money to spend on advertising, but when ten thousand McDonald's locations spend 10 percent of their gross on various marketing and advertising campaigns, everybody knows the McDonald's name. They have local campaigns that allow all the McDonald's franchisees in a certain geographic location to participate in advertising buys, and they also have larger national buys they can participate in as well. The national buys always get better placement during TV programs—usually in the middle of the show—which means there are more eyeballs on them. The regional buys are typically at the end of the program or in between programs. When you understand this dynamic, you can see that more really is better.

THE IMPORTANCE OF CREATING A RECOGNIZABLE BRAND

I've got a lot of stories about creating success, and quite a few about my failures too. The failures are where I learned most of my greatest lessons. By now, you know that the first three years of RE/MAX were a total disaster. The headwinds were incredibly strong. And yet, that's when I discovered the value of never quitting. You won't always get things right out of the gate, and that's okay; don't let it get you down. Just keep going.

An interesting aspect of human nature is that people tend to resent those who win at everything. That's why some people mock the rock stars in their field when they fall. They love to hate the success of others, and enjoy watching them falter even more. This is true in both business life and personal life—whether they're getting a divorce, experiencing bankruptcy, have gotten a DUI, or are going to jail for anything from tax evasion to buying their kid's way into college. People relate more to someone who admits that they've made mistakes than to someone who can't or won't.

I owned a NASCAR racetrack in Georgia at one point. While I ran it successfully, I couldn't make it profitable. Why? The track was located in a dry county. If we couldn't earn revenue from alcohol, there would be no profit. Because the cost of beer is so low, the profit in selling it is high, which made it critical to our success. People buy four or five beers during a race, but only one or two Coca-Colas.

Another business we were involved in was drilling oil wells. We went into that venture with zero experience but managed to make it a financial success before selling it for a handsome sum. I also built houses and commercial buildings, bred Arabian horses, built a golf course in Colorado, and helped launch a plethora of businesses by investing in founders I believed in. One thing I learned from each and every one of those businesses was the value of creating a brand. RE/MAX never underestimated the power of branding. But a brand is more than just a logo or a name; it represents the overall perception and reputation of a company, product, service, or individual in the minds of customers and the market. A brand encompasses the unique identity, values, personality, and promises associated with a particular entity, and as such, a strong brand is vital for several reasons.

In a competitive marketplace, a strong brand helps your business stand out from the competition. It creates recognition and unique positioning, distinguishing you and making it easier for customers to choose your products or services over alternatives. Repeat customers and brand advocates become valuable assets for your business. There's simply no greater compliment you can receive than a referral. When customers are familiar with your brand and have positive experiences with it, they're more likely to develop trust and loyalty. Trust is particularly important when entering new markets or introducing new products and services.

A compelling brand story and a strong company culture foster employee engagement, pride, and a sense of belonging. If you cultivate this atmosphere, employees become brand ambassadors who embody and promote the values and vision of the brand.

Building a strong brand requires consistent communication, delivering on promises, and maintaining a positive brand experience. It involves understanding and aligning with the needs and desires of the target audience while staying true to the company's identity and values. A well-established brand can ultimately contribute to the success and growth of a business or individual.

BRANDING RE/MAX

When we first launched RE/MAX, the fact that we had no brand identity yet, and consequently no brand recognition, posed constant challenges for our brokers, especially when it came to recruitment. Aside from those within the organization, nobody had heard of us. Agents from other firms weren't familiar with our company, and our potential customers weren't either. Every region was experiencing the same identity crisis. Until we could figure out how to create awareness, it would continue to be an uphill battle for our agents.

We made it a point to get the regional directors together four times a year to talk about their experiences, ideas, challenges, and possible solutions. Those meetings also helped each region compare where they were in relation to one another's progress. At one of those meetings, the idea of creating an advertising committee was raised. At the time, we had no group advertising, mainly because we didn't have the money, but our biggest brokers were vocal about the need for it. Bill Echols and Darrel Stillwell, regional co-owners in New Mexico, were appointed chairs of the committee, as they'd spent several years in radio and had the most experience in the advertising arena.

It was such a pressing issue that by the next meeting, advertising was our top priority. Our competitors were launching emotionally engaging campaigns, and they were good. Their messaging conveyed the notion that real estate was all about kids, neighborhoods, families, *and* one's "neighborhood professional" real estate agent. We were desperate to find a way to reach our clients and make RE/MAX a household name. We contemplated the most effective ways to do this. Slogans? Feelings? Logos?

I'll be honest: I love a good logo. And when you have one, people remember it. Think about Nike, Apple, McDonald's, Starbucks, Google, Disney, Uber . . . all these companies have a logo you know. When you see that image, you immediately connect it with their name. That's the instant recognition we sought.

Bill Echols knew that if we tried to force the concept, we wouldn't be putting our best foot forward. We needed time and space to think about it and let the ideas come to us. He was convinced that our logo was right in front of us; we just hadn't seen it yet.

A week later, Echols was driving in New Mexico when he came upon four hot-air balloons in the sky. Seeing hot-air balloons wasn't that unusual in New Mexico—but seeing them while contemplating ways to visually connect people and real estate made this a seminal moment in our company history.

Later that afternoon, Echols was in his office when Tommy Thomson, his office manager, asked if they could meet. He had an idea. His neighbor was a district representative for Kodak and a sport balloon pilot. He had sold his balloon and was looking to buy another one, and wanted Tommy to partner with him. Although Tommy was intrigued by the idea, it wasn't his thing. However, he thought Echols and Darrel Stillwell might be interested. He wondered if there was a possible advertising opportunity in it.

Without a pause, Echols said, "Yes, we'll do it." It was serendipitous and aligned with what Echols had been thinking earlier in the day. Stillwell wasn't so sure, however. He questioned Echols, who insisted that this was precisely what we'd been looking for: a RE/MAX hot-air balloon, complete with our red, white, and blue colors, hovering in the blue sky. It was better than a banner; it was an entire balloon bearing the RE/MAX name. They would debut the balloon at the annual hot-air balloon fiesta in Albuquerque. In 1997, it was still a relatively small event—certainly not the popular festival it is today, but still a rather memorable way to unveil our balloon.

I'm a big believer in fate, and often, we get exactly what we need, when we need it. As I like to say, the universe unfolds exactly as it should. And this time, the universe had delivered not one but two people who saw the same thing that day, albeit in different ways.

They loved the idea of having a company balloon, even if they weren't sure what to do with it, where to put it, how to care for it, or how much it would cost. Instead of buying the balloon, they decided to lease it—but there was one glitch they hadn't anticipated. The actual RE/MAX logo had red letters with a blue slash. The balloon designer explained that red letters on a white background wouldn't show up in the sky, so Echols told him to reverse the colors.

They finished the balloon just one day before the opening of the fiesta. Tommy's neighbor was the pilot, and Tommy filmed the launch and flight. Their idea was to edit the footage and bring it to the regional owners' meeting in Chicago the following weekend, and that's where Echols first approached me with his idea. He wanted to show the reel to the group. I was interested in hearing his thoughts, but I also had a lot of other pressing matters to attend to, so I suggested we take a look at his film after our break, if we had time. I wasn't terribly excited, but I reluctantly agreed.

When they turned on the projector, there it was—an eight- or nine-story-tall red, white, and blue RE/MAX balloon in a wide-open field filled with other hot-air balloons. Everyone in the room thought it was fabulous. Everyone, that is, except me. I didn't like it at all. The name was printed in the wrong colors, and I didn't understand what balloons had to do with the real estate business. The reversal of red and blue on the letters bothered me—a lot. I was incredibly protective of our brand and felt that swapping those colors was wrong. I didn't care why it was done; to me, it felt like a mistake. After I voiced my concerns, the group agreed. I told Echols and Stillwell that they could do whatever they wanted in their region, but we would use the colors as they were originally set everywhere else.

I was unhappy and decided to take a few people to the hotel bar during our break. While we were sitting there nursing cocktails, I looked up at the television and noticed that damned RE/MAX balloon on the screen. I didn't understand how that could have happened. I hadn't approved it. I asked the bartender what he was watching. He told me it was *The Dinah Shore Show*. She was broadcasting from the balloon fiesta in New Mexico. The bartender said that every time they went to a commercial, they showed the RE/MAX balloon.

Hmm.

Interesting.

We gathered up the rest of the regional leaders to hold a spontaneous vote on whether the balloon should become the official logo of RE/MAX, and if the colors should be reversed.

The group unanimously declined.

Echols and Stillwell returned to New Mexico feeling defeated, yet they didn't give up hope. They knew their gut instinct was right. It might take some time, but they both felt they could turn everyone around, including me. So they went to work in the hope of persuading us. They took the president of the board of Realtors for a balloon ride. They took agents, VIPs, and the media too. A RE/MAX agent even got married in the balloon. One thing was becoming very clear: The balloon always drew a large crowd. It had become a community attraction, and as a result, our organization was becoming more recognizable to the people who came to see it.

I began to wonder, *Is the balloon becoming synonymous with our company? And is the exposure somehow working?* It was getting hard to ignore the obvious, except for one thing: We needed a slogan to make it work. Echols felt that way too. He had solicited help from his team of brokers to work the next annual balloon fiesta and wanted to have jackets made for them to wear at the event. He knew they needed something more than the RE/MAX logo. Eventually, he came up with "Above the Crowd." He was consistently recruiting the best agents to join his team, so he loved the idea of sending a message that we were tops in our field, especially regarding our commission structure. It just clicked. And soon people were talking about us, how much they liked working with us, how much fun they were having, and how successful they were becoming. In the process, we as a company shifted our brand from being the place to work for 100 percent commission to being a fun and growing company where people enjoyed working. That minor alteration in perception changed everything for us.

Once other regions saw how successful Echols, Stillwell, and their team were at utilizing the balloon, they followed suit. A year later, our corporate region in Colorado got on board too. Their dedication and persistence persuaded me. Here's what I came to understand: Although we were becoming the top firm in the region, we still had visibility issues. If I embraced this concept, it could help us grow and become more recognized.

That's when we figured out that we needed to be on television. The Colorado region pooled its resources, and after a year of contributing fifty dollars a month, they had an advertising budget of $180,000. Gail and I connected with an outside firm who told us we'd have to spend about $150,000 for an effective commercial. However, that didn't include the budget to buy the space and time to run the ad. If we were going to do this, the spot had to be good. It had to deliver a powerful message. As we brainstormed ideas, someone suggested that since I was a pilot, I should take a cameraperson up in a helicopter to get some footage of our branded hot-air balloon from every vantage point in the sky. We could then use that footage with a voice-over that said, "RE/MAX: Above the Crowd."

The image had to be clean, with nothing identifiable in the background—no mountains or terrain. We wanted our teams all over the country to benefit from the ad regardless of where they lived. It took a couple of hours to get what we wanted, but we finally got the "money shot." We cut the commercial and ran an eight-week campaign that cost us every penny we had raised and budgeted. It aired just in time for our annual survey of consumers in Colorado. When the numbers came back, they told the entire story: 66 percent of the people who were polled could identify our corporate symbol as a red, white, and blue balloon. A little more than one-third knew the slogan. The research consultant we worked with was blown away by these numbers. In all his years of advertising, he had never seen anything with a more significant impact. It was hard to argue with those findings, so I gave the go-ahead to utilize the balloon as our official company logo. Suddenly, it was everywhere—on signs, business cards, stationery, you name it—from that day forward.

While I'd strongly resisted the idea of the balloon initially, I always understood the power of branding. It's what builds market presence and global recognition. And, in our case, it also accomplished something else: It built momentum for our agents, something they wanted and needed, especially in the early days. It was also fun—it literally lifted people's spirits. We did everything we could to support them, including allowing them to do their own advertising. If it weren't for Echols's and Stillwell's ingenuity, we might not have discovered the logo that put us on the map. Once we had our colors and symbols, they permeated everything we did going forward.

WHEN RE/MAX AND I GOT INTO THE RACE

In the mid-1990s, RE/MAX was one of the five largest customers of the Marriott hotel chain. One day, I received a call from Bill Marriott. He wanted to see if I would be interested in being part of an outing for their best customers. The experience he planned for us included a couple of days of high-performance driving at the Bondurant Racing School in Phoenix, Arizona. Founded in 1968, Bondurant is considered the premier driver training school for anyone seeking a winning edge behind the wheel, whether they're a professional race car driver or someone just looking to be more proficient in the driver's seat. The track is very safe, with run-off areas and no place to crash your car while you're going one hundred miles per hour. There are no concrete barriers either—just gravel between the track and anything that could possibly hurt you. If you slide off the track, the gravel stops you and keeps you safe. I didn't hesitate to say yes. I've always had a great love for adventure, especially adventure that involves high speeds.

On day one, they put us in a hopped-up Mustang. That was fun and an excellent place to start, but I yearned for something a little more exotic—and, yes, faster. On day two, they put us in open-wheel cars, known as Formula Vs, which are similar to the cars you see in Indy racing. That was a little more like it!

We drove on a well-put-together road course, and as I made my way around the twists and turns of the track, it felt like I was flying. All the instructors were full-time NASCAR drivers who drove mostly in the Winston West Series, the Busch Series, and the Feather-Light series, but not the big races like Daytona. They were drivers who were just trying to make a living, doing something they loved until they could someday get a ride, meaning sponsorship.

They were great instructors, ensuring that we learned as much as possible about safety and performance. They taught us what to do if we spun out, including how to drive out of the spin, where to look, and how to plan for where we wanted to go from there.

By the end of the first day, I matched the full-time drivers' lap times. By the second day, I was hooked. I was already a fan of NASCAR, having attended races over the years, but I'd never given much thought to becoming a professional driver. Sure, I'd developed a passion for driving the sports cars I owned, including Ferraris and Porsches, fast and hard, but up until Bondurant, my only experience with racing had been relegated to the streets.

When I returned home, I began thinking, *I'm not too old to go have a ball. This could be fun*, though there were many who disagreed with that line of thought. As it happened, a vice president at RE/MAX had experience helping out on various drag racing teams, so he understood motorsports. I approached him with the idea of racing at NASCAR, and he was immediately in.

We needed a few late-model cars to drive at our local track. One of the best manufacturers was in Hueytown, Alabama, so we took a trip down there, bought two cars, and were off and running. As they were building the cars to spec, we returned to Denver so I could start putting together my team. I needed people who knew tires and engines, and I needed a pit crew. I had no real experience, so I went to those who did.

While waiting for the cars, I got involved with a couple of racing schools and went to Florida to practice during the winter months. I rented short tracks, which are about half a mile long, to get in some track time, and hired instructors. I ran two hundred to three hundred laps a day, mostly on weekends. I'd be back in Denver to run RE/MAX by late Sunday night or early Monday morning.

One weekend, I approached Roger Avants, a seasoned champion who'd won many races in the super-late-model, top-of-the-line cars that can go 120–200 mph, depending on the length of the track. The longer the track the faster the speed. I asked Roger if he would spend an hour or so with me and give me some pointers. In return, I offered to buy him dinner.

He looked somewhat surprised by my offer. "Well, you know, Dave, you're a little long in the tooth for this game. These cars are a handful and have almost seven hundred horsepower. It's very dangerous, so perhaps you'll consider starting with something smaller. How about bunker cars? Give that a year or two to gain some experience," he suggested.

While he might have been giving me what he thought was solid advice, one thing he said rang very true to me. "Roger, you're right. I am a little bit older and don't have all the time left in the world." I thought my reasoning would get him to say yes, but it didn't. He declined to help, saying he didn't have the time, so I went to another guy who told me much the same thing, reiterating that I was too old and was likely to kill myself driving one of those cars. Within a year, I was beating that guy at every race. When he finally ran out of money, he decided to race motorcycles.

The third person I talked to for advice was John Metcalf. John had been racing for thirty years. He was two or three years younger than me, so he didn't question my age like the others. He was a grizzled veteran of racing, and I liked that. John heard me out, understood what I wanted to do, and said he'd help me if he could.

"Good. Let me take you to dinner," I said. We arranged a night out, where I listened while he talked about all kinds of things having to do with racing, cars, teams, and such. That was the start of a very long and interesting friendship.

When my first season started, I took all my practice runs on a track by myself, not on a short, three-eighths-mile track with forty other cars racing side by side. I even qualified on a track by myself—I was a medium qualifier out of the fifty or sixty other cars that tried independently. But once they waved the flag on race day, holy crap! Nothing I'd experienced during practice or qualifications felt anything like what I was experiencing then, driving among forty cars that were all banging and bumping into one another. Much to my surprise, there was a lot of debris on the track. We eventually got up to speeds of 110 mph, and for the first few laps, I was in a daze. Drivers were spinning out, and the leaders were coming up fast behind me. I was getting passed by everyone. It was fantastic! Exhilarating! And totally bewildering.

This was the beginning of something I'd never expected. My first thought was, *Oh God, what have I done?* My second thought was, *I can't quit now.*

After that race, we rented the track and practiced, practiced, practiced, and then practiced some more so I could be better prepared for the next race and the one after that. By the middle of summer, we were finishing in the top fifteen out of sixty cars.

Most of the races I participated in during those early days lasted thirty-five or forty laps. The longer races were more like 125 laps. Those were grueling; I had to work my way up to them. I certainly had my eye on getting there, and wouldn't stop until I did.

In the meantime, I wrecked my car. Often. Thankfully, I usually raced with two cars in the garage so I would have a spare. One weekend—I believe it was the Fourth of July—I was racing in a two-day event. The first race was on the Friday night, and sure enough, I crashed. Unfortunately, I had wrecked my other car the week before, so I didn't have a backup. The whole team stayed up all night and rebuilt the entire thing. A couple of the other teams came over and helped us. Now, that's good sportsmanship. We were still painting the car and detailing it in the truck as we took it over to the track to qualify. Lo and behold, we did. And, as it turned out, I ran a pretty decent race.

After every race, John Metcalf tried to help me improve. I would fire off questions and he would answer them one by one. I wanted to know everything about cars, tracks, gear, you name it. I was relentless and eager, and John was so kind about my inquisitive ways. After one particular race, he said, "Dave, I've never seen a man try as hard as you. You know, I work for a different team. I don't own the car, but as far as I'm concerned, from now on, your team parks beside my team. And I'll try to skip between the two teams and help you get your car set up right."

Slowly, we began to get better. We qualified for the Championship. I was just outside the top ten, somewhere around eleventh or twelfth, but I was in the race—the only place I wanted to be. Before the main event, they ran what's called a trophy dash race, which is eight laps with the eight fastest cars. They try not to hit each other—if they do, they're out of the main race—but accidents sometimes happen. John Metcalf was one of those racers that day. I was parked on the apron, waiting to come onto the track, and my spotter radioed and told me Metcalf was out. He'd totaled his car—the only one he had. I remember thinking, *Damn. That's too bad.* And then my radio cut out. I couldn't hear my team trying to tell me I should give him my car. But I had the same thought, so I radioed my team to tell him to get out of his car and meet me at my trailer. "Dave, I don't have the money to pay you for your car if I wreck it," John said.

"I've wrecked my car every damn week since I started racing. Don't worry about it. Go win us a trophy. It would be nice to see RE/MAX win once this year!" I said with a grin and a slap on the back.

The NASCAR officials knew I was giving my car to him, and instead of allowing the usual three-lap warm-up, they stalled and gave the drivers eight laps, which gave John time to get into the car, put on his seatbelt, and drive onto the track. He had to start from the back because it was a new car that he hadn't used earlier to qualify for the race. One hundred twenty-five laps went by before he caught the leader with half a lap to go and won the race. The team was ecstatic! Up until then, we'd had an unqualified driver with a fairly qualified team. John, on the other hand, had brains and thirty years of experience. He knew how to race. That night, the track opened the pits and thousands of fans came down, lining up to take pictures with or get autographs from the drivers. By the end of the night, we had a few drinks in us, and I said, "John, I don't want to be a townie. I want to go on the road to all the tracks in the United States. I've got the financial ability. What if I build a race team? We could start with fifteen or twenty cars. We'll take two pit crews with us to every track, and we'll drive identical cars. You'll teach me over the next year, and I'll put you on salary. You'll be in charge of the whole team. And if we can make a go of it, then the next thing you know, we'll move up in these various brackets, get into more expensive cars, and see if we can get to the very top."

He was thrilled. Not only would he have his winnings, he'd be on salary, and he'd also have income from merchandise too.

I wanted to go to a couple of superspeedways, but NASCAR wouldn't give me a superspeedway license because I'd been licensed for only one summer on a three-eighths-mile track. The two superspeedway tracks in America, Daytona and Talladega, are 2.5 and 2.66 miles, respectively. To get my license, I needed to practice on those two tracks and take some of the drivers from the Cup teams with me. If they would sign off on racing against me, NASCAR would give me the license. I'm not saying strings were pulled, but I'm not denying it either.

One of the reasons I loved racing was the return RE/MAX got when it came to exposure. In addition to sponsoring my race team, RE/MAX also sponsored one of Rick Carelli's Craftsman super truck teams for three years. In the racing industry, there's a company called Joyce Julius that will track all the TV, radio, print, and other media mentions your race team gets. They do it for all the big teams; leading up to the Daytona 500, they review every article, interview, and advertisement to see if the drivers have been mentioned. Were the sponsor companies noted? Were there pictures or videos showing the race cars with the company logos on them? How many times did different reporters interview the drivers on television and/or radio? How much print coverage was there? How many actual minutes were the cars visible during a four-hour race? They proved that for every dollar put into advertising and sponsorship for the car and driver, you can get back ten to twenty dollars in exposure. That's at least a tenfold return on investment. Today, to field a top-ten NASCAR team in the Infinity series, there's a minimum sponsorship fee of $20 million paid to the car owner and a commitment of at least $20 million to television advertising. And if you want to be a title sponsor for any of the big races—meaning your name is added to the title of the series, as in the NASCAR Craftsman Tool Series, for example—that will set you back hundreds of thousands of dollars more. For some of the biggest races in the Cup series, with the top drivers, that title fee could go as high as $500,000 or more. RE/MAX sponsored the ARCA series and several other races for NASCAR around the country, and it was a good investment for us with a tremendous return. We paid a lot of money to be the title sponsor, but it was worth it because we got coverage—lots of it. And the more cars we drove in the race, the more exposure RE/MAX got. During a single race, if we had three cars, were the title sponsor, and also had the RE/MAX hot-air balloon present in front of one hundred thousand people in the stands and millions of viewers at home, the publicity was exponential. Looking back, we probably did better than a tenfold return on investment (ROI).

I was in a unique position as the oldest driver in the race and the owner of RE/MAX. At the time, we weren't a public company yet, so I could still make decisions without board approval. We could make all our races the center of attention. Not only did we sponsor some races but we often bought tickets in bulk so we could host VIPs. We always had a hospitality tent where we could entertain and network. We'd have at least one of our cars there, whether it was a previously wrecked vehicle or a show car. We would paint it to look brand-new, even if it wasn't suitable for racing anymore. People loved to get into the RE/MAX car and sit behind the wheel or have their picture taken next to it. We sometimes had more than a thousand RE/MAX customers and agents come to a single race to cheer us on.

In addition to the branding on the cars, we utilized the RE/MAX balloon whenever and wherever we were permitted to. For one race, I suggested to the television network that they film the start and finish of the event from our balloon. They thought that was the cat's meow. Of course, it was dependent on the weather and wind conditions, but thankfully we were able to pull it off, getting the shot right over the start/finish line directly above the cars. We were about even with the tower where they waved the green and checkered flags. This went over well with the crowd and the network, but the CEO of Kmart was none too happy. They were a big sponsor of the race, and he was throwing a fit as the cars were speeding down the track toward the green flag—and the RE/MAX balloon—to start the race. As a result, we got hundreds of thousands of dollars' worth of television coverage that day without having a car in the race. Now, that's what I like to think of as a great ROI.

WHAT RACING NASCAR TAUGHT ME ABOUT BUSINESS

At first glance, you might not think driving a race car has much to do with starting or running your own business, but it does. For us, launching a race team was the same as launching a new business from the ground up. The steps of building the team were no different than when we started RE/MAX. Okay, to be fair, I had a little more startup capital going into racing than I did real estate, and there's no doubt that gave me a decided advantage. Even so, when I started, I didn't know much about racing, let alone the business of racing—and it is a business.

I never lost sight of that fact, and in fact I approached it that way from the start. Everything I learned from one business I used to succeed in the other. I continuously worked to get better at my craft all the time. The first two years of racing felt more like an apprenticeship—lots of learning, rookie mistakes, and frustration. If you're the founder of a startup, you know exactly how that feels.

And, frankly, the first year was absolutely terrifying. I felt out of place, in over my head, and perhaps like I didn't belong on the track with the younger drivers. By year two, though, I started settling in and getting more comfortable. My fear had disappeared, and I began to lean into the experience. I also learned that everyone wrecks in racing, so I wasn't awfully concerned about getting hurt, but every time I totaled a car, it was like throwing away $180,000. Now, the average driver loses five or six cars a year; that's part of the cost of the sport, and I was no exception. I totaled six cars a year for ten years. You can do the math on that if you'd like. I prefer not to.

When you're driving at such high speeds, you quickly learn that everyone can be impacted when someone makes a mistake. But by the second year, when the terror had subsided, the experience went from being a little scary to loads of fun. It was literally as much fun as you could have with your clothes on. I could finally really get into racing, and once I built my skills, that made all the difference in the world.

Another great lesson from racing was the importance of team building and teamwork. When you drive a car, you rely on your crew to keep you in the race. My job was to drive, and theirs was to keep the car on the track. Everyone involved could make or break the outcome—and the same is true when it comes to your team in business.

Once I started racing, we made it a point to take all our RE/MAX officers—about thirty of them—to Bondurant for a four-day driving experience. They got to feel what it was like to drive a race car, and I could share something I was deeply passionate about. As a bonus, they got to blow off some steam and turn it loose on the track for ten hours at a time. Some of the best drivers on the track were our woman executives. Drivers weren't allowed to pass each other, but many of the women were clocking speeds upward of 140 mph. Everyone got to experience the excitement of driving at high speeds, and it made avid fans of all of them.

The biggest impact racing had on me was its effect on my attitude toward marketing. In business, everyone looks to get the most bang for their buck. If you're a sole proprietor and don't have a marketing department filled with experts, you must learn to figure things out for yourself. You'll learn quickly that everyone wants to sell you marketing, whether in the form of television, digital, radio, billboard, or print ads or some other medium. What you need to do is cut through the clutter and say, "I have a limited budget. What's the absolute most I can get for my money?" I hadn't expected the exposure and return on investment RE/MAX got from racing any more than I'd expected it from our company's hot-air balloon, but both certainly made the dollars stretch and delivered tremendous brand awareness. And, personally, I had an awful lot of fun being a race car driver as well as the CEO of RE/MAX during those years. We never had the budget to be the top team, nor did I have the skill, but we competed, gained wonderful fans, and had the adventure of a lifetime.

If you lead a single-faceted life, it's pretty easy to burn out. It's unusual for the founders of a company to remain at the helm for fifty years. If Gail and I hadn't had other interests such as motorcycles, golf, or car racing to pour ourselves into, we likely would have sold our company years ago. Especially if we'd continued to work the number of hours we did when we started. As I've noted earlier, there was a thirty-year period of my career when I was traveling 250 days a year. Two hundred of those days were spent doing seminars. It was nonstop. So, I promised myself I would make it a point never to burn out. That meant I had to stay fresh and curious by becoming involved in select activities unrelated to the office. You can't sustain a lifestyle where you begin work at 6:00 a.m. and end at 9:00 p.m. seven days a week; you, your family, and those around you will eventually pay a high price. The 180 days a year I spent driving during the decade I was involved in NASCAR were gifts that renewed me and infused our business with so much energy. It was an investment that paid back in so many ways.

MARKETING MYOPIA

Marketing myopia is a term that was coined by Theodore Levitt in a *Harvard Business Review* article in 1960 referring to a shortsighted focus on a company's products or services over the underlying needs and wants of its customers. It occurs when a company defines its business too narrowly, leading to limited awareness of consumer interests and, potentially, to missed opportunities for growth. Companies like Kodak and Polaroid are great examples of how marketing myopia can lead to a decline. Both were in the film business and failed to adapt their marketing strategies and business models to changing market dynamics. Kodak's story is particularly frustrating, as they had developed an early digital camera prototype in the 1970s but opted not to fully embrace digital technology, partly because of concerns about cannibalizing their lucrative film business. This led to a significant missed opportunity to capitalize on the growing demand for digital photography and related products. Kodak serves as a reminder that complacency and failure to adapt to market shifts can have detrimental effects on even the most well-established and successful entities.

To overcome marketing myopia, companies need to adopt a customer-centric approach. This involves conducting market research, understanding consumer behavior, and continuously adapting to meet evolving customer needs and preferences. Rather than focusing solely on their existing products or services, companies should be open to exploring new opportunities and finding innovative ways to deliver value to customers.

There is immense danger when it comes to looking at your business through a narrow lens. When you don't understand the industry you're in, you lose out on unforeseen opportunities. Another example of this is the railroad industry of the 1800s. Those companies were quite wealthy, and the federal government gave them free land on both sides of their tracks, sometimes up to a mile on either side, which the companies used to lay more track.

At that time, there were no regulations for slaughtering animals, and so it wasn't unusual to move herds of cattle from one place to another, sometimes over thousands of miles, via cattle drives. With the advent of the railroads, however, those herds could be moved by railcar instead. Trains could also take cows straight to newly emerging slaughterhouses in places such as Chicago. Because their initial focus was on laying track, the railroads thought they were in the railroad business, but as their purpose evolved, they found they were actually in the *transportation* business. When automobiles emerged in the early 1900s, the first cars were hand built in somebody's garage. None of the producers had a lot of money. The railroads, by contrast, were flush with cash, and could have purchased all the early automobile and truck dealerships, bus lines, and airlines—and yet they didn't. They couldn't see past being railroad businesses. They were stuck in marketing myopia, and eventually they no longer remained incredibly wealthy. They missed their chance to own the transportation business.

Walt Disney's claim to fame was that he drew a picture of a mouse and then animated it. He created a two-minute cartoon that was shown at movie theaters along with the coming attractions before the regular feature played. That mouse helped build an empire. Although Disney's first full-length feature was 1937's *Snow White and the Seven Dwarves*, the company eventually created *Fantasia* in 1940, a full-length movie featuring Mickey Mouse. Audiences loved that mouse and all the Disney characters. They still do. Backers banked him, and it worked. He made his mind up that he was in the *entertainment* business. Thinking two steps ahead of consumers' interests, he started developing other ideas, such as a family-oriented amusement park. As we all know today, his dream became the magical places known as Disneyland and Disney World, complete with world-class hotels. Eventually the company grew to include international theme parks, entered into television, broadcasting, streaming media, consumer products, and publishing. Disney's early expansion set the tone for the company's future and proved that he knew what the railroad executives hadn't: He wasn't just in the cartoon business; he was in the entertainment business, in all of its many diverse forms. Disney didn't have marketing myopia; he had 20/20 vision, and some would even say he could see into the future.

REPUTATION AND PERCEPTION MATTER

No chapter on marketing would be complete without mentioning the importance of community involvement. A lot of small businesses look for ways to support their communities while marketing their companies or products to nearby residents. For example, think about those businesses that provide jerseys to local Little League teams. Not only does that gesture give back to the community, it also gets their name out there. There's an unending number of good causes you can become involved in. A note of caution, though: With the political climate we all live in these days, it's important to choose your charities wisely so that your involvement doesn't have a negative impact on your business or franchisees. Many founders choose to support organizations that push their political views, which can sometimes be controversial—and let's face it, everything is controversial these days. One wrong move and your company can end up being boycotted or canceled. Budweiser, Target, and Disney are all recent examples of companies that paid a high price for marketing choices they made. For us, it has always been important to work with organizations that are nonpartisan. In March of 2004, I received a call from Senator Ben Nighthorse Campbell telling me he wasn't going to run again. He said they were looking for someone to fill his seat and thought I would be a good choice based on my business and philanthropy efforts. I was humbled and honored, so much so that I seriously considered it. I thought I might be able to help the country get back on track. Boy, did I have that all wrong. When word got out that I was considering a run for Senate, the pushback I received from our agents was vociferous. Because I would have been running as a conservative Republican, they were worried I would cost them business, as they had customers who were Democrats. While I'm a conservative when it comes to the police, military, and budget, I consider myself to be a liberal on all other matters, which makes me more of a conservative independent these days. I had never been partisan in my career, and I wasn't looking to become polarizing. I hadn't really thought it through, but I heard what the agents were saying, and they were right. So, I decided not to run for office. In retrospect, a run for governor might have made more sense, but I decided to keep my focus on growing RE/MAX and our people.

The first time I realized that Gail and I had accumulated personal wealth was several years after we'd founded our company. For the first few years, we poured every dollar we made right back into the business. We weren't drawing salaries for quite some time, as we were riddled with debt. We were frugal about most things. So, by the time I was making $2 million a year, I still didn't feel secure or wealthy. I knew business was cyclical, and I always wanted to live below our means. It wasn't until we had somewhere in the neighborhood of $80 million that I thought, *I've made it.*

Well-loved companies are expected to use their influence for good; to whom much is given, much is expected. Thirty years ago, Gail and I sat down and discussed how we wanted to divide up our wealth. We came up with the idea of putting it into three different buckets. We'd give a third to our philanthropic endeavors, put a third away for taxes, and hold on to a third for ourselves and our family. We stayed with that formula for the next twenty years or more. We also established our own foundation with a focus on helping returning combat veterans earn their degrees. So far, we've awarded more than one thousand scholarships to combat veterans. It's our pleasure and privilege to do so. And because I've been a reserve police officer for more than forty years, it's also a priority for us to support the police force by providing resources for better training. One of those projects was to design and build one of the best tracks for driver training in the country. More police officers die in auto accidents than from any other cause. It was important to Gail and me to provide a place where officers could receive the very best training to help preserve their lives. The track we built is now used by multiple police agencies throughout Colorado.

In the 1970s I had a financial planner who wrote a book called *Enough*. In his book, he said that a person who had $25 million in assets had achieved enough. They never needed to worry about money again. After five years of working together, he came to me and said, "Throw away everything I said in that book; twenty-five million dollars will never be enough for you." And he was right.

His idea was self-limiting, especially for someone like me. Gail and I had higher aspirations and goals, but they were all rooted in the same idea—to change the world. We had done that in business with RE/MAX, and with many other companies since. We were equally committed to doing that through philanthropy.

One of the ways Gail and I challenged the norm in philanthropic giving was by building the Sanctuary Golf Course near my home in Colorado. I've mentioned this club several times already in this book, but I don't think I've explained how or why it came about. Simply put, the golf club was never intended to *make* money—well, at least not for us. It was actually built to *raise* money for the many charitable causes my wife and I care about.

At the time, there were a lot of rumors suggesting that had I tried to join the Castle Pines Golf Club, then owned by the late Jack Vickers. It's a beautiful club with two Jack Nicklaus courses. Back in the day, it cost $300,000 to join one course and $40,000 to join the other, and the players on each course were very different. I had never played golf before, but because I lived near the tenth fairway, I liked to walk the course in the morning at daybreak, before any carts were on the paths, or in the early evening when they were all gone.

One day I asked Gail if she had any interest in taking up the sport.

"Oh, no," she said. "My first husband was a golfer, and I was a golf widow. I hate the game." Even so, I decided to give it a go. I walked over to the less expensive course and told them I was interested in joining. I had never swung a club in my life and was looking for someone to take me out to play nine holes. They assigned me a twenty-seven-year-old, beer-drinking, fun-loving guy, and off we went, pounding balls. I hit one good shot for every ten I took. I actually enjoyed the game, so much so I joined that club on the spot.

When I got home, I told Gail what I'd done. She wasn't about to sit at home while I played golf, so she said she would like to take lessons. If I'm being honest, I wanted to play without her, but what could I say except "Of course, dear"?

After Gail's accident in 1983, she was determined to continue living her life as she had prior to the crash. That meant months of rehabilitation and outpatient therapy. During that time, several doctors told her she would likely never walk again. Well, they didn't know Gail or her fierce determination. You see, not only did she prove them wrong by walking but she also learned to play golf using one arm. Golf became an ideal escape from the day-to-day grind at the office. Gail has always loved the outdoors, and the camaraderie and competitive challenge of any game, but especially those of golf.

At the time, there were only about forty or fifty homes scattered around the course, but there was still a lot of land available. It was no secret that Jack Vickers was running out of money. To quickly raise capital, Jack was going to open up several vacant lots for $100,000 each. Our home was on a three-acre lot for which we paid $500,000, and in my mind, that meant people were going to build homes for one-fifth the cost of ours, bringing the value of our home down. This news didn't sit well with the rest of the group either. I jumped in and said, "Jack, I've got a lot of connections. We'll get through this down market, but you can't do that."

"I've already done it," he said.

Eventually, we were able to talk him out of it, and somehow that started a rumor that Jack and I were mortal enemies. This wasn't true. Jack and I were good friends, and remained so until he passed away.

Around this time, I was in the process of buying land to use as a ranch for our collection of Arabian horses. Instead, I had the idea to build one of the most beautiful golf courses in Colorado, if not the world. Today, it's not unusual to see a variety of wildlife on our course, as the nearly thirteen thousand acres of dedicated open space is meant to preserve its sanctity, and the two hundred acres that comprise the golf course have remained pristine. The extreme terrain features dramatic elevation changes and exquisite panoramic views. It's breathtaking. The course was built by one of the only architects that could handle such a project, Jim Engh.

I met Jim while playing in a golf tournament at Castle Pines. Jim Engh Design had an excellent reputation for building spectacular golf courses on rugged and difficult land, and I offered him the job of building our new course, which we would call Sanctuary. It would be more than private; in fact, it would only have *two* members: Gail and me. The only mandate I gave Jim was to make the course fun for Gail. And he did, creating special tees just for her. My request also forced him to think about players who don't hit the ball as far as others do.

When we opened Sanctuary in 1997, *Golf Digest* named it the year's Best New Private Course. After I built it, no one really cared that I had founded RE/MAX; people from all over the world just wanted to come and play this masterpiece. Suddenly, I was the guy with his own private golf course. But that wasn't the reason we'd built Sanctuary. Far from it. As I said, Sanctuary was created primarily as a venue for hosting charity events, as our aim was to raise money for good causes—and that's what we've done with the property ever since. Gail and I personally receive more than one thousand requests for donations every year. It's not easy to say no, but no one has unlimited resources or the managerial capacity to participate in everything. Having the club, however, in addition to our own private giving, helps us do as much as we can.

But the focus on giving doesn't end there; it extends to our company as well. Over the course of fifty years, RE/MAX has grown to over 140,000 agents all over the world. As a company of this size, you can only imagine how often we're asked for money. For decades we gave to a variety of charities for different reasons, but there's one major charity in the US and Canada that we've been consistently committed to, and that's the Children's Miracle Network.

When I look back at the history of RE/MAX, I can see a number of moments that defined us as a company. One of those moments occurred in 1992, when we became a corporate sponsor of CMN. As you'll see, there was synchronicity in our involvement.

The Children's Miracle Network was developed in 1981 by Mick Shannon. The idea was to create a national telethon across a network of local television stations in North America to benefit children's hospitals. It was broadcast live for twenty-one straight hours from Osmond Studios in Utah, and each hospital owned its local market and received 100 percent of the funds raised there.

CMN was founded on three principles: Kids always come first; 100 percent of the funds raised remain local so they benefit hospitals in the donors' areas; and the organization always operates with dignity and class. They also believe that it's never okay to exploit sick or injured kids.

Joe Lake, John Schneider, Mick Shannon, and Marie Osmond were all deeply committed to CMN. In fact, Marie loved the concept so much that she became a cofounder. Together, with their contacts, they approached every actor, athlete, and entertainer they could to appear on the telethon. Mick, Joe, John, and Marie also sought out corporate sponsors, and they eventually created the biggest telethon ever. It's raised over $7 billion since its inception.

As a successful business, we wanted to find a single charity that would appeal to everyone. While we understood that our agents supported their own charities, and we completely embraced that, this would be something we could do as a company. Our Canadian regional owners convinced us that CMN was a very worthwhile project and that we should meet Mick Shannon personally.

Mick subsequently came to Denver to talk with our team. He had already met Jess Jesperson, senior executive for RE/MAX, and laid out his presentation about why we were a good fit with CMN and why we should get involved. Shannon believed that because real estate agents are independent by nature, and good salespeople, they could create their own fundraising campaigns for their local children's hospitals while also drawing attention to RE/MAX as a business that cared about the communities it served. Jesperson got the idea right away. He started doing the math and calculated that seventy thousand agents, at one hundred dollars each, could raise $7 million. He loved it so much that he wanted to share the idea with Gail. He walked Shannon down to Gail's office, introduced the two, and casually said, "We're going to raise $7 million for children's hospitals!"

Gail loved it too.

We announced our partnership with CMN that year at our annual convention at the Fox Theatre in Atlanta. There were 4,500 RE/MAX agents present. When we explained the important work CMN did in saving kids' lives, there wasn't a person in that room who wasn't moved by their mission. They all gladly embraced the partnership.

Two nights later, Marie Osmond performed for us at our awards show dinner. Marie is one of my favorite people in the world. She's an incredibly charismatic woman with a good heart, and truly one of the most delightful people I've ever met.

Our company was built on a foundational belief that we're not only invested in building strong relationships but also committed to having a powerful impact in the communities where our brokers and agents live. Partnering with CMN gave us the structure to benefit the lives of local kids, their families, and the hospitals that treated them.

During our inaugural year, we held many fundraisers and live auctions to raise money for CMN. RE/MAX agents stepped up and donated generously. Even more important was the impact this had on them: They took the concept back to their teams and offices, where they were able to get others excited about this organization too. Richard Phillips, the owner of several RE/MAX franchises in Texas, was the first to embrace our Miracle Home Program, in which every agent who sold a home would donate one hundred dollars from the sale to CMN. The concept worked. We averaged $7 million a year in donations and became one of the top five donors to CMN over the years. One hundred percent of the money raised from that campaign has come straight from the pockets of our real estate agents.

RE/MAX agents and brokers began raising money for CMN in other creative ways too. They were committed to helping however they could. One of our agents, Bruce Johnson, raised more than $180,000 for CMN during a motorcycle trip across North America. Trudy Wilson swam all 386 kilometers of the Trent-Severn Waterway in Ontario and raised more than $30,000 in memory of her daughter, Lauren, who was treated at CMN. And we as a company came up with a further way to raise money for CMN that was really unique too.

We'd flown the first RE/MAX hot-air balloon in 1977 at the Albuquerque Balloon Festival. The fabric for those balloons lasts for between four hundred and five hundred one-hour flights. The constant heating and cooling of the fabric renders it unstable after that. You don't want to be a few thousand feet in the air and have it rip.

Since the original fabric couldn't be FAA certified and we didn't know what to do with it after it was discarded, we simply stored it when we retired a balloon from flight. Fifteen or so years ago, I received a call from a friend who said he had the balloon fabric in his storage unit. Apparently, we had just left it there.

"Do you want it?" he asked.

"Hell yes," I quickly responded.

I wasn't sure what I was going to do with it, but I knew there was a way to take that fabric—which originally cost us $14,000—and use it to raise hundreds of thousands of dollars for the kids.

When the balloon arrived, I took it to a seamstress and asked if she could make three different varieties of flag out of the material. One was the American flag, one was the Canadian flag, and one was the original Betsy Ross version of the American flag. We had enough fabric to make ten versions of each. We kept a first-edition set for ourselves, but the rest were auctioned off each year at the CMN auction. They usually went for somewhere around $50,000 apiece. Whoever bought one would take it to the local Children's Miracle Network Hospital with a plaque that read, "Donated by the men and women of RE/MAX."

There are countless stories of how our agents joined together on this mission of ours—too many to list here. But each is a testament to the generosity of our RE/MAX agents and the importance of the CMN mission. To date, RE/MAX agents have donated more than $157 million to CMN. Again, these donations don't come from a corporate fund; they come directly from the pockets of the agents themselves. While individual offices support other charities of their choice, no one could have imagined the kind of financial participation we would get from them when we joined forces to support CMN. And none of this would have been possible without the extraordinary organization on the other side of the partnership.

Having the right idea, the right reason, and the right timing are essential for creating something special, but having the right people makes it all come together—and for us, it started with CMN. Being involved with this organization has been one of the great honors of my life. Gail and I are truly grateful for every person who has been a part of it with us.

IN THE MIDST OF EVERY CRISIS THERE IS GREAT OPPORTUNITY

In August 2005, Hurricane Katrina decimated the southeastern United States, including Mississippi, Alabama, parts of Texas, and, of course, New Orleans, which was especially battered. When the storm hit land, it destroyed everything in its path. More than 1,800 people lost their lives, and Katrina is ranked as one of the costliest natural disasters in the history of the United States.

We lost contact with hundreds of RE/MAX agents. Anybody who was close to the coast lost their buildings and whatever was inside that made their businesses possible. Up until then, we hadn't prepared for a disaster of this magnitude. We immediately sat down and talked about setting up a foundation so when a future disaster occured, we could take care of our people. Our attorney got right on it. It usually takes 90 to 180 days to get a foundation approved, but we didn't have that much time. Our people were in need of support and funding to rebuild. We flew to Washington, DC, to plead our case. Miraculously, the government gave us approval the next day. With that in hand, we were able to put out a notice to all RE/MAX agents that a lot of our friends were hurting and we were mobilizing to send help. We created the foundation with an initial $1 million donation from Gail and me. We were asking other agents to donate whatever they could, assuring them that we would get the funds dispersed without any cost and that they would go right into the hands of the people who needed them. Our RE/MAX family donated several millions more.

When we set up the foundation, we called our bank in California to let them know we would need $500,000 of prepaid $5,000 Visa credit cards. Adam took our corporate jet to California to pick up the cards, which they made overnight for us. With the half million in credit cards and another half million in cash I withdrew from our account, we were ready to go help our colleagues.

Adam and I flew to New Orleans, and through a patchwork of efforts, including outreach to anyone with cell phone service, we managed to start finding RE/MAX people. Since both Adam and I are police officers, we wore our badges. We also carried our pistols, which we were licensed to do. We kept the money with us at all times. Besides, there were no hotel rooms to be had. If they hadn't been destroyed by the storm, they were occupied by those who had nowhere else to go. We ended up sleeping on the floor of the airport we flew into.

Somehow, we were able to arrange three meetings in three different cities along the coast. At our first stop, we set up a room at a local Holiday Inn that had all of its windows blown out. There, we were able to connect with fifty or sixty RE/MAX agents. Someone was able to get a gallon of pure bottled water and a large coffee cake too. That sounds so basic, but under the circumstances, it was nothing short of miraculous. We cut the coffee cake into one-inch squares so everybody who was there could have a piece. Then we stood up and explained that they had a choice between a credit card with $5,000 loaded onto it or $5,000 in cash. Almost everyone at the first location took the cards.

One by one, they shared their stories of survival with us, each one more gut-wrenching than the last. One young single mom came with her little girl. They had lost their house and office, and had no wallet or any access to money. They were staying at a Red Cross tent, sharing a gallon of water a day between them. All they had were the clothes they were wearing. She told me they washed their clothes with the water they had left before sleeping on a cot and letting them dry overnight. When I handed her the Visa card, she began to cry. I asked, "What's wrong?"

"We can now buy underpants for my daughter." She was humiliated and scared. This was someone who had been making a few hundred thousand dollars a year. She had money in the bank, but she couldn't access it—she had no ATM card or ID, and for the most part, the banks were closed. Like so many of the others we met throughout that trip, she was a successful businessperson who had lost everything.

We kept this assistance going for about ten years, as other tragedies occurred. We were like the Red Cross within RE/MAX, but it became overwhelming to handle these crises. At the time, we were only supporting events in the United States, but when our overseas offices heard about the foundation, they also sought support when there was a devastating earthquake or some other catastrophe in their country. Eventually, we had to let the charitable organization go, but we continued to support other organizations who could help.

What we learned over the years was that people liked to be a part of companies that care about their communities. This has been proven many times over on a small scale in local offices and with large-volume Realtors too. While RE/MAX as a company chose the Children's Miracle Network as our North American charity of choice, we never forced a broker or agent to support that charity if they didn't want to. We always encouraged them to find something they believed in and wanted to be involved with. Staying active in their communities in whatever way they chose to was what mattered. The more freedom we allowed, the more impact we as a whole would have. Every one of us has our own purpose: our mortgage company, Motto Mortgage, supports local food banks; some of our brokers support breast cancer and others prostate cancer; the list is endless. And that's a good thing, because *everyone wins.*

$5 MILLION CHARITY CHALLENGE

Occasionally, there will be times in life when good intentions backfire. In 1993, the twentieth anniversary of RE/MAX, we decided to do something called the $5 Million Charity Challenge. When

I started my speech at the opening of the general session, I talked about how all real estate companies brag that they have the best agents, the highest customer satisfaction, sell more real estate than anybody else, are the best innovators, and so on. Now, if everyone is saying this, it can't be true. Fifteen minutes later, just as I was wrapping up my speech, I got a signal from the side of the stage to stretch out my remarks. I wasn't sure what was going on, but soon discovered that our guest of honor was missing. We had hired George Foreman to participate in a skit with me in which we were both going to get into a boxing ring, "take it to the enemy," and fight. I kept stalling for over an hour. Finally, the lights went dark, except for a single spotlight. All of a sudden, a voice could be heard over the loudspeaker. "Liniger, if you're going to fight, you've got to dress like a fighter."

I was wearing a suit and tie, but before I knew it, a bevy of beautiful Vegas showgirls surrounded me. They had boxing trunks, a cape, and gloves on. The spotlight followed me across the stage, where I entered a mock dressing room with a big star on the door to change. All the while, I kept talking to the audience, tossing articles of clothing out of the dressing room. First came my suit coat, then my tie, and then a pair of pink panties just for fun.

While all of this was going on, a huge fight ring was moved to center stage. Famed announcer Michael Buffer stood in the ring with the spotlight directly on him.

"Ladies and gentlemen, lllllllet's get ready to rumbllllle!" The crowd went nuts. "In this corner, we have Century 21." We had a little lightweight guy standing there.

"And in this corner, we've got Coldwell Banker," where yet another scrawny boxer stood.

"In this corner, we've got the great pretender—welcome, ERA."

And finally, the theme from Rocky blared from the speakers as the doors in the back of the room opened. The figure who entered was surrounded by thirty security guards in yellow jackets. The presumption was that it was me, but it wasn't. It was George Foreman. He stepped into the ring and threw his hood back as Michael announced, "Former heavyweight champion of the world, George Foreman!" He stood in the ring while the crowd went crazy. They couldn't believe it. They were raucous and definitely ready to rumble.

George took the microphone and said, "Where's my buddy Dave?" I stepped into the ring, and Foreman grabbed me. My head came to just below his armpit. His fists were bigger than my head. It was a great skit, and everyone seemed to enjoy it.

It was then that we announced the $5 Million Charity Challenge. We backed a Brink's armored car filled with $5 million in $100 bills into the room. We had SWAT teams from Las Vegas all around.

"I'm going to put my money where my mouth is," I said. "I'm announcing to my five biggest competitors that I want to place a bet. I'll put $1 million on each of these five categories: who has the best agents, the highest customer satisfaction, the most transactions, the best innovation, and the most brand-name awareness. The winner chooses the charity, and the loser gives the money."

It was a hell of a deal and a great marketing opportunity. The story made every newspaper. We thought our competitors would bite. Well, not so fast. Prudential was classy about it; when reporters called them, they said, "RE/MAX has their way of measuring success and we have ours. We wish Dave the best, but we're not participating in the contest." Coldwell Banker was also really classy, saying pretty much the same thing. Century 21, however, referred to me as the "P. T. Barnum of the real estate industry." They said no one took me seriously and that I was full of shit.

Not only did this not go exactly as we'd planned but, in fact, it got even worse. Not long after that event, we started a new advertising campaign with the slogans "RE/MAX is out in front" and "RE/MAX is #1." In response, Century 21 sued RE/MAX headquarters and several brokers for false advertising in four jurisdictions, and we countersued in Denver. Over the next several years, we won in three of the jurisdictions where Century 21 had sued, leaving two federal cases to be litigated.

The first federal court case was litigated from March through August 1997 in Santa Ana, California. I sat in the courtroom with my attorneys every day, watching the jurors on the case take the brunt of this stupidity. We started with sixteen jurors, but over the course of the trial, we lost several of them for various reasons. A six-month case is financially devastating for everyone, but especially to the jurors, who cannot work and often will not be paid. For federal cases, the court pays somewhere around fifty dollars a day, often adding an extra ten for trials that last more than ten days. For our part, we spent many millions of dollars defending all the lawsuits.

During the trial, Century 21 tried to settle with me, but I told them, "I want my day in court". After many days of deliberations, the jury came back with a verdict for RE/MAX. In a later order, the judge ordered Century 21 to pay RE/MAX its attorneys' fees and costs.

We still had our case in Denver federal court. Century 21 approached me again to settle. Having beaten them in all four cases that they had filed, I was prepared to settle for a substantial payment from Century 21 to RE/MAX. Century 21 made me an offer I couldn't refuse, and we settled the last case and the California case which was then on appeal.

Now that's bringing a gun to a knife fight. Make that a full battalion! What they didn't know was, metaphorically speaking, we'd brought in a legal SWAT team. We were going up against a foe who was twice our size and better capitalized than we were. All we had was a slingshot and a rock, but we knew we had to hit them between the eyes. We had to fiercely defend our reputation and our company. That's why we hired the best of the best, from our jury consultant to our legal team. We conducted several mock trials at substantial expense to prepare for any possible scenario in court. We had them outclassed every step of the way. If we'd lost those trials, it could have put us out of business. A few thousand offices would have closed, and all our franchisees' investments would have been lost. I wasn't about to let that happen without a fight. The purpose of litigation is to win, but you never know how a jury will respond. We wanted the best representation we could get so we could save our company. It was do or die. What's more, all the marketing we'd done over the years had helped establish a true and authentic reputation for our company, and I couldn't have us be remembered in such a bad light. I was determined that these trials not discredit us in any way or tarnish our good work.

I can't tell you how grateful I was to that team of excellent lawyers and to the astute jurors who saw the situation for what it was. Our agents—and theirs—didn't want the lawsuit. Throughout the trial, they continued to sell one another's listings. That's how it works. All but a few brokers, officers, and agents weren't involved in this frivolous lawsuit, and frankly, we didn't want to be either, but sometimes you can get dragged into things and wind up having to fight. That's the world we live in.

PIGS GET FAT, HOGS GET SLAUGHTERED

In life, everything, big or small, centers around negotiation. Business deals, lawsuits, marriage agreements, even simple day-to-day decisions about where to eat and what movies to see involve some kind of give-and-take. Maybe you don't want to go see the in-laws, but you also don't want an unhappy spouse. Or perhaps when you're buying a car, you go to the dealership prepared to haggle over the sticker price until you feel as though you've gotten a deal.

Throughout my career, I took many different courses on negotiating, and there are as many ideas about how to do it well as there are books that have been written about it. Everybody has their own opinion. Mine is simple: At some point, you have to draw a line and say, "This is what I'm willing to do, but no more." That's it.

There are other people who just love to talk; they want to argue with vendors to get the best price on everything. Not me. I ask the price, and if I want it, I'll buy it. If I don't, I won't.

When we first started selling franchises, our agreements were typed, double-spaced documents. They weren't typeset. The prospective franchisee would take our agreement to their attorney, who would then mark it up with his notes. It was an argument every time—a battle to determine who had the best attorney or who could argue more effectively.

I thought we presented a contract that was fair to both sides. There were valid reasons for why the contract was set up the way it was. We didn't want to spend all our time renegotiating the agreement or all our money paying attorneys' fees. This was our deal, take it or leave it. Very quickly, my attitude became, "If you want to buy the franchise, buy the franchise. If you don't, then don't. But if you choose to do the deal, you'll sign the exact same contract everyone else signed before you." Eventually, we figured that the way around this was to typeset the contract and not leave any spaces where someone could write notes. Of course, this was long before computers and PDFs.

Gail and I have taken numerous courses on negotiating techniques. When you negotiate, everybody must win. It's a give-and-take proposition. The negotiator who tries to get every last cent out of a deal, to the point where it's no longer good for both sides, is ruining future relations. Remember this: *Pigs get fat, and hogs get slaughtered.*

When it comes to negotiating, I believe in two things: 1) Negotiate to win, and 2) Never sell an empty box. Here's what I mean:

There's an old carnival trick in which the huckster has three boxes in front of him. He'll sell you any one of the three for five dollars. One of the boxes holds items valued at more than ten dollars, and the other boxes are empty. The carnival barker says, "Which one do you want?" Inevitably, the person chooses an empty box. They don't get their ten dollars, but they knew before they played that there was a chance they might not get anything. Nevertheless, the game leaves them with a bad taste in their mouth. Now, if somebody gives you their money, you have to give them something of value. There must be an exchange. If you negotiate so hard that one side gets everything and the other side gets nothing—or one side perceives that the other side got everything and they got nothing—there will never be a good feeling about it in the end. In some negotiations, you'll think you've come to an agreement, but just as you're about to shake hands, the other party says, "Oh, by the way, one more thing." That's called a "nibble." Depending on how badly you want to close the deal, you'll either agree to the last request or not. This is why it's so important for you as a business owner to have a set standard in your mind when you're negotiating. (Hopefully, your stance isn't to kill the other party.) Make sure that you have a system that can be considered a fair deal by both parties.

I include this advice in the marketing section because everything from your pricing strategy to your customer service policies involve a kind of unspoken negotiation. They demand that you carefully consider in advance what constitutes a fair exchange.

ARTIFICIAL INTELLIGENCE AND MARKETING

One final thought on marketing: We're at an inflection point when it comes to marketing and the use of Artificial Intelligence (AI). In fact, marketing is an area of business where it's widely predicted that AI will drive enormous change. A recent McKinsey study found that, along with sales, marketing is the business function where AI will have the biggest impact financially. If you're not using AI, especially in marketing, you won't reap the benefits of what could be the most transformational technology we've ever seen.

Chances are, you're already using AI tools without being aware of it. Social media channels, e-commerce platforms and solutions, and tools designed to assist with content creation are all examples of AI use in business today. There's a plethora of AI tools out there, and marketing teams are becoming increasingly more comfortable using them. However, most marketing departments lack a coordinated, strategy-focused approach, which means those tools aren't being used to their fullest capability. When Paul Roetzer, founder and CEO of the Marketing AI Institute, searched the media for connections between AI terms and the world's top fifty chief marketing officers, he found that only four of the CMOs had spoken publicly about their use of AI or were associated with it in media mentions.

It's extremely early in our understanding of the applications and adaptations of AI, but all indications are that it will impact advertising, public relations, content marketing, and email marketing in measurable ways. For example, the biggest online advertising platforms are Facebook and Google. Both offer tools that combine audience segmentation and predictive analytics, which allow businesses to target thousands of potential customers based on gender, age, income, interests, and much more. Traditional methods of advertising, such as television, newspapers, and magazines, simply cannot provide the same data that correlates ads with actual sales the way AI-driven advertising tools do.

AI can help enhance marketing for companies in several ways, offering valuable insights, automation, and personalized experiences. The use of AI tools can assist in product development by analyzing market trends, consumer preferences, and competitive landscapes. These tools can help identify new opportunities, optimize product features, and support innovation efforts. AI can also aid in the design process, generating simulations or prototypes and automating testing procedures. It can analyze large volumes of customer data, including demographics, behavior, preferences, and purchase history, enabling marketers to gain actionable insights, identify patterns and trends, and make data-driven decisions. AI-powered analytics platforms can provide real-time data analysis, predictive modeling, and targeted recommendations.

AI algorithms can also analyze customer data to create dynamic customer segments based on specific characteristics, interests, or behaviors. This allows marketers to deliver personalized content, offers, and recommendations to individual customers or specific segments, enhancing customer engagement and satisfaction. And AI can generate content, such as product descriptions, blog posts, or social media captions, based on predefined templates and guidelines. Other tasks like writing press releases, shaping external messaging points, and researching the best outlets (online or digital) for gaining coverage can be augmented by AI as well.

When it comes to online advertising and marketing, the landscape has grown massively, providing opportunities to promote your company and its goods and services through paid or unpaid social media posts or through influencers and third-party content creators. AI can match products with people who have large audiences and are branded in some way. It can also curate and recommend relevant content to share with your target audience, saving time and effort. AI algorithms can analyze customer data to optimize marketing campaigns, determine the best timing for interactions, and personalize messaging based on individual preferences. It analyzes historical data to predict customer behavior, identify high-value leads, and prioritize sales efforts. By employing predictive analytics and lead scoring models, marketers can focus their resources on leads with the highest potential for conversion or engagement. AI can also analyze customer interactions, feedback, and sentiment to improve the overall customer experience. By monitoring customer journeys and sentiment analysis, these tools can identify pain points, recommend improvements to make, and personalize touchpoints that can be used to enhance customer satisfaction and loyalty.

To implement effective AI marketing in your business, you'll likely need to hire someone who has the knowledge and skills to make an impact on your business, or train someone within your business to learn and understand the importance of technologies like AI. Those who are currently using AI but aren't talking about it much are likely silent because they believe they have a competitive edge, and those who aren't willing to find out what AI is capable of will be so far behind by the time they realize they need it that their businesses may never recover. We're on the precipice of the most exciting and potentially transformative time ever in business and commerce, so be sure to take advantage of it.

9

Embracing Change

Charles Darwin has often been quoted as saying it's the strongest that survive. But that's not true; not only did Darwin not coin the phrase "survival of the fittest," he argued against it. What he said was that those who survive are the ones who most accurately perceive their environment and successfully adapt to it. After all, the dinosaurs died sixty-five million years before humans evolved, but mosquitoes—contemporaries of the dinosaurs—are still here. It isn't the strongest or the most intelligent who survive but those who can best manage change.

As I mentioned earlier in the book, the 1960s were an era when the real estate industry really started to transform, not only in ways that assured it would survive but in ways that helped it thrive too. At that time, being a Realtor was an old, white-haired white man's job, largely because there was no salary and no way to get started unless you had some money in the bank. It essentially attracted retired people who already had an annuity income. For example, they might have been civil servants, teachers, police officers, or in the military and had stability because of their pensions, so they could make real estate work. Right after the Greatest Generation came back from

World War II in 1945, they started having children, so by the time the 1960s came along, there was an entirely new generation of people getting married, having their own children, and needing housing.

There's an economic theory called the Pig in the Python, which the *Oxford English Dictionary* describes as a "sharp statistical increase represented as a bulge in an otherwise level pattern." This indicates a degree of pent-up demand, which is what created the housing boom in the early 1960s, along with the Fair Credit Act, which allowed married couples to qualify for a home loan that was up to 60 percent greater than the amount they would have merited based on the husband's income alone.

The 1970s brought even more change. Women started working in real estate, and the industry was ripe for disruption. RE/MAX was founded on January 30, 1973, and as major regional brands such as ours started to become larger and larger, we put a lot of pressure on the smaller brokers, because the biggest brands attracted the best agents. If you were a successful agent, you started gravitating toward companies with more market share, more brand awareness, and more customers. Franchises started exploding as ERA and Century 21 actively explored the format. By 1978, there were 178 so-called national real estate companies. All the franchise salesmen were running around talking about how 80 percent of the business would be done by five or six companies in the next five years, and sure enough, public companies came in and started scooping up real estate companies. Sears bought Coldwell Banker, then turned it into a residential empire. Merrill Lynch came in, and so did Prudential. As all these changes were happening, every company said they were going to be the biggest—but in reality, it was the adaptability of the best brokers and the best agents that made the system work, and it continues to do so today.

Of course, you now know that our competition tried to run us out of business because their executives feared they would lose some of their own earnings if their agents demanded a commission structure similar to ours. I went from president-elect of my board of Realtors to being thrown off the board the next day. The rumor mill was very active. Our financial backers bailed on us, and when they did, I was left sitting on a massive pile of debt. Bill collectors were everywhere. Even so, we managed to adapt and overcome. The RE/MAX success story is an amazing display of ambition, grit, focus, persistence, and adaptability.

Earlier, I provided some historical examples of industries and companies that failed to adapt and innovate and therefore missed out on sizeable growth opportunities. A more recent and dramatic example comes to mind here: Blockbuster. Blockbuster was a company whose failure to adapt its marketing strategies and business model to changing market dynamics ultimately led to its downfall. As you may know, it was a leading video rental chain that experienced significant setbacks when it neglected to recognize and respond effectively to the rise of online streaming and digital content delivery. Its marketing myopia was evident in its narrow focus on the traditional brick-and-mortar video rental model while new technologies were emerging and consumer preferences were shifting. As the internet and digital technologies advanced, companies like Netflix embraced the concept of online streaming and subscription-based models. They allowed customers access to a wide variety of movies and TV shows from home, while Blockbuster still promoted the in-store experience and tried to profit off late fees.

Interestingly, Blockbuster passed on an opportunity to acquire Netflix in the early 2000s when it was still primarily a DVD-by-mail rental service. Blockbuster introduced its own online rental service later, but it was unable to compete effectively with Netflix's expanding streaming offerings. Ultimately, Blockbuster filed for bankruptcy in 2010, closing all but one of its nine thousand stores, while Netflix continued to expand and lead the market. Blockbuster's sole surviving store has become a tourist attraction, especially for movie buffs. In a way, it's an ode to a bygone era.

BlackBerry is another example of a company that failed to adapt to changing technology. It was once one of the leading names in smartphones, with over 50 percent of the US market and 20 percent of the global market. At its height, BlackBerry had eighty-five million subscribers worldwide. Users were so addicted to its products that they nicknamed the company CrackBerry. But in 2007, Apple introduced the iPhone and changed the game with such features as the multitouch screen and a built-in camera. While Blackberry couldn't have anticipated the novel developments at Apple, its failure to update its product with touchscreen technology when it proved to be so popular badly hurt its sales and standing in the marketplace. The 2023 movie *BlackBerry* chronicles the tribulations of a company that missed the curve when it was once so far ahead of it.

Both BlackBerry and Blockbuster serve as reminders of the continued importance, especially today, of adapting to new market dynamics and evolving customer preferences. Companies must stay attuned to emerging technologies, consumer behavior, and industry trends to remain competitive. When companies are blind to these changes, it hinders their ability to innovate and meet the changing needs of their customers. By focusing on understanding and meeting customer needs, businesses can achieve long-term success and avoid becoming obsolete or irrelevant in the marketplace.

Several companies have demonstrated a strong commitment to innovation and have successfully adapted and evolved over time. Apple, of course, is one such company. From the introduction of the Macintosh computer in the 1980s to groundbreaking products like the iPod, iPad, and iPhone, Apple has consistently pushed the boundaries of design and functionality. It has also expanded into new areas such as wearable technology with the Apple Watch and services like Apple Music and Apple Pay.

Amazon was initially an online bookseller that later transformed into a global e-commerce and technology powerhouse. The company has consistently innovated to enhance the customer experience, introducing services like Amazon Prime, one-click purchasing, and its own line of consumer electronics, including the Kindle e-reader and Echo smart speakers. It has since diversified into cloud computing with Amazon Web Services (AWS) and made significant investments in areas like AI and logistics.

Tesla has transformed the automotive industry with its electric vehicles (EVs) and sustainable energy solutions. It has pushed the boundaries of EV technology, offering high-performance vehicles with long-range capabilities and developing an extensive network of charging stations. Tesla's innovations in self-driving technology and battery storage have also positioned them to be leaders in the future of transportation and renewable energy.

Google has continuously expanded its offerings beyond its original search engine platform. It has ventured into areas such as online advertising, cloud computing, mobile operating systems (Android), smart home technology (Nest), autonomous vehicles (Waymo), and other innovative projects through its research and development arm, Google X. Google's focus on innovation and acquisition has allowed them to diversify and maintain their position as a technology leader.

These are just a few examples of companies that have demonstrated a strong commitment to innovation and adaptability. Their willingness to embrace change, anticipate customer needs, and leverage emerging technologies has enabled them to stay at the forefront of their respective industries. Continuous innovation remains a critical factor in their ongoing success and growth. In today's uber-competitive and ever-evolving world, no one can afford to let moss grow under their feet or to let opportunity pass them by.

In 1998 I had a memorable experience with innovation. I was among an esteemed group of thrill-seeking men who attempted to set a world record by flying a balloon 24,900 miles at an altitude of 130,000 feet without stopping. It was the greatest adventure *and* the greatest disappointment of my life. Twenty-one others had tried and failed before us, including Sir Richard Branson, who had ended his attempt over Hawaii the week before ours, and Steve Fossett and Per Lindstrand, who ditched their balloon in the Pacific Ocean halfway to their goal. They had all encountered weather patterns they couldn't get around. Team RE/MAX had a crew from the United States (including me) and Australia; Dan Pedersen, an all-around great guy and the founder of the US Navy Top Gun training program, was our team's mission control director.

Our goal wasn't just to fly a forty-story manned balloon higher than any other before it; we also planned to hit the stratosphere, where we would be able to see the curvature of the earth. Once our helium balloon was inflated, it would be big enough to fit the Houston Astrodome inside it! This was a truly novel approach for balloon flight. In the stratosphere, there are no significant weather features, so once we reached 130,000 feet, we knew we wouldn't encounter the types of storms that brought down all those who had previously attempted this mission.

But just because we wouldn't run into a wall of weather didn't mean the unprecedented height wouldn't present other dangerous challenges. The atmosphere at fifty thousand feet and beyond is significantly different than it is at sea level. Think of the climbers who summit Mt. Everest: at 29,032 feet, they can hardly breathe, and many require oxygen. Now, imagine Mt. Everest being four and a half times taller; that was the altitude we were attempting to reach. Above fifty thousand feet, you're reliant on artificial means of life support. Our cabin had to function like a miniature spacecraft, and it did. Inside the capsule, which was no bigger than seven feet by eight feet, we wore specially designed spacesuits, at a cost of $500,000 each. They were the same designs as the ones used in the Soyuz and

Mir space missions, so you know some of the best technology of the time was at our disposal.

Weather permitting, we planned to launch our balloon on December 29 from a weather balloon launching facility in the middle of the Australian outback. The biggest risk typically occurs at takeoff and landing, so if we could successfully launch and then reach our intended altitude, we thought we had a good chance to make history. Although ideal weather conditions were predicted through the middle of January, there were two potentially problematic fronts moving in that could kick up winds. If all went as planned, however, we would land near Alice Springs, Australia, anywhere from sixteen to eighteen days after launch.

Weight was an incredibly important issue for us, so we weren't allowed to bring any superfluous items that might add additional pounds. Once we took off, we would have a couple of weeks to float around the world. We had limited electrical capacity, although we had solar panels on the capsule to keep the radio and satellite phone operable and the heating and cooling systems running. We could only listen to the radio in certain places, but not over the ocean. One of my friends bought me the *Encyclopedia Britannica* on CD-ROM. At the time, we all had CD-ROM drives on our laptops, and this would give me hundreds of thousands of pages to go through to keep me busy. There were no e-books yet, so this was our best option.

We had a four-week window to launch. At the last minute, the NASA team who oversaw our launch said we couldn't make it. They wanted us to reposition our solar panels. We scurried around and changed the panels accordingly, which took a lot of time. When we were set, Australia endured four of the windiest, rainiest days it had seen in more than one hundred years. On the final day we could launch, despite a thunderstorm coming at us, the NASA team said it looked like a go. At midnight, we dressed in our spacesuits, climbed into the capsule, and got into our prone positions. NASA wanted to get us up in the air before the storm rolled in. Once we were on the launch pad, we ended up sitting there for four hours. I'm a multi-engine and instrument-rated commercial jet pilot. I understand complex machinery, and believe it or not, our balloon was very complex. The capsule had a lot of communication and navigation instruments. As we were going through our checks, I kept thinking, *I know I can fly this bird.*

We were down to T-minus fifteen seconds when NASA scrubbed the launch. We were very disappointed. So much time, engineering, and planning had gone into this venture. As we were being pulled back to the hangar, I looked out through the porthole of the capsule and saw that a crowd of twenty thousand people had gathered outside the fences of the airport to cheer us on. We couldn't see them when we were lying in our launch positions, but it was a wonderful sight to behold when we glimpsed the crowd. Once we were away from the cameras, I broke down. I was bitterly disappointed. My second-in-command was terrified to try again. The NASA-requested changes and the weather conditions had spooked him. He made it clear that he had no intention of getting back into the capsule if we were going to make another attempt. He was so upset that he wanted NASA to say the balloon had design flaws and was unsafe to fly. They weren't going to do that, though, because it wasn't true. As it turned out, the Australian press somehow had a hot mic in our cockpit and heard him freaking out. For three years, this man had grandstanded to the press, and now he was panicking and afraid he was going to die. He was worried about leaving his wife and child, which I totally understood, and so never said a word to the press about his fears. Instead, we said he had high blood pressure and that I would make the journey myself.

"I can do this. I have an alarm clock that will wake me every two to four hours to make sure the O_2 levels are correct and everything is fine. I'll do it," I said.

We stayed another week to see if we might be able to launch again, but that launch failed too. At that point, I made the decision that we would come back in a year and try it again. When we ordered the balloon, we ordered a second as backup. We had unrolled one for the attempted launch, which became unusable after that night. However, we had the second one we could use a year later if the conditions were right. I had another balloon bag and thought we'd use the time to further innovate and make our prospects for success even greater. That evening we all went to a crazy cowboy bar, with saddles in the rafters. As you can imagine, a drunken good time was had by all. Later that night, members of the Australian press asked me if they could buy me a drink. Well, I've never been one to decline such a kind offer, so I said sure.

"Hey, mate," one of them said, "we had a mic in your launch command system. We heard every argument, and we heard that gutless Australian who chickened out and wanted everyone to lie for him. You took the risk. You said you would do it by yourself, and didn't bloody up that coward Australian's nose."

I took a deep breath and said, "I have no idea what you're talking about. I just wanted to go for a balloon ride."

A few days later, the press wrote glowing stories about us, and never once mentioned our copilot. It was all about my family, my friends, and the scientists who worked tirelessly to accomplish our goal. They were grateful that we'd tried to launch from their country, and made a point to say, "You're welcome back anytime, mate."

That was pretty cool.

Sometimes, even when you put in all the hard work, you'll find yourself in circumstances where you just can't prevail. But if you look intently enough, there's always a win of some sort. We got all that free publicity, which was a win. And I didn't die, which was a win too. It may not always be the win you're looking for, but there is *always* a win.

Four months later, the team from Breitling made it around the world in a balloon, setting the record. But they did it in a regular helium balloon at about thirty thousand feet. When they completed their mission, the challenge and glory were gone for me. Sixteen hundred volunteers had worked on this mission with us, and we were all heartbroken. I'd spent three years of my life training with cosmonauts, preparing for the trip and making a $3 million investment. Now, that might sound like a lot of money to throw at a failed adventure—and it was, except for one thing: RE/MAX ended up with over $1 billion worth of PR worldwide. Every time CNN, the BBC, or any other news outlet did a story on our preparation and attempt, our company logo was front and center, whether it was on our hats, spacesuits, capsule, or balloon. The return on investment was fabulous—and I'm still alive to tell the story.

The reasonable man adapts himself to the world. The unreasonable one persists in trying to adapt the world to himself. Therefore, all progress depends on the unreasonable man.

—George Bernard Shaw

Real estate developer and homebuilder Eli Broad wrote a book called *The Art of Being Unreasonable: Lessons in Unconventional Thinking* in which he writes about important lessons he learned throughout his career. Broad notes that there's often a perception that many who've attained a high level of success can be too demanding or unreasonable, and that whatever we're endeavoring to achieve may come at too high a cost. This material resonated with me—a lot. If you're an entrepreneur or thinking of becoming one, you have to be willing to make sacrifices and hard choices, some of which you may not be able to correct later. In my case, I gave up a lot of time with my kids. I wasn't the dad who attended Little League games or school science fairs; I was on the road 280 days a year, for many years—certainly throughout all my kids' childhoods. There's a part of me that regrets some of what I had to do to get to where I am today, but there's also a part of me that would do it all over again without changing a thing. Every important event in my life happened for one reason or another, and from those events, I've been able to procure a volume of lessons that are more valuable to me than the balance of my bank account.

When you think about it, what does "unreasonable" really mean? Well, for most people, it's the pursuit of something no one else believes can be done. I don't think that's unreasonable. In fact, it's what gets my motor running. What's more, being too reasonable can be dangerous, because it shifts all your focus onto figuring out why something new and different can't be done. Those who willfully embrace unreasonable thinking are able to come up with innovations that lead to success. Tell me something can't be done, and I'll show you that it can. Tell me no, and I'll figure out a way to turn that into a yes. These actions didn't always make me the most popular guy in the room, but they almost always garnered respect. I suppose I'd rather be respected than loved.

Startups are often founded by experimenters—those unreasonable-thinking doers who have a good idea and actually take the steps to get it off the kitchen table and into motion. Now more than ever, these are the people capable of creating tremendous innovation and change. They're the ones who tend to speed up the process of innovating more than others in the face of major events, such as a global pandemic. They're the leaders of companies that are racing ahead as less capable and more inefficient companies fall to the wayside.

In the opening of this book, I talked about the wisdom of our elders. I want to come back to that notion again here as we close in on the final chapter. There is, to my mind, simply no replacement for experience. I know so much more today than I could ever have imagined when we started RE/MAX more than fifty years ago. Add to that the lessons I learned from growing up on a farm and later serving in the military, and you can now see that I'm the culmination of seventy-seven years of learning—sometimes the hard way, and occasionally just as I planned.

When you align your purpose with your actions and emotions, you can accomplish anything. Remember, you get what you focus on.

THE PANDEMIC AND ITS FORCED CHANGE

Whether we were prepared for it or not, Covid has had a significant impact on business. Even in the best of times, good business leaders know they must constantly adapt their companies as markets, consumer habits, and the economy change. But this was especially true during the pandemic. In the spring of 2020, more than three million businesses ceased operation, with four hundred thousand of them closing permanently by June. Those were devastating times for all of us, but especially for small businesses and their employees.

The pandemic forced thousands of businesses to rethink their strategies and focus on ways to grow and become resilient. The *International Journal of Disaster Risk Reduction* did a study in May of 2020 that found 63 percent of small businesses in the United Stated had changed how they served their customers, while 56 percent changed how they got their supplies, 49 percent increased their social media presence, and 41 percent shifted to online sales.

So, what this tells us is that some were quickly able to figure things out, pivot, and keep serving their customers, while others simply couldn't. The businesses that were able to withstand the short-term pain of such changes most likely ended up stronger and more resilient, meaning they adjusted in ways that made their companies better off. This doesn't necessarily mean that they were more profitable, but it does mean that those companies remained in the game and became better prepared and more ready to endure the next unexpected, potentially catastrophic shock. Like anything in life, you have to figure out a way to turn a negative into a positive, and when you do, you'll come out of that experience with more confidence and the belief that you're capable of surviving any challenge the universe has in store for you.

There's no doubt that the lockdown hit businesses so fast that many couldn't withstand the shock. But the pandemic also created new opportunities for those who were able to see a way through the ominous circumstances. In fact, many businesses ended up becoming more successful because of their ability to adapt to the new home-based lifestyle, consumer habits, and other shifts that took place. Red Roof Inns, for instance, began offering day rates to those who needed a change of scenery or a quiet space to work, perhaps away from their children's Zoom classes or their spouse's work calls. Best Buy increased their access to virtual support and technology repair. Walgreens, among other retailers, began to offer delivery of groceries and personal-care items by partnering with Postmates.

Applications for new businesses in late 2020 hit their highest rate in seventeen years, with those numbers staying consistent well into 2021. One reason for this spike was the flood of laid-off or unhappy employees who were looking for new ways to make a living. Another reason was the new opportunities the market presented, especially in the field of business-to-consumer direct marketing. Companies large and small had to figure out alternative ways to reach their customers. A good example of this was studios with films set for theatrical release before the pandemic. When theaters were shuttered, the studios had to reconsider how to make that content available to the public, so they released their films on streaming services for an extra fee. Ultimately, when theaters reopened, the studios gave audiences a choice about how to watch new releases—at home or in theaters—and in the process, they changed the way people are entertained.

One of the biggest changes we saw during the Covid pandemic was the adaptation of new or previously underutilized technologies such as Zoom, Webex, Team Meeting, and others. A McKinsey survey of nine hundred executives from around the world found that companies transitioned much quicker to these digital solutions than expected, and certainly more seamlessly than they would have before the pandemic. And once those changes were made, they lasted and have now become common.

Navigating these types of difficult shifts once can make doing it again much easier. Retooling these strategies, becoming flexible enough to find new ways to keep the doors open, and leading with confidence through challenging times will greatly benefit your business and the people who work there.

TECHNOLOGY AND BUSINESS

The only constant in life, of course, is change. This is also true in business. To thrive, you have to embrace change. You don't have to be first in line, but eventually you'll have to get in the game. Interestingly, the people who are out there first, leading the way, often make the most mistakes, some of which can be hard to come back from. That's especially true in land development, commercial real estate development, and housing development. Usually, it's not the first person in who makes the money; in fact, they typically run out of money. It's the second or third person who rescues the project from bankruptcy and reaps the rewards, while the others contend with their losses and debt.

Activision Blizzard is one of the leading gaming companies in the world. They're the creators of *World of Warcraft*, *Guitar Hero*, *Candy Crush*, and many others. The company has evolved brilliantly over time; if it hadn't done so, it would likely have become obsolete. To remain relevant and stay in the game (literally), companies must continuously adapt.

Bobby Kotick has been the CEO of Activision Blizzard since 1991. He bought the business in 1990 for $440,000. In October 2023, Miscrosoft acquired Activision Blizzard for $69 billion where it became a sibling division to Xbox Game Studios and ZeniMax Media. The company now has a market capitalization of more than $74 billion. Running a gaming and technology business over the course of three decades requires flexibility and tremendous perseverance, because the industry is always changing, and rapidly. During a CNBC interview in 2019, Kotick was asked what he did during that time to sustain the business and keep it growing that other video game companies were unable to do. He said, "We are ruthless prioritizers of opportunity; we don't get distracted, we know what our business is, we find the best talent, and we make sure that we keep our talent focused."

According to Kotick, Activision Blizzard's top priority was making great games and figuring out how to reach the biggest audiences to play them, and he did an outstanding job. In 2019, the company had more than 350 million customers in 190 countries, and it's still growing today. The company continues to capture audiences by providing content more frequently and growing their franchises on new platforms. At one time, to play video games, you had to own a PlayStation or an Xbox, or you could use your computer. When games became available on phones, the market exploded. The audience grew from a few hundred million potential customers to billions. Within a month of Activision Blizzard's launching *Call of Duty* on mobile devices, one hundred million consumers signed up. That's when the company realized that taking their existing games from consoles to PCs to phones would create staggering growth. Today, the company is moving forward by continuing to push the envelope of innovation, creating new ways to fulfill their mission of bringing people together through epic entertainment. There are many emerging technologies that are changing the gaming business, including virtual reality (VR) and augmented reality (AR). Both VR and AR are immersive technologies that enhance the user's perception of the real world or create entirely virtual experiences.

VR games create simulated experiences that can either be similar to or completely different from real-world experiences. They typically require VR headsets that cover users' eyes and track their head movements to create a 3-D computer-generated environment. Users can interact with this virtual environment using specialized controllers or other input devices. AR, on the other hand, overlays digital content onto the real world, augmenting users' perception of their surroundings. AR can be experienced through various devices, such as smartphones, tablets, smart glasses, or heads-up displays. It typically utilizes the device's camera and sensors to detect and analyze the real-world environment, then superimposes digital elements like images, text, or 3-D objects onto the user's view. AR technology aims to blend the real and virtual worlds, allowing users to interact with both simultaneously.

Both VR and AR have applications across various industries, including gaming, entertainment, education, training, healthcare, architecture, and more. They offer unique and immersive experiences that can revolutionize how we interact with digital content and the world around us. While the current audience for these technologies is relatively small compared to that for gaming, there's no doubt that the market will grow and become the next frontier in gaming and devices.

A company like Activision Blizzard was built on taking chances and calculated risks. It also changed and adapted its products as consumers' wants and needs changed. Nothing great has ever happened without someone taking a risk, big or small. You cannot conduct today's business with yesterday's methods and expect to still be in business tomorrow. One of the best examples of this truth was the introduction of the internet.

Many of you may not realize that the internet started in the 1960s. It was initially created as a way for government researchers to share information. Computers in the '60s weren't compact or easy to move, so to make use of information stored in any one computer, you had to either be in the physical location of that computer or receive magnetic tapes with the information encoded on them through the mail. It was hardly convenient like it is today.

When the Soviet Union launched the Sputnik satellite, the US Department of Defense began to consider new ways information could be disseminated in the event of a nuclear attack. This ultimately led to the creation of the ARPANET (Advanced Research Projects Agency Network), the network that eventually became what we know as the internet. Although ARPANET was successful, it was still a very limited system.

January 1, 1983, is considered the official launch date of the modern internet. A new communications protocol called Transfer Control Protocol/Internetwork Protocol (TCP/IP) was created to allow computers on different networks to "talk" to each other, making it possible for all networks to be connected by a universal language.

When I first heard about the internet, I was on a panel of CEOs of the five biggest companies in the real estate industry. There were eight thousand people listening to us. One of the panel members was a man named Brian Buffini. Brian is a special guy who's been a close friend of mine for more than twenty years. He immigrated to the United States from Ireland without a single cent to his name. He got into a devastating motorcycle accident, and when he could finally get around, he joined RE/MAX and became a top producer. He was so good that he became a business performance coach, and eventually grew his team to well over one hundred coaches. The panel we were on had been convened to talk about technology, and at one point Brian pulled out his phone and said, "For all you Realtors in this room, this is the only technology you really need. Pick it up and call someone. Call for a listing, call to get a buyer, call to get a referral. This is real technology." And he believed it.

At the time, the industry was abuzz with this new app or that new app. It was all about the next bright, shiny thing. There were 1.6 million Realtors out there whom every technology company was trying to sell to.

While I believe in keeping abreast of all the latest trends so you aren't caught off guard when the next big thing happens—and, more important, so that you're one or more steps ahead of change—I do think you also need a healthy dose of skepticism from time to time. You can't open your mind indiscriminately to *every* shiny new thing, or your brain might fall out.

When the technological revolution started, I made fun of it. Call me old-school or closed-minded, but I didn't get it. I was pretty vocal about how I felt too. "Most people don't need technology. They need a customer," I would say. Of course, at the time, technology wasn't set up to bring us customers. It eventually morphed into that with the advent of the internet, online postings, Zillow, and Trulia, among other developments, but the tech industry thought of me as a Neanderthal. Now, I understood technology; I had the latest and greatest gadgets and devices. But my emphasis remained on building RE/MAX, selling franchises, recruiting and retaining agents, and collecting the money. At the time, I wasn't interested in technology or evolving with it unless I could see how it would serve my primary purpose of selling more real estate.

Eventually, around 2018, we hit a roadblock. We'd outsourced our website to a company called Homes. They created and hosted a lot of sites in the industry, and they were reliable—until they weren't. Our site started crashing, and at one time there were thirty thousand work orders in process to fix everything that was wrong with it. So, we made a huge financial commitment and bought our own web processing system, which has been extremely effective. Today, we have $60 million or more invested in data and technology, and I consider that money well spent because it furthered our sales efforts.

When Adam Contos took over as CEO, the board kept pushing him to acquire more technology. I didn't think it was necessarily a good plan. Some of the technology we bought worked as we thought it would, but most of it didn't pan out. We spent more than $100 million on various technology acquisitions, most of which turned out to be nothing but a money drain. We did, however, buy an outstanding artificial intelligence company called First, which analyzes seven hundred different points of contact with our past customers. We can take a contact list and upload it into the application, and the algorithm searches it every day for anything that indicates someone might be thinking of buying or selling real estate. These might include marriage certificates, hits on Zillow, inquiries about the price of a home or homes in a specific neighborhood, and data from all the MLS listings in the United States. It's a fascinating program that's about 90 percent accurate. Realtors will tell you they get 90 percent of their business through referrals, but actually it isn't nearly that high for most people. When you have hundreds of contacts, you're busy making today's deals, but you have a hard time following up with the other deals. But when we made the First app available exclusively to our RE/MAX agents, we found that the average agent increased their number of transactions by at least eight to ten a year. That's a phenomenal increase in money.

At one point, we wanted to revamp our fee rates with agents and brokers. We thought we could recoup some of our investment in this and other systems we'd bought if we charged them for the system's use. The buy rate was only 5 to 10 percent, but the agents didn't want to pay that. They wanted us to provide the systems to them for free. Even though First worked and increased sales, no one wanted to pay $500 a year for it. It made no sense. By turning it down, they were throwing away the opportunity to pick up an extra commission that would have more than covered the cost. The amazing thing is that while we spent all that money on technology, our agent growth in the United States had slowed to a trickle, or even a minor loss. Acquiring this system took our focus off marketing and doing what we knew how to do best.

At the time, we'd just gone public. The leaders of the company were telling Wall Street that our margins were 50 percent and we were set to increase them to 55 percent. It was unreal to have a company that grosses $300 million with pretax revenue of $160 million a year. Unfortunately, hyping our performance so we would keep our margins up to the Street's expectations backfired. After we acquired First, we had no money to reinvest in marketing and further building the business, so that $100 million was wasted. We had to reallocate our assets in a different fashion. We no longer had a growth story for the suits on Wall Street. All we were was a cash cow—meaning we were making money, but we weren't growing.

All the real estate companies that touted themselves as technology companies have failed in that regard. Compass, for example, didn't recruit people to their company because of their technology; they actually paid people to leave their former agencies to come and work for them. They lost $500 million in 2021. Keller Williams tried to imitate Redfin and Compass by calling themselves a technology company and boasting about investing $1 billion over the next five years to become the tech giant of the real estate world. Zillow, which is a pure technology play, never had that kind of money to invest. Of course, in 2022, Gary Keller had to stand in front of his company at their family reunion convention and admit that they'd failed in their efforts to develop technology and would be buying it from outside vendors going forward.

I call this the monkey brain of the entrepreneur. It's when someone isn't being analytical. When they aren't counting on people. When they're so used to working with numbers that they forget to exercise any people sense. Real estate agents are salespeople. We're flighty. We want to chase the next dream. When someone comes and shows us the next doodad, we want to buy it. Then, most times, we never use it, or it doesn't work as promised. Have you ever wondered how many unused BowFlex machines there are in the world, just sitting in basements serving as expensive clothes hangers? It all sounds good when you buy it, but after a week or two the novelty wears off and you realize that using it is hard work . . . and then you buy something else. That's the vicious cycle we've all fallen into at one time or another.

If you're going to spend money on technology or innovation, ask yourself what the return on the investment is going to be. If you're looking at a specific technology, question what the value is and how you can measure it once you purchase it. If you've already spent the money, be sure you know what you're getting back for it.

Back in the 1960s and early '70s, everyone working in real estate had an answering service to field calls if they were out of the office. Most of the employees working those services were part-time housewives looking to earn extra money. They would be on duty from 6:00 a.m. to midnight, taking messages and passing them along. It's the way we all did business for decades.

Then, in 1971, the first answering machine was introduced. It was called PhoneMate Model 400 and it weighed ten pounds, so it was quite bulky. This new technology could screen calls and hold up to twenty messages on a reel-to-reel tape. Then, in 1979, Gordon Matthews produced the first commercial voicemail system and founded his company, VMX (Voice Message Express), in Dallas, Texas. He sold the first system to 3M. According to Matthews, the reason he sold his patent was simple: "When I call a business, I like to speak to a human," he said.

When I learned about voicemail, I thought it was genius, but our agents didn't immediately embrace the new technology. Like

Matthews, they also wanted their clients talking to a human and not a machine. Four years later the answering services went out of business, and five hundred thousand part-time message-taking employees were out of a job. Eventually, people embraced voicemail, and we use it widely today.

Technology continues to introduce new ways of revolutionizing our work and lifestyles. During the Covid lockdown, technology pushed purchasing practices forward by at least ten years. An unbelievable number of people who had never considered ordering their groceries online suddenly found themselves using Instacart and other apps. Prepared-meal delivery was also impacted. Everyone was living in fear of contracting the virus, so out of necessity, they were ordering food online through Door Dash, Uber Eats, Grubhub, or Postmates. This quickly and drastically changed buying habits, especially around food.

Knowing this, we built our own exclusive technology suite for Daddy's Chicken Shack. It was custom designed for us, which required a sizable investment up front. There are several ways you can order food with the app. You can come to the store and order at the counter, where you'll use an iPad to place your order. If you have the app on your phone, you can preorder for pickup. If you've previously ordered, the app knows your history and will ask if you want to order the same thing as last time. If you want it delivered, you can order through Grubhub or Uber. If you're picking up your order, we provide an arrival time so your food will be ready, hot, and tasty when you arrive. Prepaid orders are also distributed via our drive-through window, which allows us to move cars unbelievably fast compared to McDonald's or Chick-fil-A, where you might sit in the queue for several minutes before you pay and pick up your food. Our app stores your payment information, so there's no cash involved. The idea is to make ordering and delivery as seamless as possible. The technology benefit is expected to be exponential. Sixty percent of our stores will

image generation. AI also plays a crucial role in robotics, enabling machines to perceive their environment, make decisions, and manipulate objects. Robotic systems can leverage AI techniques for tasks like autonomous navigation and human-robot interaction.

If you're wondering how AI has already impacted your life, think about Google. How often do you log on to look for information? How many times do you ask Siri, who uses Google, a question? Google can be incredibly helpful, and it has changed not only how we receive critical information but the speed with which we receive it.

In 2021, I got a call from a customer who lived in Saudi Arabia. He oversaw a $100 million fund whose goal was to bring restaurants there. I didn't get the connection at first, but then I found out that he had eaten at Daddy's Chicken Shack in Pasadena. Once he and his partner learned that we were getting ready to franchise, they said they wanted to bring Daddy's not only to Saudi Arabia but to locations throughout the entire Middle East, including Israel.

Nothing, however, is as easy as it looks. After opening RE/MAX branches in 110 countries, I'm well aware of the number and kinds of problems that come with expansion. The minute I heard about their interest, I went straight to Google to figure out how many units we could put in Saudi Arabia. When we launched Daddy's, we figured out that our saturation point was going to be about a fourth of what McDonald's is, mostly because we're fast-casual dining. We weren't going to be at every interstate intersection or service station. I Googled how many McDonald's locations there are in the Middle East and discovered that as of 2018, there were 1,435 stores across eighteen countries in the region. Having this information at my fingertips helped me have a meaningful and knowledgeable conversation about what was realistic with regard to the deal.

Our smart devices are another great example of AI at work. Have you ever noticed that after talking about something you suddenly find ads on your phone for that particular product? That's AI's doing. Alexa and Siri, Amazon's and Apple's respective digital voice assistants, are not just convenient to use, they're very real applications of artificial intelligence that have become vital to our lives. To operate most effectively over time, they similarly rely on natural language generation and processing and machine learning. We've all come into contact with AI-powered chatbots and virtual assistants that handle customer inquiries, provide support, and assist with basic tasks. They offer prompt responses and personalized interactions, enhancing customer service and reducing human agents' workload.

If you think AI won't impact your business in some way, think again. For example, in the real estate industry, numerous companies, including Zillow, Realtor.com, Trulia, Opendoor, and others, claim that they generate leads. If you've ever clicked on any of those sites, whether you were in the market for a new home, just looking to see what someone was asking for a certain property, comparing your home against others, or simply browsing, you can appear to be a potential buyer or seller. When you look at a property on those sites, the system captures your email address, but you don't become an actual lead until you request more information and they can then gather more data. In return for these leads, these companies want a 20 to 25 percent referral fee from the agent. A significant number of the six million properties sold last year, however, were from repeat customers or traditional and verifiable referrals. Two hundred million leads were generated in that year, and most were worthless. At RE/MAX alone, we likely provided a minimum of one million to one and a half million leads each month to our agents, yet 60 percent of the people we followed up with wouldn't even open an email from us because, like so many other digital captures, the leads weren't worthwhile. The best leads in real estate still come from bona fide referrals or a signage call, meaning someone saw a For Sale sign on a property and was interested enough to follow up with an agent. But who knows what the future will hold as AI continues to be refined and perfected? We all have a responsibility through critical thinking and ongoing measurements to make sure the technology is developed and applied to serve its best function in our respective industries.

AI, of course, has numerous applications across fields such as healthcare, finance, manufacturing, transportation, and education, just to name a few. When implemented effectively, it has the potential to improve efficiency, enable automation, enhance decision-making, and deliver personalized experiences to consumers. For example, AI can automate repetitive tasks, allowing businesses to streamline their operations and increase productivity. AI-powered systems can handle data entry, customer support, data analysis, and other routine processes, freeing up human resources to focus on more complex and strategic tasks. It can also analyze large volumes of data quickly and accurately, extracting valuable insights and patterns. Businesses can leverage AI algorithms to make data-driven decisions, optimize methodologies, identify trends, and predict outcomes, enabling better strategic planning, improved customer targeting, and enhanced operational efficiency. AI also allows businesses to personalize their products, services, and marketing efforts. Through machine learning algorithms, businesses can analyze customer preferences, behavior, and feedback to deliver relevant recommendations, targeted advertisements, and tailored experiences. This helps improve customer satisfaction, loyalty, and engagement.

AI can also be useful in business security, an area of critical concern for all companies as most businesses deal with sensitive and valuable material, including customer information, financial records, trade secrets, and proprietary data. Robust security measures, such as encryption, access controls, and regular backups, help protect this data from unauthorized access, data breaches, and cyberattacks, preventing significant financial, legal, and reputational damage to the company. By prioritizing business security, organizations can safeguard their assets, protect sensitive data, build trust with customers, comply with regulations, maintain employee safety, and ensure continuity of operations. AI can enhance security by identifying potential threats, anomalies, or fraudulent activities; monitoring network traffic; detecting suspicious patterns; and alerting security personnel to potential breaches. It can also aid in user authentication, fraud detection, and data protection. These next few years will be pivotal for this technology, and it will be interesting to see where it leads . . . and where we take it.

BELLY BUMPING YOUR WAY INTO CHANGE

Change is often about seizing opportunities, but sometimes it's also about disentangling yourself from arrangements that are no longer working. When I was younger, I had a tendency to settle disagreements by taking someone outside and fighting them. Today, of course, you can't really do that, especially in business. Belly bumping is a term I came up with when I realized I was going to come across people in business who were impossible to deal with. When you physically belly bump someone instead of getting into a fistfight or threatening to throw them out of the room, you invade their personal space and slowly maneuver them out the door. In business, belly bumping is finding a way to gently but persuasively push someone into making a decision to leave an organization on their own. You belly bump them out instead of firing them.

This has happened many times throughout my career. Years ago, I sold the California region for RE/MAX to a gentleman in his sixties who was a health fanatic. When he bought the region, he told me he was able to get SBA loans for all our brokers, especially in California. I didn't buy his story. None of our people had ever applied for an SBA loan, and I wasn't sure this was the best path for them, even though the Small Business Administration is one of the most well-known business-related organizations in the United States, offering funding options, educational resources, connections to mentors, and more.

This man went to some of our existing brokers and got them $250,000 SBA loans anyway. It turned out that one of his best friends was the head of the SBA in Southern California and had recently hired him to be on his staff. He knew the ins and outs of the SBA and how to get things done. A year later, he was telling his cronies there that RE/MAX was a great place to work and pushed me to hire them while he arranged for loans. I knew at that moment I was going to get rid of him. I didn't want to be in bed with a snake, so I found a way to belly bump him out of the company by applying extreme pressure from every direction until he finally knew his time was up. Eventually, we resold the region to two partners who did a fabulous job.

A lot of franchisors talk about this, although they may not call it belly bumping. They have groups they secretly call the Dirty Thirty. They look at their thirty worst-performing offices or outlets and say, "You're not making it. Our contract says we can terminate you, but we would like to save you. We'll assign one of our top outlets to be your mentor for the next three months. We'll build a business plan to get you out of the trouble you're in, and let's see if we can salvage our relationship." Doing this is basically allowing the franchisee one final chance to save their business before the franchisor closes their doors. Occasionally, someone will succeed; but the vast majority of the time, these businesses are on their way out anyway. They won't make the changes necessary to survive.

In 2007, RE/MAX went through a terrible period in California when the market collapsed. In Santa Barbara, there was a month when, despite employing three thousand agents, we had only *two* property closings. It was abysmal. At the time, there were brokers who were failing even though they had started at RE/MAX with one office and grown their business to include as many as seven offices with four hundred agents. They owned their houses free and clear. Their second homes were free and clear too. Their 401(k) accounts contained $1 million or more. They had good cash flow. But then the housing collapse happened, and their agents couldn't afford to pay the fees because there were no deals being written. We immediately went to the brokers who were at risk—especially those with multiple offices—to help them figure out what to do. In some cases, they had three offices that were still making money and two that were draining them, wiping away whatever profit the other three were making. We explained that they needed to close the offices that were bleeding cash, sell the furniture, and get the agents to merge into one of their successful offices to weather the storm. These weren't easy conversations. Egos were hurt. No one wanted to be seen as nearly bankrupt, and the fear of their agents going to competitors was very real. We lost many offices under those circumstances because they couldn't handle the perception of change or loss. In the end, most of those brokers gave up good people because they weren't willing to listen to our suggestions. Whether they knew it or not, these brokers were belly bumped. We threw them a lifeline with our business plan, and they failed to take it. They couldn't embrace short-term change for the sake of long-term survival.

As an investor, I have, on occasion, had to belly bump the founders of a company because they turned out not to be the people I thought they were. As we like to say in the West, they were all hat and no cattle, meaning all talk and no action.

Here's what I know for sure: Just because you made money in one business doesn't necessarily mean you can make it in another, especially if you're investing in unknowns. When you're an investor, it's critically important to put your money to work. You don't want it sitting in a savings account at a 1 percent annual interest rate. But people often make mistakes with mergers and acquisitions. They're too anxious to do the deal immediately instead of waiting.

At RE/MAX, we've made six technology acquisitions in the last five years, one of which I mentioned earlier. Unfortunately, none of them have lived up to our expectations, but we don't regret buying any of them. Each represented the prospect for positive change. We might have overpaid a little on a few, but we took our eye off the ball when we concentrated on those businesses more than on selling franchises and recruiting agents—our bread and butter. What we learned from these collective acquisitions was that change has to accelerate growth, not impede it.

I recently took an online mergers and acquisitions class that was outstanding. The course had some of the best M&A experts in the country. Even now, at my age and career stage, I got so much out of that course. (Always keep learning!) Thinking about the class, I was reminded of a frequent saying on Wall Street that implies 90 percent of all mergers and acquisitions go bad. That's actually not true, but somewhere around 50 percent or more don't pan out for one reason or another. Different corporate cultures, different expectations, greed, and an inability to find cost savings are just some of the reasons. The biggest reason a merger or acquisition doesn't work out, however, is that one or both parties were too anxious to make the deal instead of thinking their way through it. You may find yourself in a bidding contest if you wait too long, which means you might overpay, but being prudent will likely help your deal turn out to be a better investment.

We teach who we are.

—Parker Palmer

HOW KAIZEN LEADS TO LASTING CHANGE IN BUSINESS

Kaizen is a Japanese term that means "better for change." As a concept, it generally refers to business conduct that constantly improves all functions and involves all employees, from entry-level positions to the C suite. It equally relates to processes that touch everything from purchasing to logistics and the supply chain. Kaizen has been applied in many fields, including healthcare, psychotherapy, life coaching, government, manufacturing, and banking. It says that your goals should be to operate better and more efficiently each and every day, in some small way. It's all about incremental improvements that, over time, translate into huge gains. I think sometimes people assume that change has to be radical, but it can be gradual and stealthy and still have enormous impact.

When people talk about scaling a business, they often think that spending money will get them the growth they need. But building a staff, adding technology, and ensuring that the supply chain is able to handle your growing needs is important too.

If you're looking to grow or to partner with someone else or another organization, don't get stuck on the numbers and the processes of merging, acquiring, or partnering. Focus on the people, because they're the ones who will get you your *future* numbers. Leaders often overlook their people as they worry about the internal rate of return, growth opportunities, or future valuation of a company. This is a big mistake, as people will get you to where you want to go.

As you become more successful, opportunities to grow will naturally present themselves. Always be a work in progress and use your success as a stepping stone to your next goal. I once heard an analogy that suggested if you pitted a Super Bowl team with no all-stars on its roster against a Pro Bowl team, the Super Bowl team would beat the collection of all-stars any day. Why? There's no synergy among the all-stars, no shared culture. The same holds true for business. You can go out and find the highest performers in your business, but if they're in it for themselves—if they're Pro Bowlers but not team players—your organization will lack heart and soul, that great balance between personal accountability and shared purpose that binds a team together. Despite the promise of change, RE/MAX has walked away from deals because the leadership of the prospective partner firm appeared to only be chasing money. When weighing an acquisition or partnership, we always consider whether a firm just wants to enrich themselves or they want to help grow the concept of the business, idea, or philosophy and make their community better for it. The latter are the kind of people we want to be in business with.

10 Reasons Why Embracing Change Is Crucial

1. Innovation and Growth
   Change often brings about new ideas, technologies, and processes that lead to innovation. Embracing change encourages a culture of continuous improvement and fosters creativity, driving business growth and development.

2. Competitive Advantage
   Adapting to change allows businesses to stay ahead of the competition. Being responsive to market shifts and customer demands enables companies to offer unique products or services that set them apart from their competitors.

3. Customer Satisfaction
   Embracing change can—and often does—lead to better customer experiences. Understanding and responding to evolving customer needs and preferences ensures that your business remains relevant and valuable to its target audience.

4. Efficiency and Productivity

   Change often involves optimizing workflows and adopting more efficient technologies or systems. This can streamline processes, reduce costs, and increase overall productivity within an organization.

5. Resilience and Adaptability

   Businesses that embrace change are better equipped to face unexpected challenges, disruptions, or economic downturns. They can quickly pivot and adjust their strategies to cope with changing circumstances.

6. Talent Attraction and Retention

   Change signals to potential employees that your company is forward-thinking and open to innovation. This can help attract top talent and retain existing employees who value growth and development.

7. Market Relevance

   Markets are constantly evolving, and customer preferences change over time. Embracing this change allows businesses to remain relevant and avoid becoming obsolete or outdated.

8. Risk Management

   Ignoring change can expose a business to greater risk. Embracing change allows a company to proactively identify and manage risks, ensuring that better risk mitigation strategies are in place.

9. Improved Decision-Making

   Change helps foster a data-driven and evidence-based decision-making approach, which allows businesses to better analyze market trends, customer feedback, and performance metrics and make more informed choices.

10. Long-Term Sustainability
    Businesses that resist change risk stagnation and eventual decline. Embracing change is essential for ensuring the long-term sustainability and viability of a company.

Embracing change isn't just about adapting to the current environment; it's also about preparing for the future. It's about being proactive, open-minded, and willing to continuously evolve to meet the challenges and opportunities that come your way.

10

Personal Development

Og Mandino's 1968 book *The Greatest Salesman in the World* is a fictional story that imparts valuable lessons about success, personal development, and the art of selling. The story revolves around Hafid, a poor camel boy who dreams of becoming the greatest salesman in the world. Hafid's life takes a significant turn when he meets a wealthy and wise trader named Pathros. Pathros recognizes Hafid's ambition and potential and decides to mentor him. Pathros entrusts Hafid with ten ancient scrolls, each containing a nugget of wisdom that can transform one's life. Hafid is instructed to spend a month with each scroll, immersing himself in its teachings and mastering its principles. As Hafid progresses through the scrolls, he learns essential lessons about persistence, love, faith, and the power of positive thinking.

Throughout his journey, Hafid encounters various challenges and setbacks, but he persists by applying the principles from the scrolls. Eventually, he achieves remarkable success in his sales career and becomes renowned as the greatest salesman in the world.

Along with chronicling Hafid's personal growth, the book also emphasizes the importance of serving others, cultivating good habits, and maintaining a positive mindset. It encourages readers to adopt these principles in their own lives and to pursue their dreams with determination and integrity. I love this book, for obvious reasons. At heart I'm a salesperson who has tried to live a principled life.

Since we spend so much of our time at work, our personal development and career development are intrinsically entwined. One cannot effectively write a book about business and not include advice about personal growth as well.

I also love the thinking behind the following quote, as it reflects my philosophy too:

> ***The people who care less about what other people think about them tend to have a better life. It's just liberating.***
> **—Gary Vaynerchuk**

Gary Vaynerchuk, a.k.a., Gary Vee, has spoken at our conventions a few times over the years. Today, he runs a digital marketing company with locations in New York, Los Angeles, London, and Chattanooga, Tennessee. Gary personifies drive, determination, and integrity, and he encourages others to do so as well. He attributes much of his success to extreme self-confidence, believing that self-esteem is the ultimate drug in life. And as the quote indicates, he doesn't put much stock in what other people think of him. Gary is bold and direct. He likes to tell it like it is. I suppose we share that in common.

Gary was an entrepreneur from an early age, beginning with cutting flowers from his neighbors' yards and selling them and moving on to "franchising" lemonade stands and dealing in used baseball cards. He was always hustling. In college, he grew his parents' wine business from $3 million in annual sales to $60 million in just over five years by taking it online. In the process, he became a wine expert and created an online show called *Wine Library TV* that became extremely popular. A true entrepreneur at heart, Gary knows how to build businesses and leverage his expertise. As his notoriety grew, so did his audience—some of whom loved him and some of whom didn't. He puts no credence in the opinions of naysayers who've never met him. He has mastered the art of building a personal brand, becoming one of the leading thinkers on what's most culturally relevant and what's coming next. He based his thriving empire on his strong sense of self, and helps others find strength from within and understand the difference between confidence and security. He believes insecurity can be a killer in life and in business. It holds people back, taints office culture, and leads to weak decision-making. He also advocates fearlessness, as it can give you the courage to make a leap of faith and go after your dreams. He's written numerous bestselling books, including one of my favorites, *Crush It!: Why NOW Is the Time to Cash In on Your Passion.*

As you know, I love reading. When I was starting out in business, I read a book called *The Magic of Thinking Big* by David J. Schwartz. The messages in this book reminded me of Dale Carnegie's *How to Win Friends and Influence People*: Both are full of basic business advice such as "Believe you can succeed and you will," "Treat others how you'd like to be treated," and "Stop making excuses," which might make them seem lightweight and passé today—if not downright hokey—but there are a few takeaways from them that made a big difference in the way I operated, and I believe they will for you too. One of my favorite sayings in business is "No one cares how much you know until they know how much you care." I think the genesis of that belief can be traced back to one of the lessons Schwartz imparts in his book, that we need to remember to *be human*—to treat people as well as we can, whether they're the CEO or the janitor. He encourages us to be kind and generous with our time, money, and resources and to give people the benefit of the doubt; to listen when they speak; to be patient, especially while people are learning;

to be a good teacher; and to know that when we offer grace, people generally rise up.

Another takeaway from *The Magic of Thinking Big* is a really simple one, but don't underestimate its value. It's the notion that *believing something is possible makes it possible.* Believing in something—anything—helps you chart a clear course to achieving your goals. When you believe something is possible, your thoughts lead you onto the path that helps you do it. If you believe there's a solution to a problem, you'll find one. It's really that simple. We tend to overcomplicate things by ruminating on them and believing the stories we tell ourselves. We say things like "I'll never make it," "This is too hard," or "I'm not cut out for success." Now, these stories may or may not be true, but they do create a narrative our minds believe. You see, the brain can't differentiate between a real or an imagined thought. You can convince yourself that your idea will never see the light of day, or you can say it will succeed. Both can be true. To achieve the right mindset, you have to switch your thinking from *might be* or *could be* true to *will be* and *is* true. Crossing that bridge is the difference between success and failure.

Several years ago, when I was lying in a hospital bed in a coma, there were all sorts of rumors about my whereabouts. I had disappeared, and for a while, Gail and I didn't really share why. We thought we might be able to keep my illness a private family matter. And to be certain, when I first arrived at the hospital, I don't think anyone thought I would be there for an extended period of time. We definitely hadn't planned on my being in a coma. As far as we were concerned, I had gone in for treatment of a chronic back problem. Within days, though, I was fighting for my life. But as those days turned into weeks, something had to be said, especially to the team at RE/MAX. As so often is the case when people don't have information or answers, they create their own. There was talk that I was in rehab, that I'd run away with a secretary, or that I was dying from cancer. The wildest of these stories was that I'd been bitten by a shark. When the mighty fall, there are usually lots of people who are eager to prey on their misfortune. Haters will hate.

Managing the inquiries became a full-time job for my top leadership team and my family. My daughter, Mary, and my son, Dave Jr., did an excellent job of keeping our inner circle well informed, but even those updates were kept a little cryptic to protect my privacy. There were lots of reasons for this, especially when it came to our company. While my family saw their husband and father suffering, I was also the chairman and cofounder of a very large corporation, and the dynamics of the company had to be considered with every update we provided.

I share this with you because another lesson from *The Magic of Thinking Big* is that we should *ignore the haters.* Throughout my career, people have come after me, whether it was during the early days of launching RE/MAX or when I was getting into racing, and at many points in between. Some people doubted me, some hated me, some gossiped about me, and some were just plain mean. You know what? I didn't care. None of that was more important than keeping my focus on my goals. I certainly couldn't and wouldn't give more merit to their stories than I did my own. If I'd given any credence to the absurd things that were said about me while I was growing our business or while I was ill, it would have been extremely damaging to the outcomes.

Eleanor Roosevelt once said, "You gain strength, courage, and confidence by every experience in which you really stop to look fear in the face. You are able to say to yourself, 'I have lived through this horror. I can take the next thing that comes along.'" Never once did anyone in my inner circle say that I might not make it through my fight to stay alive. I'd been a fighter my entire life, and there was no way I would give up on myself then, let alone abandon the people I loved the most.

I've never quit at anything in my life. I've been in combat and airplane crashes. I've driven in NASCAR races and survived dangerous Class V rapids while whitewater rafting. I've done every adventurous thing known to mankind, including feats that could have killed me, and never once did I stop myself out of fear that I wouldn't survive.

There were so many people fighting to keep me alive, giving of themselves in unimaginable ways. All I could think about was not giving up. I remember saying to myself as I lay in my hospital bed, *That would make you the worst kind of hypocrite. If you give up now, you'll wash away forty years of delivering speeches to tens of thousands of people, encouraging them to never throw in the towel, to find the courage to face whatever obstacles have been put in their way head-on. Screw it; I won't quit. Not now, not ever!*

That's the mindset of a fearless leader. And even in my most difficult hours, I clung to being such a leader.

If you're green, you're growing. If you're ripe, you rot.

—Zig Ziglar

LOCUS OF CONTROL

When something goes wrong, it's human nature for most people to cast blame on some perceived external cause. Where an individual casts that blame is often related to a psychological construct known as "locus of control." Locus of control is a term that's been around since the 1950s and was coined by social learning theorist Julian Rotter. It refers to how much control an individual believes they have over the events and outcomes in their life versus how much control external forces exert upon those events. In today's terminology, it's how much "agency" a person has.

Those with an *internal* locus of control believe that they have a significant amount of power over their lives and that their actions and decisions directly influence the outcomes they experience. They attribute success or failure to their own abilities, efforts, and choices. People with an internal locus of control tend to be more self-motivated, proactive, and confident in their ability to shape their own destiny. They might say, "I take responsibility for myself. I will either succeed or fail on my own merits."

In contrast, individuals with an *external* locus of control believe external forces, such as luck, fate, or powerful others, determine the outcomes in their lives. They think that events happen due to circumstances beyond their control, and they may feel more influenced by chance or outside factors. People with an external locus of control may feel more helpless or dependent on outside factors and may exhibit lower motivation or initiative. For example, if you're trying to build a company and have experienced a lot of challenges and problems—running out of money, financial errors, competitors trying to put you out of business, and so on—you might say, "It was the wrong time, there was a recession, the industry changed, consumer habits shifted, it's their fault that I failed, etc." if your locus of control is external.

It's important to note that locus of control isn't an all-or-nothing concept, and individuals can exhibit a mix of internal and external beliefs in different situations. Additionally, locus of control doesn't include any judgment of character or ability but rather reflects an individual's perception of how much command they have over their circumstances.

Understanding where your locus of control lies can provide insights into how you approach challenges, take responsibility, and adapt to change. It can also influence the effectiveness of certain interventions or strategies in areas such as education, therapy, and organizational behavior, as people may respond differently based on their locus of control beliefs. Eighty percent of people, in fact, fall into the external locus of control group, blaming bad outcomes on others.

They won't look in the mirror and take responsibility themselves or move proactively to correct a situation they find themselves in.

Knowing where a person's locus of control is can be very useful, especially when it comes to hiring. If you can find people who readily admit their mistakes, who understand where they're going, and who are willing to lead the charge to get there, hire them!

Locus of control can also be very helpful in life-threatening scenarios, as it can dictate how you respond. I have a very internal locus of control, so I didn't let anything keep me down. I've had a lifetime of major and minor setbacks, just as I've had major and minor accomplishments. Each one taught me that whatever was happening wasn't the end of the world. No matter what, I had to move on and keep fighting.

Recovering from my coma and its underlying cause—a type of staph infection called MRSA, which is resistant to the antibiotics typically used to treat staph bacteria—certainly made me a more patient man. I probably developed MRSA as a result of my exposure to Agent Orange while serving in Vietnam. Statistically, younger people have better immune systems, but some veterans with weaker ones showed symptoms of infection when they were younger and went on to develop cancer and other horrific diseases. Even those of us who had strong immune systems would often come down with MRSA in our sixties and seventies, as our immune system health naturally declined.

During my recuperation, I also came to understand that most people are kind. There were many times when total strangers offered assistance. When they saw me walking with a cane or struggling to open a door for myself, they would say, "Let me help you with that door." Theirs were simple acts of kindness—the type I was taught to perform as a Boy Scout—but they really made a difference.

When you're helpless like I was, you become humble really fast. I couldn't walk, couldn't wipe my own butt, and couldn't feed myself because my hands didn't work. Somebody had to do everything for me, as if I were a three-month-old baby. It was very difficult for me to accept help at first. Everybody wants their independence, and I was someone who'd never had to depend on others until then.

Looking back, I'm extremely grateful for the experience. My kids came to the hospital every day for nine months, as did eight or nine of my closest friends. They were by my side seven days a week for all that time. I was never alone. I quickly found out who was naughty and who was nice—and who was kissing my ass, only acting like a friend, and who really was my friend. I also met eight of the most beautiful women in the world: my nurses, who led with compassion at all times. As hard as it must be, those women show up, day in and day out, and do their jobs—and they're damn good at it too. They understand the meaning of hard work and, above all, dedication.

I remember reading in *The Magic of Thinking Big* that every big endeavor in life requires small steps. When you look at anyone whose actions appear heroic, you must realize that they got to where they are one step at a time, and more often than not those steps were very small. In fact, I called my last book *My Next Step* because I knew I had a rough road ahead of me after I awoke from my coma. I was told I would never walk again, that I'd be a paraplegic. You know what? I was okay with that. I was alive, and that's all that mattered. I made up my mind that if I were going to spend the rest of my life in a wheelchair, then by God, I'd learn to play wheelchair hockey or basketball and become the best paraplegic I could be. I was as tough as any able-bodied person and determined not to lose myself just because I lost the use of my legs, and I would do it one step at a time. That's how real progress is made. Every great accomplishment is a collection of small achievements. I always knew this to be true, but it especially resonated with me during my recovery.

There have been many terrible times throughout the course of my life. I was not an overnight success. I worked very hard and made a lot of mistakes that I've had to pay for along the way. There have been so many make-or-break moments in our company's history when I've stood back and wondered whether I'd thrown away twenty years of my life. Through all the life events I've experienced, from being in combat to building my business to suffering extraordinary financial difficulties during downward markets, I somehow persevered. I managed to live through each challenge, overcome it, and ultimately learn that what doesn't kill you makes you stronger. Those life experiences gave me the fortitude, the toughness, to face the hardest battle of my life—and so I committed to getting out of bed and finding my determination to walk again. I was told it would never happen, but by now, you should know I don't accept defeat easily. It took nearly a year, but I won that battle.

One last lesson I learned from *The Magic of Thinking Big* is that *if you want something done, ask a busy person to do it.* As someone who works seven days a week, I simply don't know any other way to live. Being busy forces us to become exceptionally efficient and very good at prioritizing what needs to get done. Over the years, I've found myself on the road, giving speeches, recruiting agents, and selling franchises, all while building RE/MAX and spending what time I could with my family. Maybe it was my military service that gave me the discipline to work crazier hours than anyone else and still manage to have playtime too. Work breeds order, and order brings results. If you find yourself spending more time on social media than you do at your desk, you're not busy enough, or you don't think being productive is important. If you want to be an entrepreneur or to be the best person you can be, it's time to rethink your priorities.

THE THREE BOXES OF LIFE

In 1981, I read a book called *The Three Boxes of Life* by Richard Bolles, the author of *What Color Is Your Parachute?* This fascinating book explores Bolles's notion that three stages (or boxes) of life—education, work, and retirement—have become the respective stages for learning, achievement, and leisure. In the first box are the learning years. These are the years from birth to the time you complete your formal education, whether that be high school, trade school, or college. In the second box are the earning years, when you start at the bottom and work your way up throughout your career. You should have achieved your highest level of earning at the end of these years. Finally, in the third box are the yearning years, a.k.a., the retirement years.

Bolles makes a convincing case that the majority of people live in only one box at a time. His thinking on this is straightforward. When most people are learning, that's all they're doing. For the most part, they aren't earning. They aren't giving back to the community. They're not being philanthropic because they don't have the money or know-how to be financially supportive of others yet. But Bolles contends that we should be learning, earning, and giving back throughout the entirety of our lives. Doing so leads to a more fulfilling life.

Most of us spend our earning years focused on climbing the ladder of success, figuring out how to make more money, and surviving the financial strains of raising our families. We put our kids through college, buy homes, and save for retirement, often putting off things that might make our yearning years better. But once we reach retirement, we aren't necessarily able to enjoy participating in life the way we could have when we were in our prime. Bolles believes that the biggest mistake most of us make is putting things off for so long that it becomes too late.

This hit home for me. Not only did I incorporate some of his ideas into my seminars after reading about them but I also took up his ideas in my personal life.

I didn't want to be the guy who got to a certain age and could no longer enjoy himself or celebrate his successes. I didn't want to stop living just because of a number that suggested I was old, so I came up with a fourth box—or, I should say, a friend of mine did, and it stuck.

Gail and I received an award for our philanthropy and service to the real estate industry. When my friend Larry Kendall, cofounder of The Group Inc. Real Estate, introduced us, he reflected on our history and noted that for the prior thirty years, he'd sat in a room and listened to me teach the three boxes of life. He paused, turned to me, and said, "The thing is, I've added a fourth box, and so has Dave. I call it 'sudden death overtime.'"

He then explained that none of us knows what tomorrow may bring. We aren't even guaranteed to wake up in the morning. And yet he and I are still very active in our industry, our philanthropy, and with our hobbies, friendships, and relationships. Because we don't know how much time we have, we view every day as a period of overtime. We know that we must do as much as we can until our time is up.

It was a remarkable observation, and it got me thinking. It also made me ask myself some very big questions, especially about the significance of my lifetime experiences and achievements and their effect on myself and the rest of society. Suddenly, that became more important to me than the wealth and success I'd achieved. What was I doing in that moment of my life that would create a positive impact and add significant value in the world?

In 1995, I read the book *Halftime* by Bob Buford. In it, Buford talks about "moving from success to significance" in the second half of life, which he defines as being over fifty. Through his research, Buford discovered that most people work for their entire lives to achieve financial success without considering their happiness or purpose. His solution was to encourage those people to find meaning and impact during the second half of their lives.

While I was in a coma, my family was told I should be placed in hospice. Yes, the doctors were ready to count down the days. Boy, did they misjudge me. When I came out of the coma, my recovery was long, so I had a lot of time to think about the past, present, and future. I wasn't done living. Whether I was in halftime or overtime, I knew there were things I had to do while I still had the time to do them. I certainly wasn't finished building RE/MAX. I wanted to take our company public. I also intended to grow other businesses, investing in and guiding those entrepreneurs to help them reach their pinnacles of success so they could do the same for others coming up behind them.

Bronnie Ware wrote *The Top Five Regrets of the Dying* after she worked in palliative care for many years. Spending the last weeks of life with those who are dying changed her perspective on life, so much so that she decided to share what she'd learned from the dying in an article, which eventually became a book.

Ware found that most people have five common regrets as they face their mortality:

They regretted their lack of courage to live a life that was true to themselves, rather than the life others expected of them.

They regretted working so hard.

They regretted not being able to express their true feelings.

They regretted not staying in touch with their friends.

They regretted not allowing themselves to be happier.

Ware discovered that very few people cared about money, fame, or power as much as they thought they would. True success is about flourishing and what the Greeks referred to as *eudaimonia*. While that term translates roughly to *good spirit*, it also means living a life full of purpose and prosperity. Ultimately, we all have a choice about how we spend our time right up until the moment of our passing, and about the legacy we want to leave behind.

I know a lot of people who don't have to work anymore. They sold their businesses and made good money. They've gotten royalties and are generally set for life. But for many, idle hands equal an idle mind. A lot of professors are that way. They don't want to give up teaching because they enjoy the experience and the interaction.

As of this writing, I'm seventy-seven years old. In my current physical condition, I can no longer operate a race car. I drove professionally well into my sixties and competed against thirty-year-olds, and I had a damn good time doing it. I certainly held my own.

I can no longer fish.

I can no longer camp.

I sold my fighter jet because I can no longer pass the physical to be a jet pilot.

I could give you a long list of things I can no longer do, but I'd be cheating myself if I focused only on what's missing instead of all that remains. Because what remains is critical. I have a brain that functions at the highest level. I can finance ventures, mentor other entrepreneurs, and teach all those who wish to learn from my experience.

I'm happy with that position.

I would never utter a single word of complaint or say that I'm sorry I'm handicapped. That's the world. That's my life. And for sixty-five of my seventy-seven years, I had one hell of a ride.

Even so, I'm not going to sit on my ass binge-watching sitcoms and drinking booze. Okay, I might drink the booze, but I have so much left to do and to offer. I want to help the next generation succeed. At this point in my life, when I help build a company, I want no money from it. I want no profit at all. I'll finance the whole thing because I want my partners to reap those benefits.

That is my legacy.

So my mission in the world is now to actively answer this question: "How can we take young, innovative entrepreneurs and guide them along, push them, encourage them, and teach them so they get to achieve the American dream too?"

Since 2012, I've overcome being paralyzed, learned how to walk again, taken back the reins of RE/MAX while going public, bought a three-thousand-acre ranch, extended my speaking tours, and invested in several other companies and startups. And I'm proud to say that I'm having the time of my life doing so. My relationships with friends, family, therapists, and nurses have never been better. And dammit, I'm still enjoying the ride.

There's a famous saying in boxing: "You never see the punch that knocks you out." This is absolutely true. There will be blows in life you never see coming. You can't prepare for them any more than you can try to avoid them. Those punches will land when and where they choose. It's up to you to get off the floor, stand up, dust yourself off, and continue the fight.

Personal development is a lifelong journey of self-improvement and growth. Here are ten of my favorite tips to help you on your personal development journey:

1. Set Clear Goals
   Setting specific, achievable, and time-bound goals for yourself is important in all aspects of your life. Don't overlook the value of having clear objectives, direction, and motivation to grow.

2. Keep Learning
   Cultivate a thirst for knowledge and never stop learning. Read books, take courses, attend workshops, and seek out experiences that expand your skills and your understanding of anything that interests you.

3. Embrace Change
   Be open to change and view challenges as opportunities for growth. Embracing change allows you to adapt, learn new things, and turn your setbacks into comebacks.

4. Practice Self-Reflection

   If anything has taught me the value of self-reflection, it's been writing this book. Take time to regularly reflect on your thoughts, actions, and behaviors. Self-awareness helps you identify strengths, weaknesses, and areas for improvement, and it will make you a happier, more productive person too.

5. Develop Emotional Intelligence

   Enhance your ability to understand and manage emotions, both in yourself and others. Having high emotional intelligence fosters healthier relationships and effective communication in all aspects of life.

6. Stay Positive

   Maintain a positive outlook on life, even during difficult times. Positive thinking can enhance resilience and attract opportunities.

7. Take Care of Your Well-Being

   No matter how busy life gets, prioritize your physical and mental health. Exercise regularly, get enough sleep, practice stress-reduction techniques, and nourish your body, mind, and spirt.

8. Practice Gratitude

   Cultivate gratitude by acknowledging and appreciating the positive things in life. Gratitude fosters contentment and a sense of abundance.

9. Seek Feedback

   Be open to constructive criticism and feedback from others. Feedback, both positive and negative, provides valuable insight and helps you grow in areas that you may not have noticed need improving.

10. Surround Yourself with Positive Influences
    Surround yourself with supportive and like-minded individuals who inspire and motivate you. Your environment and the people around you can greatly impact your personal development journey.

Remember that personal development is a continuous process, and it's okay to take small steps toward improvement. Celebrate your progress and be kind to yourself when you have setbacks. By investing in your personal development, you'll lead a more fulfilling and purposeful life.

Here I am, on the road again. There I am, up on the stage. Here I go, playing the star again. There I go, turn the page.

—Bob Seger

Something that a lot of people don't know about me is that I love music. I like all types, from folk to country to rock. One of my favorite songs is "Turn the Page" by Bob Seger, from his album *Back in '72*. The song came out just before we founded RE/MAX. If you read the lyrics, it's a song about a performer on the road—but it also perfectly describes my early years of growing RE/MAX and the relentless seminar circuit I went on, presenting in ninety cities over 120 days, with virtually no breaks except for Sundays, which were travel days. By Sunday of each week, I was exhausted, and I would often ask myself, *What am I doing this for?*

My fifty-year journey has taken me to speak in front of more than three million people in more than thirty countries. Not unlike a rock star, right? I'll admit that I loved every minute of it. I loved the applause, but I loved changing people's lives even more.

I believe "Turn the Page" can be as relevant to you as it has been to me on your quest to achieve the perfect 10—*your* perfect 10. Not my idea of what that means but rather the things that give you perfect balance in all areas of your life. Believe me, these are exciting, challenging times. You'll experience successes and failures. Embrace them all. Without the lows, you can never truly appreciate the highs.

So there you have it. While I could write many more volumes about all that I've learned over the past fifty years, this is as much as I could share in 450 pages about what it takes to achieve a perfect 10: to knock it out of the park in business; to be a standout entrepreneur and leader; to be the stellar individual you wish to be; and to be an example for those who come after you.

Now, go make your own luck.

Make your mark.

Make your every dream come true.

EPILOGUE

As I write this book, we're approaching the end of 2023. After fifty years of experience building the RE/MAX organization, the business continues to evolve to meet the political and economic challenges facing the United States and the entire world. The companies that are most adaptable will persevere through this cycle of change, and the evolution of business will continue. Those who pivot correctly will have a great future, and those who fail to change or to implement the right changes will be at a tremendous disadvantage.

It's important to ask yourself as you look at your own organization and your personal life whether you're open to making the necessary adjustments to continue to be successful. It's often said in sports that if your opponent is younger, stronger, and faster, you must work harder and smarter to make up the difference. There are always solutions to a changing environment if you put in the effort to find them.

As mentioned earlier, we are currently in our eighth recession since the founding of RE/MAX, and after each one, the company has emerged as a stronger, more successful organization. As a leader, put your faith and trust in the people you're in charge of. Remember that one theme in this book is that most of the time, your best ideas come from the field and the people doing the day-to-day work. Also remember the theory of Kaizen, which says it's better to make a series of small, daily changes than one giant change.

The number one attribute people like about a leader in tough times is that they sell hope—not false hope but the hope that comes from keeping your eye on the dream and the reason you're doing what you do—every single day.

At the time this manuscript is being finalized, the real estate industry itself and many of its players have been charged with alleged antitrust activities related to real estate commission rates. In the real estate industry, it has been traditional for the seller to pay the agent's commission. If there's a buyer's agent representing the buyer, the seller's commission is commonly shared with the buyer's agent. The plaintiffs in these nine and counting various lawsuits are claiming that this type of commission sharing is an antitrust violation. Plaintiffs make this allegation despite the fact that agents and brokers followed the National Association of Realtors' Code of Ethics and the MLS's (Multiple Listing Service) rules of how commissions were split between the seller's agent and the buyer's agent.

The first three major lawsuits were filed several years ago against HomeServices of America, Keller Williams, the National Association of Realtors, Anywhere Real Estate, and RE/MAX. While writing this manuscript, the first trial was to take place in Kansas City, Missouri, in October 2023.

Prior to the trial starting, Anywhere agreed to settle for $83.5 million. A week later, RE/MAX agreed to settle for $55 million. This was a big decision and a painful one as RE/MAX continued to deny any wrongdoing. But I believed that the settlement was the best thing for the RE/MAX network, protecting it from costly litigation and allowing RE/MAX agents and brokers to do what they do best—help consumers buy and sell real estate. After all, I couldn't forget that franchisees invested their life with us.

The settlements took Anywhere and RE/MAX out only weeks before the rest of the defendants were going to trial. The trial lasted two weeks, and RE/MAX and its attorneys did not participate in the trial. The jury came back in less than three hours and awarded the plaintiffs the maximum amount requested. The jury awarded $1.78 billion in damages against HomeServices of America, Keller Williams, and the National Association of Realtors, which can be automatically tripled to more than $5 billion by federal antitrust rules.

While the non-settling defendants have publicly said they are going to appeal, when you've lost a trial like this, you usually have to put up a ten percent cash bond to do so, which means posting a bond of over $500 million. All of this leaves a great amount of uncertainty.

As I put the final additions in this book, all of this is up in the air—and likely will remain that way for years to come.

Many people have asked why we settled, especially when we didn't do anything wrong. It was an exceedingly difficult decision, one I didn't take lightly. In the fifty plus years I've been with RE/MAX, there were various lawsuits filed against us many times. Some were vicarious liability cases, meaning they didn't involve us at all, like the time a RE/MAX agent in California murdered their grandparents and their house was listed with RE/MAX. Vicarious liability can be disproven, but you spend big money to do so. In these types of cases, everybody goes for the perceived deepest pocket. The other cases were fought to the end. We won most of them.

When it came to the class action cases, if I had owned one hundred percent of RE/MAX at the time, I could be a riverboat gambler, throw the dice, and see if we could prevail. However, I couldn't do that. I had many stakeholders to protect, including our public shareholders, employees, vendors, and thousands of franchisees worldwide—with more than 140,000 agents who owned signs, business cards, and stationery, because they had a business that supported their families.

The stakes were high—too high to be a risk taker. As I've said, it was a difficult leadership decision—one of the toughest decisions as a leader I've ever made. I wrestled with whether I wanted RE/MAX to pay the $55 million or take the risk and bet on winning. While I love to throw the dice, I wasn't willing to gamble with the fate of our company and team members. I had to put their needs over my ego. And I had to go for the best for everybody, which meant obtaining a nationwide settlement and stopping any future litigation involving similar claims against our agents or brokers, our franchisees, our officers, our directors, or our employees. There really was only one option—spend the money and move forward.

Did it hurt?

Professionally, it was the correct decision to make.

Personally, I hated it. I made the decision, recommended it to the board, and the board unanimously agreed to support it.

God hates a coward.

So do I.

We settled anyway.

As of late 2023, the judge has given preliminary approval to our settlement. We have paid 50% of the $55 million to date, even though I adamantly feel we did absolutely nothing wrong.

Like it or not, this is the way the world sometimes works. I thank God we are not facing billions and billions of dollars of expenses or penalties that would have bankrupted the company.

Unfortunately, there's a second case set for trial in Chicago and a third class-action in Boston. Once the Kansas City trial ended, there were immediately six more cases filed for a total of nine and counting across the country.

Whether I made the right decision or not won't be known for years, as it looks like the trials will proceed and go through the appellate process. But our company is on a solid foundation. And our people are free to go ahead and do their business.

I might not even be alive when the final decision comes down, but the decision I made to settle so that we could move forward is behind us, and we will continue to do what we do. We sell real estate. We walk. We talk. We tell the story. We sell franchises, recruit and retain the agents, collect the money, and provide the services. That's a hell of an epilogue to a 450-page book.

"Was I right or was I wrong?"

ACKNOWLEDGMENTS

There are countless people who've had a hand in helping us build RE/MAX into the most successful real estate company in the world, and who've been part of the other companies I've been involved with over the years, including Area 15 Ventures. I would mention each of you individually, but it would more than double the size of this already substantial book. So instead, I want to say thank you to everyone at the RE/MAX organization, the officers and staff at RE/MAX headquarters and all our broker owners and agents. All of you have made us the team we are at RE/MAX and have helped create great success for so many people across 110 countries. I'm grateful for your contributions and the lessons I've learned from you over the years. And to Sue Rogl and Patti Corrigan, who've worked by my side for many years, I couldn't do what I do without you both. Thank you for knowing what I need before I do and for always keeping this train moving forward.

There have been many mentors, teachers, coaches, and leaders I've met who have deeply impacted my life and my success. I've written about some of those remarkable inspirations throughout this book, although there are many others I've met along the way who've also left indelible marks on my path. You never know how or when you might make an impact on someone else's life, but we all have the capacity to do so. Thank you to those who've influenced mine in so many ways.

When I think of family, I have to admit that I'm one lucky guy. My wife, Gail, has been with me on this journey for five decades and counting. I spent most of my years at RE/MAX traveling and on a stage. Gail spent those years in leadership in my absence. Together, we built something pretty amazing. She is, no doubt, my better half, and my inspiration to get up and do it all over again every single day. My children make me incredibly proud, as they have each grown up to carve their own path and to find success in their own way. I don't say it nearly enough, but I love you.

My friends, many of whom have become my family of choice, have stood by my side through thick and thin, in good times and in hard times. Adam Contos, our friendship means the world to me. Darren Hardy, I greatly respect you and the wisdom you've offered over the many years of friendship we've shared.

Writing a book can be a daunting task, and I've been fortunate to share that process with the extraordinary coauthor of both my books, Laura Morton. Without her talents, guidance, and hard work, this book would still be only a dream. Thank you so much for making it a reality. Behind every great author is an even greater team that takes what they've written and makes it shine. Thank you to Adam Mitchell, for his excellent research and assistance along the way. A debt of gratitude goes to Hope Innelli, our line editor, whose commitment to this project allowed us to go from good to great. To our copy editors, Benjamin Holmes and Phil Newman, who fine-tuned this work and helped clarify my message. And to everyone at our publisher, Forefront Books, including Jonathan Merkh, Jennifer Gingerich, and Landon Dickerson, thank you for believing in the value of this project. Thanks also to the sales team at Simon & Schuster, our PR team at JConnelly, and our marketing team at the Gray + Miller Agency.

And, finally, thanks to all of you for being a part of my life. It's been one heck of a ride!

BIBLIOGRAPHY

"10 Examples of Long-Term Business Goals to Set Now." Dividends Diversity online. Accessed May 13, 2022, https://dividendsdiversify.com/examples-long-term-business-goals/.

"10 Strategies and a Step-by-Step Guide to Find Customers." Indeed Editorial Team online. Last modified March 28, 2022, https://www.indeed.com/career-advice/career-development/how-to-find-customers.

"18 Eye-Opening Immigrant Business Owners Statistics That You Must Know in 2022." BusinessDIT online. Last modified April 10, 2022, https://www.renolon.com/immigrant-business-statistics/.

"20 Compelling Women Entrepreneurs Statistics for 2022." What to Become online. Accessed May 13, 2022, https://whattobecome.com/blog/women-entrepreneurs-statistics/.

"35 Women-Owned Business Statistics You Need to Know in 2021." Great Business Schools online. Last modified May 18, 2021, https://www.greatbusinessschools.org/women-owned-business-statistics/.

"39 Statistics that Prove the Value of Employee Training." Lorman online. Last modified September 1, 2021, https://www.lorman.com/blog/post/39-statistics-that-prove-the-value-of-employee-training.

"5 Characteristics of Entrepreneurial Spirit." *Inc.* online. Accessed May 14, 2022, https://www.inc.com/matt-ehrlichman/5-characteristics-of-entrepreneurial-spirit.html.

"5 Ways to Use Technology in Your Business Growth Strategy." YOH online. Last modified March 2, 2022, https://www.yoh.com/blog/5-ways-to-use-technology-in-your-business-growth-strategy.

"8 Reasons to Consider Franchising." *Business News Daily* online. Accessed May 14, 2022, https://www.businessnewsdaily.com/7970-franchising-benefits.html.

"A Study of 2.7 Million Startups Found the Ideal Age to Start a Business." TFX Capital online. Last modified July 16, 2018, https://tfxcap.com/a-study-of-2-7-million-startups-found-the-ideal-age-to-start-a-business/.

"Avoid Burnout Before You're Already Burned Out." *New York Times* online. Last modified November 6, 2019, https://www.nytimes.com/2019/11/06/smarter-living/avoid-burnout-work-tips.html.

"Children's Miracle Network Hospitals." Wikipedia. Accessed May 12, 2022, https://en.wikipedia.org/wiki/Children%27s_Miracle_Network_Hospitals.

"CNBC Transcript: Becky Quick Interviews Bobby Kotick." CNBC online. Last modified November 19, 2019, https://www.cnbc.com/2019/11/19/cnbc-transcript-cnbcs-becky-quick-interviews-activision-blizzard-ceo-bobby-kotick-from-the-cnbc-evolve-conference-in-los-angeles-today.html.

"Core Beliefs and Culture-Chairman's Survey Findings." Deloitte online. Accessed May 13, 2022, https://www2.deloitte.com/content/dam/Deloitte/global/Documents/About-Deloitte/gx-core-beliefs-and-culture.pdf.

"Disney: World's Largest Media Company Becoming Even Stronger." Khaveen Investments online. Accessed on May 13, 2022, https://seekingalpha.com/article/4450008-disney-worlds-largest-media-company-becoming-even-stronger.

"Everyone Has a Plan Until They Get Punched in the Mouth." Commit Works online. Accessed on May 13, 2022, https://www.commit.works/everyone-has-a-plan-until-they-get-punched-in-the-mouth/.

"Franchising in the U.S.—Statistics and Facts." Statista online. Last modified November 18, 2022, https://www.statista.com/topics/5048/franchising-in-the-us/#topicHeader__wrapper.

"Future Workforce Report 2022: Leveraging Independent Talent as a Key Workforce Strategy." Upwork online. Accessed May 14, 2022, https://www.upwork.com/research/future-workforce-report-2022.

"Gary Vaynerchuk Builds Businesses." Gary Vaynerchuk online. Accessed May 14, 2022, https://www.garyvaynerchuk.com/biography/.

"Goal Setting." *Entrepreneur* online. Accessed May 13, 2022, https://www.entrepreneur.com/encyclopedia/goal-setting.

"Grow Your Business by Growing Your People." Grow 360 online. Last modified February 20, 2020, https://grow360.com/blog/grow-your-business-by-growing-your-people.

"Grow Your People, Grow Your Business." *Forbes* online. Last modified January 17, 2017, https://www.forbes.com/sites/aileron/2017/01/17/grow-your-people-grow-your-business/?sh=7bb7de3423e6.

"How COVID-19 Has Pushed Companies Over the Technology Tipping Point and Transformed Business Forever." McKinsey & Company online. 2020, https://www.mckinsey.com/~/media/McKinsey/Business%20Functions/Strategy%20and%20Corporate%20Finance/Our%20Insights/How%20COVID%2019%20has%20pushed%20companies%20over%20the%20technology%20tipping%20point%20and%20transformed%20business%20forever/How-COVID-19-has-pushed-companies-over-the%20technology%20tipping-point-final.pdf.

"How to Manage the 5 Generations in the Workplace." Paychex online. Accessed May 15, 2022, https://www.paychex.com/articles/human-resources/how-to-manage-multiple-generations-in-the-workplace.

"Job Burnout: How to Spot It and Take Action." Mayo Clinic online. Accessed May 13, 2022, https://www.mayoclinic.org/healthy-lifestyle/adult-health/in-depth/burnout/art-20046642.

"Management Styles." Valamis online. Last modified. February 21, 2022, https://www.valamis.com/hub/management-styles.

"Marketing Myopia Definition: 3 Examples of Marketing Myopia." MasterClass online. Accessed on May 14, 2022, https://www.masterclass.com/articles/marketing-myopia#what-is-marketing-myopia/.

"Mirroring Body Language: 4 Steps to Successfully Mirror Others." Science of People online. Accessed May 14, 2022, https://www.scienceofpeople.com/category/body-language/body-language-for-rapport/mirroring/.

"Mr. Gordon Matthews." IT History Society online. Accessed May 14, 2022, https://www.ithistory.org/honor-roll/mr-gordon-matthews.

"Net promoter score." Wikipedia. Accessed May 12, 2022, https://en.wikipedia.org/wiki/Net_promoter_score.

"Pros and Cons of Small Business Financing from a Bank." TD Bank online. Accessed May 13, 2022, https://www.td.com/us/en/small-business/pros-cons-business-loan-credit-from-bank/.

"Red Roof® Offers 'Work Under Our Roof' Day Rate to Provide a Comfortable and Quiet Space for Remote Workers." PRNewswire online. Last modified March 30, 2020, https://www.prnewswire.com/news-releases/red-roof-offers-work-under-our-roof-day-rate-to-provide-a-comfortable-and-quiet-space-for-remote-workers-301031912.html.

"Storytelling and Cultural Traditions: Storytelling Is as Old as Culture." *National Geographic* online. Accessed May 12, 2022, https://www.nationalgeographic.org/article/storytelling-and-cultural-traditions/.

"Systems Approach Meaning, Importance, Factors & Example." MBA Skool online. Accessed May 13, 2022, https://www.mbaskool.com/business-concepts/marketing-and-strategy-terms/18238-systems-approach.html.

"Systems Theory of Organization." Harappa online. Last modified May 17, 2021, https://harappa.education/harappa-diaries/systems-theory-of-organization/.

"The Great Resignation Update: Limeade Employee Care Report." Limeade online. Accessed May 13, 2022, https://www.limeade.com/resources/resource-center/limeade-employee-care-report-the-great-resignation-update/#:~:text=Top%20reasons%20employees%20left%20their,Insufficient%20benefits%3A%2019%25.

"The Race to the Pole: Roald Amundsen and Robert Scott—1911–1912." Cool Antarctica online. Accessed May 14, 2022, https://www.coolantarctica.com/Antarctica%20fact%20file/History/race-to-the-pole-amundsen-scott.php.

"The Race to the South Pole: Scott and Amundsen." Royal Museums Greenwich online. Accessed May 14, 2022, https://www.rmg.co.uk/stories/topics/race-south-pole-scott-amundsen.

"The Richest Man in Babylon." Wikipedia. Accessed May 14, 2022, https://en.wikipedia.org/wiki/The_Richest_Man_in_Babylon.

"The State of the Global Startup Economy." Startup Genome online. Accessed May 14, 2022, https://startupgenome.com/article/the-state-of-the-global-startup-economy.

"The Ultimate Guide to Setting Business Goals." MasterClass online. Last modified August 30, 2021, https://www.masterclass.com/articles/the-ultimate-guide-to-setting-business-goals#how-to-set-objectives-to-help-you-attain-your-business-goals.

"Today's Parents Spend More Time with Their Kids than Moms and Dads Did 50 Years Ago." UCI News online. Accessed

May 13, 2022, https://news.uci.edu/2016/09/28/todays-parents-spend-more-time-with-their-kids-than-moms-and-dads-did-50-years-ago/.

"Top 5 Characteristics of Sales Hunters, Sales Closers, and Sales Farmers." Asher Strategies online. Accessed May 13, 2022, https://www.asherstrategies.com/b2b-sales-training/top-5-characteristics-of-b2b-sales-hunters-closers-farmers.php.

"Walgreens and Postmates Expand On-Demand Delivery Service Collaboration to Thirteen New Cities." Walgreens online. Last modified March 9, 2020, https://news.walgreens.com/press-center/news/walgreens-and-postmates-expand-on-demand-delivery-service-collaboration-to-thirteen-news-cities.htm.

"Watch: Compass's 2-Year Losses Exceed $1B." The Real Deal online. Last modified March 6, 2023, https://therealdeal.com/national/2023/03/06/watch-compass-2-year-losses-exceed-1b/.

"What Is Locus of Control?" USMC Online. Accessed May 14, 2022, https://www.usmcu.edu/Portals/218/What%20is%20Locus%20of%20Control%20by%20James%20Neill.pdf.

"What Is Myopic Marketing? (With Definition and Marketing Tips)." Indeed Editorial Team online. Last modified April 8, 2021, https://www.indeed.com/career-advice/career-development/what-is-myopic-marketing.

"What Made Shackleton a Great Leader?" Shackleton.com. Last modified February 5, 2020, https://shackleton.com/blogs/articles/shackleton-great-leader.

"Why Emotional Intelligence Is Important in the Workplace." Ottawa University online. Last modified October 15, 2020, https://www.ottawa.edu/online-and-evening/blog/october-2020/the-importance-of-emotional-intelligence-in-the-wo.

"Why Investors Are Looking at Your HR Practices." *Inc.* online. Last modified April 19, 2022, https://www.inc.com/velocity-global/why-investors-are-looking-at-your-hr-practices.html.

"Why Is Training and Development Important?" Ottawa University online. Accessed May 14, 2022, https://www.ottawa.edu/online-and-evening/blog/january-2021/5-benefits-of-training-and-development.

"Workforce Generations." Lumen Learning online. Accessed May 14, 2022, https://courses.lumenlearning.com/wm-organizational behavior/chapter/workforce-generations/.

"Ziglar: 10 Steps to Serious Goal Setting." Sound Wisdom online. Last modified May 20, 2019, https://www.soundwisdom.com/blog/10-steps-to-serious-goal-setting.

Agarwal, Dr. Pragya. "How to Create a Positive Workplace Culture." *Forbes* online. Last modified August 29, 2018, https://www.forbes.com/sites/pragyaagarwaleurope/2018/08/29/how-to-create-a-positive-work-place-culture/?sh=4e6f2f9e4272.

Akal, Nellie. "To Grow Your Business, Start Focusing on Your Employees." *Entrepreneur* online. Last modified April 14, 2016, https://www.entrepreneur.com/article/270625.

Alexander, Lucy. "The Who, What, Why & How of Digital Marketing." HubSpot online. Last modified November 30, 2022, https://blog.hubspot.com/marketing/what-is-digital-marketing.

Alhanati, Joao. "Follow Your Passions, and Success Will Follow." Investopedia online. Last modified November 5, 2022, https://www.investopedia.com/articles/pf/12/passion-success.asp.

Amaratunga, Ovin. "What Is Marketing Myopia?" LinkedIn online. Last modified August 5, 2021, https://www.linkedin.com/pulse/what-marketing-myopia-ovin-amaratunga.

Anderson, Bob, and Bill Adams. "The Six Systems of Organizational Effectiveness." Leadership Circle online. Last modified March 5, 2022, https://leadershipcircle.com/en/the-six-systems-of-organizational-effectiveness/.

Baker, Colin. "Emotional Intelligence in the Workplace: What You Should Know." Leaders.com. Last modified March 22,

2023, https://leaders.com/articles/personal-growth/emotional-intelligence-in-the-workplace/.

Barone, Emily. "The Pandemic Forced Thousands of Businesses to Close—But New Ones Are Launching at Breakneck Speed." *Time* online. Last modified July 22, 2021, https://time.com/6082576/pandemic-new-businesses/.

Beattie, Andrew. "Walt Disney: How Entertainment Became an Empire." Investopedia online. Last modified November 27, 2022, https://www.investopedia.com/articles/financial-theory/11/walt-disney-entertainment-to-empire.asp.

Beck, Randall J., and Jim Harter. "Why Great Managers Are So Rare." Gallup online. Accessed May 14, 2022, https://www.gallup.com/workplace/231593/why-great-managers-rare.aspx#:~:text=It%27s%20often%20hiding%20in%20plain,job%2082%25%20of%20the%20time.

Bisio, Rick. "How Franchising Helps Immigrants Live the American Dream." Franchise Gator online. Last modified June 15, 2019, https://www.franchisegator.com/articles/immigrants-american-dream-12755/.

Boehm, Mike. "Eli Broad Offers Life Lessons in 'The Art of Being Unreasonable.'" *Los Angeles Times* online. Last modified May 4, 2012, https://www.latimes.com/entertainment/arts/la-xpm-2012-may-04-la-et-eli-broad-book-20120504-story.html.

Boitnott, John. "4 Ways Your Company Benefits from Giving Back." *Entrepreneur* online. Last modified January 27, 2015, https://www.entrepreneur.com/article/241983.

Bolles, Richard N. *The Three Boxes of Life: And How to Get Out of Them*. Ten Speed Press, 1981.

Bradford, Jeff. "How to Write a Marketing Plan." *Forbes* online. Last modified August 5, 2021, https://www.forbes.com/sites/forbesagencycouncil/2021/08/05/how-to-write-a-marketing-plan/?sh=61048e993353.

Brower, Tracy, PhD. "Empathy Is the Most Important Leadership Skill According to Research." *Forbes* online. Last modified September 19, 2021, https://www.forbes.com/sites/tracybrower/2021/09/19/empathy-is-the-most-important-leadership-skill-according-to-research/?sh=5f7eb0d93dc5.

Bruce, Robin. "Discovering Your Purpose in Business and Life." *Forbes* online. Last modified August 23, 2015, https://www.forbes.com/sites/robinbruce/2015/08/23/discovering-your-purpose/?sh=24df91a374ac.

Bryant, Adam. "Google's Quest to Build a Better Boss." *New York Times* online. Last modified March 12, 2011, https://www.nytimes.com/2011/03/13/business/13hire.html.

Buford, Bob. *Halftime: Moving from Success to Significance*. Zondervan, 1995.

Burns, Stephanie. "What 'Finding Your Why' Really Means." *Forbes* online. Last modified May 24, 2021, https://www.forbes.com/sites/stephanieburns/2021/05/24/what-finding-your-why-really-means/?sh=4bd6749373f4.

Canfield, Jack, Les Hewitt, and Mark Victor Hansen. *The Power of Focus: What the World's Greatest Achievers Know about the Secret to Financial Freedom & Success*. HCI Books, 2000.

Cassell, Warren Jr. "Gary Vaynerchuk's Net Worth Report: How He Built His Fortune." Capitalism.com. Last modified November 17, 2022, https://www.capitalism.com/how-gary-vaynerchuk-built-his-fortune/.

Cates, Bill. "Discover Whether You're a Sales Hunter, Farmer, or Trapper." HubSpot online. Last modified April 27, 2021, https://blog.hubspot.com/sales/sales-hunter-farmer-trapper.

Cheng-Tozun, Dorcas. "Pick Your Purpose: Are You Driven by Money, Fame, or Impact?" *Inc.* online. Last modified October 11, 2016, https://www.inc.com/dorcas-cheng-tozun/money-fame-or-impact-why-do-you-want-to-be-an-entrepreneur.html.

Clark, Domini. "Top Five Hiring Best Practices for 2022." *Forbes* online. Last modified February 16, 2022, https://www.forbes.com/sites/forbeshumanresourcescouncil/2022/02/16/top-five-hiring-best-practices-for-2022/?sh=dcd84ed5f5d1.

Clason, George S. *The Richest Man in Babylon.* Penguin Books, 1926.

Clifford, Catherine. "Self-Made Millionaire Gary Vaynerchuk: This Is the Real Secret to Success." CNBC online. Last modified March 13, 2017, https://www.cnbc.com/2017/03/13/self-made-millionaire-gary-vaynerchuk-shares-real-secret-to-success.html.

Coleman, John. "Finding Success Starts with Finding Your Purpose." *Harvard Business Review* online. Last modified January 11, 2022, https://hbr.org/2022/01/finding-success-starts-with-finding-your-purpose.

Collins, Jim. *Good to Great: Why Some Companies Make the Leap . . . and Others Don't.* Harper Business Publishing, 2001.

Colvin, Geoff. "For the Next Generation of Star CEOs, Experience Alone Isn't Enough. Here's What They Need to Reach the Top Rung." *Fortune* online. Last modified May 31, 2023, https://fortune.com/2023/05/31/next-generation-star-ceos/.

Conger, Jay A., and Allan H. Church. "The 3 Types of C Players and What to Do about Them." *Harvard Business Review* online. Last modified February 1, 2018, https://hbr.org/2018/02/the-3-types-of-c-players-and-what-to-do-about-them.

Cook, Amy Osmond. "4 Ways to Nurture the Entrepreneurial Spirit at Your Company." *Entrepreneur* online. Last modified November 15, 2017, https://www.entrepreneur.com/article/302088.

Corley, Tom. *Rich Habits: The Daily Success Habits of Wealthy Individuals.* Langdon Street Press, 2010.

D'Angelo, Matt. "The Small Business Owner's Guide to Getting an SBA Loan." *Business News Daily* online. Last modified July

31, 2023, https://www.businessnewsdaily.com/15763-sba-loan-guide.html.

Dean, Kevin. "The Role of Social Media Influencers." Manobyte online. Last modified August 2015, https://www.manobyte.com/growth-strategy/the-role-of-social-media-influencers.

DeLuca, Fred, and John P. Hayes. *Start Small, Finish Big: Fifteen Key Lessons to Start—and Run—Your Own Successful Business.* Mandevilla Press, 2012.

DeMerceau, John. "Advantages & Disadvantages of Bank Loans." *Houston Chronicle* online. Last modified March 5, 2019, https://smallbusiness.chron.com/advantages-amp-disadvantages-bank-loans-47377.html.

Drucker, Peter. *The New Realities.* Routledge Publishing, 2003.

Drucker, Peter, and Nan Stone. *Peter Drucker on the Profession of Management.* Harvard Business Review Press, 1998.

Echevarria, Desiree. "If You Want More Applicants in 2022, Change the Way You Hire." CareerPlug online. Last modified April 6, 2022, https://www.careerplug.com/blog/change-the-way-you-hire-in-2021/1.

Economy, Peter. "Jeff Bezos Became the Wealthiest Man on Earth with the Help of This Remarkable Book." *Inc.* online. Last modified August 12, 2019, https://www.inc.com/peter-economy/jeff-bezos-became-wealthiest-man-on-earth-with-help-of-this-remarkable-book.html.

"These 14 Amazon Leadership Principles Can Lead You and Your Business to Remarkable Success." *Inc.* online. Last modified November 8, 2019, https://www.inc.com/peter-economy/the-14-amazon-leadership-principles-that-can-lead-you-your-business-to-tremendous-success.html.

Eliot, T. S. "Philip Massinger." *Times Literary Supplement*, May 27, 1919.

Ferguson, Donna. "The Secret of How Amundsen Beat Scott in Race to South Pole? A Diet of Raw Penguin." *Guardian* online. Last modified May 16, 2021, https://www.theguardian.com/environment/2021/may/16/the-secret-of-how-amundsen-beat-scott-in-race-to-south-pole-a-diet-of-raw-penguin.

Fernández-Aráoz, Claudio. "Jack Welch's Approach to Leadership." *Harvard Business Review* online. Last modified March 3, 2020, https://hbr.org/2020/03/jack-welchs-approach-to-leadership.

Frankl, Viktor. *Man's Search for Meaning*. Beacon Press, 1946.

Freedman, Marc. "What Happens When Old and Young Connect." Greater Good online. Last modified April 22, 2019, https://greatergood.berkeley.edu/article/item/what_happens_when_old_and_young_connect.

Freiberg, Kevin, and Jackie Freiberg. "20 Reasons Why Herb Kelleher Was One of the Most Beloved Leaders of Our Time." *Forbes* online. Last modified January 4, 2019, https://www.forbes.com/sites/kevinandjackiefreiberg/2019/01/04/20-reasons-why-herb-kelleher-was-one-of-the-most-beloved-leaders-of-our-time/?sh=333818b4b311.

Gleeson, Brent. "A Navy SEAL Commander's 3 Pillars of Authentic Leadership." *Forbes* online. Last modified July 1, 2021, https://www.forbes.com/sites/brentgleeson/2021/07/01/a-navy-seal-commanders-3-pillars-of-authentic-leadership/?sh=31b6b9441018.

Griffin, Keith. "Hiring Differences Between the Three Generations." Recruiter.com. Accessed May 13, 2022, https://www.recruiter.com/recruiting/hiring-differences-between-the-three-generations/.

Gustavsen, Alexa. "What Are the 8 Types of Digital Marketing?" Southern New Hampshire University online. Last modified August 2023, https://www.snhu.edu/about-us/newsroom/business/types-of-digital-marketing.

Gutoskey, Ellen. "Why 'Relentless.com' Redirects to Amazon." Mental Floss online. Last modified January 21, 2022, https://www.mentalfloss.com/article/654621/why-relentless-redirects-amazon.

Haden, Jeff. "Want to Be More Successful? This PayPal Cofounder and First Outside Facebook Investor Says Embrace a Definite Optimist Mindset." *Inc.* online. Last modified September 22, 2020, https://www.inc.com/jeff-haden/want-to-be-more-successful-this-paypal-co-founder-first-outside-facebook-investor-says-embrace-a-definite-optimist-mindset.html.

Hall, Tanya. "7 Ways Companies Can Give Back to the Community." *Inc.* online. Last modified February 20, 2020, https://www.inc.com/tanya-hall/seven-ways-companies-can-give-back-to-community.html.

Hansen, Max. "Seven Hiring Practices to Implement Today to Set Your Company Apart." *Forbes* online. Last modified July 6, 2021, https://www.forbes.com/sites/forbeshumanresourcescouncil/2021/07/06/seven-hiring-practices-to-implement-today-to-set-your-company-apart/?sh=220fda2c658c.

Hardy, Darren. *The Compound Effect.* Success Media Books, 2010.

Harkins, Phil and Keith Hollihan, "Everybody Wins—The Story and Lessons Behind RE/MAX." John Wiley & Sons, Inc 2005.

Harrell, Melissa, and Lauren Barbato. "Great Managers Still Matter: The Evolution of Google's Project Oxygen." Google re:Work online. Last modified February 27, 2018, https://rework.withgoogle.com/blog/the-evolution-of-project-oxygen/.

Herrity, Jennifer. "7 Management Styles for Effective Leadership (With Examples)." Indeed online. Last modified July 31, 2023, https://www.indeed.com/career-advice/career-development/management-styles.

———. "The Importance of Training Employees: 11 Benefits." Indeed online. Last modified March 29, 2023, https://www

.indeed.com/career-advice/career-development/importance-of-training.

———. "What Are Business Goals? Definition, Steps and Examples." Indeed online. Last modified July 31, 2023, https://www.indeed.com/career-advice/career-development/business-goals.

Hittelet, Pierre-Yves. "12 Leadership Lessons to Learn from the Navy SEALs." *Inc.* online. Last modified May 25, 2017, https://www.inc.com/pierre-yves-hittelet/navy-seal-leadership-lessons.html.

Horowitz, Ben. "Why It's Crucial to Train Your Employees." *Business Insider* online. Last modified May 17, 2010, https://www.businessinsider.com/why-its-crucial-to-train-your-employees-2010-5.

Hougaard, Rasmus. "Connect with Empathy, But Lead with Compassion." *Harvard Business Review* online. Last modified December 23, 2021, https://hbr.org/2021/12/connect-with-empathy-but-lead-with-compassion.

Joe, Alexander. "Importance of Technology in Business." Market Business News online. Last modified November 17, 2021, https://marketbusinessnews.com/importance-of-technology-in-business/241669/.

Jones, Jenn. "The Pros and Cons of a Home Equity Loan." Lending Tree online. Last modified March 31, 2023, https://www.lendingtree.com/home/home-equity/pros-and-cons-of-home-equity-loan/.

Jones, Stephen. "Amazon's New Management Principles Are a Sign of the Times for Corporates." *Business Insider* online. Last modified July 5, 2021, https://www.businessinsider.com/what-amazon-management-principles-change-means.

Judy, Jim. "Immigrant Entrepreneurs Flock to Franchising Opportunities." *Entrepreneur* online. Last modified May 5, 2017, https://www.franchise500.com/article/293452.

Kaado, Bassam. "Why You Need to Create a Fantastic Workplace Culture." *Business News Daily* online. Last modified April 28, 2023, https://www.businessnewsdaily.com/15840-create-a-great-company-culture.html.

Kassel, Amelia. "How to Write a Marketing Plan." Marketing Library Service online. Accessed on May 13, 2022, https://www.infotoday.com/mls/jun99/how-to.htm.

Kastenholz, Christoph. "The Importance of Influencer Marketing in the 'New Normal' Digital Sphere." *Forbes* online. Last modified May 2, 2021, https://www.forbes.com/sites/forbesagencycouncil/2021/03/02/the-importance-of-influencer-marketing-in-the-new-normal-digital-sphere/?sh=1672efc14483.

Kim, Jihye, and Minseong Kim. "Rise of Social Media Influencers as a New Marketing Channel: Focusing on the Roles of Psychological Well-Being and Perceived Social Responsibility among Consumers." *International Journal of Environmental Research and Public Health*. February 2022, https://www.ncbi.nlm.nih.gov/pmc/articles/PMC8872418/.

King, Brittany K. "36 Statistics on the Importance of Employee Engagement." *Lorman* online. Last modified August 30, 2021, https://www.lorman.com/blog/post/36-statistics-on-the-importance-of-employee-engagement#:~:text=Companies%20with%20happy%20employees%20outperform,more%20profit%20than%20disengaged%20ones.

Kohll, Alan. "How to Build a Positive Company Culture." *Forbes* online. Last modified August 18, 2018, https://www.forbes.com/sites/alankohll/2018/08/14/how-to-build-a-positive-company-culture/?sh=3c5aaab749b5.

Kolaski, Robert. "The Role and Importance of Technology in Business." Industry Today online. Last modified June 21, 2018, https://industrytoday.com/the-role-and-importance-of-technology-in-business/.

Kroc, Ray, and Robert Anderson. *Grinding It Out: The Making of McDonald's*. H. Regnery, 1977.

Laoyan, Sarah. "Setting Business Goals: The First Step to a Successful Business." Asana online. Last modified October 13, 2022, https://asana.com/resources/business-goals-examples.

Legace, Martha. "Ernest Shackleton: The Entrepreneur of Survival." Harvard Business School online. Last modified December 5, 2014, https://www.hbs.edu/news/articles/Pages/shackleton-anniversary.aspx.

Levitt, Theodore. "Marketing Myopia." *Harvard Business Review,* July–August 1960.

Lopez-Garrido, Gabriel. "Locus of Control." Simply Psychology online. Last modified September 13, 2020, https://www.simplypsychology.org/locus-of-control.html.

Manahan, Rowan. "Where Am I Going? How to Put Your Life in Context." LifeHack online. Last modified March 9, 2023, https://www.lifehack.org/articles/featured/where-am-i-going-putting-your-life-in-context.html.

Mathers, Connie. "You Are the Average of the Five People Quote: 5 Lessons." Develop Good Habits online. Last modified March 9, 2022, https://www.developgoodhabits.com/five-people/.

McWhinney, James. "Franchise vs. Startup: Which Way to Go." Investopedia online. Last modified December 7, 2022, https://www.investopedia.com/articles/personal-finance/110215/franchise-vs-startup-which-way-go.asp.

Merchant, Priya. "Pivoting During the Pandemic: How These Businesses Succeeded." *Entrepreneur* online. Last modified January 12, 2021, https://www.entrepreneur.com/article/362003.

Merle, Andrew. "The Reading Habits of Ultra-Successful People." *HuffPost* online. Last modified December 6, 2017, https://www.huffpost.com/entry/the-reading-habits-of-ult_b_9688130.

Miller, Derek. "Despite COVID-19 Crisis, 2020 Was Biggest Year for New Entrepreneurs." LendingTree online. Last modified

April 5, 2021, https://www.lendingtree.com/business/small/coronavirus-new-entrepreneurs-study/.

Moldavskiy, Vlad. "How Your Company Benefits from Giving Back." Business Collective online. Accessed May 13, 2022, https://businesscollective.com/how-your-company-benefits-from-giving-back/index.html.

Mollman, Steve. "Blockbuster 'Laughed Us Out of the Room,' Recalls Netflix Cofounder on Trying to Sell Company Now Worth over $150 Billion for $50 Million." *Fortune* online. Last modified April 14, 2023, https://fortune.com/2023/04/14/netflix-cofounder-marc-randolph-recalls-blockbuster-rejecting-chance-to-buy-it/.

Moore, Catherine. "Learned Optimism: Is Martin Seligman's Glass Half Full?" PositivePsychology.com. Last modified December 30, 2019, https://positivepsychology.com/learned-optimism/.

Moreira, Fabrizio. "Seven Ways Technology Makes Your Small Business Grow Faster." LifeHack online. Last modified October 7, 2016, https://www.lifehack.org/482038/seven-ways-technology-makes-your-small-business-grow-faster.

Morrison, Bob. *Why S.O.B.'s Succeed and Nice Guys Fail in a Small Business*. Generic Publishing, 1976.

Pancholia, Harsh. "Why Opening a Franchise Business Is Better Than Starting Your Own." *Entrepreneur* online. Last modified March 26, 2017, https://www.entrepreneur.com/article/291914.

Parker, Kim, and Juliana Horowitz. "Majority of Workers Who Quit a Job in 2021 Cite Low Pay, No Opportunities for Advancement, Feeling Disrespected." Pew Research Center online. Last modified March 9, 2022, https://www.pewresearch.org/fact-tank/2022/03/09/majority-of-workers-who-quit-a-job-in-2021-cite-low-pay-no-opportunities-for-advancement-feeling-disrespected/.

Perry, Elizabeth. "Do You Have an Entrepreneurial Spirit? 10 Characteristics to Lean Into." BetterUp online. Last modified January 25, 2022, https://www.betterup.com/blog/entrepreneurial-spirit.

Pillemer, Karl A. "Why Should We Listen to Old People? A Very Good Question." *HuffPost* online. Last modified December 6, 2017, https://www.huffpost.com/entry/why-should-we-listen-to-old-people_b_1207996.

Pourron, Antoine. "10 Steps to Build a Successful Company Culture." LumApps online. Accessed on May 14, 2022, https://www.lumapps.com/blog/corporate-culture/how-to-build-company-culture/.

Repko, Melissa. "Why Best Buy's CEO Thinks the Appointment-Only Shopping Strategy Was the Best Approach." CNBC online. Last modified May 21, 2020, https://www.cnbc.com/2020/05/21/why-best-buys-ceo-thinks-the-appointment-only-shopping-strategy-works.html.

Schooley, Skye. "Your Guide to Creating a Small Business Marketing Plan." Business.com. Last modified May 16, 2023, https://www.business.com/articles/sample-marketing-plan-outline-and-template/.

Schwartz, David. *The Magic of Thinking Big*. Touchstone Publishing, 1987.

Seid, Andrew. "Brokers for Beginners: Are Franchise Brokers Right for Your Emerging Brand?" Franchising.com. Accessed May 13, 2022, https://www.franchising.com/articles/brokers_for_beginners_are_franchise_brokers_right_for_your_emerging_brand.html.

Semczuk, Nina. "5 Lifelong Lessons from 'The Magic of Thinking Big' by David Schwartz." Medium.com. Last modified October 9, 2018, https://medium.com/@nina.semczuk/5-lifelong-lessons-from-the-magic-of-thinking-big-by-david-schwartz-6b33f5b21fae.

Severson, Dana. "The 8 Rules of Leadership by Jack Welch." *Inc.* online. Last modified November 13, 2017, https://www.inc.com/dana-severson/these-8-simple-rules-of-leadership-from-jack-welch-are-more-important-now-than-ever-before.html.

Shavitz, Jeff. "Learning, Earning and Returning: The 3 Stages of a Fulfilling Life." *Entrepreneur* online. Last modified November 13, 2016, https://www.entrepreneur.com/article/284706.

Shoenthal, Amy. "How Today's Top Marketing Leaders Are Approaching AI." *Forbes* online. Last modified August 10, 2023, https://www.forbes.com/sites/amyshoenthal/2023/08/10/how-todays-top-marketing-leaders-are-approaching-ai/?sh=276de24561e4.

Shontell, Alyson. "When You Type in the URL 'Relentless.com,' You'll Be Surprised Where It Takes You." *Business Insider* online. Last modified February 12, 2022, https://www.businessinsider.com/amazon-was-almost-named-relentless-2014-2.

Silva, Christianna. "Influencers Aren't Going Anywhere. So What Does That Mean for Today's Teens?" Mashable.com. Last modified October 26, 2021, https://mashable.com/article/influencers-are-toxic-to-kids.

Sims, Calvin. "THE MEDIA BUSINESS: Walt Disney Reinventing Itself." *New York Times* online. Last modified April 28, 1994, https://www.nytimes.com/1994/04/28/business/the-media-business-walt-disney-reinventing-itself.html.

Singh, Sandeep. "The Importance of Building Systems within Your Work System." iTechFever online. Last modified June 6, 2021, https://www.itechfever.com/importance-of-building-systems/.

Smith, Lauren, Jamie Kohn, and Iga Pilewska. "What Stops Employees from Applying for Internal Roles." *Harvard Business Review* online. Last modified May 10, 2022, https://hbr.org/2022/05/what-stops-employees-from-applying-for-internal-roles.

Solomont, E. B. "Keller's Second Coming." The Real Deal online. Last modified April 17, 2019, https://therealdeal.com/magazine/la-april-2019/gary-keller-second-coming/.

Spinella, Adam. "NBA Team-Building: The 3 Pillars Approach." The Box and 1 online. Last modified June 17, 2021. https://theboxand1.weebly.com/draft-philosophy/nba-team-building-the-3-pillars-approach.

Stoller, Paul. "The Wisdom of Elders: How the Wisdom of Elders Can Promote Social Well-Being in Troubled Times." *Psychology Today* online. Last modified June 30, 2020, https://www.psychologytoday.com/us/blog/the-path-well-being/202006/the-wisdom-elders.

Sutton, Jeremy, PhD. "How to Prevent Burnout in the Workplace: 20 Strategies." PositivePsychology.com. Last modified April 19, 2021, https://positivepsychology.com/burnout-prevention/.

Thompson, Ben. "The Relentless Jeff Bezos." Stratechery online. Last modified February 3, 2021, https://stratechery.com/2021/the-relentless-jeff-bezos/.

Thompson, Jeff, PhD. "Mimicry and Mirroring Can Be Good or Bad." *Psychology Today* online. Last modified September 9, 2012, https://www.psychologytoday.com/us/blog/beyond-words/201209/mimicry-and-mirroring-can-be-good-or-bad.

Umoh, Ruth. "Black Women Were Among the Fastest-Growing Entrepreneurs—Then Covid Arrived." *Forbes* online. Last modified October 26, 2020, https://www.forbes.com/sites/ruthumoh/2020/10/26/black-women-were-among-the-fastest-growing-entrepreneurs-then-covid-arrived/?sh=2fed11906e01.

Uzialko, Adam. "Everyone Is Not Your Customer: That's OK." *Business News Daily* online. Last modified February 21, 2023, https://www.businessnewsdaily.com/15109-identify-your-customer-base.html.

Van Doorn, Maarten. "You Are the Average of the Five People You Spend the Most Time With." Medium.com. Last modified June 20, 2018, https://maartenvandoorn.medium.com/you-are-the-average-of-the-five-people-you-spend-the-most-time-with-a2ea32d08c72.

Vasel, Kathryn. "Covid: These U.S. Companies Decided to Go Fully Remote." *Mercury News* online. Last modified January 27, 2022, https://www.mercurynews.com/2022/01/27/covid-these-u-s-companies-decided-to-go-fully-remote-permanently/.

Vitez, Osmond. "The Impact of Technological Change on Business Activity." *Houston Chronicle* online. Last modified February 12, 2019, https://smallbusiness.chron.com/impact-technological-change-business-activity-2191.html.

Wallace, Alicia. "US Worker Productivity Fell at the Fastest Rate in Nearly 75 Years." CNN online. Last modified May 5, 2022, https://www.cnn.com/2022/05/05/economy/us-productivity-first-quarter-2022/index.html.

Ward, Lauren. "Pros and Cons of Small Business Loans." Lantern by SoFi online. Last modified February 11, 2022, https://lanterncredit.com/small-business/pros-and-cons-of-small-business-loans.

Ware, Bronnie. *The Top Five Regrets of the Dying: A Life Transformed by the Dearly Departed.* Hay House, Inc., 2011.

Welch, Jack, and Suzy Welch. *Winning.* Harper Business, 2005.

Weller, Chris. "9 of the Most Successful People Share Their Reading Habits." *Business Insider* online. Last modified July 20, 2017, https://www.businessinsider.com/what-successful-people-read-2017-7.